D0772546

Marketing by Agreement
Second Edition

Marketing by Agreement

A Cross-Cultural Approach to Business Negotiations
Second Edition

J. B. McCall
McCall Consultancy Services
Eyemouth, Berwickshire

and

M. B. Warrington
Eyetech Group
Thornby-on-Tees

JOHN WILEY AND SONS
Chichester · New York · Brisbane · Toronto · Singapore

Library of Congress Cataloging-in-Publication Data:

McCall, J. B.
    Marketing by agreement: a cross-cultural approach to business
negotiations / J. B. McCall and M. B. Warrington. — 2nd ed.
                    p.   cm.
    Bibliography: p.
    Includes indexes.
    ISBN 0 471 92151 3.
      1. Export sales contracts.   2. Marketing—Law and legislation.
    3. License agreements.   4. Negotiation in business.   I. Warrington, M. B.   II. Title.
    K1030.4.M38   1989
    343′.084—dc19
    [342.384]   88-33642
                                                                                            CIP

British Library Cataloguing in Publication Data:

McCall, J. B.
    Marketing by agreement. — 2nd ed.
    1. Marketing. Applications of behavioural sciences
    I. Title   II. Warrington, M. B.
    658.8

ISBN 0 471 92151 3

Typesetting by K-DEE Typesetters, Fareham, Hampshire
Printed and bound in Great Britain at the Bath Press, Bath, Avon

02/26/90

To Brenda and Pauline

Contents

Preface ix

Preface to the second edition xi

PART I The Nature and Function of Negotiation 1

CHAPTER 1 A NEGOTIATION APPROACH TO MARKETING 3

CHAPTER 2 THE ANATOMY OF NEGOTIATION 11

CHAPTER 3 COMMUNICATION, CULTURE AND
             NEGOTIATION I 40

CHAPTER 4 FRAMEWORKS FOR ADAPTIVE BEHAVIOUR 77

CHAPTER 5 COMMUNICATION, CULTURE AND
             NEGOTIATION II 98

CHAPTER 6 MAKING COMMERCIAL AGREEMENTS
             WITHIN LEGAL FRAMEWORKS 118

PART II Negotiating Marketing Agreements 155

CHAPTER 7 THE SALES/PURCHASE AGREEMENT I 156

CHAPTER 8 THE SALES/PURCHASE AGREEMENT II 184

CHAPTER 9 THE AGENCY/DISTRIBUTORSHIP AGREEMENT 226

CHAPTER 10 THE LICENSING AGREEMENT 258

CHAPTER 11 THE JOINT-VENTURE AGREEMENT 282

CHAPTER 12 MANAGING THE NEGOTIATION PROCESS 304

Bibliography 311

Author index 317

Subject index 320

Preface

This book presents an approach to marketing which emphasizes the implementational aspects of marketing plans. It seeks to redress an imbalance which has developed in marketing in recent years. As new planning and strategic concepts have been developed, these have been embraced within the marketing literature. Yet the means by which marketing plans are given effect have been grossly neglected by comparison.

Commercial agreements of all kinds describe a framework within which a business organization's marketing operations take place. All require to be negotiated, most of them in the context of interpersonal business encounters. A negotiation theme has been adopted because it has special relevance for such marketing aspects, and because it makes people central to the process and highlights the skills necessary for effective performance.

Negotiation research has been enriched in recent years by various contributions from the social sciences. Research in the fields of communication, organizational behaviour, sociology and social anthropology, socio-linguistics and social psychology have been identified as contributing particularly to the negotiation literature. These various researches have been integrated in Part I in a representation showing the factors affecting negotiation outcomes. A 'negotiation skills model' has been derived which provides a framework within which specific skills can be identified in the process. It provides a basis for relating negotiation to communication and culture and to further concepts for the development of negotiation skills. Part II is concerned with the application of these concepts to sales purchase, agency/distributorship, licensing and joint venture agreements.

Because marketing is increasingly international in its nature a cross-cultural perspective is adopted. People who negotiate across cultural boundaries require special skills if they are to make a noticeable impact on outcomes. While the approach is cross-cultural, it subsumes negotiations within specific cultures. This can include organizations which tend to develop their own sub-cultures. The skills identified are equally applicable to the domestic situation since the skills model is a conceptual one which can be related to all types of situation.

Negotiators and would-be negotiators, whatever their existing or future company role, would be less than effective if they had to rely solely on past experience or a 'how-to-do-it' approach by way of preparation for negotiations. Such is the complexity of the negotiating process that those who employ an approach embodying a series of pre-planned steps leading to conclusion of an agreement, are likely to be confused when negotiations do not follow the planned-for stages. Those who rely on experience and intuition alone equally close the door to many possibilities. To maximize their potential impact in negotiating situations, those involved in the process must know not only what they are doing but also why. A knowledge of concepts underlying the negotiation process can provide a frame of reference which allows people to interpret past experience and respond in a creative way when unforeseen problems occur.

No practitioner training is complete without the opportunity to exercise skills and to receive feedback on performance. Just as case studies, role-playing exercises and other forms of small group work are used in various kinds of management training and development, so the would-be negotiator or negotiator updating his skills will require to be exposed to actual and simulated negotiating situations. While this book will not of itself do that, it provides necessary concepts liberally and simply illustrated in Part II with practical examples, which the authors believe will lay a sound foundation for professional competence.

The authors wish to acknowledge the very considerable help received from colleagues who have willingly given of their time to read drafts of the chapters which follow. In particular they would like to thank Lillian Carmichael and Michael Wright for their comments on Chapter 5 and Pat Flynn for his view on Chapters 6 and 7. Peter Turnbull of the University of Manchester Institute of Science and Technology made helpful comments on Chapter 2, as did John S. Wright of Georgia State University on Chapters 2 and 3. Robin Rae's advice on Chapter 9 was invaluable.

No book of this kind would be complete without the help of the unnamed many whose opinions, research and experience have contributed to what follows. These are the businessmen, students, educators and trainers who have enriched our experience through our associations and interactions with them. Any deficiencies are entirely our own.

J. B. McCall

M. B. Warrington

November 1983

Preface to the second edition

Since the publication of the first edition, a number of developments have taken place that are important for marketing and other negotiators. It has long been recognized by practitioners that what goes on within organizations affects, and is affected by, what goes on between organizations. Organizational culture, touched on in the earlier edition, has been enriched by a fast-growing literature. This has facilitated a greater understanding of what goes on inside organizations and provides new insights emphasizing the importance of this for external relationships; it also provides frameworks for greater understanding of customer, intermediary and joint-venture organizations. This provides a basis for communicating with members of these organizations in a way that is meaningful to them.

To take account of those developments a new chapter has been included which addresses communication, culture and negotiation within the organization. It includes intra-organizational aspects of preparation and support for negotiators and implementation of any subsequent agreement. In the last few years implementation of marketing strategy and plans has been observed to receive a wide treatment in the literature. Much of this relates to the people and political skills of managers as negotiators, within the organization as well as in external relationships.

A new last chapter has been added to consolidate and integrate the perspectives used throughout the book. While the thrust of the first edition, in terms of focus and example, inclined to emerging markets, the present edition brings a greater balance to the book by the inclusion of a greater number of examples from American and European markets.

Apart from the updating of obvious aspects like the law within which negotiation takes place, and endeavouring to support further the text with relevant and current examples, this edition includes a wider selection of readings to reinforce chosen aspects of the text.

A package for teachers with teaching notes, case studies and negotiation exercises is available from the first author.* Included is a data disk for use with standard micro-computers to provide feedback to students from a behavioural analysis of role-play negotiation situations. There is a support material for the behavioural aspects of negotiation. The book, however, can stand on its own, liberally illustrated as it is in Part II with practical examples of the concepts developed to give a firm foundation for developing and reinforcing professional competence.

The authors wish to acknowledge the help received from a large number of people. In particular, they would like to thank John Cox of Buckinghamshire College of Higher

* Ian McCall, Greenburn Cottage, Auchencrow, Eyemouth, Berwickshire TD14 5LS, UK.

Education for comments on the teaching manual referred to above; Graeme Drummond of Napier Polytechnic of Edinburgh for his contribution to the very practical exercises in the same manual; Marko Ilešič of the Edvarda Kardelja University, Lubljiana, for his comments on Chapter 11; Peter Lawrence of the University of Loughborough for so readily making available to us his researches on the characteristics of management in various European markets; and Ottmar Wernecke of the Fachhochschule, Bielefeld, for his advice on examples of German language usage in Chapter 3.

Our thanks also go to those thoughtful members of Faculty, students, businessmen and other interested parties who took the time to provide feedback on the first edition. We are indebted to them for what follows. The responsibility for what is written remains our own.

June 1988   J. B. McCall
                                                 M. B. Warrington

PART I

THE NATURE AND FUNCTION OF NEGOTIATON

In Chapter 1 marketing plans are conceptualized in terms of agreements and the negotiation approach to marketing is introduced. These factors affecting negotiation outcomes are interrelated and integrated and a 'negotiation skills model' presented in Chapter 2 which is related to the sales/purchase situation and, by association, to other forms of exchange agreement. The concepts reviewed and developed provide a framework within which the issues and processes of negotiation can be examined from the separate standpoints of the parties involved. The buyer, the executive licensing-in, the distributor/agent, the company officer seeking to strengthen operations by a form of joint activity, are as much involved in marketing as are the seller, the executive licensing-out, the manufacturer/supplier/principal or the company officer seeking to expand activities via a joint venture.

The frameworks are useful for considering the relationship of language, culture and negotiation in Chapter 3. Negotiation is seen to hang on two-way communication. This is a multi-channel process involving the spoken language and the way it is used, the associated non-verbal language, the situation in which it takes place, the social context and social structure. The chapter looks at language as culture to provide insights into cross-cultural negotiation.

In Chapter 4 the theme of culture is developed further by an examination of a single culture and by relating negotiations to it. It being shown that a very different culture is legitimate in its own context, a view of social relations is established against which those in the reader's own culture can be compared.

The chapter concludes with general frameworks which provide directions along which single country or comparative studies can be placed. The emphasis throughout the book in terms of focus and example is on emerging markets, but traditional markets are not neglected. While an emphasis on emerging markets is believed to be justified in itself, these markets happen to be 'high-context' cultures. It is held that an intensive review of one of these cultures as in Chapter 4, and extensive coverage of others, highlights significant aspects of our own culture and enables us to function better in all cultures by assisting us to overcome cultural bias.

Chapter 5 addresses the social reality of organizations, how differing viewpoints are normally held on particular issues by different functions or sections and the way in which negotiators can handle the conflicts arising from such viewpoints. This has implications not only for meeting task objectives, but also for negotiations that take place between organizations.

All agreements are made within legal frameworks. Chapter 6 is a new synthesis of the law in relation to agreements in international transactions. This brings the law in relation to domestic transactions into sharper focus. It views the law as it affects the various kinds of agreements covered and parties involved, and addresses itself to the reality that agreements are not necessarily made under the law of one's own country.

CHAPTER 1

A negotiation approach to marketing

Conceptualizing marketing plans as agreements................................... 3
What the book is about... 3
A significant antecedent... 4
The cross-cultural dimension... 5
The people dimension.. 5
Plans as agreements... 6
The negotiation focus... 6
The pervasiveness of negotiation.. 6
Key role for negotiation.. 7
Factors affecting outcomes.. 8
Integration of the factors.. 9
The negotiation skills model.. 10

CONCEPTUALIZING MARKETING PLANS AS AGREEMENTS

What the book is about

This book is about the inter-organizational negotiations which are crucial to marketing operations, the intra-organizational negotiations which affect them, the interpersonal interactions which are central to negotiations, and the skills which lead to effective negotiation outcomes.

The face-to-face elements in marketing have been largely ignored in the literature, and yet there is increasing evidence that they are key aspects of the marketing task which have not to date received the attention which they merit. While there has, rightly, been a readiness to embrace new planning and strategic concepts within the marketing literature, there has been a reluctance to focus on the means by which these are given effect. Yet a marketing strategy is only as good as its implementation, and that implementation depends on the people who span organizational boundaries and whose work is aimed at creating various kinds of agreements for which negotiated support within the organization is needed before, during and after the making of such agreements. It is punctuated by the negotiations through which such agreements are made and put into operation, revised or terminated. Because implementation becomes

3

increasingly difficult — through growing professional competence, pressures of competition arising from industrial concentrations, changes in organizational relations, changes in international relations, and differing economic and organizational ideologies — the negotiations through which implementation is largely carried out take on an increasing importance.

A significant antecedent

The interaction of organizations and their effect on each other has been well illustrated by the IMP Group research. The group has developed an interaction model which has grown out of inter-organizational theory and a micro-economic approach characterized as the 'New Institutionalists' (Hakansson 1982). Based on research in five European countries and drawing on earlier research in marketing and purchasing, the study analyses relationships between firms buying and selling in industrial markets and describes the nature of the relationships in different circumstances. Seen as an interaction process between parties in a particular environment, it identifies four basic elements:

1 the interaction process
2 the participants in the process
3 the environment in which the interaction takes place
4 the atmosphere affecting and affected by the interaction.

The interplay of these elements is conceptualized in terms of the complexity of episodes and the extent of relationships, the structural fit between the parties and their knowledge of each other, the degree of homogeneity and dynamism of the market and the relationships of atmosphere to these. The inter-organizational personal contact patterns are explored in terms of roles such as information exchange and social enhancement. Progressive institutionalization of these patterns is reflected in the expectations built up of the frequency and style of contacts. It becomes increasingly difficult, in the face of intercompany meetings becoming incorporated into the procedures of the separate companies, for one party to withdraw from these arrangements.

The IMP research was confined to industrial products. There is some evidence to suggest that the kinds of developments in industrial products equally affect consumer products, in that the interdependence of suppliers and resellers has grown. The interactive approach questions the emphasis on selling and purchasing as separate processes. It also questions the value in industrial markets of the current emphasis on the marketing mix which implies a passive buying organization. It stresses the importance of relationships and the constraints which these place on freedom of action. The process can be likened to continuous negotiations between the organizations concerned. It needs only a short step to extend the interactive approach beyond the sales/purchase relationship to other forms of agreement and relationships.

The interaction approach is extended by combining it with a systems analysis approach, resulting in the concept of markets as networks (Hammarkvist 1983). In this the resources of the company are not confined to the organization itself, but also embrace those other supplier and customer organizations in surrounding networks. The perspective is very much one which views the development of relationships with other organizations as a necessary condition for the effective harnessing of resources across organizations.

This approach is reinforced by the concept of value chains developed by Porter (1985). The value chain 'disaggregates the firm into its strategically relevant activities in order to understand the behaviour of costs and the existing and potential sources of differentiation'. A firm gains competitive advantage by performing these strategically important activities more cheaply or better than its competitors. To achieve this it has to interact with the value chains of suppliers, customers and channels of distribution. The interdependencies arising from these interactions are the source of competitive advantage and as such inhibit withdrawal from evolved arrangements.

The cross-cultural dimension

It was no coincidence that the IMP research was carried out on an international basis. Today's business spans countries. In order to establish competitive advantage or to generate the returns required to justify investment in the first instance, many organizations require to operate on an international scale. They buy or sell or make arrangements which are concerned ultimately with purchase or sale on a worldwide or restricted geographic basis. As their overseas operations expand they develop new strategies and seek new means of putting their products or services on the market which match these strategies. International competition is a fact of business life. This book therefore adopts a cross-cultural perspective. While the approach is cross-cultural it subsumes negotiations within specific cultures. Indeed the propensity of organizations to develop their own sub-cultures supports this cross-cultural view. The skills identified are directly applicable to the domestic situation at both corporate and personal levels.

The people dimension

While the IMP research examines the interpersonal contact patterns in terms of intensity and styles of interaction, and indeed isolates personal contacts as being at the heart of interaction between organizations, it does not examine the nature of these personal relationships, how they can be crucial to the management of inter-organizational relationships and how they relate to situations, issues and skills.

When we adopt a negotiation approach, people are given a focal position in the implementation of strategy. They have to negotiate relationships with their opposers and with their constituents or the management group they represent; they engage in seeking information about the needs and preferences of their opposers prior to formal negotiations, to put forward appropriate proposals at the optimum level of offer; they have to employ skills to elicit information in the course of a negotiation and to identify changes in the power relationship which they may have to use to revise their objectives for the negotiation; they are required to use appropriate behaviours and language to achieve interaction goals across cultures. The whole conceptual basis of problem-solving, conflict resolution, change agent and decision-making skills within the interaction is considered through the negotiation function.

Plans as agreements

Using the idea of negotiation and interpersonal interaction it is possible to conceptualize the output of marketing planning in international markets in terms of agreements to be negotiated.

Some of these agreements are more important than others in their overall contribution to company performance. Agreements of purchase/sale, agency/distributorship, licensing and joint venture have been selected as those most important, and from which most benefit can be gained from consideration in a marketing negotiation context. Minor agreements not treated separately are those concerned with information sharing and exchange, joint purchasing, specialization, joint and contract product research, consortium and group selling, franchising, joint advertising and promotion.

The agreements that are made between organizations, the people who are responsible for their negotiation, interpretation, execution and revision, and the skills needed to do this, represent a structure of activities which is an essential complement to the strategic and marketing mix elements traditionally concentrated on in the marketing literature. It is an emphasis which merits the widest consideration for it is the reality which confronts the vast majority of marketers. Executives returning to their jobs and graduating students taking up jobs will be the better for having developed the bases for negotiation skills, for these are increasingly required in the marketplace and the workplace.

THE NEGOTIATION FOCUS

The pervasiveness of negotiation

Increasingly, negotiation has come to be viewed as a universal phenomenon. Abell (1975) regards organizations as bargaining and influence systems, while Zartman (1976) sees negotiation as one of the basic processes of decision-making. Another author has developed a paradigm which presents a framework for studying individuals, organizations and societies through the key role of negotiation. It is viewed as a widely-used method of working towards individual and collective ends (Strauss 1978). This 'negotiated order' approach takes into account 'alternative approaches which include persuasion, threat, appeal to authority and force'. Strauss maintains that most theories of negotiation are deficient because they are based on single areas of research like industrial relations. Whatever the theoretical foundation, power lies at its heart.

It is within a power framework that Bacharach and Lawler (1981) develop a theory of bargaining in organizations relating it to outcomes. What goes on within the negotiating organization has been connected to the managerial process and the working relationships of managers from colleagues and superiors to customers and suppliers (Lax and Sebenius 1986). This acceptance of the negotiation process as a given is evidenced in Macmillan (1978) in the development of the political element in corporate strategy. In relating the nature of marketing tasks to the organization, Spillard (1985), drawing on the work of organizational theorists, identifies a conflict-resolving role for marketing to handle the political element in the integration of what would other-

Marketing itself with its emphasis on the environment highlights the importance of legal, political, economic, technological and social factors.

Integration of the factors

Environmental influences, influence strategies and skills, behavioural predispositions of negotiators and situational influences all interact with each other to give emphasis to the complexity in the determination of negotiation outcomes. These factors interact with each other to make the negotiators act in a particular way. The interaction of the negotiators themselves will also affect outcomes (see Figure 1.1).

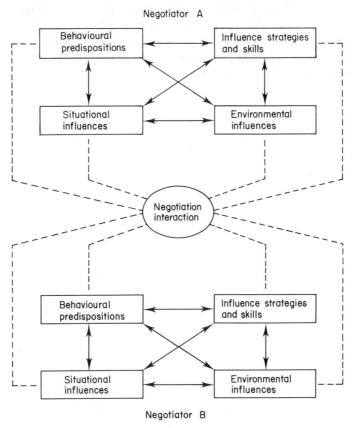

Figure 1.1   Model of factors affecting negotiation outcomes

The representation is useful in a number of ways:

1 It integrates factors within a single conceptual viewpoint which other authors have looked at in other perspectives.
2 It provides a reference point for negotiators who can relate it to particular issues on which they seek to resolve some conflict.

3. It is an essential accompaniment to the 'negotiation skills model' which follows. Together they represent powerful tools for negotiators.

The negotiation skills model

The model (which is given in full in Figure 2.4) uses a well-known three-stage approach drawn from labour negotiations. It is extended to include a preparatory or pre-negotiation stage and a post-negotiation stage. Those skills are identified which provide maximum effectiveness at each stage.

Perhaps the most important part of the model is the isolation of those skills required to effect movement from one stage to another, such movement having been identified by observers and empirical researchers as crucial to the process.

The following chapter develops the model which is central to subsequent chapters, providing a framework for both conceptual considerations in the rest of Part I and implementational considerations in Part II.

CHAPTER 2

The anatomy of negotiation

The nature of negotiation for agreement... 12
  Mixed motives.. 12
  Widely varying situations.. 12
  Ostensibly incompatible expectations...................................... 13
  Interaction-dependent outcomes.. 13
  A definition... 15
Behavioural predispositions of negotiators.. 15
  Interpersonal orientation... 15
  Basic individual differences... 16
Situational influences on negotiation.. 18
  Interdependence.. 18
  Distribution of power... 19
  Factor interaction... 20
Environmental influences on parties... 20
Influence strategies in negotiation.. 20
  Initial proposals... 21
  Moves and countermoves... 21
  Explicit persuasion attempts.. 21
Stages of negotiation.. 24
  Distributive bargaining stage.. 24
  Integrative bargaining stage... 26
  Decision-making and action stage... 30
Marketing negotiations.. 31
  A negotiation skills model... 31
  Sales/purchase negotiations... 34
Culture and negotiation... 37
Summary.. 37

This chapter sets out to provide the concepts around which marketers can frame the negotiations which are the stuff of everyday marketing activity — negotiations leading to agreements of purchase/sale and other channel arrangements aimed at creating and maintaining sales.

THE NATURE OF NEGOTIATION FOR AGREEMENT

Mixed motives

Potential buyers and sellers, licensors and licensees, principals and agents, manufacturers and their distributors, and prospective partners in a shared enterprise, would not be in contact long if they did not feel they had something to negotiate about. The research literature indicates that negotiations are mixed-motive situations and that each party has a motive to enter into negotiation to reach a mutually acceptable solution; also that simultaneously they have a motive for competition.

In international negotiations conflicts of interest can be heightened by varying national commercial practices and differing political philosophies and economic doctrines.

The conflict which is inherent in such discussions results in an attempt to compromise or to create a situation in which resources can be exchanged or divided. Failure to agree can involve an organization in heavy costs. There are costs of disagreeing in that a seller, for example, invests time and money leading up to a negotiation. Equally there may be costs of agreeing, as where business is done on unfavourable terms which may mean a shift in a buyer's anticipations in the next negotiations, or where agreement is made but basic problems have not been resolved.

Where interdependence of the parties is perceived to be high, supra-organizational mechanisms for resolving conflict are seen as appropriate, for example by establishing superordinate goals, by the employment of conciliation and mediation, or by submitting to arbitration or committees of enquiry. At a slightly lower level of interdependence, resolution or reduction of conflict can be seen as a function of interpenetration mechanisms such as exchange of persons. At a still lower level of interdependence organizational boundary mechanisms such as diplomacy are seen as conflict-resolving strategies.

Bargaining and negotiation can be said to take place in the resolution of all conflicts, irrespective of what management mechanisms are used (Stern 1976). The main thrust of this chapter is towards the negotiation situation in which the parties normally attempt, without the assistance of third parties, to settle the basis of their future behaviour across national and cultural boundaries. These cultural boundaries can include micro-cultures, as where organizations within the same cultures with differing philosophies and styles seek agreement on issues on which they hold differing views or where members of organizations originating from differing national cultures have to communicate across national and organizational cultures.

Widely varying situations

Negotiation involves talking about a relationship before doing something about it. However, negotiation situations vary considerably. At one extreme it may involve a complete discussion to consensus; at the other it may involve minimal conflict which may be resolved by the unsophisticated process of making a token or uncontested oral or written concession. It is necessary to examine the former to provide the basis for a conceptual background to negotiation.

The situation in which negotiations take place can vary in respect of the number of persons involved, varying from two individuals to two negotiating teams; of the number of parties involved, varying from a minimum of two to where several parties are privy to the same negotiations, as for example where governments are interventionist in business; of the countries of origin of the negotiation parties, which can be any two or more of some 140; of the degree of newness of the negotiating relationship, which can vary from the first-time agreement to existing agreements of differing duration for renewal, extension or revision/termination; of the interdependence and power relationships between the parties, which may change over time; of the nature of the disagreement, as where it can arise from an attempt to resolve a new conflict by agreement or from the interpretation of an existing agreement. Changes over time in the internal environment of organizations and in their external environment will alter the negotiation situation because of their effect on the aspirations and attitudes of the participants.

Ostensibly incompatible expectations

Most individuals involved in commercial negotiations act on behalf of organizations. There is much in the research on negotiation to show that representing a group may affect subsequent negotiating behaviour as a result of the perceived role obligations of individuals representing the group. It might therefore be claimed that the greater the authority of the negotiator, the greater the flexibility he has and the less likely he is to be inhibited by his role obligations in his attempts to reach agreement.

Few salesmen have complete authority to reach a compromise, and dilemmas abound because the salesman finds himself subject to sets of incompatible expectations. Buyers are equally inhibited by their role obligations. A purchasing agent for a large international company will have greater authority than an official of a state purchasing organization in a planned economy country.

A critical relationship for negotiators to manage is that with the groups or organizations whose interests they serve. The negotiator's role colours his perception. The same set of facts seen from the point of view of the opposer will be different. This is a form of selective perception whereby each sees what he wants to see. The way a negotiator perceives his opposer affects his interactions with him. These perceptions are, in turn, affected by his role *vis-à-vis* the opposer and his view of the opposer's role.

Differing expectations are a way of life in negotiating situations, the more so in intercultural situations where each party's view of the other's role can be conditioned by the norms of his own country. The good negotiator seeks creative solutions to these apparently incompatible expectations.

Interaction-dependent outcomes

Interorganizational interactions

The quality of agreement, that is the extent to which the joint outcomes, in the view of the negotiators, approaches the optimal, is dependent on how they react to, and on, one another. They are in a mixed-motive situation in which there is incentive both to cooperate and compete. Parties to a bargaining relationship are in dynamic interaction with each other, and tangible issues like how resources might be shared are affected by others arising from the relationship. When a negotiator perceives an opposer to be unjustly demanding, resistant or punishing, either as a result of making excessive demands and insufficient concessions or inhibiting movement to what he considers to be his proper share of available outcomes, it is likely that intangible issues related to the anticipated or actual loss of public image, face or self-esteem will emerge.

These issues often stem from the social implications of failing to appear competent and strong to the opposer and to the group of which he is a member in his company, whose expectations may not match up with the realities of the actual negotiation.

The need to appear strong and competent appears to be grounded in the supposition that a negotiator should look like that to obtain a satisfactory outcome, and that he should protect himself against injury to his self-esteem that may arise from being evaluated negatively. Dispositional characteristics such as low self-esteem, and high need for power and social acceptance, may make some negotiators particularly susceptible to intangible issues related to public image and face. By the same token, a highly competitive motivational orientation — which may arise from personality factors or in response to a foreign opposer's apparently odd behaviour, with its implications for misperception and mistrust — may operate in a similar way. It is therefore important for the negotiator to understand what underlies an opposer's actions. He can then adapt his behaviour to the situation.

Intra-organizational interactions

Negotiation between organizations does not take place in a vacuum. Prior experience of buyers with sellers or agents, of distributors with suppliers, of licensees with licensors and joint-venture partners with each other, colours the experience of the parties. Failure to deliver in the time originally promised is a common reason for jaundiced views of a buyer in subsequent negotiations. Such problems usually arise within a selling company's work-place.

To overcome, for example, delivery and product-related problems, it is often necessary for negotiators or their associates to resolve these problems through peers in the organization over whom they have no direct authority. Such is the nature of modern organizations, that people at managerial level retain the responsibility for specific tasks but do not have the hierarchical authority to require a particular course of action. Such problems have to be resolved across functions. Because these functions view problems and issues from different viewpoints but believe the lens through which they observe is an objective one, it is important for the negotiator within the organization to understand what underlies the viewpoints of peers on whom he or she has to rely. By so doing he or she can communicate in a way meaningful to them and so be more likely to influence them in a way which facilitates external negotiations with customer organizations.

Intra-organizational negotiations are less formal than those between organizations and are not sustained by legal sanctions as in commercial agreements which often hold organizations to them after one or other of the parties sees the costs of maintaining the agreement as exceeding the advantages stemming from it. Informal relations are characterized by the principles of exchange and by the establishment and maintenance of relationships through which effective marketers achieve their task objectives.

A definition

Any definition of negotiation has to take cognizance of the various types of agreement negotiated, informal as well as formal, has to embrace written as well as oral communication, has to take account of the fact that agreements may be renegotiated from time to time as well as made for the first time, that not all negotiations lead to agreement, and that certain agreements are not supportable by law. In an international context, cultural considerations and commercial interests are often interrelated. For our purposes the following is a working definition of negotiation:

> *Negotiation is any sequence of written and/or oral communication processes whereby parties to both common and conflicting commercial interests and of differing cultural backgrounds consider the form of any joint action they might take in pursuit of their individual objectives which will define or redefine the terms of their interdependence.*

BEHAVIOURAL PREDISPOSITIONS OF NEGOTIATORS

Interpersonal orientation

Negotiators entering relationships with one another bring to their interaction variations in prior experience, background and outlook. Indeed they bring all the predispositions which they have, such as the internal pressures bearing on them which drive each of them to perceive their environment in different ways. They shape the way an individual reacts to the negotiating environment, as it is to this environment he brings his inherent personality in terms of, for example, cooperativeness, complexity of cognitive structure, authoritarianism and willingness to take risks. All these aspects will differ to some degree from country to country, creating the possibility of widely varying negotiation behaviours.

It is the environment which provides the external pressures like the negotiator's need for positive evaluation, to look strong and competent, to satisfy both his opposers across the table and the group he represents in his organization, and raises issues that block agreement.

A negotiator's enduring predispositions therefore shape the information he seeks about his opposer's intentions and preferences. They also shape what each chooses to disclose about his own preferences, intentions and the extent to which his information represents an open and trustworthy disposition to the other, as well as the kind and quality of agreement they normally ask for and accept.

In order to integrate the various researches into the variables concerned with individual differences, a distinction has been made to aid understanding by conceptualizing a bargaining world comprising two different people who reside at or near opposite poles of a dimension called *interpersonal orientation* (IO). Depending on their location on this continuum, negotiators can be expected to view their environment and to bargain in very different ways (Rubin and Brown 1975:158).

The negotiator at the upper end (the *high* IO) is responsive to the interpersonal aspects of his relationship with the other. He is both interested in, and responsive to, variations in the other's behaviour. Such variations provide the high IO individual with the important information he seeks about the other party — what his opposer prefers and expects, how he intends to behave and what he is really like. One consequence of this perspective is that where changes take place in negotiation situational factors, the high IO individual is likely to attribute the resulting change in the opposer's behaviour to his personality rather than to the particular situation in which the parties are involved.

To understand the consequences of this perspective for the way in which negotiation develops, it is useful to consider how a negotiator whose basic predisposition is either cooperative or competitive might be expected to behave. The high IO who is *cooperatively* disposed enters the negotiating relationship with a posture that is both trusting and trustworthy in that he expects cooperative gestures to be reciprocated. In turn, he responds to cooperative overtures with reciprocation rather than exploitation. If the opposer acts cooperatively, it can be expected that the relationship will flourish. The high IO who is *competitively* disposed enters the relationship with an eye to taking advantage of his opposer. He is both suspicious and untrustworthy. If his opposer behaves cooperatively the competitive high IO attempts to exploit him. Where the opposer is also competitive, the competitive high IO will develop the impression of the other as similar to himself and will behave competitively to defend himself against the possibility that the opposer will fare better than himself.

When the negotiator is a *low* IO he is characterized by a non-responsiveness to interpersonal aspects of his relationship with his opposer, being neither interested in cooperating nor competing with him but in maximizing his personal gain. He sees the other's behaviour as being induced by a set of environmental constraints. The low IO's behaviour is aimed solely at achieving as much gain for himself as he can, regardless of the other's behaviour or disposition.

Basic individual differences

The variables internal to individuals that determine their behaviour differ from person to person and the same is true of behaviour in the negotiation interaction. The basic determinants of behaviour in the individual are related to one another by the *self-image*, or feelings and beliefs an individual has about how he looks in his own eyes and the eyes of others.

An individual with a positive self-image tends to have greater self-esteem and self-acceptance and less anxiety about how he looks in the eyes of others than does a person with a more negative view of himself. Persons with a negative self-image tend to bargain more competitively than do those with a positive view of themselves.

The individual's self-image is related in the first instance to his *needs*. The individual is stimulated to action by his *motives*, and a negotiator's motivational predisposition and subsequent behaviour have usually been examined in relation to one or more of three basic motives — his motivation towards a standard of excellence or achievement, towards friendly relations or affiliation, and towards power or dominance. Those negotiators high in achievement motivation tend to act like low IO s, while those high in affiliation and power motivation tend to act like high IO s.

The individual's needs and motives are what he perceives them to be. *Perception* is the entire process by which an individual becomes aware of his environment and interprets it so that it will fit into his own frame of reference. It uses both the sensations aroused by stimuli and the learning gained from past experience. *Attitudes* can be taken to be the state of mind that results from these interpretations. They point to a structuring of awareness which derives from social experience and is referred to as *cognitive structure*. Cognitive structures and associated perceptions and attitudes vary from culture to culture and influence the course of social interaction, as they will do within a heterogeneous culture like our own.

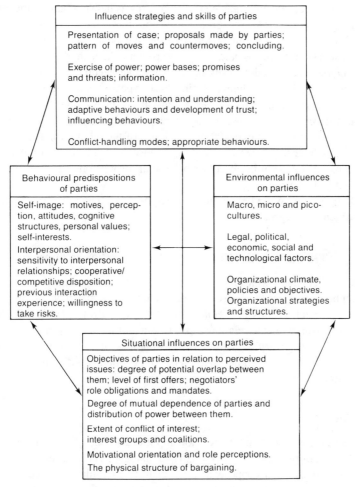

Figure 2.1 Factors influencing negotiations and their outcomes

Research has shown that negotiators who have developed trusting attitudes behave more cooperatively than those who are less trusting. Cooperators behave like high IO's and competitors behave more like low IO's. In one study of negotiators' perceptions of intentions it was found that cooperators behave like those with whom they interact, that is they behave cooperatively with cooperators and competitively with competitors.

Attitudes are important for negotiations because attitudes have a strong effect on behaviour. *Attitudinal structuring* is the expression given to activities which are directed towards bringing about specific relationship patterns between the negotiating parties. Each time negotiators meet it provides an opportunity for them to reinforce or change existing attitudes. Previous episodes provide the historical precedents which influence a meeting and bear on the current issue.

The kinds of behaviour adopted by the negotiators will influence any future meeting.

Because of the relationship between trust and cooperative attitudes in bargaining, the establishing of a certain measure of trust — and the implied resolution of conflict — is a necessary prerequisite to any negotiation. Trust is indispensable to the influencing and negotiating process. No agreement is possible without it (Pedler 1977a,b). Agreement implies a commitment on future negotiating behaviour when conflict issues are under discussion. If trust is defined as an expectation that another will do a certain agreed thing, then the precedent resulting from previous negotiations, and in particular most recent negotiations, will help to define these expectations at the next negotiating episode. For these reasons difficulties arising at the negotiating table from basic individual differences are themselves affected by the interaction itself and previous interactions in terms of the expectations each has of the other. It is the failure of a negotiator to deliver the expectations of his opposer which leads to a breakdown in trust. Failure to promise or imply future behaviour through one's actions may create concern and lack of trust.

The relationship between behavioural predispositions of negotiators and the other factors influencing negotiation outcomes are shown in Figure 2.1.

SITUATIONAL INFLUENCES ON NEGOTIATION

Quite apart from content issues in negotiation, the principal situational influences on negotiation behaviour are the degree of dependence the parties have on one another and the power relationships between them (Rubin and Brown 1975:197). This is reflected most strongly in the relationship between multinational companies and host countries, where they vary over time as the stream of benefits to the host country decreases and nationals accumulate experience of negotiating with representatives of the multinational companies.

Interdependence

Because negotiation is a voluntary relationship it is also one of mutual dependence. Where a negotiator presses for as personally advantageous an agreement as possible, he runs the risk of driving his opposer away from the relationship which seeks to resolve the conflict of interest between the parties. This would put an end to the process in which both choose to participate in the first instance, and perhaps eliminate the possibility of mutual gain. Personal advantage is accorded low priority, for example, in Oriental countries where individuals identify more with community and organizational goals than do Westerners.

The variables which affect the nature of negotiators' interdependence, and the consequence of salient patterns of interdependence for negotiating effectiveness, have been usefully conceptualized whereby the parameters of negotiators' interdependence are viewed in terms of their motivational orientation, distribution of power and interpersonal orientation.

By motivational orientation (MO) is meant one negotiator's cluster of attitudes towards another. It has been usefully categorized in terms of cooperative, competitive and individualist orientations. A negotiator with a *cooperative MO* has an interest in his opposer's welfare as well as his own. A *competitive MO* is indicative of an interest in doing better than the other, while at the same time doing as well for himself as possible. A negotiator with an *individualistic MO* is only interested in maximizing his own outcomes, irrespective of how his opposer fares. Regardless of variations in reward structures, attitudinal predispositions and payoffs, a cooperative MO tends to lend itself to more effective negotiation than does an individualistic or a competitive MO.

Distribution of power

Power refers most generally to the ability of a negotiator to move his opposer through a range of outcomes. Thus the broader the range of outcomes through which a negotiator can move another, the greater his power is said to be. Equal power exists where negotiator and opposer can move each other through an equivalent range of outcomes. By distribution of power is meant the degree to which the power in the interaction relationship is equal or unequal. Despite variations in actual or perceived status of the participants and in reward structure and payoffs, equal power among negotiators tends to result in more effective bargaining than does unequal power. Under conditions of unequal power among negotiators, the party with the greater power tends to behave exploitatively, while the less powerful tends to behave submissively. Another associated generalization drawn from the research is that the smaller the total amount of power in the system, the more effectively bargainers are likely to function.

Relative power is an important concept in terms of the aspirations and expectations of the parties. It is seen in its most extreme form in relation to the nature of the relationship of a large customer and a small supplier which has been described as 'vertical quasi-integration' (Blois 1972). The supplier is often dependent on the customer for absorption of his output. He is therefore unlikely to pitch his initial price of asking at a level which the customer might not like and which might not deter a supplier of more equal power.

The kind of power which stems from economic or other leverage a company might have is referred to as *objective power*. When parties meet for the first time and the power balance between them has not yet been fully established, they often try to alter the opposer's definition of the power relationship. Such tasks, which may involve actions like manipulating information, bluffing and projecting images to change the opposer's perception of the power balance, is referred to as *subjective power* (Bacharach and Lawler 1981).

Factor interaction

Interpersonal orientation has already been looked at in relation to whether negotiators are high or low in their sensitivity to interpersonal aspects of their relationship with each other and their relationship with regard to being cooperatively or competitively disposed. Just as each of the parameters, that is interpersonal orietation, motivational orientation and distribution of power has its effects in relation to bargaining effectiveness, so too do these factors interact with one another. Negotiators will tend to function more effectively when they share a cooperative MO and are of equal power; when they share a a cooperative MO and are high in interpersonal orientation; and when they share a cooperative MO, are of equal power and are high in IO. They will tend to function least effectively when they share a competitive MO and are of equal power; when they share a competitive MO and are high in IO.

ENVIRONMENTAL INFLUENCES ON PARTIES

The influence of the environment on negotiations is one that is not unfamiliar to marketers. The general literature on negotiation, particularly that stemming from social psychology and communication theory, tends to neglect this aspect. Nevertheless, it is one which must have a bearing on any negotiation outcome. In international negotiations for the establishment of overseas subsidiaries and joint ventures, characterized by massive investment and considerable power in the system, it is seen as critical.

At the level of the organization, organizational cultures will influence negotiation outcomes in so far as they place constraints on people representing the organizations who are in negotiation. Organization structures, policies and objectives may also be seen by the parties as constraints on their activities, and therefore as variables affecting outcomes.

INFLUENCE STRATEGIES IN NEGOTIATION

Through the verbal exchanges which they participate in, the proposals and counter-proposals and concessions they make and the social posturing they invariably display, negotiators shape the outcomes of their interaction in a strategic way. The quality of their outcomes is influenced by their mutual dependence. As well as exchange or division of resources, dependence in relation to outcomes rests also on intangible issues, having to do with how a negotiator looks or is perceived in his opposer's view. It also rests on the various influencers on the negotiations, whether or not they are physically present at the negotiating table.

In deciding the negotiating position to take up, each party has to obtain information about the other's true preferences, intentions and social perceptions. Even as he acquires the information, the negotiator must adopt a particular posture and disclose information about his own intentions, preferences and perceptions which may be used by the other to shape his own strategy. It is this exchange of information and what can be imputed from the information and the ways it can be used for mutual influence, that represents the fundamental strategic issue in negotiation. The view has been put forward that there are several interrelated ways in which the intentions, preferences and perceptions are conveyed (Rubin and Brown 1975:259−288), and we shall now look at these.

Initial proposals

It is the initial proposals and counter-proposals that largely determine the course of negotiation. Early moves and gestures are critical in the creation of the setting in which the negotiation is to be played. This is where rules and norms are first established, where previous negotiation experience of the more recent kind may be seen as the benchmark against which present discussions will be measured and where issues such as trust and hardness in bargaining are considered. The division of resources to which each party aspires is presented at this time for the other's consideration.

Moves and countermoves

Opening claims and postures apart, it is through the arrangement of proposals and counter-proposals that negotiators seek to arrive at an acceptable agreement. These show the extent to which a negotiator is cooperative. The detailed patterning of proposals and counter-proposals in the form of packages and concessions provides the negotiating parties with important information about the other's preferences and intentions. Also, to the extent that the opposer's moves appear to be made in response to the negotiator's own behaviour, information is conveyed about the negotiator's ability to persuade systematically.

Explicit persuasion attempts

To make it more likely that an offer will be acceptable to an opposer, a negotiator may support his proposals with a number of more explicitly conveyed attempts at persuasion. The different bases of social power have been defined.[1] Originally written for interpersonal interactions, it has been extended in the literature to organizations.

1 Information power

This draws on the special information an individual or organization holds as a result of the operations he/it performs and his/its special relationship with sources of information which are of significance for the performance of another individual or organization. By indicating relevant information of which his opposer is unaware, a negotiator can try to gain acceptance of his proposals.

2 Reward power

This is based on the belief by one individual or organization X that another individual or organization Y has the ability to mediate rewards for him/it and will deliver such rewards if X cooperates. It can provide a negotiator with important information about the perceptions, preferences and intentions of his opposer.

3 Coercive power

This is similar to reward power in that it is based on an individual's or organization's control of resources or ability to facilitate another individual's or organization's goal achievement. It relies on the belief that punishments will be forthcoming or rewards withheld unless the requested behaviour is exhibited. As with reward power it can provide the negotiator with information about an opposer. By carefully observing the frequency, intensity and timing with which promises and threats are made, an attempt can be made to gauge the other's preferences and intentions.

4 Legitimate power

To the extent that a negotiator can convince an opposer that he has a right to make a particular demand or proposal, the likelihood of an offer being accepted is increased. By appealing to rules, procedures, past relations or norms of reciprocity and reputation, each party can seek to get the other's agreement.

5 Referent power

This results from the willingness or desire of one individual or organization to be associated with another and to maintain such an association. Such a desire may result from the demonstration of desirable behaviour on the part of the second individual or organization, from similarities in characteristics of the two, or merely from the fact that they have been closely associated over time. Such a willingness may make it easier to get a proposal accepted in pure or modified form.

6 Expert power

This is based on the belief that an individual or organization has special knowledge or expertise within a given area, and that it can confer advantages on a second individual or organization which sees these advantages as significant for its operations.

7 Communicative power

This form of power stems from the ability of the negotiator to communicate with an opposer in a way in which the interpretation of the message by the opposer reflects the intention of the speaker. Other forms of communicative behaviour are associated with interactive skills, addressed in the next chapter, which can be influential in shaping a predictable reaction from an opposer. The bases of social power listed at 1−6 above each implies a persuasive message strategy (Miller 1983). This form of power can be significant in influencing negotiation outcomes (see pp. 42–44).

Reward and coercive power, in terms of promises and threats, can be made by either party. They have entered into a voluntary relationship and can decide how long to remain in interaction with the other or whether to remain involved at all. A negotiator can threaten to leave unless a particular proposal is agreed, or he can promise to stay in the relationship if a particular concession is made by his opposer. Such persuasion attempts are possible only because the parties have the power to impose beneficial and harmful outcomes on each other.

Promises and threats are likely to be used when in the negotiator's perception he cannot exert persuasion in other ways. Studies indicate that negotiators tend to make more promises than threats, while threats tend to increase the likelihood of early compliance. As might be expected the use of promises in the course of a bargaining relationship tends to increase the likelihood of negotiators reaching a mutually beneficial agreement, whereas the use of threat tends to reduce this likelihood. It would appear that threats either need not be used when negotiators are cooperatively disposed towards each other, or should not be used, as when a conflict of interest is perceived by the parties as relatively large.

Another useful framework of influence is Kelman's (1961) three processes of social influence. Like French and Raven's framework it has been extended in the literature to include organizations.

The three processes are:

1 *Compliance:* this occurs where a person or organization accepts an influence attempt because the person or organization being influenced expects to elicit a favourable reaction from the influencing individual or organization. The behaviour will only be maintained in special public situations and the personal or organizational values and beliefs may be quite different.

2 *Identification:* this happens where a person or organization identifies with another and attempts to establish or maintain a desired association with the individual or organization. Identification involves a belief that the behaviour is maintained privately but only in the appropriate role, e.g. shop steward, boss or supplier or customer firm.

3 *Internalization:* Influence is accepted because the influencing individual's or organization's demands are consonant with the individual's or organization's values. The content of the behaviour is intrinsically rewarding. The behaviour becomes part of a personal or organizational system and is exhibited independently of any external source.

A useful synthesis

The French and Raven (1959), together with the Kelman (1961) studies, underline that a firm's total power is a combination of several power-bases and that these supplement more widespread focus on the economic aspects of power. The need to distinguish between the various power-bases has been cogently argued by Kasulis and Spekman (1980). They maintain that the use of different power sources has different consequences in terms of understanding on the part of the organization receiving the influence attempt which, in turn, results in different levels of long-term cooperation. They demonstrate this by combining French and Raven's classification of power resources with Kelman's three consequences of influence attempts as in Figure 2.2. They break down French and Raven's 'legitimate' base into its 'legal – legitimate' and 'traditional – legitimate' components.

Power-base	Likely consequence of an influence attempt	Expected level of long-run cooperation
Coercive	Compliance	Low
Reward	Compliance	Moderate
Legal – legitimate	Compliance	High
Referent	Identification	Low
Expert	Identification	High
Traditional – legitimate	Internalization	Low
Informational	Internalization	High

Figure 2.2 Sources and consequences of power in relation to long-run cooperation: Based on Kasulis and Spekman (1980).

The importance of this synthesis lies in the fact that it establishes the power source best used where a high level of long-term cooperation is desired. It has significant implications for long-term seller/buyer arrangements as well as for those long-term arrangements between organizations like agency, distributorship, licence and joint-venture agreements addressed in Part II.

STAGES OF NEGOTIATION

Writers on negotiation and bargaining have sought to simplify analysis of the process by breaking it down into sub-processes or stages. One such useful framework views the process as comprising three stages.[2]

Distributive bargaining stage

At this stage the parties are concerned with establishing the negotiating range by taking up their extreme positions in relation to the issues about which they are in conflict. These extreme positions reflect the most hopeful objectives of the parties — as distinct from those they would like to settle at or at which they would settle *in extremis* — and represent the starting point for the assessment of the feasibility of demands. Some of these objectives will not be known prior to the negotiation and will have to be established during the negotiation process, either at this or the following stage.

Most negotiators will seek to convince their opposers that their opening position is their limit. The reality is that a negotiator's behaviour is rarely accommodating to the extent that he will move all the way towards his opposer's position. It is more likely that the implications of the positions taken up will be assessed.

Every conflict in issues has implications for costs and outcomes. The more issues there are, the greater the opportunity there will be to explore how resources will be exchanged or shared.

Research into the effects of early cooperative or competitive attitudes on the course of negotiation leads to the conclusion that the early initiation of cooperative behaviour tends to promote the development of trust and a mutually beneficial cooperative relationship. Early competitive behaviour tends to induce mutual suspicion and competition. Negotiators tend to initiate a pattern either of mutual cooperation or of mutual competition early in a relationship, and then to persist in one or other of the patterns for the remainder of their interaction. One of the reasons adduced for the importance of this early period in a negotiating relationship is that, despite the extreme positions taken up, which in some senses can be viewed as a form of ritual, the negotiating positions of the parties are relatively fluid. Commitments have not been made or unretractable positions taken up that restrict movement in the subsequent bargaining exchanges.

Negotiators often consider it appropriate for this stage of negotiation to be used to test limits and a variety of behaviours with their opposers before committing themselves to a particular stance. It has been established that a hostile act in the early stages of a relationship is far less likely to induce a retaliatory response than one performed at a later stage. So the potential psychological costs involved in trusting the other party, great as they may be, may not be as considerable in the early stages of the relationship as they are once positional lines have been drawn. Once established, mutual trust may help negotiators to a cooperative pattern of behaviour that may prevail throughout their interaction.

Opening moves in negotiating may be used to convey information not only about each party's disposition to the other, but also about his intangible preferences and intentions. They also inform the parties about the division of resources to which each aspires, and in so doing specify the range of outcomes that are possible in the relationship. Different groups of nationalities tend to have differing levels of aspiration and cooperativeness, identification of which will be predictive of the action which negotiators should take and the behaviours they should adopt. Experimental research studies conclude that negotiators attain high and more satisfactory outcomes when they begin their interaction with extreme rather than moderate demands. This puts into perspective the conflict-resolving behaviours open to negotiators.

A useful representation of these has been developed on two dimensions of behaviour, assertive/unassertive and uncooperative/cooperative (Thomas 1976). The former measures the extent to which a party seeks to satisfy his own objectives and the latter the extent to which he attempts to satisfy the other's objectives (see Figure 2.3).

Avoiding and accommodating behaviours are not normally expected in negotiating. If they do occur, behaviour of the avoiding kind will result in breakdown and behaviour

26

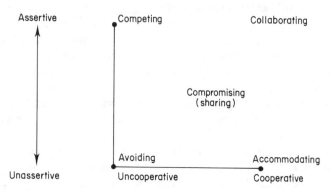

Figure 2.3   Conflict-handling behaviours open to negotiators (based on Thomas 1976)

of the accommodating kind in agreement being made immediately by acceptance of the accommodating behaviour. Competing is a behavioural state whose outcome is based on power. A *competing* approach has to be matched by a complete accommodation by the other side, otherwise agreement is unlikely. *Collaborating* behaviour rests on the premise that a joint problem-solving operation provides for the most mutually advantageous outcome. Such an approach is seen to have the ability to create alternatives which increase the total benefits from which both parties share more than they would from a compromise outcome. *Compromising* is a strategy which is directed at resolving conflict by give and take on both sides. To the extent that movement has to be made by both parties in each other's direction to achieve agreement, while meeting the broad objectives of the parties, this is also a problem-solving approach.

The examination of the effects of early cooperative or competitive attitudes also puts into perspective these factors which inhibit movement of one or both parties in the direction of the other. Fears of position loss (where once a concession has been made it is difficult to go back on it) or image loss (where making a concession implies flexibility where previously there may have been a commitment to the original position) can inhibit progress towards agreement. A concession may make a party appear so flexible that the opposer's target is upgraded and he readjusts his objective in the light of the wider possibilities which his perception of the concession might raise.

Integrative bargaining stage

This second stage is characterized by a movement towards agreement which constitutes a period of problem-solving. To arrive at this stage, if it is the wish of the negotiators to do so, it is necessary to overcome the so-called 'concession dilemma'. In this, the inhibiting factors of position and image loss mentioned above, together with the danger of antagonizing an opposer through becoming more and more committed to an original position, make retraction increasingly difficult. To escape from this situation it is necessary to adopt an approach which is encapsulated in the phrase 'to convey without commitment' (Morley and Stephenson 1977:39)

While there are no absolute rules of negotiation, one way to break out of such non-conclusive argument is by means of signalling behaviour. By verbal and/or non-verbal cues parties indicate their willingness to negotiate. Such indicating behaviour does not guarantee that agreement will ensue. What it does do is to create the possibility of agreement. A skilled negotiator rewards indicating behaviour, for example, by asking questions where he will give his opposer the opportunity to develop aspects of his opposition to the negotiator's original position. When there is no response an indicator or signal can be used again or made in another form. Where necessary the negotiator can be a little more specific. When there is still no response the negotiator can disengage from the proceedings or sit out the argument.

The course of a negotiation is shaped not only by early gestures but also by moves and countermoves. When indicating behaviour is reciprocated it usually takes the form of a claim or offer which results in a move from the original position taken up in the distributive bargaining stage.

A proposal is the means by which movement is made from entrenched positions. A negotiator who is invariably cooperative is reacted to very differently from one who never departs from a competitive stance. Cooperation, it is claimed, begets cooperation, and conversely non-cooperation begets non-cooperation. It is argued that in the presence of an opposer who behaves in a consistently competitive fashion, the need to maintain face, or at least not to lose it, emerges as a central theme in the relationship and drives the negotiator to defend himself through competitive behaviour. On the other hand, where an opposer chooses to be cooperative, a negotiator's need to maintain face is dramatically reduced and he can and often does risk that the cooperation will not be reciprocated. Given the development and maintenance of mutual cooperation negotiators are in a better position to work for a synergistic joint payoff. Failing the cooperative approach, it is still possible to resolve conflict through the process of sharing the exchange or division of resources in a form of compromise by a trade-off of concessions.

Opening proposals are therefore tentative. The laying of cards on the table is not a normal strategy. Cultures in which pride is taken in such forthrightness tend to produce businessmen who are poor negotiators. The formalities have to be gone through, otherwise the negotiator who takes a shortcut to his final position may find his opposer upgrading his objectives. Tentative proposals reassure both sides. A negotiator tells his opposer what might be on offer if equally interesting movement is made by the opposer away from his own position and in the direction of the negotiator's.

The position is always clouded by changing pressures of competition, resulting in shifts in the relative power positions of the parties and by recent experience of negotiations, not necessarily between the same parties. When the parties know each other and have built up a working relationship over a period, the uncertainty of information, preferences, attitudes and intentions which exist in any bargaining situation may well be reduced if not eliminated. An opposer's expectations will still be contained within the negotiator's behaviour and the opposer's perception of it.

Reduced uncertainty can aid agreement. The surer an opposer is of a negotiator's commitment, the more he can react rationally to the latter's moves. If two parties meet with any regularity, they will be aware of each other's negotiating styles. If a negotiator's style is known, for example, to be one in which he makes only a slight shift from a declared position, his opposer can interpret the moves with greater accuracy. If, on the other hand, the negotiator has no consistent style and varies his approach, settlement will be that much more difficult. Although joint outcomes are believed to be the highest under conditions of cooperation, sharp decreases in joint outcomes occurred in negotiation experiments when a violation of trust which had been built up took place in the form of an attack mechanism (Hornstein and Deutsch 1968).

Where there has been no previous pattern of interaction, or where interactions are at long intervals of time between which fundamental changes can have taken place in the negotiating environment, agreement can be assisted by pre-negotiation contact. It has been shown that where negotiators have been deprived of an opportunity for pre-bargaining interaction, they took longer to reach agreement, remained further apart on the issues involved and were less yielding than those who had an opportunity for pre-bargaining bilateral discussion (Druckman 1968). The implications for negotiations are clear. If contact for pre-negotiation discussions either directly or through well-primed intermediaries or associates is not possible, then written communications assume an increasing importance. The trouble with letters or telex messages is that the emphasis which can be given by speech or non-verbal gestures in clarification of a point or position is denied the parties. Such written exchanges have to be sufficiently lucid and practised if the path to agreement is to be smoothed.

If a proposal is made, a detailed response even in the face of an outright rejection can provide opportunities for indicating behaviour, perhaps pointing to those parts of a proposal which are of interest and those which are not. A counter-proposal attempts to establish some common ground. This does not mean that individual items in the counter-proposals should be agreed to individually at this time.

On the contrary, it is usually best to keep issues linked. A mutually favourable agreement is more likely to be reached if all issues are juggled simultaneously, thereby presenting to the other an integrated rather than segmented picture of one's shifting preferences. It has been pointed out that premature agreement on any issue or sub-set has the effect of limiting the negotiator's latitude for subsequent trade-off, so reducing the total number of available options for agreement. From this it has been concluded that the generation of such options is only possible by treating the outcome as a package rather than individual sub-agreements.

The trading-off of concessions on one or more issues in return for concession on these or others by the opposer is more efficient because it leads to a significantly higher joint outcome distribution. The greater the number of issues, the greater will be the pressure to differentiate between them and separate them into different packages according to their importance or some other form of grouping.

In international negotiation, pressures towards differentiation are reflected in the emergence of 'package deals' and 'tie-ins'. The package deal involves proposals to settle general related issues simultaneously. Tie-ins involve the introduction of issues that may be extraneous to a given set, with the stipulation that settlement of the set is dependent on the satisfactory agreement of the extraneous issues as well. Issues control or the formulation of issues, as distinct from the substance of issues, is seen as the basis of being able to lead a negotiation.

In an empirical study of commercial negotiating behaviour, it was found that the most skilled negotiators made fewer counter-proposals than did average negotiators (Rackham and Carlisle 1978). The difference suggests that the common strategy of meeting a proposal with a counter-proposal may be less than effective. The reasons evinced are additional complication, submission at a time when the other party is least receptive (being occupied with his own proposal), and perception by the other party of a blocking or disagreeing tactic.

It is probably for a combination of these reasons that a skilled negotiator avoids immediate countering with his own proposal. The skilled negotiator is more likely to avoid certain phrases and words to describe his own proposal which irritate without persuading, words and phrases which say favourable things about himself, and by implication unfavourable to his opposer. He is more likely to seek information either as a basis for bargaining, as a strategy to give control over the discussion, as a more acceptable alternative to open disagreement, or a ploy to keep the other party active and so retain the initiative. Equally he is more likely to let his opposer know in the negotiating exchanges what his feelings are. This may or may not be genuine, but it has the effect of appearing explicit and above-board. It can also be used as disagreeing behaviour to avoid direct disagreement language.

The principled approach to negotiation
Fisher and Ury (1983) have established four key actions for conducting *principled nego-tiations* which they claim provide a greater likelihood of successful outcomes for both parties.

1 Separate the people from the problem. This entails accurate perceptions of the problems or conflict which lie, not in objective reality but in people's fears, hopes and emotions. Any solution has to address this in terms of the opposer's needs. In the process, the problem should be separated from the people, for example not reacting by 'that is totally unacceptable', but by articulating in a more self-directed manner: 'I am very concerned that we have different interpretations of that point — I would like to give you our interpretation now.'
2 Focus on interests not positions. Negotiators can talk just as hard about their interests as about their positions. It is the combination of support and attack which is most effective in achieving satisfactory outcomes: support in terms of trying to meet both parties' interests which may be related to their security, recognition or sustenance of self-image; attack in terms of fighting hard on the substantive issues.
3 Invent options for mutual gain. This is the creative aspect of negotiation and seeks to broaden the options of the parties. If, for example, agreements cannot be made on substantive issues, then it can possibly be made on procedural issues; if comprehensive agreement cannot be made, perhaps partial agreement can; if unconditional agreement cannot be achieved, then perhaps a contingent agreement can.
4 Insist on objective criteria. This focuses on principle not pressure, and involves a joint search for objective criteria which would include fair standards and fair procedures. Such an approach produces wise agreements and protects a relationship which would be threatened by an approach in which there is a constant battle for dominance.

Adapted from Fisher and Ury (1983).

The movement we have seen from the hard-line stage of distributive bargaining to the problem-solving stage of integrative bargaining is paralleled by a transition from the 'party line' to interpersonal relationships. Proposals are made and evaluated in the light of the original positions taken up. By means of these proposals and counter-proposals put up, or by putting these proposals into a package, progress is eased from where the negotiators are to where they might settle. Such parcelling of proposals and counter-proposals does not necessarily conclude an agreement. What it does is to invite the opposing party to bargain away what is unacceptable to him by making concessions. The less that has been given away in the early stages, the more is available for trade-off and achieving a satisfactory settlement. The exploration of possible settlement points with a view to agreement is a function of the third stage.

Decision-making and action stage

Instead of making a concession and asking for agreement, a negotiator can make agreement conditional on acceptance of a package. This avoids the situation where a concession is offered and accepted without reciprocation. If the condition is accepted, there is an agreement. If the opposer has other points of difference which have to be settled before he can agree to the package, he can be asked to state the differences in full and the negotiator can then modify his position accordingly.

Concessions provide vital information on both tangible and intangible issues. They allow each party, for instance, to gauge the other's preferences and intentions and, in turn, give each party the opportunity to present or misrepresent information about his own. For example, a negotiator who concedes frequently will probably be viewed as willing to settle for less than one who concedes only occasionally. In the same way a negotiator who makes concessions up to a certain point, and refuses to go beyond it, will be likely to be perceived as close to some limit or cut-off point beyond which he will leave the relationship rather than settle. Concessions also convey information about a negotiator's perceptions of his opposer — how he looks in the other's eyes. To the extent that he believes he is seen to be capable and effective, he may be expected to behave in an increasingly cooperative manner. An opposer who initially takes up a hard and extreme position and follows it with an easing of demands may be viewed as indicating a perception of the negotiator as an effective and worthy adversary to whom concessions must gradually be made. On the other hand, a failure by the opposer to make any real concessions may be viewed by the negotiator as a reflection of his incompetence. A negotiator wants to believe he is capable of changing his opposer's behaviour.

Promises and threats are also means by which one party seeks to influence another, probably because they have the power to impose beneficial and harmful outcomes on each other. They also convey information about a negotiator's preferences and intentions. By observing the frequency, strength and timing with which threats and promises are made, the recipient can attempt to determine what these are. Threats and promises convey information, too, about the sender's perceptions of the other.

Two behaviours with a similar function, *testing understanding* and *summarizing* (Rackham and Carlisle 1978), are used significantly more often by skilled negotiators than by average ones. Testing understanding is a check to establish whether a previous contribution or statement in the negotiation has been understood. Summarizing is a short restatement of previous points raised in the discussion. Both these behaviours reduce misunderstanding and clear the way for agreement.

There is always a temptation to settle consciously, leaving certain points unclear. This can only be done at the cost of the efficiency of the agreement. Problems swept under the carpet at the agreement stage tend to emerge when attempts are made to make the agreement operational. The summary is one way to avoid this. It is also one of the principal means by which a negotiator seeks to close the discussions. This will normally be done after the testing of understanding.

Both behaviours can be used at all stages of the negotiation but they take on a greater significance as agreement is approached. Neither the negotiator nor his opposer is absolutely certain what the other party's limit really is. A negotiator on his limit will want to close, but is unlikely to wait until this is reached, although he will want his opposer to think he is at that limit. His opposer has to decide whether he is at it or not. If the opposer feels he has conceded more than the other party, he will wish to continue bargaining. Therefore to attempt to close too early is to increase the risk of no settlement. The summary close is an initiative by one of the parties which takes the points already agreed and the concessions which are on offer, parcels them according to his perception of an acceptable package and makes agreement conditional upon its acceptance.

A summary close may precede or follow on an attempt to bring discussion to a mutually agreed conclusion by means of a concession if this is felt necessary. Such a concession must be large enough to encourage acceptance. What is considered large enough may vary within the commercial practices of different cultures. If it is perceived to be too big it may be interpreted as a sign that the negotiator is still well within his limits and may encourage the other party to try for a bigger share of the division of resources. If a concession close is envisaged, the negotiator has to have sufficient margin in hand to make it. This underlines the importance of not conceding too much in the early stages. What constitutes too much will be determined by the custom established in different cultures.

MARKETING NEGOTIATIONS

A negotiation skills model

It is now possible to take the three-stage framework and enlarge it to take account of the effects on outcomes of pre-negotiation contact. Also, the need for an agreement which is efficient — one which provides a sound foundation for a working relationship based on complete understanding of the parties entering it — suggests a post-negotiation stage to complete the cycle of negotiation (see Figure 2.4). This also provides a starting point for renewal or revision.

Additionally, it should be possible to derive the skills required at each stage of what can now be envisaged as a five-stage process. As has been shown earlier, progression

		SKILLS PREDOMINANTLY REQUIRED WITHIN EACH STAGE OF THE NEGOTIATION PROCESS
	PRE-NEGOTIATION STAGE	To determine objectives in relation to environmental and known or likely situational factors; to establish best level of first offer where appropriate. To identify where possible nature of issues to be resolved, if necessary by the interactive process; to identify possible intangible issues. To plan the negotiation, e.g. by identifying or building in trade-offs; to prepare alternative courses of action to meet different contingencies; to establish authority limits.
FACE-TO-FACE INTERACTION	DISTRIBUTIVE BARGAINING STAGE	To push for the most advantageous outcome. To test limits and further isolate issues; to identify factors in the situation which affect relative power. To identify whether cooperative or competitive strategies should be used. To establish preferences and needs of opposer.
	INTEGRATIVE BARGAINING STAGE	To be aware of own and opposer's style of behaviour; to adopt appropriate conflict handling mode(s). To exercise the range of interpersonal skills, especially those concerned with communicating and influencing. To maintain flexibility of movement by keeping issues linked in face of proposals and counter-proposals. To elicit information regarding tangible and intangible issues and reformulate, as necessary, objectives and strategy.
	DECISION-MAKING AND ACTION STAGE	To assess the interaction of factors bearing on outcome and to make a judgment, by means of a package or packages, of what is acceptable in terms of exchange or division of resources. To test for understanding and agreement. To select appropriate closing technique, e.g. by summarizing or making a concession.
	POST-NEGOTIATION STAGE	To draw up or accept a contractual or other agreement which reflects the established understanding and the realities of legal interpretation where appropriate. To provide for review or revision in the light of factor changes.

Figure 2.4 Negotiation Skills Model. The cycle of negotiation showing the skills required within each stage and for progression between stages. The same individuals would not necessarily be involved at the pre- and post-negotiation stages, but would be party to the continuity.

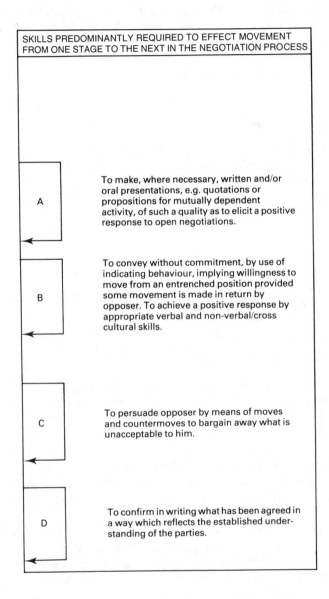

SKILLS PREDOMINANTLY REQUIRED TO EFFECT MOVEMENT FROM ONE STAGE TO THE NEXT IN THE NEGOTIATION PROCESS

A — To make, where necessary, written and/or oral presentations, e.g. quotations or propositions for mutually dependent activity, of such a quality as to elicit a positive response to open negotiations.

B — To convey without commitment, by use of indicating behaviour, implying willingness to move from an entrenched position provided some movement is made in return by opposer. To achieve a positive response by appropriate verbal and non-verbal/cross cultural skills.

C — To persuade opposer by means of moves and countermoves to bargain away what is unacceptable to him.

D — To confirm in writing what has been agreed in a way which reflects the established understanding of the parties.

(Figure 2.4 *contd*) The stages are a conceptualization of the real situation. In practice, negotiations do not always fall into such neat categories. For example, where the number of issues is small and the negotiators know each other's stles, the participants may move almost directly to the integrative bargaining stage. Where a negotiator attempts to 'tie in' extraneous issues, the process may be gone through again. In international negotiations cultural issues can de-emphasize certain stages.

from one stage to the next does not necessarily happen by itself. Indeed, it often needs very considerable skills of sensitivity, communication and judgement on the part of the parties to effect movement through the stages. The skills derived for this purpose are shown in the model.

Many of the skills referred to are applicable to negotiations that take place within organizations and are referred to in Chapter 5.

Sales/purchase negotiations

While the model is applied here to the sales/purchase interface, it could equally be applied to other forms of exchange behaviour — such as negotiations between licensors and licensees, regulating arrangements between manufacturers and their intermediaries, between wholesalers and retailers and prospective parties in a shared enterprise.

Pre-negotiation stage

Here the broad, environmental factors likely to influence a negotiation are assessed by buyer and seller in the determination of their objectives. A seller with a long order book or a highly competitive product or a monopolistic supply position can set himself a higher objective than can a seller who does not enjoy these advantages. A purchaser desperately requiring a product will be prepared to settle for less than one who can postpone the decision to purchase.

Each will be concerned to decide his own aspiration level in terms of what he will ask or pay. By increasing the level of his initial demand or offer the buyer/seller will reduce his chances of settlement. If a possibility of opening negotiations exists both parties should be seeking some idea of problems to be resolved which could possibly make them re-assess their objectives. When a seller can establish that a customer, for example, has to operate within a restricted power supply, he is in a better position both to focus his sales pitch and identify areas of specification which are likely to be open for trade-off. Such activities call for pre-negotiation contact between the parties, the initiative for which often resides with the seller.

Before entry into a face-to-face negotiation, buyers and sellers may require to negotiate the extent of their negotiating authority with the groups they represent. People involved in purchase and sale rarely have absolute negotiating authority and will consequently wish to know the limits within which they have to operate.

Facilitating stage A

Although the pre-negotiation stage often leads straight into the distributive bargaining stage, as when it is part of a continuing dialogue, it will sometimes be necessary for a seller, and occasionally a buyer, to make a presentation which will attract a willing response from the opposing party to enter into across-the-table negotiations.

Distributive bargaining stage

Buyers and sellers indicate strongly, often by the use of positive and uncompromising language, the outcomes they wish to achieve; which, in fact, represent their most hopeful objectives. Each is likely to test the other's limits. Eventually limit positions are as far as possible identified.

At the same time buyers and sellers are, or should be, looking for clues as to whether the other is showing signs of being cooperative or competitive. Indications are sought as to any particular idiosyncrasies or personal needs of the opposer which can be used in remaining stages of the negotiations.

Facilitating stage B

Fears of position loss and image loss may make it difficult for a seller to make concessions in case the buyer's target is upgraded and he employs more ambitious tactics. Similar conditions could, of course, apply to the buyer. Yet if no movement can be made there is a possibility that stalemate will ensue and place agreement in jeopardy.

By use of signalling behaviour, either party can indicate, without committing himself at this stage, his willingness to make a move from his extreme position provided there is equal movement made by his opposer. The language used to indicate this can be verbal and/or non-verbal. There is therefore a need to be able to identify readily such cues and respond to them. When this has been done buyers and sellers are in a position further to explore possibilities.

Integrative bargaining stage

Having now moved into a more interpersonal relationship, buyers and sellers can establish with more confidence the type of conflict-handling mode to adopt. Whether a cooperative or competitive or compromising stance is taken up will depend on the perceived reactions to any overtures that are made.

At the same time sellers will be seeking further information about the buyer's requirements, the urgency of his need for the product on offer (taking competitive suppliers into account), the buyer's ability to pay, constraints affecting his activities, and his personal vanities and aspirations. Simultaneously the buyer will be seeking information about such matters as the level of the seller's order book, whether there will be other customers competing for his services, the importance to the seller of the business under negotiation, and the needs and preferences of the salesman as well as the company he represents. Information so obtained can then be used to revise objectives and/or strategies as circumstances dictate.

In the face of proposals and counter-proposals, both buyers and sellers will give themselves more scope for advantageous settlement if they keep issues linked. When issues are picked off one by one, it is usually because the buyer — and sometimes the seller — believes it is in his interest to do so. In the process, communication skills, to influence outcomes, become critically important. Language can be used to shape predictable reactions by providing negotiators with a range of behaviours drawn from the breakdown of overt behaviour into its separate elements. Non-verbal communication can assume a greater significance than verbal in relation to expressions of emotion and the communication of the attitudes and feelings of a negotiator to his opposer. The consideration of attitudes and feelings are important in that if a buyer, for example, brings his own social drives and skills to a particular situation, then the seller has to adopt a corresponding behaviour. If both generally persist in asking questions and seek to be dominant, social interaction will be limited. It is therefore up to the seller to adapt his behaviour in such a way that there is no clash of techniques which might lead to discomfort and lack of harmony.

But parties' attitudes and feelings are not always what they seem. A buyer does not always wish to convey how keen he is to have a particular product, nor a salesman how much his company needs a particular sale, in case his opposer revises his objectives upwards. Ability to spot deception is therefore a useful skill in the negotiator's armoury, as is an ability to deceive if such deception is indeed deemed necessary. At the same time buyers and sellers may choose to project images of themselves which are not true. Nevertheless, each should refrain from making and emphasizing points which make it clear that he knows this to be so. If we destroy an opposer's face, we destroy the relationship necessary for effective interaction.

Facilitating stage C

Given that movement has been made allowing proposals and counter-proposals to be put forward, how can these be organized and presented to arrive at an agreed conclusion? Here again the quality of the buyers' and sellers' communications are paramount. Giving advance indication of the behaviour they are about to use makes a statement or question less equivocal when clear understanding is important, provides social pressure to force a response, and gives the other party time to clear his mind of his own previous statement or proposal. To maintain clarity of understanding, and so clear the path for agreement, testing of understanding and summarizing should supplement these moves and counter-moves so that the opposer is persuaded to bargain away what is unacceptable to him by clarifying what could otherwise be vague or dubious.

Decision-making and action stage

Having established beyond doubt the principal issues as seen by buyer and seller, and having kept issues linked in the light of the moves and countermoves made, buyer and seller will now each make a judgement of what is acceptable. This is likely to take the form of a package which the opposer may or may not immediately accept. One or other will seek to close the agreement by summarizing the situation through the package. Once agreement is reached ambiguities must be checked out as in the case of the individual issues involved.

Facilitating stage D

When agreement has been reached it is not unusual to record the principal issues agreed.

This has the effect of confirming the understanding of the negotiators. Whether this is given legal effect through the offer and acceptance procedure or via a formal contract will depend on circumstances.

Post-negotiation stage

When a contract is drawn up precision is an essential requirement. The skill is therefore required, if indeed the negotiator is also the writer of the contract, for sufficient knowledge of the language of the law to enable this to be done. Where circumstances are likely to change within the context of the agreement, this can be written into the document. Where the law, as is usual, is that of the seller, then it must be the seller's initiative which does this.

CULTURE AND NEGOTIATION

It has been claimed that in boundary-spanning activities, of which negotiation is arguably the most important in international business, the crucial problem is not coordination of variables under control but adjustment to constraints and contingencies not controlled by the organization. This arises from the interdependence of some part of the organization with organizations not subordinated to it. The negotiator spanning organizational and international boundaries has a very considerable task in adapting his behaviour, not only to constraints and contingencies in a familiar environment comprising different kinds of organizational cultures, but also to a different dimension of constraints which stem from operating across different national cultures. The less familiar that culture, the greater is the problem of adjusting to it and communicating within it in such a way that the understanding of an opposer reflects the negotiator's intention. The negotiator's difficulty is compounded by the fact that his intention must also be culturally appropriate and acceptable. It is to this problem of communicating within and across cultures in negotiating situations that the next chapter is addressed.

SUMMARY

Negotiation is characterized by conflict of interest where there is simultaneously a motive for entering negotiations, by widely varying situations, by incompatible expectations and interaction dependent outcomes.

Negotiators entering relationships have certain behavioural predispositions, such as degree of cooperativeness, complexity of cognitive structure, authoritarianism and willingness to take risks. These can all be conditioned by different cultural influences.

Some individual differences are related to one another by the negotiator's self-image, which is related in the first instance to his needs and motives in terms of his motivation to achievement, affiliation and/or power. Needs and motives are what the negotiator perceives them to be. Perception is the process by which the individual interprets his environment so that it will fit into his frame of reference. Attitudes are the state of mind resulting from these interpretations. They point to a structuring of awareness which derives from social experience and is referred to as cognitive struc-

38

ture. The nature of this social experience varies from country to country and culture to culture and influences the course of the interaction. Attitudes are important for negotiators as they can have a considerable effect on behaviour. Attitudinal structuring is the expression applied to these activities aimed at bringing about specific relationship structures between negotiators. Change of an opposer's attitude is what the negotiator is seeking to achieve. If a negotiator is to effect this change in attitude, the establishment of trust and cooperative attitudes is a necessary prior requirement.

Quite apart from issues for settlement in the negotiation itself, and associated factors like task-related information, history of relationships and other environmental constraints, the principal situational influences on negotiation behaviour are the degree of dependence the parties have on each other and the power relationships which exist between them. In deciding the negotiating position to take up, each party has to obtain information about the other's intentions, preferences and perceptions. Explicit persuasion attempts to support proposals are based on one or more of the different bases of social power. Promises and threats can sometimes aid coordination of mutual expectations, but are seen as inappropriate where negotiators are cooperatively disposed and undesirable where conflict of interest is perceived by the parties as relatively large.

The negotiating process can be regarded as comprising three stages. The first stage, or *distributive bargaining,* is concerned with establishing the negotiating range as the parties take up their extreme positions regarding issues in conflict. Limits are being tested and each party tries to move the other to his own position. A second stage, or *integrative bargaining,* is associated with movement towards agreement; it constitutes a period of problem-solving. There is a shift from the hard-line relationship of the first stage to an interpersonal relationship in which attempts are made to resolve the difficulties between the parties. A third stage, *decision-making and action,* is where the implications of possible points of settlement are explored with a view to reaching agreement. Within this three-stage progression, there are practical problems to be resolved and examples were given of these.

The behaviours open to negotiators in attempting to resolve conflicts have been developed on two dimensions of behaviour — assertive/unassertive and uncooperative/ cooperative, and the behavioural choices identified as avoiding, competing, compromising, collaborative and accommodating. Settlement is assisted by a consistent approach when the parties meet from time to time. Where there has been no previous pattern of interaction, agreement can be assisted by pre-negotiation contact. When proposals and counter-proposals are made, it is advantageous to keep issues linked rather than agree on them individually. This gives the negotiator greater latitude for subsequent trade-off by increasing the available options for agreement and making agreement conditional on acceptance of a package.

Testing understanding and summarizing reduce misunderstandings and clear the way for agreement. The summary is also one means by which the negotiator seeks to close a discussion. A summary close may precede or follow an attempt to bring discussions to a mutually agreed conclusion by means of a concession if this is felt necessary.

The chapter discussed the development of a 'negotiation skills model'. This embraces the stages of negotiation and extends it to include pre-negotiation and post-negotiation stages. Importantly, it relates to the movement between stages, which is where the negotiators' greatest difficulties lie. While applicable to all forms of agreement, it is related by way of example to the sales/purchase agreement. It underlies the discussion in the following chapter and in the chapters which comprise Part II.

At nearly all points, culture will impinge on the negotiation in terms of varying commercial practices, differing dimensions of constraints, the aspirations and attitudes of the participants, the role obligations of the parties, changing environmental aspects affecting the relationships between parties, and differing world-views of parties affecting their approach to the negotiations. Of considerable significance is the ability of negotiators to handle the problems of communicating across cultures in negotiating situations.

Notes

1 Points 2−6 were developed by French and Raven (1959). Point 1 was developed later. Communicative power has been derived from the concept of communication in relation to behaviour-shaping skills developed in the next chapter.
2 The framework is that of Douglas (1962), adopted and enlarged by Morley and Stephenson (1977).
3 Examples of signalling behaviour are given in Kennedy *et al.* (1980:55).

Questions

1 Refer to Fig. 2.1 and give examples of the interaction of the factors affecting the way negotiators behave in the face-to-face situation. For instance, the exercise of power under 'influence strategies and skills' can interact with the technological base of the organization under 'environmental influences on the parties' to give an organization a bargaining advantage and encourage a negotiator to ask for a premium price.
2 Distinguish between subjective and objective power, giving examples of each and of the circumstances in which they might be used.
3 What factors are likely to highlight the distributive bargaining stage of a negotiation?
4 Evaluate the laying of cards on the table as a negotiation strategy.
5 Using the negotiation skills model at Fig. 2.3, give examples of the language a negotiator might use at each of the face-to-face stages and the facilitating stages B and C.

CHAPTER 3

Communication, culture and negotiation I
The interorganizational perspective

Communication and the negotiation process.. 41
Language in negotiation... 42
  'It's what you say . . .'.. 42
  '. . . and the way that you say it'... 44
  Flagging behaviour to come.. 45
  Shaping predictable reactions.. 46
  Checking out ambiguities... 46
Negotiation and foreign languages... 47
  Negotiating the foreign language barrier... 47
  . . . and the cultural/linguistic barrier... 49
  Prerequisites for oral communication... 52
Non-verbal sign systems and negotiation... 52
  Expression of emotion.. 52
  Communicating interpersonal attitudes and feelings.............................. 53
  Deception and its detection.. 54
  'The believability scale'.. 55
  Under- and over-reactions.. 56
  Managing impressions of self... 56
Social context and structure.. 57
  Situation and negotiation.. 57
  High- and low-context cultures... 58
  Social structural constraints.. 58
  Differences in cognitive structures 59
  . . . is not confined to East/West differences................................... 60
A total communication system.. 61
Language as macro-culture... 61
Cultural sensitivity: key to interpersonal communication............................ 63
  Overcoming cultural bias... 63
  Learning how people in other cultures behave..................................... 64
  Approaches to culture.. 65
Perspectives assisting interpersonal communication.................................. 65
  The growth process of the firm... 65
  Group or individual orientation.. 66
  Education.. 67
  Ideological background... 68

Summary.. 69
Reading I.. 72
Reading II... 74

Communication is at the heart of negotiation. It is influenced by the wider culture of a people and the narrower but no less significant culture which develops or is created within organizations.

This chapter views communication behaviour and negotiaton behaviour in the context of the wider culture. The term macro-culture is preferred to national culture on the grounds that a culture can reach across national jurisdictions as in the case of the Flemish culture in northern Belgium; or the Arab culture which impinges more strongly on peoples of the Arab-speaking countries than does any other factor affecting national identity. Also within national boundaries it is possible to find strong ethnic minorities with a distinctive culture as in Canada or some of the African countries south of the Sahara.

COMMUNICATION AND THE NEGOTIATION PROCESS

An international business strategy is only as good as its implementation. Failure to negotiate effectively can undo careful prior planning, and this failure can often be blamed on ineffective communication on the part of the negotiator.

To understand fully the potential and problems of language and persuasion in negotiation communication it is first necessary to understand the process of negotiation. This was examined in the previous chapter and was viewed as comprising five stages. The first stage addresses the determination of objectives, level of first offer, and the preparation of courses of action to meet different contingencies. The second stage is concerned with establishing the negotiating range as the parties take up their extreme positions in relation to issues about which they are in conflict; limits are tested as each tries to move the other to this position. A third stage is associated with movement towards agreement; this constitutes a period of problem-solving and there is a transition from the impersonal power relationship of the second stage to an interpersonal relationship in which attempts are made to resolve the issues at conflict. A fourth stage of decision-making and action is where the implications of possible settlement points are explored with a view to reaching agreement. The fifth stage is where a contractual agreement is drawn up or other agreement ratified.

Within this five-stage progression there are practical problems to be resolved. How can we ensure that the preparation work of the pre-negotiation stage will elicit a positive response to enter face-to-face negotiations in the distributive bargaining stage? How is progress to be made from the hard-line position of the distributive bargaining stage to the integrative bargaining stage in which proposals are made which reflect movement by the parties from these positions? Fears of position loss and image loss may make it difficult for a negotiator to make concessions in case the opposer's target is upgraded and he becomes more ambitious in what he wants. Yet if he does not he may put possible agreement in jeopardy. Once movement is made how can the moves and countermoves by each party be organized and presented in order to arrive at an agreed conclusion; that is, how do we get to the decision-making and action stage? Finally, how do we get from verbal agreement in the decision-making and action stage to the post negotiation stage where we have an agreement that sticks, and reflects the realities of legal interpretation as well as reflecting the understanding of both parties? In particular, how can the negotiator communicate in order to assist these processes?

LANGUAGE IN NEGOTIATION

'It's what you say . . .'

It was stated in the last chapter that the bases of social power each implies a persuasive message strategy. They imply but do not spell out types of symbolic inducements. Therefore to transform a specific basis of power into a specific package or message content is a necessary further step for developing sets of persuasive message strategies (Miller 1985) which can then be used in the negotiation situation.

Using just such an approach Marwell and Schmitt (1967) developed a list of compliance-gaining strategies (see Figure 3.1). These, with the exception of liking

| Message Strategy | PERSUASIVE MESSAGE STRATEGIES | | |
	What the Strategy Implies	Manufacturer	Agent
1 Promise	If you comply, I will reward you	If you agree to reduce your rate of commission, we will revoke the annual renewal of the agreement and replace it with one for five years	
2 Threat	If you do not comply, I will punish you	If you feel you can't reduce your rate of commission, we feel the market demand will be negligible and perhaps we should discontinue our relationship with immediate effect	
3 Positive expertise	If you comply, you will be rewarded because of the order of things	If you reduce your rate of commission, the stimulation of demand will result in a greater aggregate commission	
4 Negative expertise	If you do not comply, you will be punished because of the nature of things	If you don't reduce your rate of commission, our market share will fall even further and so will your annual commission	
5 Pre-giving	You reward target before requesting compliance		
6 Aversive stimulation	You continuously punish target to obtain compliance by making cessation contingent on compliance	We would certainly consider some way of speeding up commission payments on extended credit contracts if you were to reduce your rate of commission	

7 Debt	You owe me compliance because of past favours I have done you	We have regularly reduced our price under pressure from you, but have paid you full commission. We would hope that you will now reduce your rate of commission to . . .	We have built up your business here as a result of our hard work and expertise. Surely you're not going to punish us for . . .
8 Liking	You are friendly and helpful to get target in good frame of mind so that compliance will be achieved		
9 Moral appeal	A moral person would comply		You must agree a principle is a principle and not for negotiation
10 Positive self-feeling	You will feel better about yourself if you comply		If you accede to our request, you will live in the realization you have acted in an honourable way
11 Negative self-feeling	You will feel worse about yourself if you do not comply		If you were to insist on going back on your word, do you think you could live with yourself?
12 Positive altercasting	A person with 'good' qualities would comply	You are experienced and professional businessmen who, I'm sure will agree to the proposal in our mutual interest	
13 Negative altercasting	Only a person with 'bad' qualities would not comply	We know that when the chips are down your commercial judgment wouldn't let you make an ill-advised decision	
14 Altruism	I need your compliance very badly, so do it for me	It's important for you *and* us that we get the price down. I need your help and I'm asking for . . .	It's important for you and us that our relationship is maintained. I need your help and I'm asking for . . .
15 Positive esteem	People will think highly of you if you comply	If you agree to this reduction in commission, your associates will respect your judgment in the light of subsequent events	
16 Negative esteem	People you value will think worse of you if you don't comply	If you don't agree to this reduction events may well lose you the professional respect of your associates	

Figure 3.1 Compliance-gaining message strategies: The examples are drawn from a situation in which a manufacturer, because of appreciation of his country's currency in relation to that of the agent's country, is seeking to become more price competitive there. He is asking the agent to accept a reduced commission in line with his own reduction in margin in the belief that his business will be increased and that the agent will obtain a greater aggregate commission than under the previously agreed rate. The agent feels that there is a matter of principle involved and that his rate of commission should remain inviolate. Adapted from Marwell and Schmitt (1967) by McCall and Cousins (1989)

and pre-giving, are readily translatable into specific inducements. These have been operationalized in relation to a specific negotiation situation by McCall and Cousins (1989). These sixteen compliance-gaining strategies have been only minimally varied and classified on the reward/punishment and persuader/persuadee dimensions by Miller and Parks (1982) and this is shown in more detail in Chapter 5.

. . . and the way that you say it'

Different kinds of language behaviour can be matched to the needs of the negotiation situation once these needs have been established. At the opening of a negotiation the language is that which reflects distributive bargaining — strong, positive, uncompromising. The words may be the same as those used in more cooperative situations, but the 'paralanguage', that is the stress and speed of speech, the intonation and the pitch, are used in such a way that an unyielding stance is implied.

In Figure 3.2 this kind of language is illustrated from the viewpoint of pitch (the nearer to the upper line the higher the pitch) and the stress (the bigger the dot the greater the stress).

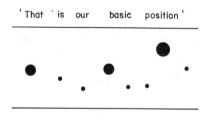

Figure 3.2

In the early exchanges a negotiator may try out various behaviours to test the opposer's limits. If these limits are not expressed in a correspondingly positive and strong manner, the negotiator, in an attempt to move for example an American opposer to his position, may be tempted to try as one of his behaviours a 'hard-sell' in which the syllables are dramatic, terse and rapid. In an English environment a 'soft-sell' approach might be used with related gentle, melodious and leisurely tones.

Eventually, if limit positions are identified and no movement ensues, one of the parties may indicate by signalling language a willingness to move without involving commitment at this stage, as in Figure 3.3.

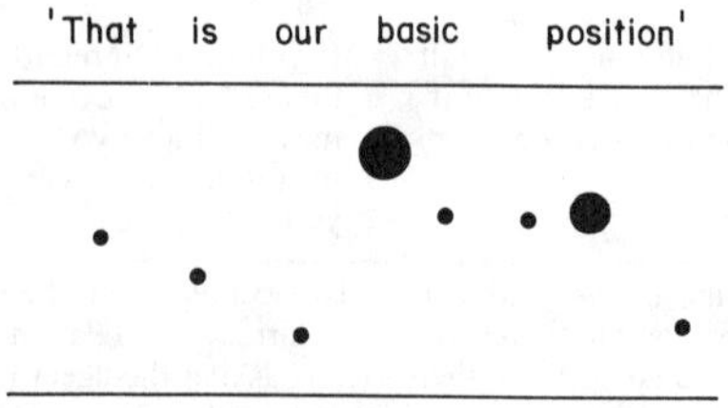

Figure 3.3

Here the indication is that the position is negotiable and invites responses like 'Under what circumstances would you be prepared to extend the period of credit?' Indicating behaviour, like all behaviour, relies not only on the words used, the stress, rhythm and pitch given to them by the user; it is also supported by other non-verbal language such as appropriate facial expressions and hand movements.

The transition from stage I to stage II is eased if irritating language is avoided. A licensing executive representing a would-be licensor who volunteers the opinion that the substantial downpayment in addition to royalties which he is seeking 'will be quickly recouped in a buoyant market like yours' is likely to antagonize a would-be licensee who probably considers that he is the person best qualified to pass judgement on the possibilities in his own market. If the negotiator interrupts or is perceived not to have considered well the other's view, or rejects it out of hand, he is liable to alienate his opposer. The implication is that the negotiator whose language indicates such behaviour considers his opposer incapable of deciding for himself or deems his views unworthy of consideration. Communication is a two-way process in which what is said is not necessarily what is heard. The negotiator may not intend to attribute such meaning to his language, but the reality for his opposer is his own perception of it.

In the early exchanges when the negotiating range is being established and the parties are making their most extreme demands, such demands are often couched in strong language and reinforced by repetition. The great danger in such a situation is that the interaction dynamic will take over and the parties find themselves in what has been called *attack/defend spirals* from which it can sometimes be difficult to escape, although agreement is still possible technically. This is most likely to happen in cultures which encourage competitiveness and confrontation.

Flagging behaviour to come

As the negotiation moves fully into the stage of integrative bargaining, so interpersonal forces come into play and the language used becomes more conducive to problem-solving. As the parties spell out the conditions under which they will be prepared to treat, the need is for frankness to establish beyond doubt that each other's proposals are understood. Skilled negotiators have been shown to give advance indication of the kind of behaviour they are about to use by using such phrases as 'Can I ask you a question — what . . .?' or 'If I could make a suggestion — provided you could . . . we might consider . . .' (Rackham and Carlisle 1978).

This 'flagging' of behaviour to come makes it less equivocal when clear understanding is important, provides social pressure to force a response, and gives the other party time to clear his mind of his own proposal or other previous statement. Disagreeing behaviour is not flagged because it highlights confrontation, the outcome of which often is loss of face for one or other of the negotiators. To do so would be counter-productive. Therefore a reason or explanation is given leading to a statement of the disagreement in the least competitive terms. While less important at the distributive stage when positional lines are still to be drawn, it can be of considerable importance at the integrative stage when a mutual trust may help the parties to a cooperative pattern of behaviour. The way language is used has to reflect this. When negotiators see disagreeing behaviour to be necessary, the apparent extent of disagreement can be mitigated by revealing, or appearing to reveal, what is going on in their minds, as in 'I am very concerned that we seem to be so far apart on . . .'.

Shaping predictable reactions

The interactive skills approach to negotiation provides a negotiator with a range of behaviours derived from a breakdown of observable behaviour into its separate elements. It claims to provide a repertoire wide enough to give genuine choice in deciding how best to behave in different situations.

Shaping and seeking behaviours are most powerful in achieving interaction objectives. Among the behaviours which are influential in shaping a predictable reaction are those which are concerned with such activities as making and seeking proposals and suggestions and seeking clarification and information (Honey 1978). Language is the vehicle for these influencing behaviours and has to be appropriate to the intended behaviour.

A negotiator does not hold a monopoly in articulating shaping behaviours. He will equally be involved in responding behaviours, also conveyed in terms of language. Behaviour supportive of a previous suggestion, for example, can be useful in encouraging an opposer to talk, whether for the purpose of encouraging his cooperation or gleaning information. The language which conveys the supportive behaviour is a kind of verbal headnodding; it encourages the opposer to elaborate or develop a view. Another responding behaviour is stating a difficulty. This can be used for such purposes as seeking clarification or deliberately to indicate disagreement. Difficulty stating, if consciously flagged, can in certain circumstances also be a powerful shaper of behaviour, as when a negotiator plays devil's advocate.

It should be pointed out, however, that the interactive skills approach, based as it is on observable behaviour, while providing a useful framework for negotiators, is inadequate to handle images, feelings and world-views which are also important for the communication and understanding of meaning. For this reason these factors are explored in the pages that follow.

Checking out ambiguities

The succession of moves and counter-moves leads to concessions, which are usually made conditional. To maintain the clarity of understanding necessary to clear the path for agreement, testing understanding and summarizing are techniques used to check out ambiguities prior to agreement (Rackham and Carlisle 1978). The skilled negotiator therefore uses suitable language in summarizing and testing understanding: 'Do I understand that if we agree to the credit being repaid in equal instalments, accept a four weeks' longer delivery period and agree to the supply of your standard discharge mechanism you will reduce the contract price by $15,000?' When the parties are satisfied they have spelt out their positions beyond doubt, and that each party is understood by the other, the ground is prepared for agreement.

Instead of making a concession and asking for agreement, a negotiator can make agreement conditional on acceptance of a package. This he can do if he has kept issues linked until brought together in the package. When agreement emerges precision is an essential requirement. An eventual contract based on a verbal agreement or an agreed summary of the substance of the verbal agreement, has in the event of a dispute to be interpreted either at arbitration or in the courts in terms of the applicable law. A gap often exists between the courts who interpret a contract and use language as a precise instrument, and laymen like uninitiated buyers and salesmen who use it in a more general way. There is therefore a need, certainly for businessmen concluding agreements without legal assistance, for sufficient knowledge of the language of the law, so that they are able to achieve precision in making agreements.

NEGOTIATION AND FOREIGN LANGUAGES

From the foregoing it should be obvious that to negotiate in a foreign language it is not enough to know it intimately or to have mastered its business language or register. It is at least as important to know what is involved in the negotiation process and the behaviours which can direct and influence negotiations. It has been claimed by one highly respected authority that human communication equals translation, and that therefore a study of translation is a study of language (Steiner 1975:44). Appropriate behaviour objectives will be couched in language terms and, whatever the spoken language, it can then be matched to the stage of negotiation and the language objectives for the appropriate behaviour in a given interaction situation.

Negotiating the foreign language barrier . . .

Translation into a foreign language poses problems for both negotiating parties. Unless we know a foreigner's language well, we might easily misinterpret his English paralanguage (Crystal 1975). For example, it is not always possible to see that a foreigner is angry or upset or embarrassed. On the contrary, it is a very common reaction to misinterpret a foreigner, to assume he is being rude or belligerent or sarcastic on the basis of his tone of voice, and to respond accordingly. What we are really doing is responding to interference from the paralinguistic features of his mother tongue. For example, flat level tones in English regularly connote boredom or sarcasm. In Russian, on the other hand, the level tone is much more widely used with a natural, matter-of-fact interpretation. A Russian will therefore tend to speak English with too many level tone endings. To his own ears the sentence sounds intonationally neutral, but to the English listener he sounds uninterested and rude.

By the same token the English speaker negotiating in a foreign language has to ensure he uses the pitch, loudness, speed and rhythm associated with the meaning he intends to convey. Similarly an Arab speaking English is often thought by Westerners to be shouting, as Arabs tend to speak more loudly than Englishmen or Americans. That tone of voice in speaking a second language can be misunderstood in negotiation is shown in one study which reports that tone of voice interpreted as 'sincere' by Egyptians sounds 'belligerent' to Americans (Adams 1957). Americans speak louder than Europeans and give the impression of assertiveness not necessarily intended.

48

Whether to speak the foreign opposer's language or not will depend on a number of situational factors. If the negotiator does not have a reasonable command of the opposer's language he will have to consider whether he should use it at all. In most countries, efforts to speak the language, no matter how ineptly, are usually well received. An opposer will often indicate that he has an interpreter at hand or break into the negotiator's language if he feels more can be achieved that way. The French, however, do not like to hear their language used inaccurately and do not hesitate to give signals to that effect.

In Tunisia, on the other hand, lack of fluency in French can be a positive advantage. French has lost some of the stigma associated with it because of the colonial experience. Yet the majority of Tunisians recognize the practical necessity of some French but often insist it should only be used as a tool and need not be learned perfectly. Indeed an excellent accent in French may be resented. Because of its authoritative connotations, French allows Tunisians to maintain social distance in certain situations. All educated Tunisians speak it. In spoken contexts the preference for language in descending order is:

(i) Tunisian Arabic for as broad a range of situations as possible;
(ii) French, when Tunisian Arabic is not possible, e.g. with a foreigner or in technical contexts;
(iii) Classical Arabic when neither of the other choices is possible as in speaking with Arabs from other countries who do not know French.

In written contexts the hierarchy of preferences is nearly reversed. French is the written language of bilinguals, Arabic being confined to printed matter in official communications (Stevens 1983).

The use of Hindi to address indigenous Indians is usually met with a reply in English. To understand this, one must know something of the nature of social relationships in India and how they are marked linguistically. It appears that the use of Hindi when speaking to native English speakers denotes a relatively informal or intimate status. Indians will tend to speak in English to Westerners who are strangers in order to mark personal distance. Only when the relationship has become less formal can the language use change. This type of situation is comparable to the shift from 'Mr' to 'Bob' in English or the shift in German from 'Sie' to 'Du' (Gumperz 1966).

Despite the need to be aware of such considerations, a facility in an opposer's language is a basic factor in successful interpersonal relations and can therefore bear on negotiation outcomes. Research by the IMP Group into managers' perceptions, attitudes, opinions and beliefs in five European countries concluded, among other things, that British marketers were, despite their own perceptions, less than adequate to discuss technical and commercial matters because of limitations in their ability to communicate in the language of the other four countries (Turnbull and Cunningham 1981). Social relationships were also more difficult to establish. French buyers had particular difficulties in making social contact with British and German suppliers. It appears that the often remarked 'chauvinism' of the French in relation to their language is such that marketers wishing to operate in France must have, in any case, a good level of ability in the French language. There is no reason to doubt that the disinclination of the British to learn and speak foreign languages is shared by other English-speaking peoples. There is much opinion to reinforce this view. The difference between English-speaking and French businessmen may be, according to the research study, that the French recognize the need to communicate in the customer's language.

Ideally, the best way to negotiate the language barrier begins with a mastery of the language. Cultural aspects are then more easily assimilated and appropriate foreign language behaviours facilitated within the negotiation process.

. . . and the cultural/linguistic barrier

Language and speech are characterized by pauses between a speaker's words or sentences or between the conclusion of one party's speech act and the beginning of the other's. When two Japanese are negotiating the time period between conscious thought and speaking activity will tend to be substantially longer than with Europeans or Americans in similar situations. While the pauses are part of the Japanese communication interaction, similar pauses for Westerners can be awkward. They may interpret the silence as confusion, prevarication, lack of understanding, embarrassment or even a potential negative response by the Japanese. They might even be tempted to fill in the gaps with meaningless and insincere chatter which could make the misunderstanding worse. It should be clear to both the participating Westerner and Japanese that knowledge of the difference in perception of silence can be used to advantage by a negotiator by making simple adjustments to his behaviour to make the dialogue a more comfortable one to the other party.

There are many situations and countries in which it is necessary to use interpreters, because neither party has an adequate command of the language of the other. This is particularly so in those countries such as the Arab states and the so-called Pacific Rim countries. Some of these languages are so flexible in their translatability that it would be unwise to accept agreement in them. Arabic is one such language. Because written and official Arabic is divorced from the language of everyday life, it has a particular influence on the literate Arab (Shouby 1951). This manifests itself in general vagueness of thought and in over-emphasis on the psychological significance of linguistic symbols at the expense of their meaning by fitting the thought to the word rather than the word to the thought. Words become substitutes for thought rather than their representation. Over-exaggeration and over-assertion become natural means of expression, with the result that a simple statement in English cannot be translated into Arabic literally without losing part of its meaning. Within their own countries Arabs are compelled to over-assert and over-exaggerate, otherwise there is a good chance other Arabs will misunderstand them. If an Arab says what he means without exaggeration, other Arabs might think he means the opposite. This can lead to misunderstanding in negotiation by non-Arabs who do not realize that the Arab speaker is merely following a linguistic tradition. In the same way, Arabs often fail to realize that others mean exactly what they say if it is put in a simple, unelaborated manner. To many Arabs, a simple 'no' may be perceived as a sign to continue rather than a direct negative. Communication is made more complex by the need to interpret Arab behaviour and to behave towards an Arab in a way in which his interpretation reflects the intended meaning.

> The tendency for Arabs to over-assert in the perception of Westerners is compounded by the nature of Arabic grammar.
>
> An analysis of comparative advertising in Saudi Arabian magazines, initiated on the widely accepted assumption that advertising tends to mirror society, showed that the Arabic language was laden with 'rhetoric, puffery and exaggeration'. The high incidence of such language appears to be explained by the fact that in contrast with the English adjective, with its three forms of positive (great), comparative (greater) and superlative (greatest), Arabic has only two forms. These are the positive and the so-called elative which can either have comparative or superlative meaning (Patai 1973).
> In addition to these basic meanings of the positive and the elative, the positive can also mean superlative and the elative can mean positive. *Afkhar Al Mantojat* literally 'the best of all products' means 'an excellent product'. The use of the elative in the simple positive sense indicates an inclination to emphatic expression. The elative form is frequently used to intensify expressions. In such cases it is used for the sake of the interpretation of the basic meaning of the adjective, not for indicating the especially high degree of the quality expressed by the adjective. (Adapted from Razzouk and Harmon 1985.)

The Japanese enjoy a social organization characterized by vertical relationships supported by emotional ties and social obligations and by the concept of harmony and consensus, all of which are reflected in business encounters (Nakane 1973). Consequently, displays of naked power are seen as potential threats to harmony and face. If it is necessary to resolve a conflict, the Japanese like to do it in such a way that neither side appears to have been forced to make a concession. Compromises like splitting the difference are usually acceptable. They prefer agreement on the main points to a formal legal contract, because they see litigation also as a threat to harmony. This avoidance of confrontation can be seen in their use of affirmatives as negatives (Van Zandt 1970). When a Japanese says 'yes' he usually means 'no', or at best 'maybe'. He will use the word 'hai' frequently, meaning literally 'yes' but usually indicating understanding rather than agreement. If he draws breath between his teeth and says something like 'sah' or states 'it is very difficult', he means 'no'. If a negotiator is to communicate effectively in these circumstances, he has to adapt his language to culturally conditioned cues and responses.

In some areas of the world, for example in Germany, Austria, Hungary, Czechoslovakia and Italy, it is customary to overstate a case. In others, for example in Britain, Scandinavia and Australia, it is normal to understate it. A negotiator's expectations stemming from the attribution of his own linguistic customs to his opposer can result in a perceived violation of a sincerity condition. Where a negotiator attempts to adapt to his opposer's linguistic customs, he may sometimes overcompensate in his interpretation of a foreigner's utterance when an opposer is also trying to adapt. An Australian might decode a German's statement to be an overstatement when in fact it is an attempt at Australian understatement (Clyne 1977). Social anthropologists tell us however that power relations usually determine who adopts and adapts behaviour in a cross-cultural setting. A German in an Australian setting is likely to be the one to modify his behaviour.

Communication breakdown can arise from actual or imaginary differences in expectations arising from cultural differences, often perpetuated by education systems. These can generate tension and even conflict between negotiating parties from different countries. In one study conducted, the effect of culture on expectations of multinational companies and host governments is well demonstrated. Unlike other MNC attributes — such as size of investment, sophistication of technology, degree of diversification, period of operation, number of employees and sales volume — expectational differences contributed very significantly to the variation in the independent variable of conflict. The host government expectations are at the total system/aggregate environmental level. The MNC's expectations are concentrated at the sub-system firm/task environment level. Considered in this way the gap between expectations is quite evident. The problem is compounded by the fact that expectations generally remain unvoiced. Clarity of expectations should go a long way to reducing tension (Negandhi 1980).

Westerners negotiating in South Korea or Japan can help clarify expectations if first they can see issues as perceived by businessmen in these two countries. The ranking that takes place among individuals applies equally to institutions. Consequently, group members see their own institutions in terms of how they rank with competing institutions. Competition appears to exist between similar firms, and the loyalty of groups within organizations produces company and personal goals which stress superiority over competitors. This tends to be expressed in terms of size, which together with factors like steady employment, acquisition of technology and greater exports, usually takes precedence over profits. A blind adherence solely to the profit motive, as illustrated in Reading II at the end of Chapter 10, can lead to misunderstanding and communication breakdown. Such issues, if not brought to the fore prior to any joint-venture agreement, can virtually guarantee future problems.

There is much written about the Korean and particularly the Japanese use of the experience curve. The reality is that this is largely coincidental. Koreans and Japanese enjoy cultures which tend to put size first. This therefore inclines them to embrace market entry and ownership strategies which place emphasis on the long term. Initial prices are set at a level identified as good value by the market and sufficiently low to preclude competition entry. As market share builds up and volume increases, the typical cost savings of 20−30 per cent every time volume doubles, are not passed on in full to the market and considerable profits are created in the later stages of the product life-cycle. This strategy is facilitated by an ability to carry the delayed profitability due to the advantages inherent in the concentration of overseas trade in the hands of a few conglomerate companies.

In Korea these conglomerates are called *chaebols* and their success has been largely due to the close relationship between government and business in Korea and the control the government has been able to exert over bank lending for expansion. In Japan they are called *sogo shoshas,* and their ability to finance long-term strategies stems from their relationship with banks, insurance companies and shipping companies. Western, and particularly US companies tend to make much more short-term decisions under pressure from shareholders for 'profit now'. The two views are opposed and require to be clear to the other party before creative and acceptable solutions can be attempted.

The English and Americans, it is said, are divided by a common language.

'One trait which, it is claimed, characterizes Americans is their sincerity, spontaneity and candour. This stems from the Utopian belief that manipulative dissimulation is undesirable and that coexistence is possible without much mutual influence. Sincerity, certainly in the European view, is the dominant norm governing relationships in the US and appears to originate in the belief that everything should be comprehensible to the outside world. It has been suggested that in the presence of a sincere person, one feels assured, nothing is being withheld or masked by irony, understatement or wit, the three favourite modes of Euopean discourse.

It is speculated that anything smacking of overt dissimulation seems particularly threatening to an illusionistic society that insists on pretending to be real. Relationships with Americans are best promoted by openness without resort in interpersonal interactions to such linguistic devices as puns or double meaning which, for them, savours of covertness.' (Adapted from J.M. Evans, quoted by P. Watzlawick (1976) in *The Language of Change: Elements of Therapeutic Communication,* New York: Basic Books.)

Prerequisites for oral communication

Successful negotiation in an intercultural situation rests on an awareness of the process of negotiation as the first prerequisite. The second is the ability to understand and use influencing behaviours. The third is empathy for the culture with which the negotiator is interacting, since a responsiveness to the culture will mediate appropriately the influencing behaviours. Language is the servant of all three, and each spoken language has to meet language objectives stemming from them, supported by its own non-verbal gestures and expressions.

NON-VERBAL SIGN SYSTEMS AND NEGOTIATION

While the spoken word remains one of the most powerful and flexible tools of communication in negotiation, translation of meaning is not confined to it. Some sensory data cannot be paraphrased or even identified by speech. The spoken language is only one, although the most important in the majority of circumstances, of a multitude of graphic, olfactory, tactile, spatial, temporal and symbolic means of communication. The ambiguity of a spoken language can be reduced when read in conjunction with these non-verbal sign systems. Understanding within a language can therefore be assisted by the interpretation of verbal messages through such non-verbal signs.

In certain negotiating circumstances non-verbal aspects of communication assume a greater significance than does verbal language. These are in relation to expressions of emotion and the communicating of attitudes of a negotiator to his opposer (Argyle 1975:119).

Expression of emotion

When a negotiator takes the view that his opposer is being unjustly demanding, unreasonably resistant to proposals or punitive in the exercise of a greater power in relation to what he considers his share of available outcomes, it is likely that intangible issues related to the anticipated or actual loss of public face or self-esteem will emerge. The negotiator is likely to react in a way which will protect him from injury — for example, in terms of the expectations of his peers or those in authority in his organization — and this can manifest itself in a stream of non-verbal signals about his inner state. These will take the form mainly of facial expressions and other gestures, sometimes supplemented by vocalizations such as grunts and groans. Some cultures, for example Oriental cultures, more than others inhibit emotional expression. Other cultures, such as the Italian and Greek and all Latin American ones, are much more demonstrative. Yet within each culture there is a perfectly clear range of visual expression from mild to intense, and it is a question of being attuned to the particular culture to read the extent of emotional intensity (Morris 1978:118).

The negotiator has to be sensitive to emotions being displayed by his opposer, whether the emotion arises from a state such as anxiety or from milder states or moods like feelings of displeasure or shame. Emotions are often difficult enough to handle without compounding the difficulty with misperception. It is up to the negotiator to ensure that he does not, through insensitivity to such emotions, drive his opposer away from the relationship while settling within his own objectives remains a possibility.

Communicating interpersonal attitudes and feelings

In order to handle the negotiating relationship and decide the negotiating position and behaviour to adopt, each party has to obtain information about the other's attitudes towards him — whether he is cooperative or competitive and what his true feelings, preferences and social perceptions are. It is what can be drawn from the exchange of information by the parties and the way it can be used to influence each other that constitutes the fundamental strategic issue in negotiation. In communicating attitudes to other people, non-verbal signals have a much greater impact than verbal signals and are more likely to reflect a true mood.

In any consideration of interpersonal attitudes it is useful first of all to look at the main dimensions of these which have emerged in studies of interpersonal relations (Argyle 1983).

People who have a high affiliative motivation have a variety of positive attitudes. They need and seek friendship, acceptance and warmth in relationships with their peers. At the opposite end of the axis are those who are aggressive and reject any attempt to establish relationships. As hostility is often concealed it may be difficult to perceive this kind of attitude.

People who are motivated to be dominant in relationships, where there is no clear difference of status or power between the parties, exhibit this attitude partly by a general pattern of bodily relaxation. Whereas affiliation relations are communicated by a greater degree of gaze often combined with a smile, by facial expression, soft tone of voice, direct orientation and bodily relaxation, dominance relations are characterized by relaxation also, asymmetrical position of arms and legs, leaning backwards away from the vertical and a tendency to speak more than the other party. It is quite possible, indeed likely, to have combinations of attitudes — for example, friendly dominance.

The significance for negotiators of these considerations of attitudes is that when they meet they bring to the interaction their own social drives and skills. If both talk all the time or both persist in asking questions and generally seek to be dominant, social interaction will be limited. For a dialogue to be successful, there has to be a coordination of techniques. If an opposer wants to use his own favoured social skills the negotiator has to adopt a corresponding behaviour (Argyle 1983). If both parties produce their preferred skills, they will not in general find there is a perfect fit. Where there is no coordination of the skills of the negotiators the clashing of techniques will lead to discomfort and lack of harmony. It is therefore up to the negotiator to adjust his behaviour as necessary.

If an Indian or Chinese, or any other negotiator, insists on adopting skills which reflect his own attitudes, then it is up to the foreign businessmen to adopt a coordinating set. An international salesman or a buyer who has a creative role in making international contracts for alternative sourcing would be expected to behave in a way similar to his overseas counterpart, such as meeting his affiliative needs by sharing his emotional state; or in a complementary way, as being dominant while the other is dependent. By such accommodation can a meaningful interaction take place.

Deception and its detection

Emotions, attitudes and feelings of one party towards the other are not always what they seem. For strategic reasons signals are often sent which are not genuine. A buyer does not always wish to convey how keen he is to have a particular product or service nor a salesman how much his company needs a particular sale, in case his opposer revises his objective upwards. Personal inclinations and interests of one or both the negotiating parties may be at odds with the interests of the organizations they represent. Opening moves and concessions allow each party to gauge the other's preferences and intentions and, in turn, give each negotiator the opportunity to present or misrepresent information about his own. Deception is frequently practised in all social interaction, and negotiation is no exception. Negotiators who feel it necessary to practice deception should be able to do it well. This they can learn by becoming adept at detecting its practice in others.

When an individual practices deception, his behaviour tends to fragment. Verbal and non-verbal components of a message conflict and it is possible to detect the deception as a result. Non-verbal leakage of deception has been studied and the findings are important for all executives involved in face-to-face activities in various kinds of exchange relationships. Experiments in the USA suggest lying is characterized by a number of non-verbal behaviours (Ekman and Friesen 1969):

1   Hand actions normally used to emphasize verbal statements are significantly reduced.
2   Touching the face with the hand increases dramatically, particularly covering the mouth and touching the nose. This does not mean that a person covering his mouth must be lying. It does mean that he is more likely to be lying at times when he covers his mouth than at times when his hand does not cover it. The same applies to the touching of the nose. Variations include stroking the chin, scratching the eyebrow and pulling the ear-lobe.
3   There is an increase in the number of body shifts of the person concerned. These are slight changes in the resting posture of the trunk as the speaker moves from one sitting position to another.
4   The hand shrug becomes more common as other gesticulations decrease in frequency.
5   What distinguishes facial expressions when lying from when telling the truth are micro-expressions so small and so quick that only trained observers can detect them.

'[If you must lie] the best way to deceive is to restrict your signals to words and facial expressions. The most efficient means of doing this is either to conceal the rest of your body or keep it so busy with a complicated mechanical procedure that all its visual deception clues are stifled by the demand for physical dexterity. In other words, if you have to lie, do it over the telephone or when peering over a wall; alternatively when threading a needle or manoeuvring a car into a parking space. If much of you is visible and you have no mechanical task to perform, then to succeed with your lie you must try to involve the whole of your body in the act of deception, not just your voice and face.' (Desmond Morris in *Manwatching*, Triad Granada, 1977)

'The believability scale'

When contradictory signals are received it is the non-verbal signal which should be trusted. In the face of contradictory signals it is useful to refer to the 'believability scale' developed by Desmond Morris (1977). This is a seven-point scale in decreasing order of believability:

1   Body stress signals: These are signals resulting from stress to which the nervous system automatically reacts and produces involuntary changes in the body of the individual. Sweating or licking of dry lips or heightened pitch of the voice are signals indicating this stress, which may stem from lying or fear or excitement. These are the surest signals because they cannot be controlled even when the individual is aware of them.
2   Lower body signals: It is the lower parts of the body that are least easily controlled. Foot-tapping, for example, can indicate impatience when verbal and facial behaviour betoken interest.
3   Body posture signals: General body posture is often a giveaway, as when one party nods, murmurs accord and even leans forward in an attentive position, but his body sags or slumps showing boredom.

4 Unidentified gestures: Many hand actions are indefinite movements to which no names have become attached. The negotiator who makes aggressive gestures with his hands while talking of the need for cooperation is contradicting his verbal claim.
5 Identified hand gestures: Many hand gestures are deliberate and definite. Such actions are not to be trusted if they appear as part of a contradictory signal.
6 Facial expressions: People are so aware of their faces that they can exercise considerable control over them to reinforce spoken deceptive behaviour.
7 Verbalizations: When oral messages are given these can only be trusted when there is no contradictory behaviour.

Under- and over-reactions

Non-verbal behaviours are often performed too weakly or too strongly for their particular context. The reason for this is that a person's true mood is interfering with the behaviour he is trying to project. Gestures and expressions embody subtle complexities. When the performer's mood is inappropriate he fails to convey these complexities to the degree required to convince.

With under- and over-reactions there is a danger when negotiators from different cultures meet that they will misunderstand each other. The man who holds the eye too long as Westerners may believe of Arabs, or is over-familiar or personal as Englishmen may believe of Americans or Indians, may well be looked on as over-reacting. In fact they can be behaving in accordance with the norms of their own cultures where rules in relation to public display have not dampened their actions to the degree they have in the other party's culture. On the other hand the opposer who underplays the intensity of gaze, as a Japanese might do by the standards of American or West European negotiators, may well be regarded as deceitful. As trust is an essential component in effective negotiation, negotiators require to familiarize themselves with the culture with which they are interacting.

Managing impressions of self

People often deliberately manipulate clues. The ideas which the sender has about himself are converted into body signals which others have to decode. By creating a favourable impression on others, a negotiator can gain material advantages and sustain at the same time a positive and satisfying self-image.

Negotiators, through the moves, countermoves and concessions they make and the verbal and non-verbal behaviours that support them, provide information on intangible as well as tangible issues; they allow each party to gauge the other's attributes, preferences and intentions and, in turn, give each party the opportunity to present or misrepresent information about his own. It has been shown by Goffman (1972a) that interactors need this kind of information about each other's preferences and attributes to know how to deal with one another.

Attributes are not always directly evident and one has often to rely on non-verbal signals which are associated with such attributes. It is possible for negotiators to send information about themselves which is not wholly accurate but presents an improved version of the self. For example, an individual in an organization nominated to negotiate a given contract might wish to convey the impression, perhaps by his style of social behaviour or the cut of his clothes, that he holds a higher position in his company than he does in reality.

Goffman maintains that the behaviour of people in a social situation is designed to help everyone maintain the self they choose to project in that particular situation. If contradictory signals suggest that the self being presented is not the true one, a negotiator has to refrain from making and emphasizing points which make it clear that he knows this to be so. If a negotiator wishes to be seen to be strong and competent, in the eyes of his peers and superiors in his own organization as well as in the eyes of his opposer, then he must be treated accordingly. When a negotiator has taken up an extreme position and follows it with an easing of demands, this may be looked on as indicating a view of his opposer as a worthy adversary to whom concession must gradually be made. A failure to make any concessions that are perceived as real by the opposer may be interpreted as a reflection on the latter's own competence, particularly if he cannot return to his constituents with some evidence of concessions won. A negotiator who believes he is seen to be capable and effectve may be expected to behave in an increasingly cooperative manner. If we destroy his face we have destroyed the relationship.

Negotiating across cultures carries the risk of misperception arising from differences in the manipulation of clues. Misinterpretation can introduce antagonisms into a relationship. In many Western countries there is something of a taboo on verbal self-presentation. While Australians have an achievement orientation they also have the 'tall poppy syndrome' — one must not take too much credit for one's accomplishments or be seen to stand out above the crowd. Observers have noted a similar attitude in Sweden to setting oneself apart from others in terms of what is said and what is done. In countries like India and the Arab countries, on the other hand, this is acceptable social behaviour. People are not forced back into non-verbal signals as in these Western and Australasian cultures. An understanding and acceptance of these different clues can direct verbal and non-verbal behaviour in a way that can smooth the bargaining process.

SOCIAL CONTEXT AND STRUCTURE

Situation and negotiation

We have seen that people usually project the self they choose in a particular situation. That situation will mediate the verbal and non-verbal behaviours of the encounter. Differing situations will influence these behaviours according to, for example, whether the speaker is talking to the same or opposite sex, to subordinate or superior, to one listener or many, to someone directly or on the telephone, to someone directly or through an interpreter. If we want to distinguish appropriate from inappropriate behaviour in a given scene to guide our actions as negotiators, or if we want to examine the effects of a particular interaction in other situations and environments, we must know a great deal more about the social context within which the communicative act takes place (Goffman 1972b).

High- and low-context cultures

Much work showing the relationship between speaking and social conduct has been done by Hall (1959, 1969, 1983), particularly in connection with the time dimension and spatial relationships. He has also drawn a useful distinction between what he has called high-context and low-context cultures (Hall 1976). Communication in a high-context culture depends heavily on the context or non-verbal aspects of communication, whereas the low-context culture depends more on verbally expressed communications. It is noteworthy that the high-context countries are just those which, it is forecast, will feature large in future trading relations with the advanced industrialized countries of the world (Pockney 1978).

> ' [When people from two different cultures meet] there is infinite scope for misunderstanding and confusion. This may be a matter of misinterpreting the other's communications, verbal or non-verbal. There is the Englishman who deprecates his own abilities in what turns out to be a highly misleading way; there is the Arab who starves at a banquet because he is only offered the dishes once; there is the African who puts his hand on a Western knee. There may be difficulties in setting up a stable pattern of interaction — Americans and Europeans have been seen retreating backwards or gyrating in circles at international conferences pursued by Latin Americans trying to establish their habitual degree of proximity. Westerners are perplexed by Japanese who giggle when hearing or delivering bad news. American businessmen find it difficult to adjust to the more hierarchical pattern of relationships in their overseas branches where subordinates do not speak their minds to their superiors.' (Michael Argyle in *The Psychology of Interpersonal Behaviour*, Pelican Books, Fourth edition, 1983, pp. 189–190[1])

Social structural constraints

Analysis of the social structure of high-context countries can provide useful insights for negotiators. Nakane (1973), writing of Japan, sees the persistence of social structures in the modes of social relations which determine the probable variation of group organization in changing circumstances. This persistence reveals the basic value orientations inherent in society and the basis of individual behaviour and interpersonal relations. In high-context countries negotiators require sufficient knowledge of the culture to communicate understandably and acceptably. It is only if they are in a position to share the assumptions of the people with whom they are dealing that they can build up relationships and have a satisfactory interaction. These assumptions will embrace the cognitive structures of the people concerned and the world view which they hold, which derive from culture.

---

[1] Reprinted by permission of Penguin Books Ltd. © Michael Argyle 1967, 1972, 1983.

Differences in cognitive structures . . .

There is a wide gulf between the ways in which Westerners and Orientals think. Western and Chinese cognition have been compared and the following characteristics isolated (Redding 1980):

(a) Western cognition: logical, sequential connections; use of abstract notions of reality to represent universals; emphasis on cause.

(b) Chinese cognition: intuitive perception and more reliance on sense data; non-abstract; non-logical (in the Cartesian sense), with emphasis on the particular rather than the universal; high sensitivity to context and relationships, and concern for reconciliation, harmony and balance.

The concept of harmony is seen at its most significant in terms of time. In the West, at its simplest, there is a linear view of time in which scheduling and keeping to dates is given a high priority. In China time is not seen as duration constituted by succession but is rather characterized by a cyclical view which puts more stress on end-results. In the Chinese concept of relationships, the individual is closely embedded in a social network in which the family or clan and, by association, social needs are a greater motivating factor than the so-called 'self-actualizing' needs. Social controls are external and are imposed by the sensitive feelings of pride engendered, and conformity is imposed by wounding or the threat of wounding this pride. This is the basis of 'face' which is a pervasive aspect of interpersonal relationships. These relationships are extended into cliques and obligation networks characterized by patronage and nepotism which permeate Chinese society and its organizations. It is this highly developed sense of, and reliance on, relationships which tends to make the Chinese put friendship before business.

The implications for negotiators of these cognitive structures have been examined (Warrington and McCall 1983). Since time is cyclical, deadlines are not understood and are not therefore restrictive. Indeed, negotiations are protracted for a number of reasons. The Chinese see the negotiating process as an opportunity to elicit as much information as possible, particularly that of a technical nature. Would-be sellers would be advised to be prepared to conduct technical seminars. This tendency of the Chinese to draw out as much information as possible before disclosing their hand may be associated with the issue of face and their reluctance to display ignorance. As they appear to assimilate data in intuitive 'lumps' and only understand in terms of 'wholes' or 'total systems', their appreciation of technologies may be limited until they have grasped how the diverse elements fit into the system.

Chinese negotiators tend to suck up information like technological vacuum cleaners:

'It is said that the Boeing Aircraft Company prepared and presented literally a room full of literature. They had discussion of technical presentations every day for eight weeks. At the end of that time the Chinese made one response: "Thank you for your introduction".' (Warrington and McCall 1983)

The stage of distributive bargaining is therefore unimportant where the assimilation of information is a major element in the interaction. The confrontation inherent in it is in any case a potential threat to face. The integrative stage assumes a greater importance for the development of the relationships between the negotiators. The problem-solving element is not so much one of moving gradually from extreme positions to an intermediate one as of reaching an agreed position in one well-considered step. The foreign negotiator has to make his points as cogently as he can within the relationships that he can establish. Whatever the number of issues that are explored, settlement can and should only be made in a single package. A summary close is more suitable than a concession close, provided the timing is right. When a decision has been made, it is still possible for adjustments to be made. The Chinese are pragmatists in this respect.

When the Chinese take decisions, these are not made by individuals; the Chinese system and Chinese manner are against this. Decisions emerge as a result of group consensus, and delays have to be seen in that light and not as a deliberate procrastination or lack of interest. A number of experienced businessmen have indicated that the Chinese are shrewd negotiators and not beyond using negotiations as an exercise in attrition. This suggests that the Western negotiator must have some notion of what is an acceptable time for decision-making before taking final action.

The concepts of harmony and friendship in business relationships, reflected in the total absence of contract law, means that the Chinese are more concerned with a contract as a basis of relationships rather than a legalistic document. If companies feel they must have standard contract terms, then 'heads of agreement' can be an acceptable preliminary.

. . . is not confined to East/West differences

Even within Western Europe or within the English-speaking group of countries, there are differences in the ways people conceptualize their experience and hence increase the possibility of misunderstanding. It has been pointed out that our concepts structure what we perceive and how we relate to other people. Our conceptual system therefore plays a crucial role in defining our everyday realities. This system, in terms of which we both think and act, is metaphorical in nature (Lakoff and Johnson 1980).

The essence of a metaphorical concept is understanding and experiencing one kind of thing in terms of another. For example, the metaphor 'argument is war' is strong in Anglo-American culture and is reflected in such statements as 'your claims are indefensible', 'his arguments are easily shot down', 'position loss' and 'we'll attack every weak point in his position'. In other words Lakoff and Johnson maintain that human thought processes are largely metaphorical. In Sweden, which has maintained a neutrality for hundreds of years, wars have not been part of their tradition, confrontation is disliked and the cooperative mode is preferred. It is not to be wondered at that the 'argument is war' metaphor is not one which patterns how Swedes structure their perceptions and how they relate to others.

A TOTAL COMMUNICATION SYSTEM

We have seen that, in the negotiation process, interpersonal communication is a key activity which takes place at the verbal, non-verbal, situational, contextual and social structural levels. These are interrelated and lose meaning in isolation. Together they can be described as a total communication or multi-channel system which has been called the 'integrational aspect of the communicative process' (Birdwhistell 1973). In the broadest sense the integrational aspect includes all behavioural operations which:

1   keep the system in operation;
2   regulate the interaction process;
3   cross-reference particular messages to comprehensibility in a particular context;
4   relate the particular context to the larger contexts of which the interaction is but
    a special situation.

The next chapter aims to illustrate just this in frameworks for adaptive behaviour in business encounters in particular intercultural contexts. To span differing languages and cultures and achieve a fuller understanding, the international negotiator has to interpret the cultural patterns and concepts of one country in terms of the patterns and concepts of the other. It is up to him to bridge the gap between utterance and felt meaning. If the hearer understands and accepts a message then he has been influenced (Hovland *et al.* 1953).

If negotiators, because of lack of cultural awareness, can so easily fail to perceive, or indeed do misperceive words, actions and similar clues in international business encounters, then there is a need for approaches which will help to improve perception. The remainder of this chapter will address this question by considering language as culture, the development of cultural sensitivity in interpersonal communication, and different cultural perspectives which assist interpersonal communication.

LANGUAGE AS MACRO-CULTURE

Language is not a universal means of communication; rather it is a means of communication embedded in a particular culture. If language is culturally distinctive it is reasonable to expect that each language will have a correspondingly distinctive vocabulary. Examples abound of how language reflects the emphasis in a culture — Eskimos have many specific terms describing snow and its landscape and the Arabs have literally hundreds of words to describe the camel and its associated equipment. The importance for interpersonal relations of language as a mirror of a distinctive culture can likewise be shown. The Japanese concept of *amae*, unfamiliar in the West but embodied in the psychological concept of 'passive object love' (Balint 1965), refers initially to the feelings that all normal infants harbour towards the mother — dependence, the desire to be passively loved, the unwillingness to be separated from the warm mother–child circle and cast into the world of objective reality.

In a seminal work Doi (1973) established the basic premise that in a Japanese these feelings are somehow prolonged into, and diffused throughout, his adult life so that they come to shape, to a degree unknown in the West, his whole attitude to other people and to reality. This means that within his own most intimate circle, and to diminishing degrees outside it, he seeks relationships which allow him to presume on familiarity. The assurance of another's goodwill permits a certain degree of self-indulgence, and a corresponding degree of indifference to the claims of the other person as a separate individual. Such a relationship implies the blurring of the distinction between subject and object.

Amae is, as a word, peculiar to the Japanese language, yet it describes a psychological phenomenon that is basically common to mankind. It shows not only how especially familiar the psychology in question is to the Japanese, but also that the Japanese social structure is formed in such a way as to permit expression of that psychology. This implies that *amae* is a key concept for the understanding not only of the psychological make-up of the individual Japanese, but of the understanding of Japanese society as a whole. The emphasis on vertical relationships as illustrated in some detail in the next chapter, as being characteristic of the Japanese type social structure, could also be seen

---

It is not only in a culture so different from Western cultures as the Japanese that language reflects what is important in that culture. For example, the very positive West German attitudes to work and achievement are seen in the abundance of words confirming them and the incidence of their use:

'The vocabulary employed by German managers . . . does not reflect the language of the business school or the concept of management as a systematic entity which can be analysed in general terms . . . . There is *Arbeitswille*, the will to work; *Arbeitsfreude*, delight in work; *Arbeitseinsatz*, getting stuck into work; *Arbeitslust*, love of work – a very common expression; *Einsatzbereitschaft*, a willingness to engage in purposeful action; *Durchsetzungsvermögen*, the ability to get things done, see things through, and so on. The word *Termin*, delivery date or deadline, and associated words like *Termintreue*, faithfulness to deadlines, are also very much on the lips of the German manager and there is a block of derived adjectives and compound nouns based on *Termin*. Another key word is *Leistung*, performance or achievement which again gives rise to a set of derivatives: there is *leistungmässig*, compatible with performance; *leistungsfähig*, capable of achievement and *Leistungsgesellschaft*, the achievement-oriented society or meritocracy. Other common compound words related to performance or achievement are *Leistungswille*, desire to demonstrate performance; *Leistungsbereitschaft*, readiness to demonstrate performance; and *Leistungsvermögen*, capacity for achievement.

The German *Unternehmer* – the entrepreneur – is highly regarded. He is legitimated not so much in these days by risking his money as by his direct involvement and personal responsibility. If one wishes to praise a German manager for acting responsibly and in the best interests of his company, one describes his conduct as *unternehmerisch*.

Key words in the Anglo-Saxon management vocabulary which are not used much in the original by German speakers . . . are *human relations* and *job satisfaction* . . . The words *communication* and *motivation* exist but are not key words in the German manager's vocabulary . . . the fact that such phrases do not figure much in the German manager's vocabulary is a further piece of evidence that German management is not Americanized, has a low managerial consciousness and tends to think in direct and tangible terms. (Adapted from Peter Lawrence, *Managers and Management in West Germany*, Croom Helm, 1980, pp. 101–2. Reproduced by permission.)

as an emphasis on *amae*. One might be justified in seeing the susceptibility to *amae* as the cause of the emphasis on vertical relationships.

There is a whole vocabulary of related words, demonstrated by Doi, that express how pervasive the concept is in social interactions. Closely linked to *amae,* and further evidence that all the many Japanese words dealing with human relations reflect some aspects of the *amae* mentality, are *giri* and *ninjo,* roughly translated as social obligation and human feeling. *Ninjo* has come to be an unconscious awareness referring to a set of emotions that are especially familiar to the Japanese. It seems that things understood as *ninjo* are apprehended vaguely as a kind of Gestalt, and that it is the ability or failure of foreigners to fall in with this that gives rise to remarks about foreigners understanding or not understanding *ninjo.* To understand *giri* it is necessary to consider the relationship between it and *on. On* means that one has taken on a kind of psychological burden as a result of receiving some favour; while *giri* means that *on* has brought about a relationship of interdependence. To emphasize *ninjo* is to encourage the other person's sensitivity towards *amae*; to emphasize *giri* is to stress the human relationships contracted via *amae.* One might substitute *amae* with the more abstract term 'dependence' and say the *ninjo* welcomes dependence whereas *giri* binds human beings in a dependent relationship The concept of *amae* then illustrates the emotional content of interpersonal relationships in Japan through the vocabulary that the language has developed out of the unique culture which it reflects. For the foreign negotiator visiting, or resident in, Japan, an understanding of the Japanese need to *amaeru* is a prerequisite to successful intercultural social interactions.

CULTURAL SENSITIVITY:
KEY TO INTERPERSONAL COMMUNICATION

Overcoming cultural bias

We have already seen in considering the Japanese concept of *amae,* the close relationship between language and macro-culture. Goethe's celebrated saying 'He who knows no foreign language does not know his own' might well be extended to include 'culture'.

Hall (1976) has argued that what gives man his identity no matter where he was born is his culture — the total communication framework of words, actions, posture, gestures, tones of voice, facial expressions, the way he handles time, space and materials and the way he works, plays, makes love and defends himself. All these are complete communication systems with meanings that can be read correctly only if he is familiar with the behaviour in its historical, social and cultural context.

However, all man's actions are modified by learning. Once learned, habitual responses and ways of interacting gradually sink below the surface of the mind and operate from the depths of the unconscious. Man's nervous system is constructed in such a way that the patterns which govern behaviour and perception come into consciousness only when there is a deviation from the learned pattern, as can easily happen in intercultural encounters. He tends to judge against these patterns and is led easily into attitudes of cultural bias. The only way to transcend this bias is to achieve awareness of the structure of one's own system by interacting with others who do not share that system. This is assisted by the acquisition of the relevant language and of conceptual frameworks as drawn in preceding sections and in the next chapter.

Once this awareness is achieved, one is in the position to exercise the cultural sensitivity necessary for successful social interactions between businessmen of differing linguistic and cultural backgrounds.

Learning how people in other cultures behave

If a person grows up in a bicultural situation, as where father and mother originate from different countries or where two or more cultures are constantly in contact, he becomes accustomed to the fact that people are different in the way they behave.

In bicultural cases people can shift from, say, a Spanish way to a German way without knowing that the shift has occurred. This is the position to which the individual brought up in a monoculture has to aspire if he wishes to establish close contacts across cultural boundaries.

While linguistic and behavioural concepts provide insights and frames of reference for interpersonal encounters with foreign businessmen, such concepts do not give a comprehensive picture of all factors bearing on these interactions. No such neat network of concepts exists. Different organizations have different products, markets and strategies and each requires to identify those which are most applicable to their own situations. The concept of *amae* discussed above would be of little value to a company specializing in mail order or trade with West Africa. On the other hand, the extended family group still prevails in parts of Africa and Indo-China, and the concept of such a circle of relationships can explain why family or personal matters are allowed to intervene in the flow of business discussion where ownership and key positions are held by family members. The latter concept would be of little use in Japan where vertical one-to-one relationships and weak kinship ties make it irrelevant.

Learning to do business with foreign businessmen can be a life-long learning experience, particularly as companies adapt to changes in their environment and develop new strategies in traditional markets, extend the geographic base of their operations, develop new products and embrace new technologies which take them into unfamiliar markets and market segments. A company sensitive to its environment will have to change its own culture to meet these changes. It is necessary for businessmen to be guided in their behaviour in a new market by characteristics of that market that have been identified and analysed by those experienced in it or by researchers.[1] Together with the concepts referred to these help to establish the cultural pattern within which the context of a particular interaction is set.

When companies meet other companies or governments in their capacities as major buyers and the meeting of the parties is characterized by ignorance of each other's attitudes and ways, international consultants sometimes act as 'cultural brokers'. Theirs is a difficult task as attempts at reconciliation may be perceived by one of the parties as siding with the other. When this is the perception of the buyer, problems can arise in the buyer's relationship with the consultant.

Approaches to culture

The approaches that prepare a person for effective interaction and communication in foreign cultures are many and varied.[2] An historical approach may be necessary, for example, to explain the close relationship which firms have with some national governments, how these governments can exert influence on business negotiations, and the consequent need of the businessman to identify and adapt to patterns of behaviour in transactions with government officials. Reading I at the end of the chapter examines behavioural aspects of French government intervention and how it interacts with French elitist tradition to provide a base of influence.

A cultural approach may help to isolate key values and attitudes and customs in a culture to help the visitor, for example, in terms of local attitudes to time — the traditional Nigerian view that 'time no dey' (is of no importance) has not been entirely eroded by the growing sophistication of the commercial sector; also in terms of attitudes to work and achievement and towards wealth and material gain — a typical Western appeal to the profit motive might founder because objectives are political or sociological rather than economic; in terms of attitude to change, in such matters as risk perception and the transfer of technology — the events in Iran in 1979 illustrated that attempts to modernize were seen by the fundamentalist group that took over the country as a threat to the traditional values of Iran.

Social anthropology can provide frameworks which bring together the various aspects of social behaviour in a total perspective. Differing social modes explored are seen as independent parts of an underlying structure. By adopting the holistic cross-cultural treatment which social anthropology applies, we engage in cultural confrontations in which we suddenly perceive how our vision is clouded and distorted by hidden assumptions we did not know we entertained. Such frameworks and insights are illustrated in the next chapter.

PERSPECTIVES ASSISTING INTERPERSONAL COMMUNICATION

There are other perspectives which are useful in examining interpersonal communication in the intercultural setting. These are not exclusive but may be considered to be major.

The growth process of the firm

This can be visualized as following a path along which business enterprises develop from a domestic to a global orientation.

In developing new strategies to match its resources in a changing environment, the business firm has progressively to consider new forms of distribution and ownership. Where there is a permanent presence in a foreign country there is a need for a greater knowledge, on the part of the individual businessman, of both the national culture and the sub-culture represented by individual organizations. Where the stage of growth has not yet involved a presence overseas, but relies for example on intermediaries, knowledge at the national culture level will usually be sufficient.

An exception to this may be the high-technology, high-value capital goods manufacturer whose specialists move among a few customers from country to country and who require to have technical discussions with specialists of the company in the country concerned. They are confronted with the situation of ideally requiring knowledge of various languages, national and organizational cultures for maximum effectiveness. Where response to the market and its culture is deemed to be more important than communication between the man in the field and the home organization, the temptation to employ a national of the country concerned should be great.

Where a company has overseas subsidiaries, there will be problems of communications between headquarters and the subsidiaries. These problems will be of varying kinds, depending on the type of organizational structure adopted.[3] Whether the problems are between specialists in a functional structure, or between HQ product managers and subsidiary managers in a geographic type of structure, or between HQ area specialists and managers in product structured subsidiaries, or concern the ambiguities of multiple reporting in matrix organizations, or just problems in the running of a large international group, most will certainly be cross-cultural in their nature. If the subsidiary manager is an expatriate the problems between HQ and the subsidiary may be few but problems between the subsidiary and the host government, employees and others considerable. Having local managers just reverses the communication problem. The subsidiary manager is a key figure because it is he who absorbs the culture of the subsidiary and the wider national culture and interprets it for HQ. Similarly, he has to interpret policies, objectives, allocation decisions, and so on, made by HQ in terms of the subsidiary's viewpoint.

Bilingual and bicultural managers are needed to ensure good communications are maintained. Even where the subsidiary is neither supplier nor customer, the need for successful interaction is still there by dint of the continuous discussions between a company HQ and subsidiaries.

Group or individual orientation

Societies can be classified according to whether cultural emphasis is on the group or the individual. There is a strong correlation between societies oriented towards group organization and high-context cultures. Low- and high-contexting correspond to 'elaborated' and 'restricted' speech codes as propounded by Bernstein (1972). Restricted codes sensitize their users to particularistic meanings; elaborated codes orient their users to universalistic meanings in the sense that they are less context-tied. In the restricted code speech often cannot be undertstood apart from the context, and the context cannot be read by those who do not share the history of the relationships. Thus the form of the social relationship acts selectively on the meanings to be verbalized, which in turn affect the choice of words. We can say that in the restricted code, roles of the speakers are communalized. In the elaborated speech variant meanings are explicit and individualized.

Speakers are involved in particular role relationships, and if they cannot manage the role they cannot produce the appropriate speech. For as the speaker proceeds to individualize his meanings, he differentiates himself from others. 'Difference' lies at the bottom of the social relationship and is made verbally active, whereas in the restricted code it is 'consensus'. As we move from communalized to individualized roles, so the grounds of our experience are made verbally explicit and the security of the condensed symbol is replaced by rationality.

High-context cultures require considerable emphasis on context to facilitate understanding in a business dialogue. Communalized roles as distinct from individualized roles have important implications for interpersonal relations. We shall see in Chapter 5 that what would be viewed as logical by one social group (for example, a company or department) would not seem so to others. This is partly the result of the specialized 'company language' which develops.

Similarly at the national cultural level what would be seen by Westerners as logical procedure is ignored by the Japanese (Nakane 1973:35). Because the expression of opinion in Japan is influenced by the nature of the group and a man's place in it, Japanese conversations tend to be one-sided. There is little development of dialectic style. Style is guided at all times by the interpersonal relations which exist between speakers. The premises underlying thesis — antithesis are parity and confrontation on an equal footing which will develop into, or permit the possibility of, synthesis. Because of the lack of discipline for relationships between equals, the Japanese do not practise these three basic steps of reasoning and have to overcome this great handicap in order to advance any issue brought under discussion.

Education

Role relationships can be complicated by misperception where there is a mix of national cultures, or in the less obvious case of company or functional sub-cultures as in the multinational soap company referred to in Chapter 5. Specific behaviour which means one thing to one party to a social encounter can be interpreted quite differently by the other party. A significant characteristic of a role to one person may not be significant to another.

The British education system is such that many people brought up in it associate ability to articulate with intelligence and tend to think inarticulate people stupid. This leads them into difficulties when they meet an inarticulate scientist or engineer and classify them as unintelligent.

If this attitude is transferred, say to France, another dimension is introduced in the interaction situation. The French engineer has normally been brought up in a rigorous educational system which has included a liberal core of philosophy and literature. He is often an articulate man of high personal culture, much more so than his Anglo-Saxon counterpart (Ardagh 1977:470). If the French engineer wants to use his social skills in a social or business encounter, it may be desirable for the foreign party to adapt to the Frenchman's behaviour by, say, meeting his affiliative needs which may relate to his personal culture.

West German managers tend to have a very different way of looking at the business world and their own organizations from American and some other West European managers. Management education as it is known in the USA, for example, is not conducted at undergraduate or immediate postgraduate level. German managers are predominantly qualified in engineering followed by business economics and law. Whether cause or effect, this primary thrust towards engineering is reflected in an emphasis on things practical like a commitment to doing things well, to making delivery on time, to the tasks in hand, and the skills and knowledge to carry them out, as distinct from concepts of management which are less clear to them perhaps as a direct result of a heavier focus on these aspects. This is reflected in the concept of *Technik*. For the American, or other foreign negotiator, for example, concerned to adapt to the behaviour of his German opposer, an understanding of this concept is crucial; there is some evidence, as shown earlier, that the kind of language, conventions and concepts used have a direct effect on the credibility and acceptability of persons seeking to do business with organizations. The significance is increased when it is reinforced by an aspect of national culture. An explanation of the term *Technik* in a German context and its significance for this example is given in Reading II at the end of this chapter.

In perceiving and being perceived it is necessary to establish what the other party regards as significant clues to any role. A study of the education system as part of the culture of a would-be party to a commercial agreement can provide one set of clues.

In a study conducted at the European Institute of Business Administration (INSEAD) the effect of culture and education on communication is well demonstrated. French managers had very noticeably a lower rate of oral interaction than US and British managers. A low rate of interaction is indicative of a high rate of written communication which is characteristic of bureaucratic structures. A foreigner negotiating with a Frenchman need not therefore be surprised if bureaucratic procedures are adopted (Weinshall 1973).

In one recorded instance a group of Englishmen were negotiating with French partners and the moment of agreement on intentions had arrived. The French immediately pushed a document across the table for signature of agreement to the stated intentions. The English reaction was one of not being trusted and they huffily replied that signatures were not necessary. The French, reared in their bureaucratic tradition in which it is common practice for them to record by agreement the progress of negotiations at each stage felt the unwillingness to sign was a lack of trust in them. It took the intervention of an American to discern that clues to the respective roles were being misinterpreted (Handy 1985:84).

Ideological background

By focusing on the ideological background of national markets it is often possible to clarify issues likely to affect communication in business encounters.

The East European bloc representing members of the Council for Mutual Economic Assistance (CEMA) have self-sufficiency as an economic and political goal. With their centrally planned economies they lean towards autarky rather than foreign trade interdependence, which latter viewpoint makes the economy more difficult to control. The system is designed to meet the wishes of the planners rather than the needs of the market.

Because of tendencies towards a market system, technological developments take place in the West outside any formal planning system. To keep abreast of new technological developments, CEMA countries are continually in the market for such developments, and this is reflected in the five year plans that are produced. The purpose of exports is to pay for these imports. Such is the difficulty of CEMA countries in finding hard currency that 'compensation' trading is often made part of an agreement, or 'switch trading' is effected whereby arrangement is made for payment to be made in soft non-convertible currencies.

This also explains why such countries insist on carrying their goods in their own ships, insuring through the state insurance organization and supplying as much locally as possible. It is to save on foreign exchange. Acceptance of these constraints is as much part of the communication process and social interaction as understanding the behavioural patterns and procedures of centralized Foreign Trade Corporations to which all foreign trade in goods and technology in Eastern Europe is entrusted.

There are other Socialist planned economies such as those in North Korea, Vietnam, Albania, Nicaragua, Burma and Cuba. The biggest and possibly the most important for the future is China, which will need an immense injection by Western technology to catch up on the gap created during the term of Mao's chairmanship. Equally there are other countries which do not embrace a form of socialist ideology but which are sufficiently centralized to enable planning and purchasing to be carried out to meet specific objectives. Iran, until the overthrow of the Shah, was one such country. Turkey is another. In order to move from an agrarian to a mixed economy, Turkey found it necessary to establish State Economic Enterprises in which civil servants run these state industries because the private enterprise system was largely a fragmented mercantile one and could not have taken over the responsibility for these developments, although it is the ultimate intention to sell them off to private hands.

Again, acceptance of what officials see as givens — for example, delays in making decisions and delays in foreign exchange being made available for import payments — can enable business negotiations to concentrate on the real issues that lead to an agreement. Acceptance of such givens entails the proviso that precautions are taken, for example, by building into a quoted price an interest element against payment delay, to ensure no loss is incurred or margins eroded by factors beyond the control of either party.

SUMMARY

In negotiating with foreign businessmen at the interpersonal level, language is a powerful but insufficient tool. Successful negotiation rests on an awareness of the process of negotiation as a starting point following by an ability to understand and use influencing behaviours and an empathy for the culture being interacted with. Language is the servant of all three, and each spoken language has to meet language objectives stemming from them, supported by its own non-verbal gestures and expressions.

These non-verbal sign systems are seen to assist the interpretation of verbal messages. In relation to expressions of emotion and communication of attitudes, non-verbal aspects assume greater significance than the verbal. Misperception is a danger in intercultural negotiations as emotions are expressed by differing degrees of intensity in different cultures.

Attitudes were examined in relation to dominant/submissive and affiliative/ aggressive dimensions. Their significance for negotiators is that when they meet they bring to the interaction their own social drives and skills. If both seek to employ similar approaches, interaction will be limited. The negotiator has to adjust his behaviour as necessary.

Attitudes and emotions are not always what they seem to be because people sometimes send deceptive signals for strategic reasons. Deception is characterized by conflict between verbal and non-verbal behaviour, and when conflict exists non-verbal behaviour is the one to be trusted. Lying can be detected by observation of non-verbal behaviours. A 'believability scale' was described. Non-verbal actions can be performed too strongly or weakly for their particular context because the performer's true mood interferes with his social display.

When cultures meet there is the increased possibility of misunderstanding since a cultural norm of one negotiator can be viewed as over- or under-reacting by another, unless there is an awareness on his part of the cultural differences. Non-verbal clues are often manipulated deliberately.

By creating a favourable impression a negotiator can gain material advantages and sustain a positive self-image. The behaviour of people in social encounters is designed to help the parties maintain the self they choose to project in the particular situation. Face must not be destroyed or the relationship is destroyed. Again there is the risk of misperception in intercultural situations arising from differences in the manipulation of clues.

The verbal and non-verbal behaviours of an encounter are usually mediated by the particular situation. If we wish to distinguish between appropriate and inappropriate behaviour in a negotiation situation, we have to know a great deal more about the social context in which the interaction takes place. A distinction has been drawn between high- and low-context cultures and analysis of the social structure of a high-context country and a knowledge of the cognitive structures derived from the culture are seen as an essential basis for effective interaction. A comparison was drawn between Western and Chinese cognition by way of example. In the negotiation process, therefore, interpersonal communication is a key activity which takes place at the verbal, non-verbal, situational, contextual and social structural levels and constitutes a total communication system which can assist the negotiator to bridge the gap between utterance and felt meaning.

If language is a distinguishing characteristic of culture, then each language will have a distinctive vocabulary. By examining the Japanese concept of *amae* we see how the language relates uniquely to the psychological concept of 'passive object love', which goes a long way to explaining the emotional nature of interpersonal relationships in Japan. Cultural sensitivity is identified as a key to interpersonal communication, and examples have been given as guides to adaptive behaviour.

Perspectives which are useful in assisting interpersonal communication in the intercultural setting are identified as the growth process of the firm, group or individual orientation, education and ideological background.

Notes

1 See, for example, Eggers (1977); also Tung (1982, 1984).
2 A useful text for developing intercultural perspectives is Terpstra (1978).
3 A useful explanation of organizational structures is given at Chapter 16 of Robock and Simmonds (1983).

Questions

1 Refer to the sixteen persuasive message strategies shown at p. 42–3. Give examples of each from a situation in which a potential licensee with a virtual monopoly in his market is seeking a reduced downpayment and royalty from a manufacturer seeking to exploit the licensee's market with a highly original and newly patented product.
2 Give examples of the kinds of behaviour used by skilled negotiators, if possible showing the kind of language that might be used in support.
3 How far is it true that the best negotiators always speak the language of their opposers?
4 What problems are likely to arise between the parties when a Japanese seller meets an Arab buyer if neither has prior experience of negotiating with the other's nationality.
5 In what circumstances can non-verbal language be more important than the spoken language?
6 What indications can a negotiator obtain that his opposer is trying to deceive?
7 What are the implications for Western negotiators of differences in their view of the world from East Asian opposers?
8 Can you distinguish differences in ways of thinking as between (a) English-speaking countries (e.g. US and UK), and (b) different West European countries?
9 Make a sales presentation of this book to:
    a A German business/academic publisher you would wish to negotiate trans-lation rights into German.
    b A Swedish professor of marketing whom you would wish to adopt the text.
10 Distinguish between high- and low-context cultures and indicate the significance of these differences for communication with members of these two culture classifications.

READING I

The interaction of elitism and dirigisme in France: a source of influence*

The state influence in France over the whole of private industry and business has always been strong, and this is the essence of French *dirigisme* which operates through a mix of bureaucratic regulations and high-level personal contacts, together with the state's dominant control of the finance markets. The state owns most of the large credit bodies so that firms depend on it for much of their financing of loans. Additionally, many firms rely heavily on state purchases. And the Ministry of Finance has much formal power: a firm must seek its authorization over a far wider range of matters than in Britain or Germany, and certainly much more than in the USA. Under this system the state has acted as a bossy but protective nanny to private companies. Top French civil servants in the ministries have reached their positions through a very special elitist system. The concept of technocracy has always been strong in France and the upper echelons of the civil service known as *Les Grands Corps de l'Etat,* recruited mainly from two all-powerful colleges, exert a powerful influence in government and sometimes business affairs. The products of the prestigious Ecole Polytechnique and the Ecole National d'Administration (ENA), nicknamed *les 'X'* and *'les énarques'* respectively maintain tight social networks and loyalties. The Polytechnique is a Napoleonic creation and produces a technical elite. ENA is the postgraduate civil service college set up in 1946. The latter's star appears to be in the ascendant. The *poly-techniciens,* trained as engineers and not executives, find themselves in a competitive world of modern management for which they are seldom suited. While a number of younger 'X' and others have been on graduate courses in the USA to such places as Harvard Business School, these are a minority as yet. The two Ecoles attract the best brains in France, who, because of the relatively high prestige accorded to public service or industry, choose to enter these fields. While in most other West European countries and in Australasia or the USA there is little interchange of personnel between the private industrial sector and the civil service, it is not an uncommon occurrence in France. The result is that *polytechniciens* and *enarques* have close contacts in either sector.

Many firms welcome entrants to their ranks with open arms, sometimes less for their actual abilities than their previous contacts. If a firm has an *'X'* or an *Enarque* on its staff, he may be able to ring a contact in the relevant ministry to negotiate entry or

* Adapted from John Ardagh, *France in the 1980's,* Penguin Books, 1982. Reprinted by permission of Martin Secker & Warburg Limited.

influence a particular outcome. On one occasion the French branch of Sony was in dispute with the Ministry of Finance on some vital issue and found itself getting nowhere until Sony astutely appointed an 'X' its director for France: he quietly settled the problem with another 'X' in the minister's cabinet. It happens all the time.

The technocrats have not been without their critics. They have been seen as over-privileged in that their progress up the ladder is virtually assured, they have been cast as remote impersonal figures cut off from people and human needs, and they have been accused of abuse of their power. The system, it has been claimed, creates a gulf between the élite stream and the rest, and inhibits promotion on merit from the middle ranks. On the other hand, there is little doubt that it enables youngish men with modern ideas to reach positions of influence. Another virtue is integrity. The state, by paying its senior civil servants highly and treating them well, has, over the centuries, built up a body of men who, within the limits of human frailty, have qualities of honesty and integrity. While left-wing governments may seek to dilute the élitism, the system is so entrenched there is little foreseeable likelihood of radical change in the near future. Its members are a source of influence which, if tapped, can help achieve outcomes which might not be possible without their intervention.

READING II

Technik*

A dimension to the consciousness of German managers is the pervasive influence of *Technik*. This is a word and concept which has equivalents in some other languages, for instance, *Teknik* in Swedish and *Techniek* in Dutch, but not in the English language. The starting point is that there are differences in the ways in which societies perceive and evaluate skill and knowledge; differences in the way they group and label branches of knowledge.

In English-speaking countries we distinguish between Arts and Sciences. The distinction is there in common speech and assumptions, is reflected in school timetables and college prospectuses and is actually thought to connote something. The distinction was formalized, publicized and given a further thrust by C.P. Snow's famous 'Two Cultures' lecture at Cambridge over 20 years ago. The key question here is: what is the role of engineering in the two cultures scheme, or the Arts versus Sciences distinction? C.P. Snow solved the problem by fitting in engineering as 'applied science', and this is a common, if not invariable convention, in the English-speaking world.

This 'applied science' label is, however, rather damaging to engineering. It tends to accord engineering a junior, dependent and subordinate status under the aegis of science. This is unfortunate for the status of engineering in Britain. It is also misleading since it tends to suggest that any advance in engineering is dependent on a prior advance in science, and this is simply not true. Sometimes this relationship and dependency exists. Sometimes it does not. The 'applied science' label also implies some misconception of engineering work. It suggests, that is, that engineering work consists of the application of knowledge and principles derived from science, and again this is only partly and sometimes true. The 'applied science' formula also suggests a similarity between science and engineering, albeit with engineering as the junior partner. This is totally false. The output of science is knowledge; the output of engineering is three dimensional artefacts. Much scientific work takes place in laboratory conditions where the influence of undesirable variables has been controlled: most engineering work is conducted 'on site' and is subject to environmental influences. Scientists who study things, seek ideal solutions and universally valid laws. Engineers who make things, seek workable solutions which do not cost too much. In short the 'applied science' label is damaging and misleading. And it does not exist in Germany.

* From Peter Lawrence, *Managers and Management in West Germany*, Croom Helm, 1980, reproduced with permission.

It is indeed linguistically and culturally difficult to represent the two cultures thesis in German. This is not because the Germans do not make distinctions, but because they make different distinctions. Engagingly, they use the same word for Arts and Sciences. The German term *Wissenschaft* covers all formal knowledge subjects whether arts, natural sciences, or social science in the British scheme of things. And particular subjects are often designated by compound nouns based on *Wissenschaft;* economics, for instance, is *Wirtschaftswissenschaft,* literature, as a university subject, is *Literaturwissenschaft.* The Germans employ a second term *Kunst* to refer to art. Not to 'the Arts' in the British sense of the humanities, but to the end products of art — the paintings and statues and symphonies. And thirdly, the Germans use the term *Technik* to refer to manufacture and the knowledge and skills relevant to it. That is, of course, to engineering knowledge and engineering and craft skills. It was noted that more German managers are qualified in engineering than in anything else, that engineers enjoy higher status in Germany than in Britain, and a lot of reasons for this status differences were advanced. The existence in German culture of the concept of *Technik* not only avoids the demotion and misconception of engineering implicit in 'applied science', it also tends to dignify and even glamorise engineering under its distinctive rubric.

It is important to grasp that *Technik* really does not have any equivalent in English. The English word 'technique' is not a contender. It simply means a way of doing something, and the something is not necessarily technical or related to manufacture. Neither is the English word 'technology' an equivalent of the German concept of *Technik.* There are various objections to 'technology' in this context. First, it is a new-fangled and imposed word, not a culturally rooted concept like *Technik.* Secondly, it again over-stresses the engineering/science link; when examples of 'technology' are offered they are typically from the 'science based' industries such as aerospace and electronics. Thirdly, even if technology connotes some of the relevant knowledge, it does not connote relevant skills — *Technik* does. And fourthly, technology is a rather vague word; there are no agreed definitions of technology, and the word is most often used by politicians wishing to strike a modern pose, politicians who would be hard put to define it. The corresponding word *Technologie* exists in German with the same vague connotations: it tends to be used by journalists, politicians and social scientists; managers and engineers talk about *Technik.*

It is also fair to add that the word *Technik* is actually used in German, and used in quite homely ways. It is not a term for the exclusive use of those who write books on the philosophy of science. In recent conversations with German managers the present writer has come across such gems as '*die Technik ist sauber*' ('*Technik* is wholesome' — a manager denouncing the American practice of using pretty girls in machinery advertisements) and '*Ich bin eigentlich Technik Liebhaber*' ('Actually I'm a *Technik* lover' — production manager expounding on his job satisfaction). A standard German phrase is '*technisch gesteuert*', meaning technically guided or directed in terms of *Technik.* One hears of advertising departments which are '*technisch gesteuert*', or sales departments, or whole companies.

In short *Technik* exerts a pervasive influence in German firms and on German managerial thinking. The idea of *Technik,* however, affects the ethos of the typical German company as a whole, as well as the pronouncements of individual managers.

The influence of *Technik* tends to account for the uncomplicated view taken by top managers of company goals and the means to achieve them. The goals are in the German view 'technicized', to the German manager they are self-evident and there is no need to have a seminar on it. *Technik* similarly accounts for the relative lack of interest in techniques of planning, control and decision-taking. The German is more likely to feel that *Technik* is in the foreground and managerial technique and corporate strategy take second place. The standing of *Technik* again supplies the clue to German apathy on foreign investments, mergers and takeovers. These measures are outside *Technik;* they are not the way in which German firms have traditionally expected to make money.

Technik is also, all things being equal, a force for integration. The German company is *Technik* in organizational form. The skilled worker, the foreman, the superintendent, the technical director are all participants in *Technik*. Of course there are many things which they do not have in common, but *Technik* is something which transcends hierarchy. It may also transcend particular functions in the company. This is most obviously true for the various technical functions — Research and Development, Design, Production, Production Control, Maintenance and Quality Control. The fact of qualificational homogeneity in these functions (nearly everyone has one of two different qualifications and they are all engineers) tends to integrate these functions and *Technik* provides them with a cultural umbrella. It is also conceivable, though we would not press this point, that *Technik* is sufficiently pervasive to have some integrating effect as between technical and commercial functions. The first occasion on which the present writer heard the word *Technik* used by a German manager was in the observation of a public relations manager in a commercial vehicle company that '*Die Firma lebt schliesslich von der Technik*' ('After all, the firm lives from *Technik*').

CHAPTER 4

Frameworks for adaptive behaviour

Adaptive behaviour in cross-cultural encounters........................... 78
How much adaptive behaviour?.. 78
Approach to adaptive behaviour.. 78
Japan: a unique culture... 79
Why Japan?.. 79
Problems of the Japanese market.. 79
Approaches to the market... 80
The vertical principle.. 81
Japanese group formation... 81
Group maintenance.. 82
Rank... 82
The structure of vertical organization.................................... 83
Groups and the vertical principle...................................... 83
Group leadership... 84
Interpersonal relations in and between groups............................. 85
Patterns of emotion.. 85
The competitive situation.. 87
Implications for negotiations with Japanese............................... 87
Emphasis on interpersonal behaviour.................................... 87
Japanese negotiation and the 'negotiation skills model'................ 88
Status relationships and the negotiation situation..................... 89
Other frameworks.. 90
Beyond culture... 90
No single framework.. 90
Cultural analysis.. 91
Matrix approaches.. 91
Structural analysis.. 91
A four-dimensional framework... 92
General concepts and specific studies..................................... 94
Summary... 95
Reading... 96

ADAPTIVE BEHAVIOUR IN CROSS-CULTURAL ENCOUNTERS

How much adaptive behaviour?

In the face-to-face element of negotiation the interpersonal relationship between a negotiator and his opposer can influence negotiation outcomes. People come to the negotiating table with personalities of their own and with their own values and skills and social drives, as discussed in the previous chapter.

The attitudes and feelings of the negotiating parties along affiliative – aggressive and dominant – submissive dimensions were examined. It was seen that for a dialogue to be successful, where one party wants to use those social skills which reflect his own attitudes, then the other party requires to adopt a coordinating behaviour. If both parties wish to be generally assertive and dominant, the negotiation interaction will be limited. In other words, a good negotiator adapts his behaviour to the needs of the interaction and so avoids the clashing of techniques which can lead to discomfort or uncooperative behaviour on the part of one party. In no way does he deny his own personality. He creates the possibility of maximum interaction.

Similarly, when we translate the negotiation to an intercultural context, the negotiator who, from his knowledge of his opposer's culture and his sensitivity to it, can adapt his behaviour to the situation, is serving the interests of the interaction. The more and better the communication, the greater the amount of information shared or extracted and the greater the build-up of trust, the more likely is the possibility of creating the satisfaction which is what negotiators are exchanging at the end of the day. In so adapting his behaviour the negotiator can and should remain true to his own cultural standards.

In order to be effective the negotiator requires to be constantly alert to the distinctive qualities of the people with whom he is negotiating. He requires to appreciate the meaning of their actions so as not to mislead or be misled by them, and also to make his own points in a way which promotes advantageous outcomes.

Approach to adaptive behaviour

It was seen in the previous chapter that negotiators as members of society are led easily into attitudes of cultural bias. The only way to overcome that bias is to create awareness of one's own cultural system by understanding how other people behave in another system.

In an evaluation of cross-cultural research in organizations, it has been concluded that more effort should be invested in understanding behaviour in a single culture, developing middle-level theories to guide explorations and seeking the relevant questions to ask across cultures (Roberts 1970). It has been maintained by Hall that the only way to transcend cultural bias is to achieve awareness of the structure of one's own system by interacting with others who do not share it (Hall 1976).

This chapter embraces these views and takes an approach which analyses the social structure of one country, Japan, and relates it to negotiation. Japan has a culture so different from Western cultures that comparison sheds considerable light on these. Each is seen to be legitimate in its own context. Because not every culture is so well researched as is that of Japan, nor do businessmen have the time to carry out extensive research into a multitude of cultures, nor is there equally helpful literature available on all cultures, there has to be recourse to general frameworks which can provide guidance. Fortunately there are some useful frameworks to which reference can be made and which will be considered after examination of the Japanese culture.

JAPAN: A UNIQUE CULTURE

Why Japan?

Japan is a particularly suitable country for study for a number of reasons.

First, more than almost any other country Japan has a homogeneous culture. This is because Japan was cut off from the rest of the world for over 200 years during the Tokugawa period. It was not until 1868 that trade with the outside world was re-established and officially encouraged. As a result there are strong social structural factors which bear on Japanese values and group organization, on the modes of social relations, and hence on individual behaviour.

Secondly, Japan is the only non-Western country to have industrialized successfully. As a result Japan is a major trading partner of Western industrialized countries. It is a growing market in which there is growing pressure on the Japanese to open up their domestic market to these countries because of their adverse terms of trade with Japan. As an emerging market of vast potential — Japan has the highest GNP per capita in the world — it merits a close study by those involved in international business. Institutional solutions at government level have been attempted.

Thirdly, Japan is at the centre of what has been foreseen as a major shift in the hub of world culture and commerce. It has been claimed that just as the hub moved from the Mediterranean to the North Atlantic, so is it now moving from the Atlantic to the Pacific (Kahn 1971). The 'Pacific Rim' is now the subject of ongoing studies. There is additionally a growing body of research on the emerging Pacific Rim countries like China, Japan and South Korea. Japan's advance as an economic power, and the subsequent interdependence of it and other Pacific countries, both in its role as investor and as supplier and customer, makes it of prime importance for marketers.

Problems of the Japanese market

Exploitation of the opportunities in the Japanese market has been constrained by a number of factors. It is widely held that entry is difficult for many classes of product. Tariff barriers have not been dismantled at the rate at which Japan's trading partners would have wished, particularly those with large adverse balances, usually the developed countries of the West. Non-tariff barriers, such as impediments to direct investment like Government's close relationship with commerce and industry and delays caused by complicated procedural processes, also pose problems for international marketers.

Further entry problems have been identified. A Japanese advertising agency has published a book which locates the problem in the complex market structure which, once understood in its unique Japanese context, ceases to be a problem. Another view fixes the problem in the social structure and the obligations built up among individuals over the years which are difficult to overturn. This is the view considered most productive and to which this part of the chapter is addressed.

Such barriers have constrained the strategic options that companies have perceived as being open to them. Licensing has frequently been used as a means of tackling the Japanese market, assisted by intermediaries who have specialized in introducing foreign manufacturers to Japanese manufacturers and piloting the negotiations through the necessary government departments. As the realization grows that the potential of the Japanese market is largely untapped and political pressures compel easier entry, licensing is likely to become less attractive. Allocation of resources is likely to be made to alternative entry strategies, varying from direct sales to direct investment as in a joint venture with a Japanese organization.

What these alternative strategies have in common is that in the first instance negotiation with the prospective Japanese customer, intermediary or partner must take place. A satisfactory agreement in such matters is basic to the success of future operations. One authority on the Japanese maintains that the homogeneity of the Japanese and the tight, efficient organization within their own national unit has tended to cut them off in feeling and understanding from others. Their great skills in interpersonal relations within their own country turn almost to handicaps when dealing with others (Reischauer 1977:232).

Approaches to the market

A number of well-quoted articles have been written in whole or part about interpersonal aspects of relations between overseas and Japanese businessmen (Miller 1961, Van Zandt 1970, Drucker 1971, Graham 1981, Tung 1984). These focus on distinctive behavioural characteristics of the Japanese that influence negotiations; for example, their emotional sensitivity and their hiding of emotions, paternalism, group spirit and decision by free consensus. Again, no framework is available into which these various characteristics fit and interact and which would make a meaningful conceptualization to help the would-be marketer to Japan in terms of understanding and responding to patterns of behaviour.

Valuable insights are given into Japanese society and those features which distinguish it from other complex societies by Nakane (1973). She provides an interpretation of distinguishing aspects of Japanese society and synthesizes them in a novel way which gives considerable direction to the interpersonal approach of the foreign businessman in Japan. Despite the appearance of a people torn asunder by traditional and modern forces, Nakane sees the persistence of social structure in the modes of personal social relations which determine the probable variability of group organization in changing circumstances. This persistence reveals the basic value orientation inherent in society. Her approach is through a structural analysis, not a cultural or historical explanation. Concentration is on individual behaviour and interpersonal relations which provide the base of both the group organization and the structural tendencies dominating in the development of a group. Her theme is the vertical principle and the one-to-one relationships which form the basis of this group organization.

THE VERTICAL PRINCIPLE[1]

Japanese group formation

The way in which individuals in any society get together in groups is based on the concepts of 'attribute' and 'frame'. The concept of attribute applies to what an individual has in common with other individuals, for example by being a member of a professional association; the concept of frame may embrace an institution or a relationship binding a set of individuals into one group, as in being in a section or department in a particular company.

The Japanese tend to see situations in terms of frame rather than universal attribute. This coming together of different social levels provides for a strengthening of organizations. The social group structure is clearly seen in the household structure. The concept of the traditional household *ie,* is of a social group constructed on the basis of an established frame of residence. What is important is that the human relationships within this group are considered more important than other relationships. The concept of *ie* persists in the idea of *uchi,* a colloquial form of *ie. Uchi,* meaning 'my home' is used to mean place of work. So in most cases the company provides the social existence of the individual and therefore to Western eyes appears to have authority over all aspects of his life. A company is perceived as a *ie* with the employer as the household head and employees as members of the household. The employer has therefore a responsibility for his employees and their families for which the company is the first responsibility. With the advent of industrialization and the formal structures found in modern organizations, the informal, traditional structure persists in large measure.

Since Japanese social groups include people of differing attributes, any tendency to strengthening horizontal ties within these attributes is weakened by the emotional involvement of the people concerned. This emotional contact is strengthened by contact not only in the work sense, but by the human relationships developed at the personal level in social circumstances. The result is that the influence of the group not only affects an individual's actions, it alters even his ideas and ways of thinking. The family becomes identified with the company, and the group consciousness becomes so highly developed that there is little social life outside the group in which the individual works. Every problem which an individual has to cope with must be resolved within this frame. It follows that each group develops a high degree of closeness. It is the social group which exerts power to restrict the behaviour of each member, and that includes the behaviour of the household head.

There exists in large companies in Japan a lifetime employment system which has to be seen in relation to this frame. Frequency of contact increases dependence of group members and a system of payment by seniority reinforces it.

Group maintenance

The sense of unity which the groups develop nurtures the mutual dependence of group members and gives an added stability to the frame. At the same time this distances the group from others outside the frame but with similar attributes. It also brings closer within the frame people with different attributes.

This makes it difficult for people to leave the group. There is disinclination on the part of group members to move to another company and no means open to them by which they can readily make such a move.

Because there are no ties between people of similar attributes, as in craft unions or associations of clerical, technical or scientific staff, the possibility of discussion of individual problems with counterparts in other organizations, or assistance in achieving a particular outcome, is precluded.

Japanese group affiliations and human relations are very much one-to-one. For each Japanese there is one group which is paramount. There is a loyalty which is absolute. Where such emotional participation stems from and supports this one-to-one affiliation, there is no room to serve two masters. Concepts of matrix organization are foreign to the Japanese. Because the ties which bind people together are also one-to-one, the breaking of this pattern is not something that can be foreseen. The solidarity of the group is encouraged by this total emotional involvement. The cohesion among group members rests on this underlying vertical relationship. Because of the almost total emphasis on the frame and vertical relationships, even individuals with identical qualifications tend to create differences between themselves. As this is reinforced, an almost incredibly subtle system of ranking emerges. In all kinds of Japanese organization there are differences of rank based on relative age, date of joining the organization and duration of service.

Rank

The interpersonal world of the Japanese recognizes a number of clear-cut categories. Rank on the basis of seniority distinguishes three categories. *Sempai* are seniors who are normally addressed by their name and the suffix *san*. Juniors are *kohai* and are addressed by name and the suffix *kun*. Colleagues of the same rank are *doryo* who are usually addressed without a suffix.

The use of pre-names in Japan is confined to children, a point to be borne in mind by negotiators from more informal and so-called egalitarian societies. This means of addressing others is established by relationships early in a man's career and remains unchanged for the rest of his life. Whatever the change in an individual's status over time, there remains a considerable reluctance to change what has been established at an early stage. Everyone has a place in the established order and everyone has a personal stake in its maintenance. This is further evidence of how a vertical system operates against the formation of strata in a group.

Rank determination by seniority is applied to all circumstances and to a great extent controls social life and directs and constrains activity by individuals. Seniority or merit are the principal criteria for the establishment of any social order. Merit predominates in the West, seniority in Japan. There is a certain rigidity inherent in the system. Regardless of the situation there is only one ranking order for a given set of persons. In a rapidly changing environment where experts emerge and require to be encouraged, the system will require to adapt to accommodate them. Nevertheless it is as a result of the very rigidity of ranking and the stability which it induces that it functions as the determinant of social relations in Japan.

It is for this reason that when people from different institutions meet for the first time, they exchange business cards. In this way they make explicit the title, position and company of the other person, enabling them to establish the role which they will take. It is also a pointer for Western businessmen to the etiquette of reading a card on its presentation and of having a sufficient supply of their own to cope with the many introductions effected at all levels.

A Japanese businessman is unlikely to disagree openly with a senior. Even opposition at a level of triviality involves long elaborate circumlocutions. Typically, when an objection is raised, the objector extols the past work of the senior, addresses him in terms of the greatest respect, and gradually presents his own view in a way which implies minimum dissent. A junior takes care not to hurt a senior's feelings. This takes the form of avoidance of direct confrontation. Silence is a preferred behaviour to outright opposition. Since opposition and confrontation give rise to the fear that the harmony of the group would be disrupted, avoidance is an important measure. Freedom to speak out is determined by the social processes within the group. High status confers this freedom.

The accelerator on which a young Japanese will ride, and therefore his place in the hierarchy, is first determined by his educational qualifications. To this extent the Japanese system takes account of merit. Thereafter it is determined by the date of his entry into the organization. Sometimes each year's entrants into a large company form themselves into a club. This serves to distinguish them from newcomers within the company and further consolidates the seniority system. If a man from a certain year group is promoted, his year colleagues will be greatly disturbed. Such is the strength of consciousness of rank. As a result, Japanese management feels compelled to promote several individuals from the same year group. There are many acting appointments in Japan and this is the principal reason.

These year groups are not concerned with the jobs which their members carry out. This is because from the outset a man is employed for whatever job a company will eventually determine for him. Whereas there is no recognizable group consciousness among middle managers or clerical staff or skilled workers, there is in fact a strong departmentalization in the functions where the vertical relationships further weaken any group consciousness based on attribute.

THE STRUCTURE OF VERTICAL ORGANIZATION

Groups and the vertical principle

In vertical relationships in which firm personal links exist between superior and subordinate, there is a different group structure from where the attribute or horizontal relationship exists. Where vertical relationships predominate the individual cannot change his relative position within the organization. In horizontal organizations a new member enters the group on the same footing as others already there. In the vertical system it is difficult to change leaders because leadership is always restricted to one individual, whereas in the horizontal system it is relatively easy. In the vertical system it is not possible for two individuals to stand in equal positions, but it is normal in the horizontal system.

This vertical relationship is expressed in terms of *oyabun* and *kobun,* that is, in terms of the parent/child relationship. *Oyabun* may be someone in a senior position at work with whom a subordinate (*kobun*) has developed a closed personal relationship. The *kobun* is helped by his *oyabun* in such matters as receiving advice when important decisions are to be made, or generally in lending a sympathetic ear to problems. The *kobun,* for his part, puts his own services at the disposal of the *oyabun* when he should need them. Some *oyabun* can have quite a number of *kobun* while others may only have a few. The concept of *amae* discussed in the previous chapter is central to the relationship.

Group leadership

The leader is an integral part of the group organization. In comparison with leaders in other societies his authority is curtailed and controlled at a greater number of points. He does not enjoy a sphere of activity separate from the rest of the group. Indeed the Japanese language has no word for leadership. To convey the concept one has to have recourse to the *oyabun — kobun* relationship. The leader is expected to be involved in the group to the point where he has almost no personal identity. The group for its effective performance relies not so much on the ability of the leader as on his personality and skill and charm to create, in a situation with a high degree of personal involvement, the harmony (*wa*) which is seen to be the cornerstone of effective performance.

If a change in group leadership is required it is a crucial time for the stability of the group. A leader-to-be has to be capable of maintaining the relations that exist within the group. His position of leader is legitimized by his seniority. Additionally, a leader must have a personal following in terms of *kobun* attached to him.

It is possible to have an outstanding man in any group; but if he is dissatisfied with his senior or has a growing reputation as an individual, the group is likely to be hostile towards him. Individual players are seen as a threat to the group and the only path open to them is to form their own groups. The popularity of no one individual should exceed that of the senior to whom the prestige is attributed. So disruption is always a possibility in Japanese groups because of this. The development of factions is a potential feature of group life.

Such is the preoccupation of the Japanese with interpersonal relations within groups that these may take precedence over economic objectives. For example, a proposed merger between two companies to make them more competitive in international markets may depend on the relationship of groups and the persons within them. If one group does not dominate another, or unless a leader emerges acceptable to both, there will be no group harmony and the venture is likely to fail.

The group emphasis has affected the whole style of interpersonal relationships. Team players are preferred to individualists. The assertive personality familiar in the West is considered by the Japanese to be evidence of neuroticism. It is the group qualities of cooperativeness and sensitivity to others which are values much admired, not the individual drive and forcefulness exemplified perhaps by some Western salesmen. If the foreigner bends to this perception of individual behaviour, then his interpersonal relations with Japanese businessmen will be smoothed.

The key Japanese value is harmony for the group, which they seek to achieve by a process of mutual understanding rather than by creative conflict. Decisions should not be left to one man but should be arrived at by consultation. The Japanese are committee men par excellence. Consensus of groups is the goal — a general agreement as to the feeling of the meeting to which nobody continues to hold conflicting views or strong objections. The essential leader is the man who can promote this group understanding.

Without the concept of 'frame' the Japanese find it hard to form functional groups. Inevitably groups establish the vertical type of organization structure. Its strength lies in its capacity for swift mobilization of the collective power of the members — a characteristic to be prized in times when speedy adaptation to unforeseeable changes in the environment is necessary in order to compete. The continuous flow of new and modified products, from motorcycle models to video recorders to small tractors, is witness to the effectiveness of this kind of organization.

INTERPERSONAL RELATIONS IN AND BETWEEN GROUPS

Patterns of emotion

The most significant factor in the exercise of leadership is the personal ties between the leader and his immediate subordinates. These arise out of the informal structure. Where the informal structure does not coincide with the company's formal and administrative organization, the leader in the formal organization who has subordinates tied to another leader outside the formal organization is assured of a rough time. He may be able to establish new personal ties through the formal organization, but this becomes progressively more difficult as his career moves on, as personal ties are usually made at a comparatively early stage. A man moving to a post of high responsibility may take his *kobun* with him as his personal subordinates.

The vertical personal relationship is characterized by a mutuality. Protection is repaid with dependence and affection with loyalty. As this is not an equal exchange it tends to enlarge the emotional element in order to facilitate easier control of the action of individuals. The relationship binds the leader as well as the subordinate. The leader's emotional sympathy towards his subordinate can be seen as a form of paternalism and always presumes a sympathetic understanding of his subordinates. The better and greater the leader, the more strongly is the tendency revealed to consider his subordinates' wishes and opinions The dependence of *amaeru,* which has been translated as 'to depend and presume on another's love' and 'to seek and bask in another's indulgence', is often seen as the key to the understanding of Japanese patterns of emotion. The social superior may also have an *amaeru* type of emotional dependence on a subordinate, and often does.

Because they are attuned to emotional interactions, the Japanese have developed an emotional sensitivity which responds to sensitivity on the part of foreigners. Personal feelings play a large part in a Japanese's behaviour, but he conceals it so well a businessman from overseas may be unaware of it. A Japanese will often judge a visiting businessman by the way in which he can strike emotional chords in him. He is looking for an undefined quality best described as 'sincerity'. Virtue and integrity are said to reside not in a man's heart but in his stomach. Between men the most meaningful understanding is one which needs no words. The Japanese call this 'stomach talk'.

The system of consultation which has developed out of the pattern of vertical relationships is the basis of wide informal discussions involving subordinates. It is from this process that a consensus may emerge. This consensus may be embodied in a *ringi* document adapted by a subordinate at the leader's request. It is then given a wide circulation to which a large number of persons may indicate they are not opposed to what is in it. The *ringisho,* as the actual document is called, may take some time to circulate, or meetings may take place to consider the points involved. This can occasion delays which Westerners can wrongly interpret as the matter having been dropped. This knowledge should, for the Western negotiator, be a counsel of patience.

However easy the relationship between a leader and his *kobun* may be, when third parties, or others in the formal organization structure, are present, the leader is invariably treated in terms of great deference. A subordinate must in all circumstances save his leader's face.

'Face' is an important factor in Japan and in much of East Asia. The foreigner who makes an appeal over the head of a subordinate with whom he is holding discussions, as he might do in his own country, threatens loss of face for that official and is guilty in Japanese eyes of improper behaviour. Naked displays of power in negotiations are regarded as potential threats to face. If conciliation is necessary the Japanese like to do it in such a way that neither party appears to have had a concession forced.

Similarly, if a Japanese is reluctant to enter an argument, it is not because he is trying to discomfit a foreigner; it is his normal reaction to possible confrontation. Rarely does a Japanese say 'no'; he prefers to say 'yes', which in Japanese is the equivalent of 'I understand'. In fact it has the opposite meaning to 'yes'. There are records of foreigners resident in Japan which tell us that if a Japanese says 'It is very difficult' or 'It may be possible' it is odds-on he means 'no'. Similarly, if he draws in breath between his teeth this can also imply the negative.

For the Japanese the emotional content in human relations is of prime importance. Their emotionality is such that in Japan the concept of contract can be said not to exist. Japanese businessmen may sign contracts with their counterparts from overseas, but their interpretation of it may well differ. They are disinclined to trust long legal documents to which reference may be made at a later date. They view them as potentially damaging to harmony, which may end in loss of face. The contract is looked on as an agreement to enter into a general course of conduct, rather than something fixing the precise terms of performance. They prefer 'heads of agreement' to a lengthy document, and only consider an agreement valid as long as the conditions under which it was made hold true.

The competitive situation

Not only is ranking something that takes place among individuals; it applies equally to institutions. The vertical stratification of institutions stimulates competition between parallel groups of the same kind. Group members see their own institutions relating to how they rank with competing institutions. Competition between business firms is the result. In international trade foreign buyers can only benefit from the fact that many companies offer the same product to buyers. There appears to be something in the Japanese make-up that makes them want to 'follow the leader'.

The competition which results between similar firms, and the loyalty of groups within organizations and of individuals within the groups, produces company and personal objectives which stress superiority over competitors. This, together with steady jobs over the long term, usually takes precedence over profit. Japanese values are orientated to sociological rather than economic goals. The traditional Western seller's appeal to the profitability of a given course of action might well be reconsidered in the light of the priority of objectives dictated by the structure of social relations within the culture.

Market structure is affected by vertical integration in institutions. Besides links with larger and smaller institutions of its own kind, each institution has constant dealings with a wide variety of other institutions offering necessary services. So we have functional groups forming which can include a bank, an export – import organization, a shipping company, an insurance company and a manufacturing organization. Within the group duties and obligations are so prescribed that there is little opportunity for the entry of others. It is widely held in Japan that once a relationship has been established, it should be maintained despite economic loss. So it can be seen that the independence of a single organization in Japan is low, but that of a group of organizations very high. This 'one-set' pattern whereby a group of companies is involved in a wide range of interests is repeated in many aspects of Japanese life.

The difficulty of market entry owing to the way society is structured applies equally to all foreign firms trying for business in Japan. Those whose officers can best adapt their individual behaviour to the Japanese face-to-face situation are the most likely to take that business.

IMPLICATIONS FOR NEGOTIATIONS WITH JAPANESE

Emphasis on interpersonal behaviour

The Japanese concern with interpersonal relationships is reflected in their negotiation styles. This has been the subject of interesting research into the approaches to negotiations of Japanese and American businessmen (Graham 1981). The research has been carried out in a face-to-face context, and business negotiations in both countries seem to comprise four stages, as follows.

Non-task sounding

This is the stage in which the establishing of rapport takes place. Typically the Japanese spend a lot more time in this task than do Westerners. It can be associated with gift-giving which is symbolic of the Japanese pattern of mutual dependence. The exceedingly high entertainment expenses incurred by the Japanese are seen to be part of the preliminary stage of establishing interpersonal relationships. Eating has long been established as a rapport-establishing activity.

Task-related exchange of information

In this stage Americans were observed to make clear short statements of their needs and preferences. For the Japanese this stage betokens the main part of the negotiation. As with the Chinese in the previous chapter the Japanese ask question upon question while giving few or ambiguous responses. The ambiguity rises apparently from the concepts of *tatemae* and *honne*. The former can be translated as 'truthful' and the latter as 'true mind'. It is important for Japanese to be polite and to communicate the *tatemae* without giving offence, while holding back the possibly offensive but informative *honne*. Americans see this as a double standard and the Japanese view the American frankness with discomfiture.

Persuasion

American negotiators openly disagree and use persuasive tactics. Japanese negotiators avoid confrontations and respond to threat by withdrawal. For the Japanese it is of greater importance to maintain the relationships than to take up a stance that could be construed as contentious. Japanese persuasion appears to consist of volunteering information and the use of silence.

Concessions and agreement

In this final stage Americans are seen to make progressive commitment throughout, settling one issue and proceeding to the next. Progress can be measured, the final agreement being the aggregate of the total concessions. Japanese negotiators, adopting the holistic approach which characterizes them, tend to make concessions at the end. Agreement can be as speedy as the information stage is protracted.

Japanese negotiation and the 'negotiation skills model'

The research conducted by Graham is not inconsistent with the negotiation skills model shown at Figure 2.4, which can accommodate the four stages identified.

Because of their reluctance to test limits and to get involved in confrontation, the Japanese are able to forget positions right away and concentrate on interests by moving direct to the integrative bargaining stage. Here the awareness of their own and opposer's styles of behaviour is highlighted, in this instance accommodating to the Japanese non-task soundings and the different intensities of information seeking and giving shown in the research.

At the same time the persuading and influencing process is taking place in the different ways of the Americans and Japanese. The progression from the integrative bargaining stage to the decision-making and action stage is assisted by the concessions, or moves and countermoves, which each side makes. That Americans negotiate concessions throughout while the Japanese do so at the end, is reflected in the decision-making and action stage, in which a judgement is made by both parties of what is acceptable in terms of a package.

Status relationships and the negotiation situation

The pattern of vertical relationships in Japan, and the system of consultation which has grown out of it, has meant that the Western practice of trying to affect outcomes and change views at the negotiation table is not shared by the Japanese. Their decisions are made away from the face-to-face situation, and good negotiatiors will give Japanese opposers space and time to consult. This implies also the patience to give the *ringi* system the opportunity to work.

The Japanese structure of vertical relationships can be seen as an emphasis on *amae* discussed in greater detail in the previous chapter. In this the Japanese seeks relationships which allow him to presume on familiarity. The indulgent dependence generated in such a relationship assures him of another's goodwill. In the buyer/seller relationship this is reflected in the roles they play. A buyer is normally an individual with a higher status than that of a salesman, and in consequence can regularly obtain more favourable outcomes than can the seller. This is because the seller is culturally disinclined to make too great an issue of anything that might savour of asperity. But the Japanese can trust the buyer to consider his interests. While salesmen from overseas usually tend to be accorded high status than domestic salesmen, the cultural characteristics persist. For the foreigner negotiating in Japan an understanding of the need to *amaeru* is an important precondition of successful interaction.

The need for patience in negotiating in Japan obtrudes at every turn. Its exercise is often required when a negotiator believes he has given sufficient information for all practical purposes and finds that it is only the beginning of an overwhelming quest for information. It is often compounded by apparently ambiguous answers on the part of Japanese counterparts in response to a request for information. The answer appears to be to continue to supply the answers to the questions asked and to take a page from the Japanese book and ask endless questions until satisfied.

Within their own social framework the Japanese are truthful in their interactions, but not to the point where it can give offence. The tendency among Western negotiators is to draw the bottom line with some forcefulness. Limited conflict is, after all, seen as a productive process. 'Calling a spade a spade' is in some cultures seen as a quality of honesty and integrity. To the Japanese it is reprehensible boorishness. Western negotiators would be wise to avoid it.

Japanese working in the West have learnt to increase their eye contact, to smile more and to give shorter periods of silence before responding. Westerners might adopt a reverse process in order to create the comfortable atmosphere in which relationships can develop. There is a view that language barriers are less trouble than cultural barriers; that lack of cross-cultural know-how is the critical factor in interaction between individuals of different countries.

OTHER FRAMEWORKS

Beyond culture

It is hoped that the structural analysis of Japanese society drawn here will legitimize it in its own context in the view of readers. It has equal validity for the Japanese as Western cultures have for their own people. What is normal varies from society to society and a realization of this is a first step to being sensitive to other cultures. No one would be expected to deny his own culture or go native, but sufficient should now be able to be drawn from a résumé of Japanese society to show that adaptation to critical aspects of the culture is a skill which negotiators would do well to cultivate.

The analysis of another society helps to put our own into perspective and to overcome the cultural bias to which we are all liable on occasion. It is a prerequisite to looking at ways of exploring other cultures.

No single framework

International marketers, by the nature of their work, move from country to country either selling goods or creating channels of distribution through which their goods, or goods manufactured to their particular specifications, can be put into the international marketplace. These activities take place in countries at all levels of development. No two have identical cultures. It is therefore difficult for businessmen spanning a number of countries to have in-depth knowledge of them all. However, many sales staff, for example, concentrate for a period on one market or group of markets. To this extent they have an opportunity to advance their knowledge of how the people of a country or countries behave.

A large number of articles have been written about different countries and doing business with them, often by businessmen. These articles, while informative and helpful for the country concerned, do not provide conceptual frameworks which would be helpful to the marketer in terms of understanding and responding to patterns of behaviour.

Others have arisen from research into individual cultures which try to explain them to people of different cultures (Redding 1980, Doi 1973). Yet other writers have conducted empirical researches into cultural aspects of negotiation (Brunner and Taoka 1977, Tung 1982, 1984). All these provide some guidance to the reader in specific contexts. They do not necessarily provide a general frame of reference that permits the reader to interpret past experience and think for himself when unforeseen situations arise, which are the underlying strengths of a good concept. Concepts are ways of looking at reality. Some helpful concepts follow.

Cultural analysis

One approach to the cultural adaptation of the businessman to the foreign negotiation situation is the elimination of the bias contained in the 'self reference criterion' (SRC). This involves a cultural analysis which begins with a knowledge of the traits of the businessman's own culture and a similar level of understanding of the foreign culture (Lee 1966). This enables the businessman to isolate the SRC in the problem being considered, and to redefine it without the SRC influence for the purpose of best meeting a particular goal. Managerial behaviour must be altered if it is dysfunctional enough to disturb seriously the value orientations of the other party to the discussions.

This approach depends for its effectiveness on constant observation of foreign business behaviour in terms of the cultural values which govern it. At the same time the visiting businessman to the host country must be aware of the behavioural patterns of his own country. Adaptation can therefore be made to such factors as lateness for appointments, delays in getting down to business and failure to keep promises.

The approach is of limited use to the marketer who, because of the nature of his work — for example, negotiating sales or distributor agreements — is not always in a position to observe local behaviour and the cultural values governing it. It presupposes, perhaps optimistically, that the businessman is aware of cultural changes in his own country. Neither does it provide a framework within which social modes and values can be fitted and to which the visiting businessman can relate for guidance in his interpersonal relations with foreign negotiators.

Matrix approaches

Other approaches to aspects of cultural assessment are those developed by Hall and by Farmer and Richman. Hall (1959) developed a two-dimensional matrix of ten aspects of human activity which he calls 'primary message systems'. A grasp of the complex interrelationships of a culture can be obtained by beginning with any of the ten relationships and studying its intersection with each of the others. A pointer to interpersonal relations may be seen in the relationship of 'interaction' and 'association' (the organization and structuring of society and its components). It does, however, suggest that a framework could be built within which these relationships take place, but does not provide one.

The Farmer and Richman approach is also a matrix one in which they propose a list of cultural elements which are set against 77 critical elements in the managerial process (Farmer and Richman 1965). While it looks at many of the variables involved, each combination explains only a small part of the socio-cultural context in which interpersonal interactions take place.

Structural analysis

Social anthropology provides a link which brings together the different aspects of social behaviour, by studying societies whose members' mutual social relations are embedded in, and expressed through, the medium of a common culture. Different social modes are seen as interdependent parts of an underlying pattern or structure. By adopting the holistic, cross-cultural treatment which social anthropology applies, we engage in cultural confrontations in which we suddenly perceive how our vision is clouded and distorted by hidden assumptions we did not know we entertained (Lewis 1976).

This approach promises to provide the overall conceptual framework which explains various kinds of social behaviour. This is the approach adopted by Nakane (1973) in her insightful analysis of the structure of Japanese society.

A four-dimensional framework

It is cogently argued by Hofstede (1984) that people carry mental programmes that are developed in schools and organizations and form one of the bases of national culture. These programmes affect not only individual thought, but also the behaviour of individuals within organizations. Drawing on massive and sophisticated research, he sees the ways in which they affect behaviour along the four universal dimensions of 'power distance', 'uncertainty avoidance', 'individualism' and 'masculinity'.

Power distance

This is concerned with authority and the extent to which members of a society accept that power in institutions and organizations is distributed unequally. An index is derived from country mean scores on perceptions of a superior's style of decision-making, colleagues' fear of disagreeing with superiors and subordinates' preferred type of decision-making in their superior. Prior to these research data it had been widely held that in the interpersonal relationships between superiors and subordinates, the superior would always seek to maintain or increase the extent to which he could influence subordinates, while subordinates would always seek to reduce it. The level of power distance at which these tendencies will be brought into balance is seen to be determined by the particular society and culture.

Uncertainty avoidance

Accelerating change has underlined the basic fact of uncertainty in human life. Uncertainty avoidance is the degree to which members of a society feel uncomfortable with uncertainty and ambiguity, which leads them to support beliefs promising certainty and to maintain institutions which protect conformity. This is coped with in organizations by means of technology, rules and rituals. Tolerance of uncertainty among people varies across cultures. Using rule orientation, employment stability and stress as indicators, an index of uncertainty avoidance is built up. These data point up the consequences for society and for organizations.

Individualism

This describes the relationship between the individual and the groups within which he works in a particular society, and reflects the ways in which people live and work

93

together. The degree of individualism indicates whether there is preference for a loosely-knit framework in which individuals care for themselves and their immediate family or whether the social framework is tightly knit and the community becomes the primary concern. An index in relation to country individualism is developed.

Masculinity

Sex roles differ according to the society one is in. Men and women tend to have different goals based on the sex differences. A masculinity index measures how far people tend to embrace goals more popular among men or among women. For a masculine society even the women prefer assertiveness; in a feminine society even the men prefer modesty. High scores in the index indicate greater differences between men and women in the same jobs.

There are useful conclusions drawn from examination of the different dimensions. Power distance studies, for example, show that leadership complements subordinate-ship. It is not an independent trait which can be acquired whatever the situation. Given this complementarity, a key to leadership is the expectations of subordinates in a given country. Existing theories of leadership do not take this into account, although it should be clear from the analysis of Japanese society that this is so. In low power distance countries like Israel and Sweden, initiatives by subordinates are welcomed by management. Unlike his Japanese counterpart, the Israeli or Swede will not disapprove strongly of attempts by opposing negotiators to go over his head to influence a superior. The perceived leadership behaviour between 'task' and 'people' orientation as witnessed by the Blake and Mouton (1980, 1977) studies is a function of a country's power distance level.

Concern for consensus in Scandinavian countries are 'feminine' traits which are firmly embedded in the cultures of these countries. The reality for people lies in the ways in which they perceive facts and situations. Any attempt, therefore, to influence individual Scandinavians at the negotiating table has to take this into account.

Conclusions have also been drawn from correlations of the indices developed. The interaction of uncertainty avoidance and masculinity, for example, challenges the universality of Maslow's hierarchy of needs theory, McLelland's achievement theory and Herzberg's two-factor theory, and suggests they are all culture-bound. Hofstede develops a 'motivational world map' which takes account of cultural characteristics which depend on the degree of uncertainty avoidance and masculinity. From this it can be seen, for instance, that in negotiating with a Frenchman (strong uncertainty avoidance/weak masculinity) it would be advisable to make a proposal which appeals to his defensive and risk-avoiding culturally induced behaviour. In negotiating with a British opposer (weak uncertainty avoidance/strong masculinity) an appeal to risk-taking, recognition-seeking behaviour would be advisable. The cultural characteristics persist, although there will always be individuals who do not have the cultural traits to the same extent as the majority. It is part of the information-seeking behaviour of negotiators to establish when this is so and to adopt other suitable tactics.

Cultural clusters have been developed from combinations of the indices providing,

94

within this four-dimensional space, categories which serve to simplify their thinking on cultures; and they provide negotiators with a point of reference for their adaptive behaviour.

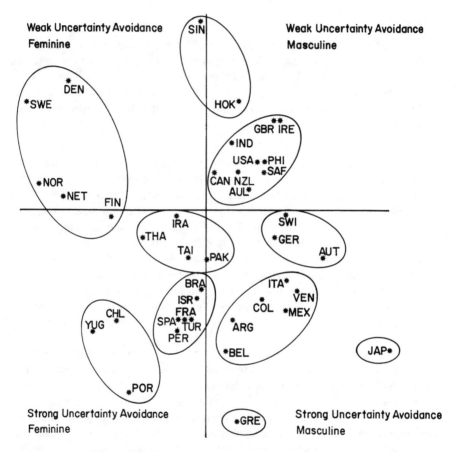

Figure 4.1   Positions of 40 countries on the 'uncertainty avoidance' and 'masculinity' scales. From G. Hofstede, *Culture's Consequences: International Differences in Work Related Values,* Inc. 1984, Sage Publications. Reprinted by permission of Sage Publications,

GENERAL CONCEPTS AND SPECIFIC STUDIES

These general concepts provide reference points against which the many useful studies into single cultures and comparative studies can be placed. The negotiator who has to move between a number of cultures and is aware of the relationship between communication, culture, human behaviour and negotiation will eventually internalize them for one culture and language. The process facilitates the internalization of these factors for future cultures in which the negotiator may be required to work.

SUMMARY

In order to allow interactions to develop to their potential, negotiators require to be able to overcome inhibiting factors which can give rise to discomfort or uncooperative behaviour. This involves adopting coordinating behaviours to facilitate maximum outcomes for the parties.

To overcome attitudes of cultural bias it has been shown that it is necessary to gain insights into a single culture so that one's own can be seen in perspective and each is seen to be legitimate in its own context. This approach is adopted and the Japanese culture is examined. It is seen to form into social groups on the basis of 'frame' rather than 'attribute', which latter means is characteristic of Western cultures. This leads to an examination of vertical one-to-one relationships in Japan, the way groups form and are maintained and the importance given to rank both in terms of individuals and organizations.

This is followed by consideration of relationships within and between groups in which the one-to-one relationships are analysed as a form of dependency relations. This in turn is related to formal organizations and to a comparison of Western and Japanese cultures in relation to negotiation.

An attempt having been made to dispose of the self-reference criterion which prevents many individuals from transcending cultural blocks, other frameworks are examined which provide the negotiator with concepts to help marketing negotiators understand and respond to patterns of behaviour. These frameworks include cultural analysis, matrix approaches, structural analysis and a four-dimensional framework. These, particularly the last, provide points of reference on which studies in single cultures can be placed.

Note

1 The discussion draws heavily on Nakane (1973). For anyone pursuing seriously an approach to the Japanese market, it is, in the view of the authors, essential reading.

Questions

1 Imagine you are going to give a talk to a small group of people going out to Japan to teach English as a foreign language. In your own words advise them of the hazards of communicating with the Japanese and indicate some ways they might make themselves more acceptable to their Japanese hosts.
2 Turn to the negotiation skills model in Figure 2.4 and show which of the face-to-face stages are more important in negotiating with the Japanese.
3 Indicate the importance of Hofstede's four cultural universals of power-distance, uncertainty, avoidance, individualism, and masculinity and show how these can assist the negotiator in his transactions.
4 The Japanese are said to be good at adapting to the ways of different purchaser countries. Do you think the Japanese will always be so adaptive?

READING

Cross-cultural negotiations*

Given this horizontal relationship between American negotiators and the vertical relationship between Japanese negotiators, what happens in cross-cultural negotiations? It is my belief that a Japanese seller and an American buyer will get along fine, while the American seller and the Japanese buyer will have great problems. Moreover, I believe this consideration to be a key factor in our trade difficulties with Japan. And my observations in the field and the laboratory provide strong evidence for such a proposition.

When the Japanese seller comes to America to market his products, he naturally assumes the lower status position and acts accordingly (with great respect for the American buyer, etc.), and a sale is made. Initially, the Japanese seller is taken advantage of. After all, he expected the American buyer to respect his needs (consistent with *amae*). But in any case, a relationship is open and the Japanese seller has the opportunity to learn the 'American way', to adjust his behaviour, and to establish a more viable long-term relationship.

Such a conception of the Japanese experience in America is supported by both my field interviews and by my laboratory observations.

Universally, Japanese executives in the United States reported to me that their company 'took a beating' when entering the American market. But they also reported adjusting their business and negotiation practices to fit the American system, just as in the laboratory the Japanese were more likely to adjust their behaviour. In cross-cultural interactions, Japanese participants dramatically increased eye contact, increased the number of smiles, and decreased the number of aggressive, persuasive tactics. The Americans were found to make few analogous adjustments. Also, there were fewer silent periods in cross-cultural negotiations. But this is apparently not due to Japanese adjustments as much as to Americans filling potential silent periods with new arguments.

There is an important implication underlying this apparent adjustment by the Japanese and not by the American negotiators. It is a consideration not brought out specifically in the findings of the study. Anthropologists tell us that power relations usually determine who adopts and adapts behaviour in a cross-cultural setting. Japanese executives in an American research setting are likely to be the ones to modify their behaviour.

* From John L. Graham, 'A hidden cause of America's trade deficit with Japan', *Columbia Journal of World Business*, Fall 1981. Reproduced by permission of the publishers.

Were this research conducted in Japan, results might be somewhat different. Moreover, in American negotiations status relations are less defined and less important. The Japanese seller can apparently fit into such a situation without offending the American buyer.

However, if an American seller takes his normative set of bargaining behaviours to Japan, then negotiations are apt to end abruptly. The American seller expects to be treated as an equal and acts accordingly. The Japanese buyer is likely to view this rather brash behaviour in a lower status seller as inappropriate and lacking in respect. The Japanese buyer is made to feel uncomfortable, and he politely shuts the door to trade, without explanation. The American seller never makes the first sale, never gets an opportunity to learn the Japanese system.

CHAPTER 5

Communication, culture and negotiation II
The organizational perspective

Introduction.. 98
Micro-culture and pico-culture...................................... 99
Negotiation and social reality in organizations...................... 99
Rationality is not enough.. 99
People create their own reality.................................... 100
Rationalities, logics and symbols................................. 101
Language as micro-/pico-culture....................................... 103
Accomplishment of tasks... 103
Organization of thought.. 104
The universe of discourse... 104
The internal politics of negotiation behaviour..................... 105
Tasks and self-interests of groups............................... 105
Organizational structure and power.............................. 106
Networks... 107
The effectiveness skills.. 108
Communication and persuasion..................................... 109
Selecting the persuasive message strategy...................... 110
Negotiating within organizations................................. 111
Communication and handling conflict............................. 111
Analysing the organizational culture................................. 112
Summary 113
Reading 115

INTRODUCTION

In this chapter we move from the consideration of the interaction between people negotiating in different macro-cultures to that culture which is created or evolves within organizations. There is a strong relationship between what goes on in the wider culture and the way people behave in organizations.[1] It was seen in Chapter 4 that the four universal dimensions of 'power distance', 'uncertainty avoidance', 'individualism' and 'masculinity' represented different ways of viewing the world which interacted to make people act and perceive as they do. This is developed in schools and organizations and is reflected in them (Hofstede 1984). Such national values as German egalitarianism (low power distance) and *Technik* (explained in Chapter 3, Reading II), come through strongly in German organizations.

People's membership of organizations makes them act in a particular way which, within the wider culture impressed on them all, distinguishes them, sometimes in a spectacular way, from each other. Given that negotiation outcomes are dependent on the interaction of the parties, it follows that if we can understand how and why people behave in a certain way in a given organization or in part of that organization, it should be possible to communicate better with them by adjusting to their behaviour and making the communication more meaningful in their terms.

Micro-culture and pico-culture

In order to assist understanding of the communication process inside organizations and between them, it is useful to consider the concept of corporate, organizational or *micro-culture* on the one hand, and the concept of sub-unit or what we shall call *pico-culture* on the other. Micro-culture assumes that the total organization shares the same value scales, ideology and basic assumptions. Pico-culture assumes that there is a plurality of sub-cultures within an organization. The term applies to each sub-culture. The problems that negotiators have to address are largely associated with the conflict that can arise from the differing viewpoints inherent in such situations and with the management of these multiple realities to ensure the achievement of any objectives (Morgan 1986).

This has implications for the management of negotiations between and within organizations. Not only does it mean that adjustment has to be made to accommodate to, and so influence, these different viewpoints within an organization, it also means that this adjustment can vary with the department involved in another organization. Where decisions are taken across functions or departments as in a major organizational buying decision (see Chapter 7) persuasive messages may have to be conveyed in different ways to different participants. In negotiations within an organization as where it perceived to be necessary to influence production to guarantee a genuine minimum delivery date should there be pressure anticipated from a potential customer in this direction, the skills to exercise this influence are more easily identified if the appropriate values, needs and assumptions of production personnel are known.

It is the function of what follows to explain the nature of these organizational realities and how an understanding of it can assist the creation of productive internal relationships in the interests of effective negotiations with external organizations. The skills in identifying the realities of organizations will help uncover key perspectives both in one's own organization and those organizations with which that organization interacts.

NEGOTIATION AND SOCIAL REALITY IN ORGANIZATIONS

Rationality is not enough

Much of what negotiators do is concerned with decision-making and problem-solving.

These have long been viewed as orderly and rational processes. Our Western tradition informs us that costs, price concessions, calculations of probabilities and all these issues for negotiation which are regarded as determinable by what is broadly termed management science, constitute an objective or *external physical reality* (Schein 1985). This rational model of decision-making is under strong attack.

In the first place the human brain can only retain about seven pieces of information in the short-term memory (Miller 1966, Simon 1979). Managers cope with multiple stimuli by employing strategies, usually unconsciously, that make their task more manageable. When they have reached their limit of information processing capability, people store new information in ways that bias it. As if this were not enough, the rational model is further challenged on the grounds that decisions are not made on the basis of all reasonably available information, but are taken when there is just enough information to make an acceptable decision — the concept of 'bounded rationality'. The challenge is further compounded by the fact that there is a wide variety of information-processing biases which show that information is subject to all sorts of conscious or unconscious manipulation or interpretation, such as selective perception, inconsistency across similar cases, undue influence of primacy and recency in a series, and the dominance of a vivid experience over valid statistical information (Hogarth and Makridakis 1981).

People at various managerial levels in different functions tend to view a problem in terms of their own functional perspectives, unless they have an awareness of how these functions view the issues. Buyers, for example, are often surrounded by sets of contradictory expectations. They themselves like room for manoeuvre in the deployment of their talents and specialist skills. They are often specialists in negotiation, and shop around for the best available terms. But finance may want it cheap, the engineers want it perfect (and are therefore reluctant to change from known suppliers), production wants it now, and sales want some tactical advantage as where they can use reciprocal purchases as a lever.

As they think about information and talk things through, negotiators become emotionally involved with the problems thrown up. This can affect how they define a problem. How they define a problem can influence choice, and this has been shown to be affected by historical solutions, by the power attributed to the individual or sub-unit which is the source of the problem statements, by previous decisions and by perceived discrepancies between an existing state of affairs and a desired one (McCall and Kaplan 1985). What price a focus on choice when the definition of a situation can easily predetermine it!

People create their own reality

To understand how meaning is communicated and interpreted in organizations, it is necessary to understand how an organization's activities create meaning for people. When opinions about suppliers, customers, the organization or how any problem in relation to these should be approached, are matters of consensus not externally testable, such matters are what Schein calls intersubjective or *social reality*. In such circumstances a group shares assumptions about which decisions are based on consensual criteria, e.g. 'Let's see what the majority favour'.

If an organization is to act coherently, it also has to share assumptions on which decisions are scientifically resolvable and which are based on consensual criteria. So it can be said that problem-solving and decision-making can be rational or non-rational. If a negotiator is to be effective within his own organization in order to get the inter-organizational outcomes he prefers, he has to be party to these assumptions. Only then can he communicate effectively and acceptably.

Very often an individual's judgement is coloured by his prior experience as where a negotiator has been tested in an earlier encounter and chooses to take a hard line irrespective of changes. Very often, too, it is coloured by his felt need for elbow-room and self-expression or desire to nurture a particular self-image or adhere to a particular value. These examples capture what Schein has described as *individual reality.*

What determines whether the rational or non-rational approach is taken is the culture of the organization. Where this applies company wide, a strong micro-culture can be said to exist. Such strong cultures have been observed in non-unionized companies like IBM and Hewlett-Packard, in organizations with only a short history before bureaucratic procedures develop, small organizations where diversity and hence interdependence is less, and in firms where professional norms and ideologies prevail like accounting and legal firms.

In large, highly specialized organizations the micro-culture may be relatively weak and the sub-unit or pico-culture strong. In such cases the pico-cultures are likely to have different rationalities or logics. People create, absorb and enact these rationalities which then provide a lens through which the world can be objectively observed. In these circumstances what is believed to be objective is in reality based on value premises. Where negotiators are involved in getting agreement across these different rationalities to obtain commitment in relation to projected external negotiations, awareness of these rationalities is the first stage in developing a strategy.

Rationalities, logics and symbols

It was Berger and Luckman (1971) who, in a seminal work, first investigated the process by which people construct their own social order and yet regard it as a reality external to themselves. This theme has been further pursued by Thompson (1980) in an analysis of the social construction of reality in organizations with different types of rationalities or logics. He sees the socialization of new entrants into an organization as involving the internalization of the various patterns and symbolic meanings that have become dominant in that organization. The new entrant learns what rationalities are important in an organization. These represent basic and long-standing assumptions which people in an organization or dominant parts of an organization share to bring meaning to their interactions. Spillard (1985) in his examination of organization and marketing, lists nine different logics for each of which he has shown the characteristic viewpoint it imparts (see Figure 5.1).

No firm possesses only one of these logics. There is, however, likely to be one or two which are dominant and which underpin the organization's whole existence. In the logics or rationalities which dominate, the words and actions which symbolize these

Logic	Characteristics
1 Raw material logic	Sees itself as exploiting particular raw materials. Their processes, technologies, rules, values, expectations and structures are all dictated by its orientation to the raw materials.
2 Process logic	May be bound as above but to a processing function. Retailing, advertising, assembling typical. It is the processing that comprises the organization's unique competence.
3 Technological logic	Technology provides the organization's strength and focus as in electronics, metallurgy, processed food.
4 Product logic	Product is central, as in cars, computers, carpets, insurance policies. All characterized by concept of product and product range for which firm is recognised.
5 Market logic	Defined in terms of market they serve. This can be a market segment. May consider making and marketing any product needed by segment.
6 Product/market logic	Defined in terms of a product and a market. Firm involved in assembling and selling a system does this as do package-tour operators.
7 Marketing task logic	Introduces a classification of possible operational stances, viz. analytic/exploratory/reactive/risk-averse or defensive/aggressive/passive or welfare/revenue-earning. These mutually exclusive.
8 Personality logic	Firm's actions are dictated by significant power-holder(s). Usually only used as veto or when culture built up over time. Small/medium firms in this category.
9 Philosophical logic	Difficult to define. May be determined primarily by values usually described in bi-polar terms, e.g. team-oriented/individual-oriented, risk-taking/mechanistic.

Figure 5.1 Some different rationalities and logics. From Peter Spillard, *Organisation and Marketing*, Croom Helm, 1985. Reproduced with permission.

logics, what is right or wrong, fair or unfair, all operate to provide a shared view of what really goes on in an organization.

In order to function as a group, either as a total organization or as separate parts of it, the individuals who come together must establish a system of communication and language that allows an interpretation of what is going on. Because people cannot stand too much uncertainty, categories of meaning which filter out what is unimportant, while focusing on what is important, become a major means of reducing uncertainty and overload.

Organizations or functions within them cannot take for granted the commitment of members to their particular viewpoints. In order to develop and sustain consensus and cooperation, senior managers attempt to manipulate or select certain attitudes and values (Salaman 1980). In the recruitment process selection is confined to these candidates who are most likely to subscribe to organizational values and ideology or who are most likely to embrace them given an adequate induction process. The principal means by which people absorb and embrace company or functional values in the process of socialization is language. The negotiator who wants to keep in good shape his relationships with those who provide him with authority and resources to get things done and those through whom he has to operate to do his job well, must have a sensitivity and feeling for the values of bosses and key peers.

LANGUAGE AS MICRO-/PICO-CULTURE

New entrants to an organization are introduced to the language associated with their jobs. This sensitizes them to observing certain kinds of events and not others. It evokes a certain way of thinking and implicitly indicates how decisions should be taken. Negotiators have to be able to understand and use the language that is most appropriate in the circumstances.

Accomplishment of tasks

Just as national culture is reflected in the language which embodies it, so is the sub-culture of a business organization mirrored in the special language which it develops, influenced by the larger culture within which it operates. This is particularly observable in large multinational companies which, as they grow, expand their vocabularies to cope with the problems of differentiating tasks and experience essential to the goals and needs of the group in given social contexts.

Language, which serves the purpose of facilitating the performance of tasks, many of which may be specialized, has two major dimensions which have been called 'technical' and 'relational'. Technical language makes possible detailed division of labour and talk about the tasks resulting from this division. A manufacturer of washing powder, for example, divides this into 'heavy duty powder', 'light duty powder', 'mixed action', 'synthetic', 'soap powder', 'enzyme', and so on. Relational language refers not to the way in which tasks are named and described, but how they are allocated among specific company officers. The relational function of language has two aspects which exist simultaneously. These are separation and integration. That is to say that for work in an organization to be performed, roles and responsibilities must be separated out, but provision made for them to be coordinated and integrated back into the whole which is the company.

Entrants to a multinational enterprise studied by Seaton (1976) are trained for a particular role by a role model or 'significant other'. By mastering the linguistic protocol, the language of the role sensitizes him to observing some kinds of events and not others. The role occupant comes to accept and expect certain meanings and patterns of experience which stem from the language which 'goes with the job'. Thus the role in a large organization inclines to the occupant existing in his own small world, and so gives rise to the separation which is a condition and an effect of specialization. At the same time, the process of linguistic naming and description reintegrates the employee into the corporate unity. Confusion is avoided because the new entrant, in addition to internalizing the detailed requirements of his own role, also partially absorbs the role demand of other performance areas in the organization in so far as they relate to him. His training is aimed at achieving this. The firm's relational practices enable an executive to be switched from one country to another and make him feel at home quickly owing to the identical namings, procedures and practices. In one sense the multinational company has created its own international occupational language. The individual is forged into a community, all the members of which are integrated into the mechanism.

Organization of thought

Language functions do more than facilitate the negotiation of tasks in an organization. They also serve to a degree to organize thought. Not only does the language suggest the habits and values of the group; it also tends to mould the self-conception of the individual within the community. Through language, culture becomes existential. This supports the contention that the multinational enterprise manifests strong evidence of providing a culture, a way of life and world-view for its employees. It meets the description of a sub-culture provided by Turner (1971) as a 'distinctive set of meanings shared by a group of people whose forms of behaviour differ to some extent from those of wider society'. Language is a significant independent variable in the determination of a distinctive world-view and may indeed be the most important carrier and evidence of it. The mastery of the sub-cultural language is what gives substance to the sub-culture. The organization member tends to become what he speaks and writes, particularly in a corporate context, although the views he develops may extend far beyond corporate boundaries.

The universe of discourse

This 'universe of discourse' which comes to exist in a large organization implicitly designates how decisions should be taken and what the verbal basis of such decisions should be.

It has been argued that there is no such thing as an abstract, absolute form of logical reasoning which is applicable to all social contexts (Mills 1939). What constitutes a 'reasonable' argument and what does not are products of specific social situational contexts. What would be acceptable as logic in one group of people may not seem so in others. The implication of this idea is that it is possible to gain insight into the particular 'universe of discourse' of a given social group by noting preferred words and terms in contrast to those that are negatively valued.

This 'universe of discourse', in which most executives in an organization use the same kind of language and linguistic justifications for their points of view, makes it particularly difficult for an outsider to gain acceptability (for example, in making sales to the organization), if he draws on verbal concepts outside the organization's 'corporate language'. Companies wishing to do business with such an organization, and in particular, company officers whose roles involve interpersonal activities with officers of the organization, have to make a conscious effort to identify key elements of the organization vocabulary. It is only when these have been identified, and related procedures and documentary formats of the organization followed as closely as possible, that a marketer's fitness as a suitable person to conduct business with the organization will be affirmed. Language, in addition to suggesting the characteristic preoccupations and intentions of an organization or occupational group, acts as a major vehicle of a new entrant's socialization to the extent that it may affect how he sees not only the firm, but also himself and the world outside. The very process of socialization, itself partly a function of language, ensures that company personnel adopt a company lexicon which determines to a large extent members' ways of thinking and decision-making and to which negotiators require to adjust in order to achieve business goals by interpersonal means. It is no coincidence that advertising agencies often employ personnel who have worked with actual or potential major accounts.

THE INTERNAL POLITICS OF NEGOTIATION BEHAVIOUR

Tasks and self-interests of groups

Given the different organizational realities implied by the differing rationalities and logics which may be embraced, and which are reinforced by language use, it is not surprising that people bargain on their interpretation of events. They bargain to find an interpretation that best serves a critical mass of self-interests including their own. Affiliate companies, departments, functions, sections and factions all negotiate their own reality. It provides each group with a common frame of reference and identity which prompts members to adopt positions on organizational issues which suit their group purpose. Negotiators, in seeking to overcome this conflicting viewpoint and promote the viewpoint of the overall organization in terms of their task or their own preferred outcomes, have to adopt strategies which will further this viewpoint. Unless there is an overarching ideology or total organizational culture which values this viewpoint the pull of the social reality in the section, function or department will mean that the negotiator has to overcome these drawbacks by his own interpersonal skills. Even where such an overarching ideology exists there will still be different interpretations or viewpoints on issues due to different priorities in specialized functions.

Organizational structure and power

These self-interests of groups and the problems they create are compounded by organizational structures. With the development of divisional and complex multilateral structures, integration of specialized activities has largely been moved out of the marketing function and into division and general management (Doyle 1979). This has resulted in a greater proliferation of interactions between people working in different functions of an organization. Whether they know it or not, the fact remains that functions and the people in them are interdependent when it comes to getting things done like implementing plans of which negotiation is at the forefront. This means that the social realities and associated logics that exist in different parts of an organization, come of necessity into conflict. At bottom, differing viewpoints are strengthened by the conflicts that specialization throws up.

Although management textbooks often urge a match of responsibility and authority, the coming together of accountability and control is not so simple. Not only do divisional and matrix organization structures make decision-making a concern that crosses functions, but the stresses and strains on these multilateral forms which derive from the difficulty of reconciling the need for specialization with the need for coordination and integration of effort, has resulted in managers becoming integrators and coordinators. They are increasingly seen to be accountable for tasks carried out through other functions for which they do not have direct responsibility. Negotiators come into this category: they have to live with the inadequacies of formal structures. In these circumstances the skills of a negotiator as persuader and politician are called on just as much as bargaining skills. They encompass the skills that have been referred to as 'indirect management' (Lax and Sebenius 1985).

In an important work, Pfeffer (1981) underlines the pervasiveness of power and its significance for what goes on in organizations. It affects decisions in respect of such processes as the allocation of resources and development of strategies. It has an effect on the organizational structure that evolves or is created in organizations, and is reflected in that structure.

Where boundary-spanning roles are carried out by functions and individuals in them, power accrues to them from coping with critical uncertainties in the environment. According to Piercy (1985) this coping is accompanied by the assumption of information processing burdens, to absorb these uncertainties for the core of the organization. By so doing they create dependencies in other parts of the organization. They may therefore have the potential to increase the political clout arising from these dependencies in the manipulation of information important to decision-making processes and on which others in the organization rely.

Negotiators, just because they exercise a boundary-spanning role *par excellence* in so far as they are the sole repositories of the information they have extracted in their inter-organizational dealings, can use the power that this very special information bestows on them to resolve conflicts, or they can use influence strategies to do so. Holding and controlling information whether through formal or informal systems, tends to provide the holders with status and influence as a result. Piercy's (1985) information – structure – power (ISP) model views the marketing department — of which commercial negotiators, whether as salesmen, licensors, overseers of distributorship and agency arrangements and partners in joint venture arrangements, are arguably a part — as a participant in competition with others to cope with the strategic contingencies facing the organization in which structure as an information-processing capacity confers power.

Information is a resource which can be used politically rather than as a component of a 'rational' approach to problem-solving. In the ensuing conflicts which inevitably arise with other departments and with general management, that boundary-spanning department which controls key information inputs in a given situation will tend to be the department whose views will prevail. A mastery of interpersonal problem-solving skills is likely to strengthen the department's position just as similar skills in another competing department will tend to counter that power. Despite being in the very special position of obtaining on-the-spot information, negotiators may or may not be in the principal and hence most powerful boundary spanning department. The Piercy ISP model fits readily into the factors affecting negotiation outcomes shown at Figure 2.1.

Networks

To get things done despite the inadequacies of the formal structure, individuals in larger organizations supplement conventional and bureaucratic systems with the influence of internal and external networks (Mueller 1986). This, however, cannot be achieved without closing the gap between the power one needs to get the job done and the power that automatically goes with the job (Kotter 1985). Sufficient power to fill the gap and the willingness to use that power to manage all the interdependencies in as responsible as way as possible, are necessary prerequisites.

Basic to the creation of resource networks and the associated good working relationships, personal skills and information power, is a close understanding of the social reality in which the job is set. It involves a detailed knowledge of the different perspectives of all the various interest groups and the realization of where these perspectives are in conflict. It means, too, knowing what power sources are available to each group in the pursuit of its own interests and the extent to which they are prepared to exercise that power.

Information of this kind is needed to identify these people in the organization who will be needed to provide support for the negotiator in planning ahead his negotiation strategy, in obtaining the necessary support and quick turn-round of requested information or other assistance in the course of negotiations and the implementation of subsequent contractual obligations where the formal structure cannot deliver.

Yet information of itself is not enough. It requires also the power associated with credible relationships with bosses, subordinates, peers in other parts of the organization, suppliers and customers. Relationships of this kind are founded on some combination of respect, admiration, perceived need, obligation and friendship. These are enhanced and reinforced by good track records. These take time to establish.

Negotiators find themselves charged with executing plans which the organization may not have the structural arrangements to facilitate. In addressing the often neglected implementation end of strategy, Bonoma (1985) has identified the four key skills of interacting, allocating, monitoring and organizing. Interacting skills concern informal allocation of talents in managing one's own and others' behaviour in a way that is contrary to the dictates of the formal organization structure. A negotiator might identify, perhaps from earlier meetings with a potential customer, a problem that will almost certainly surface in subsequent negotiations in relation to the product. The negotiator's internal network might enable him to obtain assistance in helping resolve the problem of a particular individual in R & D. The skill is to get this addressed in time for the formal negotiations through his peer relationships in R & D. Allocating skill is the art of shifting small bits of discretionary money from one budget head to another, e.g. from advertising to sales to make strategy work despite the budgetary allocation system.

Monitoring skill is one specific to the individual which can be drawn on to supplement formal decision support systems which have not produced the desired results, for example, key ratios or rules of thumb which the individual has developed in the course of his experience. The final skill of organizing or networking is the skill to build up an information organization both inside and outside the company, to meet the needs of the job where the formal organization falls short.

The allocating and monitoring skills are what might be called the technical skills. These represent the abilities to identify problems whether through formal or informal means and to pinpoint what needs to be done to obtain a short-run workable solution. Interacting and networking are the true managerial skills through which these solutions can best be effected. The networks developed provide the necessary framework within which the interacting skills can be employed.

Good interactors understand that compromise, trade-off and the principles of exchange are what dominate managerial life. In Bonoma's study successful managers treated their peers like customers. A sales manager might assist the production function to achieve cost-efficient production in a volatile market by negotiation of a given level of stocks to stabilize demand. The production manager, having been put under an obligation, is likely to reciprocate when the sales manager requires his assistance, for example in obtaining a rushed delivery to meet the special need of a customer. Negotiators are only too aware that if their company falls down on contractual requirements or fails to respond to a customer's special request, that will affect the outcomes of the next episode or transaction. Such actions point up the benefits of cooperation which is more likely to be seen as a possible solution on future occasions.

Such outcomes cannot be achieved without the help of bosses and subordinates. The support of bosses is necessary to provide the mandate and resources to get things done. Getting this support does not happen by itself. An individual has to take responsibility for making sure that his boss's backing is provided (Kotter 1985). The managing of one's boss is a necessary prerequisite to effective performance. In terms of relationship to subordinates, leaders need not only information on them but also on all the relationships among them so that the networks of subordinates can be used to advantage as well as their own.

THE EFFECTIVENESS SKILLS

Central to the whole process of getting things done are the interacting skills. Through these, influence can be brought to bear on those individuals or groups who for reasons of differing perceptions, personality clashes or sheer bloody-mindedness, seek to block what the negotiator sees as significant for his planning for negotiations with an outside organization.

Influence can vary from entreating through persuasion and negotiation to commanding. Giving orders is a strategy to be avoided where no authority exists, and entreating may work with a friend or peer who has been put under an obligation. The vast majority of situations requiring the exerting of influence fall within the persuasion and negotiation categories (McCall and Cousins 1989). These categories are not mutually exclusive. Negotiation and persuasion normally occur within the same interaction.

Communication and persuasion

It was seen in Chapter 2 that French and Raven's bases of power and Kelman's processes of social influence are grounded in differing sources of the persuader's power. Both those means of influence centre on characteristics of the persuader or the outcomes for the person being persuaded resulting from compliance, rather than on the content of the message itself. So to translate a specific basis of power with a specific message content is a necessary further step for developing sets of persuasive message strategies.

Using just such an approach Marwell and Schmitt (1961) developed a list of sixteen compliance-gaining strategies which have been classified by Miller and Perks (1982) along the reward/punishment and persuader/persuadee dimensions. They can apply to interactions between organizations just as much as they apply within organizations.

Persuader-onus/reward-oriented strategies

In this group of message strategies the persuader specifies the rewards that will be forthcoming if the persuadee complies with the message recommendation. These different messages have the following implications:

1 Promise: If you will comply I will reward you.
2 Positive expertise: If you comply you will be rewarded because of the nature of things.
3 Pre-giving: Target is rewarded before compliance is requested.
4 Positive esteem: People will think highly of you if you comply.

Persuader-onus/punishment-oriented strategies

In this group the persuader specifies the punishments that will be forthcoming to the person being persuaded if the latter fails to comply with the message recommendations. These are the implications:

1 Threat: If you do not comply I will punish you.
2 Negative expertise: If you do not comply you will be punished because of the nature of things.

3 Aversive stimulation: Target is continuously punished to obtain compliance by making cessation contingent on compliance.

4 Negative esteem: People you value will think worse of you if you don't comply.

Persuadee-onus/reward-oriented strategies

In this group of persuasive message strategies, the persuader specifies the positive self-reinforcing contingencies that will accrue to the persuadee if the persuadee fails to comply with the message recommendations. These are the implications of each strategy:

1 Positive moral appeal: A moral person would comply.
2 Positive self-feeling: You will feel better about yourself if you comply.
3 Altruism: I need your compliance very much so do it for me.
4 Positive altercasting: A person with 'good' qualities would comply.

Persuadee-onus/punishment-oriented strategies

In this group the persuader specifies the negative self-reinforcing contingency that will accrue to the persuadee if the persuadee fails to comply with the message recommendations. The implications of each are:

1 Negative moral appeal: Only a person who was not moral would fail to comply.
2 Negative self-feeling: You will feel worse about yourself if you do not comply.
3 Debt: You owe me compliance because of past favours I have done you.
4 Negative altercasting: Only a person with 'bad' qualities would not comply.

Selecting the persuasive message strategy

Situational differences can have an impact on the choice of strategy. For example, in intimate interpersonal relationships, punishment-oriented strategies are more likely to engender hostility, resentment or insecurity on the part of the target for persuasion than in low-intimate interactions. In organizational contexts much the same is true. In any case in communicating laterally across functions, a negotiator is unlikely to have the sanctions to apply punishment-oriented strategies. They are at odds too with the concept of influence networks which are created on the principles of exchange. These latter are most easily and effectively applied through reward-oriented strategies.

Irrespective of message strategies, good communicators provide other behaviours in support. Every individual in a conflict situation seeking to persuade another to his viewpoint is both a proponent trying to convince and an opponent who must be convinced if an accommodation is to be arrived at. To be persuasive, a good communicator 'should feel like an advocate who is seeking to convince an able and honest arbitrator always being open to being persuaded by reason'. Being open to persuasion is itself persuasive (Fisher 1983). By being attentive to what the other party is saying, a good communicator is in a better position to select an appropriate strategy in the circumstances.

Negotiating within organizations

Typically negotiations within organizations do not adhere to the more formal and often ritualistic patterns reflected in transactions between organizations. Where company officers, with responsibility for negotiating specific commercial outcomes with external organizations, need the support of peers in affiliate companies, other sections or departments, but lack the authority to direct that support, they require to negotiate with them to achieve it. In these circumstances informal relations are the keynote. They are exemplified by the principles of exchange (Bonoma 1985); they are also characterized by the establishment and maintenance of relationships and the use of persuasive message strategies of the kind indicated above.

For example, a sales manager may have accumulated 'credits' with the production manager by deciding to enter markets where demand will take up the slack in the troughs of production, so facilitating a steady throughput and hence production efficiency. When he wants particular information for his contingency planning for an imminent sales negotiation, like a minimum delivery time if pushed to it perhaps associated with customers' specific modifications, he calls in these credits, if necessary using an appropriate persuasive message strategy to do so (e.g. obligation). Others in his resource network in the organization might similarly provide data on cost or credit or performance.

Communication and handling conflict

Persuasive message strategies and negotiation are used within a wide variety of conflict situations. Indeed, in the vast majority of situations conflict is either present or threatens to be present. Even where relationships are cooperative, there will always be a compelling need to be competitive on the odd occasion, if only to underscore the importance of a certain position on an issue under consideration.

To enable people to communicate in a way which effectively handles such conflict, it is useful to know something about the studies that have been carried out on it. A useful framework is that of Pondy (1967) who saw conflict as having a number of distinct phases. The first phase is *latent conflict* in which two or more parties cooperate with each other and compete for certain rewards. The second phase is *perceived conflict* where, for example, groups rely on each other and one believes the other is pursuing a course of action which is harmful to its members. The third phase is *felt conflict* in which differences of interests and opinions are given expression in specific issues which take on added significance because they symbolize how the parties feel about each other. Pondy identifies a fourth phase as *manifest conflict* which arises after a conflictual situation has been activated, as sometimes witnessed in the making of coalitions to resist the forces of opposition and organizational strife. The final phase is the *conflict after-*

math which consists of the results of conflict seen in terms of future conflict. The outcome of any episode shapes the input affecting future latent conflict.

Not only are persuasive message strategies and negotiation used in a variety of conflict situations, they are also used within a wider communication strategy. These have been well summarized by Conrad (1985). *Avoidant strategies* may be appropriate where issues are trivial or where potential losses from open conflict may outweigh possible gains. It may have the effect of making the other party more hostile which can only inhibit creative management of conflict. *Delaying strategies* of the 'I don't have time to talk about it now' variety can be used, or more subtly, procedural rules can be manipulated to delay or subvert protracted confrontation. *Structuring strategies* may be important where individuals find conflicts ambiguous and complicated. People tend to become defensive in such situations in ways which can lead to escalating conflict spirals. By focusing on a particular issue and repeating or clarifying it, attention is diverted from the complexity of the situation. By such activities structure is given to the conflict. Other forms of structuring a conflict are to establish evaluative criteria, and hence de-emphasize other possible criteria, or to appeal to a relationship — 'We have worked together for a long time and in all that time I've never asked a favour of you. For once . . .'

Where avoiding or structuring strategies are not alternatives, resort can be had to confrontive strategies. Taking a hard-line position on an issue comes into this category. Where one party takes this kind of stance, the other party, even if he wishes to be cooperative, will require to adopt a similar stance if he is not to lose out. The danger is that the parties in such circumstances may get hooked on these hard-line positions and find it harder and harder to disengage.

People use various combinations of these strategies. They may seek to develop a cooperative relationship, but be forced to be competitive to underline strongly held preferences on an issue. A very important point to emerge is the importance of not becoming trapped in attack/defend spirals.

ANALYSING THE ORGANIZATIONAL CULTURE

In order to exercise influence in the most appropriate and effective way, a negotiator aiming to get maximum support for his activities before, during and after negotiations, has to be aware of the social reality in which these activities are embedded. To harness this support he has to develop the capacity to assess correctly differences in people's goals, values, perceptions and stakes and to see the subtle interdependencies among them. The skills needed also involve an ability to implement these judgements by successfully influencing people of diverse views in different parts of the organization. It means knowing where the various perspectives are in conflict and the sources of power each group has to pursue its own interests and to what extent they are prepared to use that power. The information uncovered allows the negotiator to know whose cooperation will be needed to implement any proposed line of action in external negotiations.

The intangible phenomenon of micro- or pico-cultures can be understood by consideration of the various approaches that have been adopted in relation to them. Our favoured approach is the 'shared meanings' view of culture. Sathe (1983) maintains that even if these shared understandings cannot be directly appraised, they will be manifest in *shared things, shared sayings, shared doings* and *shared feelings.* People's actions indicate what they share in terms of things. The language they use and their preferred words and their incidence say much about what things people do.

SUMMARY

The concepts of micro-culture and pico-culture were defined and it was seen that irrespective of which prevailed, conflict was inevitable given that people tend to view issues in terms of their own functional perspectives. In examining decision-making and problem-solving as issues over which conflict can arise, it was seen that the external physical reality whereby issues are seen as resolvable by rational processes, is not enough. When issues are matters of consensus not testable by rational processes, this is what is called social reality. When an individual attempts to impose his own highly subjective interpretation of events or issues on both rational and non-rational behaviour, that is what is termed individual reality.

Whether or not we are speaking of a micro-culture or pico-culture, people construct their own reality and support it with a rationality or logic which underpins the whole existence of the organization or group. Many rationalities exist but one or two will be dominant and provide a shared view of what goes on within the organization or group. The close relationship between language and micro- or pico-culture is seen in the 'universe of discourse' which can develop in a company or division or department. This can affect the way in which executives view the world and to which marketers negotiating with them very often have to accommodate.

Groups as well as individuals have their self-interests which they seek to promote. Depending on the internal and external environment different groups within an organization structure will derive power arising from their boundary-spanning roles. They compete with others to cope with the strategic contingencies facing the organiz-ation, and reduce uncertainty for the core of the organization which becomes dependent on this coping. Structuring as an information-processing capacity confers power on those who control key information and they use that power politically to achieve their own goals, for example in getting a bigger share of a fixed budget. With the growing complexity of organization structures there are increasing strains on these structures which derive from the difficulty of reconciling the need for specialization with the need for integration and coordination. Negotiators have to live with the inadequacies of formal structures. The skills of 'indirect management' call on the negotiator's skills as persuader and politican as much as on his bargaining skills.

To get things done despite the formal structure, conventional and bureaucratic systems like information systems require to be supplemented by internal and external resource networks. Bonoma has identified the four key skills of interacting, allocating, monitoring and organizing (networking) to meet the needs of the job where the formal organization falls short. Good negotiators understand that to prepare effectively for, to obtain support during, and implement agreements after negotiations, they or their associates have to compromise, trade-off and use the principles of exchange. Persuasive

114

message strategies and negotiation are used at different levels of conflict. These are used within a wider communication strategy which can include avoidant, delaying, structuring and confrontive strategies.

To get maximum support for his activities before, during and after negotiation, a negotiator has to be aware of the social reality in which such activities are embedded. This means knowing the micro- and pico-cultures in an organization and within these managing relations with bosses from whom the negotiator gets his mandate and resources; and with subordinates and, most importantly, peers in a lateral relationship through whom he has to act to meet particular task objectives. One useful approach in relation to understanding the micro- and pico-cultures is the shared meanings view of culture. Even if their shared assumptions cannot be directly appraised, these will come through in their shared things, shared sayings, shared doings and shared feelings. The language used by organizational members and their preferred words and their incidence, tell us much about these.

Note
1   A useful text putting organizational culture in a macro-culture perspective is Harris and Moran (1987), especially Chapter 6.

Questions

1   Why is the rational approach inadequate to explain the decision-making process?
2   Explain the rationalities or logics that appear in organizations and show how these can generate internal conflicts.
3   Is there a 'universe of discourse' in your own organization or business school?
4   How can negotiators overcome the problem of their accountability for their own negotiation tasks and their lack of hierarchical authority to get these tasks carried out?
5   What is the relationship between communication and the resolution of conflict?
6   What are the sources of power in organizations and how can it be used politically?
7   Familiarize yourself with the Reading on the next pages and identify in the dialogue what you have learned from this chapter.

READING

Attempting to resolve a delivery problem*

Subordinate

We're having trouble delivering disposable widgets to Techcorp.

Manager D

Oh-oh, that doesn't sound good. What's going on? Can I be of any assistance?

Subordinate

Well, I thought I'd let you know about it and run through the actions I've taken already. I think I know what to do, but I don't want to miss any bases.

Manager D

Fine. Go ahead.

Subordinate

I got a call from Dan saying we couldn't make schedule. When I asked why, he gave me a song-and-dance about poor materials. Since I know he likes to use that as an excuse, I called Ellen in purchasing, who told me the stuff was exposed to excess moisture while Dan was storing it. He, of course, denies it.

Manager D

So what did you do?

Subordinate

I haven't done anything about that part of it yet. I don't think we should get directly into a confrontation with Dan, do you?

---

* From D. L. Bradford and A. R. Cohen, *Managing for Excellence,* John Wiley and Sons, New York, 1984. Reproduced with permission.

Manager D

That depends on what our options are. In general, it's not a good idea to make anyone lose face, but let's see if there are any other choices. We've got to find a way to meet our commitments or we'll lose our edge as the most reliable manufacturing unit in the business. What else have you done?

Subordinate

I checked with Techcorp's purchasing agent about why the pressure. Turns out that their people made some promises to one of their customers without checking on actual availability. She's going to see whether she can get the customer to allow some slippage.

Manager D

Will they accept a looser tolerance on the widgets? If they would, would that help us?

Subordinate

She's going to check that too. Then we'd have to fight with our quality-control people. If I need you, would you talk to Ted's boss to pave the way?

Manager D

You expect trouble from Ted?

Subordinate

He's done it before.

Manager D

How would you approach him?

Subordinate

I've always tried to play it straight and tell him what our needs are. But he's a stubborn old coot.

Manager D

What do you suppose his interests are?

Subordinate

I don't know; I've never thought about that — I suppose he's very proud of our quality and doesn't want his reputation to be hurt.

Manager D

Besides, he's been at that job a long time and is likely to be there forever.

Subordinate

Yes, and I suppose he needs to feel valued and recognized. If I involve him in deciding how much tolerance the product can take, he'd respond better, and we'll come up with something reasonable.

Manager D

That sounds on target. Do you suppose it would help to reinforce with him the organization's theme of dependable and reliable service?

Subordinate

I think so, especially if I put it in that light. In fact, I've got another idea. I'll call him and get him together with the Techcorp buyer. That would be exciting for him I'll bet.

Manager D

Sounds good. When you put yourself in the shoes of someone who gives you a hard time, it's amazing how different things look. What else?

Subordinate

It just hit me; there may be some ways to reschedule some other production so we can concentrate on widgets. I know how to proceed now. I'll touch base this afternoon. Thanks.

Manager D

[Smiles]

CHAPTER 6

Making commercial agreements
within legal frameworks

The law, the businessman and the international negotiation of
agreements.. 119
   The pervasiveness of the law.. 119
   The diversity of the law... 120
   The unity of the law.. 120
   The individual businessman and the law.................................... 121
   The formation of contracts.. 122
Sales agreements... 122
   The offer.. 122
   The acceptance... 123
   The counter-offer.. 124
Performance of contracts... 124
   Delivery.. 125
   The passing of property.. 125
   The passing of risk... 126
Undertakings given by a seller... 126
Change of contract circumstances.. 126
The law which applies to a contract... 127
   Methods of avoiding conflict... 127
   Choice of laws.. 128
   Arbitration... 128
Some special considerations in dealing with governments................ 129
Other contractual and cooperation agreements................................ 130
   Marketing strategies... 130
Licensing.. 132
   Licences and patents... 132
   Trademarks, copyright and know-how...................................... 133
EC legislation and international licensing agreements...................... 134
   Franchising in the EC... 135
US legislation and international licensing agreements...................... 135
Agency and distributorship agreements.. 135
   Differences in treatment of agents and distributors................... 136
EC law and agency/distributorship agreements................................ 137

US law and agency/distributorship agreements.................................... 138
Agency/distributorship agreements in the Arab countries........................ 139
Joint-venture agreements... 139
Joint-venture agreements in the EC.. 140
Agreements of minor significance.. 141
Summary 141
Reading I... 147
Reading II.. 150
Reading III... 153

THE LAW, THE BUSINESSMAN AND THE
INTERNATIONAL NEGOTIATION OF AGREEMENTS

The behaviour of businessmen involved in activities leading to agreements is constrained by legal rules concerning commercial behaviour. To avoid the pitfalls which await him, the negotiator of agreements would be wise to acquire a working knowledge of the law in the context of the work in which he is engaged. In international business that context exposes him to different laws, often with different underlying philosophies.

The pervasiveness of the law

In a world in which accelerating rate of change is a predominant feature of the social environment, it is only to be expected that changes in attitudes and their interaction with technological, cultural, economic and political factors, will be reflected in the laws which regulate the conduct of business. Internationalization of trade, increasing commercial and technical sophistication, and the emergence of multinational enterprises have provided new problems and new challenges for national governments who see opportunity or threat in these developments and who legislate to exploit the opportunities or counter the perceived threats.

Consequently, government are more than ever concerned to spell out the legal basis under which goods are made, distributed and sold within their countries. Such basis embraces issues like the degree of competition to be maintained, the extent to which restrictive practices are permitted, whether and how industrial/intellectual property is to be protected, how far consumers and users are to receive protection in their economic exchanges, the relationship between industry and government in its capacities as politically motivated entity and defender of the public interest, the degree of foreign ownership and expatriate management tolerated, and the means for settling disputes in connection with agreements.

The emphasis on the issues and the ways in which governments give effect to their established aims differ from country to country. It is within the legal means adopted to reach these ends that businessmen strike their bargains.

The diversity of the law

The political and economic histories of each country have resulted in great diversity between countries in business law and practice. This diversity tends to be lessened by a number of factors. The Roman tradition of law is reflected to this day in *civil* or *code law*. It is really legislation embodying rules to which reference can be made for direction. Such laws are sometimes referred to as belonging to the 'continental' or 'Franco-German' school of legal thought.

Common law systems are based on English common law and belong to what is sometimes called the 'Anglo-American' school of thought. It was originally the law 'common to' the whole country, based on custom and declared to be the law by the courts, when so required. It is essentially 'judge-made' law as opposed to legislation. One might say that judges declare what is the common law of the land and interpret legislation. Some twenty-six countries enjoy a predominantly common law system.

Neither system entirely meets latter-day needs. Common law countries have adopted codes and statutes and civil law countries are constantly developing their law through cases. *Muslim law* systems, based on the Koran, exist in varying states of purity or dilution in some thirty more. The remaining countries tend to be economically weak and have systems of law based on tribal or *non-literate law* (Banks and Texter 1967).

Supranational law has been developed to meet the needs of regional economic and political blocs. Of the various attempts at economic and political integration among nations, the best known is that of the European Community which is seeking by 1992, to create a completely free market within the community. This will extend legislation to all manner of services not previously included, and will considerably alter the structure of markets. It will also be extended to ensure public procurement within EC countries is made on the basis of opening up government markets to competition in all member countries, see Reading III at end of chapter. It affects directly or indirectly every individual in the member countries. To make such a bloc effective, it has been found necessary to have laws which regulate inter-country activities of organizations. Where such activities, for example, affect trade between member states, the supranational law takes precedence over domestic law.

The unity of the law

All the differing national laws make it necessary, if disputes arise, to examine first of all which national law applies between an exporter and his customer or intermediary abroad. Attempts have been made to establish a world law of international trade aimed at eliminating the search for the proper law. The object of making reference here to attempts to establish international trade law is to emphasize the differences and difficulties of contracts between parties enjoying different legal systems and the issues of which individuals entering such contracts must be aware. A step forward was made in Vienna in 1980 when, under the aegis of the United Nations Commission on International Trade Law (UNCITRAL), a protracted conference agreed a Convention on Contracts for the International Sale of Goods.[1]

It is likely that by the time of going to press a sufficient number of countries will have ratified the convention to give it legal effect. It is significant that the USA has already ratified and that more developing countries have ratified than subscribed to earlier attempts to draw up a law to regulate international sales. Because their principal trade is within the countries of the Council for Mutual Economic Assistance (CEMA) the Soviet bloc countries have adopted the general Conditions of Delivery (1968 – 75) which are widely used by the Foreign Trade Corporations of the East European countries. While these have provided East European lawyers with an accessible set of norms and an advanced set of solutions, any failure to embrace the 1980 Convention may well retard international codification on a world scale.

The importance of the Vienna Convention is that its terms highlight the legal problems of doing business internationally. Reference will be made to it below to illustrate difficulties confronting and indicate possible solutions for, those businessmen who negotiate, in particular, international contracts of purchase and sale.

The custom of the merchants has been a successful source of harmonization of international trade law. Over the years, international traders have developed special trade terms like f.o.b., c.i.f. and f.a.s. which are understood by merchants the world over. That considerable harmonization has been achieved is in no small measure due to the work of the International Chamber of Commerce (ICC), a non-government organization consisting mainly of international traders in the market economy countries. The ICC special trade terms have been expanded over the years and are known as 'Incoterms'. These must be adopted by the parties if they are intended to form part of a contract of sale. Incoterms have influenced both the American Uniform Commercial Code and the CEMA General Conditions of Delivery 1968 – 75.

Not surprisingly, the international merchant community has been more successful than lawyers represented by UNCITRAL and other legal groups. The ICC has dealt with practical subjects. International lawyers, on the other hand, have the unenviable task of overcoming doctrinal and conceptual obstacles which are rooted in the traditions of different legal systems. They pursue their goal because they hope for a worldwide system of international trade law. In the meantime, those responsible for negotiating contracts should be aware of these developments as they could be caught up in them at any time, either as a party wishing to adopt them in a contract or as a potential supplier or buyer in negotiation with a businessman from another signatory country wishing to adopt them. Perhaps more importantly, a knowledge of them and why they are proposed are basic to a full understanding of the difficulties, and hence the action this knowledge indicates, in making international contracts.

The individual businessman and the law

Within the framework of national, supranational and international laws businessmen make their agreements. Many people believe that agreements and contracts are solely the province of the lawyer and that those involved in the process of purchase and sale, of licensing-out and licensing-in, of establishing supplier/intermediary relationships and of setting out the terms for cooperative action, are concerned with something quite separate. Nothing could be further from the truth.

The purchasing officer, manager or buyer, or other party or signatory to an agreement to procure supplies, is almost invariably involved in negotiating contracts, as is the sales manager, contracts manager, salesman or whoever is nominated to pursue a course of action leading to a sale. Very often they enter into contracts by the very fact of accepting a tender or an order, or even by conducting themselves in a way that the courts would assume that they had intended to be legally bound. Similarly, the research and development manager, the licensing executive, the marketing manager, or whoever elects or is delegated to negotiate a technology transfer deal or franchise arrangement, seeks to achieve agreement without the assistance of lawyers.

There are times when it may be desirable or necessary to obtain legal advice on contract matters, and indeed to include a lawyer in a negotiating team. Yet the fact remains that activities leading to an agreement are normally carried out within a legal framework by businessmen in their capacities of customers and suppliers, manufacturers and intermediaries, producers and overseas partners.

The formation of contracts

In law, all contracts stem from an offer which is made by one party and accepted by another. Unless the parties to any agreement are aware of the offer and acceptance procedure, one or other may enter into what he thinks is a contract when no contract exists or, equally, may enter into a contract without realizing he has done so, perhaps on the other party's terms.

SALES AGREEMENTS

All agreements, whether on information, manufacturing and know-how, joint research, specialization, agency and distribution, joint venture or management contract, are ultimately aimed at creating sales. Notwithstanding the marketing importance of these agreements, in terms of the number of transactions entered into, agreements of sale exceed by many times the number of other agreements made. It is particularly appropriate, therefore, that the offer and acceptance procedure,[2] which is basic to the making of a contract, should be related here to agreements of purchase and sale around which it has largely developed.

The offer

In the case of contracts which are the subject of negotiation in respect of specification, price and payment conditions, delivery, performance and other terms of concern to the parties, the negotiations are frequently opened by a prospective customer, often after discussions with a prospective supplier, asking the supplier to quote against his requirements. This is often the case with engineering products of the capital goods variety, or with products of high technology where the buyer relies on the judgment of the seller to meet his requirements. At this stage no commitment is incurred which carries the intention that, if accepted, a contract will ensue.

The resultant estimate or quotation is normally an offer subject to the seller's conditions of sale, and is open for acceptance unless qualified to show that the proposal is a negotiating step only.

However, the majority of transactions occur where the goods are standard, are sold on the open market and are not subject to detailed negotiation. They are often consumer goods or goods purchased regularly as part of a course of dealing, and can arise from the supplier's normal promotional activities inducing a buyer to place an order which is itself an offer, subject to the buyer's conditions of purchase.

When a dispute arises over an alleged contract, as where one party believes a contract has been made and another maintains he has not entered a contract, a court may adopt the traditional approach of examining whether the parties are still in the negotiating stage, whether an offer has emerged, and whether the offer has been accepted. The question arises as to when the parties pass from the initial negotiating stage to the stage where the offer has emerged. The importance of the offer being defined with some certainty can therefore be seen. The essential feature of an offer is that it is intended to result in a binding contract if the person to whom it is addressed says 'yes' unconditionally and without qualification. If the person from whom the communication emanates reserves the right to think it over when the other party says 'yes', the parties are still in the stage of negotiation.

Under English law and that of many other common law countries, an offer can always be revoked. In continental European laws based on the civil code, an offeror is bound by his offer unless he has specifically excluded its binding character. In an attempt to reconcile the differences between the common law and continental European law on offer and acceptance leading to the conclusion of an international contract of sale, a compromise was established by the United Nations Convention on Contracts for the International Sale of Goods to the effect that an offer can be revoked on price but this revocation is excluded (1) if the offer states a fixed time of acceptance or otherwise indicates it is firm and irrevocable, or (2) if the revocation is not made in good faith or in conformity with fair dealing. Where an offer is rejected, it lapses whether or nor a time limit is specified.

The acceptance

Here again there is a difference between Anglo-American law and that of continental European countries. Under English law, for example, if a supplier makes an offer against a prospective customer's request, subject to his own conditions of sale, acceptance of the offer as it stands means that a contract of sale has been made and the seller's conditions form part of the contract. However, some customers are more wary than others and often have an order form which, while apparently accepting the seller's offer, incorporates different conditions of purchase. By so doing, the intending customer is putting forward qualifications to the supplier's offer and making a counter-offer. In certain continental European countries, the acceptance may contain insignificant additional stipulations without the offer being rejected. The solution proposed in the Vienna Convention is that if the stipulations do not materially alter the terms of the offer then a contract is made on the original offer. If the stipulations are material and significant, the offer is rejected and a counter-offer made.

Another difference between Anglo-American law and some continental European laws is that, under the latter, a contract may be concluded by tacit acceptance. A statement in an offer that 'if we do not hear from you within x days, we shall assume you have accepted this offer' may result in a contract if the person offered does not notify the seller within that time. Common law countries reject silence as a mode of acceptance. In this instance, the solution proposed by the UN convention on Contracts for the International Sale of Goods inclines to the Anglo-American view and rejects this form of acceptance.

The counter-offer

The counter-offer can take the form of the prospective customer purporting to accept the offer but including his own (very different) terms of purchase, or it may suggest acceptance of the offer on slightly different terms. Subject to the different approaches of common and code law and the solution proposed in the 1980 Vienna Convention, a qualification has been made either way which operates as a rejection of the offer to which it is a reply and constitutes a counter-offer. If accepted, this will result in a contract of which the buyer's terms of purchase will form a part.

Even if the seller did not make a formal acceptance of the counter-offer but were to deliver the goods without demur, the contract would be on the customer's conditions of purchase, since the seller, by delivering the goods, would be implicitly accepting the purchaser's counter-offer. Wise sellers, while giving the impression of accepting the counter-offer on their standard acknowledgement of order form, incorporate in this form or in a separate attachment referred to in the form, their original conditions of sale. This can have the effect of rejecting the counter-offer and putting forward yet another offer. If the customer accepts delivery of the goods the acceptance of this new offer will be implicit in his action and a contract will be made on the supplier's conditions.

It is therefore possible to see why it is said that in one set of circumstances an order is an acceptance and in another it is an offer; that an acknowledgement of order can be a counter-offer, or it can be an acceptance. Once a negotiator knows how contracts are formed, he is on his way to knowing what he is committed to in contract terms. Should a dispute arise later over terms, a position of strength is more likely to have been established by the party which has acted from a knowledge of these rules and procedures.

Where the goods being negotiated are of considerable value or have to be built to the buyer's specifications, a formal contract embodying all terms of the agreement is drawn up and signed by the parties concerned. Such contracts usually include a clause invalidating any previously agreed arrangements. This means in effect that the offer and acceptance procedure, even if adhered to in earlier exchanges, can have no bearing on the outcome. The contract document becomes the basis for negotiations.

PERFORMANCE OF CONTRACTS

The making of a contract cannot be divorced from its effects. The sales negotiator has to be as concerned as the purchasing executive with the eventual contract, for the reason that the laws on performance of contract should help to determine the nature of the contract to be negotiated.

For example, the making of a contract cannot be separated from the effects of the laws concerning the disposal of goods by a supplier in performance of a contract. This has three distinct phases, namely the delivery of the goods, the passing of the property and the passing of the risk. The three do not always coincide, particularly in f.o.b. and c.i.f. contracts (Schmitthoff 1980:75-88).

Delivery

That branch of law known as the conflict of laws will resolve the question of whether an issue, in this case delivery, will be decided under the provisions of the seller's law or the law prevailing in the country of the buyer. Differences exist between national laws. For example, in countries such as France, Greece, Italy and Germany, if the seller delays the delivery of the goods and no time is fixed for the delivery, the buyer must normally demand delivery and allow the seller a reasonable time for performance before he can treat the contract as repudiated. This requirement is unknown in Anglo-American law which is much stricter in this respect and would treat the contract as repudiated automatically when a reasonable time for delivery has expired, provided time is of the essence of the contract.

If an exporter wishes to avoid the incidence of foreign law, he can do so by having embodied in his contract a specific stipulation to the effect that the contract should be governed in every respect by the law of his own country.

However, an inflexible attitude in this respect might exclude consideration of an exporter's offer where, for example, a large organization or main contractor operating on an international basis, or a national government used to making contracts on its own standard conditions of purchase, are not prepared to negotiate. A relatively large number of developing countries, including most Arab countries, have it written into their law that all contracts will be subject to domestic law.

The passing of property

Under the laws of the USA, the United Kingdom, France, Belgium, Italy and Portugal, the property in the goods sold passes when the parties intend it to pass, whether the delivery of the goods has taken place or not. In Holland, Spain, Germany, Argentina and some other countries, the property passes only if the intention that it should pass is supported by actual delivery of the goods.

It is a sound precaution for an exporter to make arrangements for the retention of the Bill of Lading, which is normally a document of title, until the purchase price is secured. Under documentary credit and documentary collection arrangements, the Bill of Lading is only released against payment, or a legal undertaking to pay in the case of release of a Bill of Lading against a tenour bill of exchange. Where it is not possible to retain the Bill of Lading until the purchase price is paid — for example, where shipment is made under documents which do not give title to the goods, as in the case of a seawaybill, airwaybill, non-negotiable Bill of Lading or data freight receipt — it is advisable to incorporate a reservation of title clause. A reservation of title clause may put the exporter in the position of a secured creditor in the event of the insolvency of an importer who has been granted credit terms. Such reservations of title are recognized in the law of many countries, particularly West European countries.[3]

The passing of risk

Under the law of most countries, and the UN Convention on Contracts for the International Sale of Goods, the risk of accidental loss passes, as a rule, on the delivery of the goods. In the United Kingdom the risk passes normally when the property passes. In international trade law generally the concepts of the passing of risk and the passing of property are regularly separated. Special arrangements between the parties are admissible. In the absence of these, the risk will generally pass in a contract when the goods leave the custody of the seller. Therefore, in 'ex-works' and 'f.o.t.' contracts, the risk passes when the goods are delivered to the buyer or his agent, or to the railway as applicable. In f.a.s. contracts the risk passes when the goods are delivered alongside the ship, and in f.o.b. and c.i.f. contracts when they are delivered over the ship's rail.

UNDERTAKINGS GIVEN BY A SELLER

Just as promises are often made by manufacturers with regard to delivery, so are they also made from time to time concerning the ability of the goods to meet a certain standard or comply with particular requirements. The parties are at liberty to provide in their contract that, in the case of non-performance or delayed performance, the party in default should pay a fixed sum calculable either as a lump sum or on a scale varying with the length of time of the default.

Clauses fixing the amount recoverable in breach are common in international standard contract forms. Under continental European legal systems, these clauses are penal in their purpose and are normally enforceable without question. In common law countries such as Australia and New Zealand, the USA and the United Kingdom, penalty provisions are normally frowned upon and will be enforced only if they are recognized *liquidated damages* — that is, a genuine pre-estimate of the damage likely to be suffered as the result of a breach. This takes little account of the fact that there are occasions when the damage can only be estimated with any accuracy after the event.

CHANGE OF CONTRACT CIRCUMSTANCES

When a fundamentally different situation emerges which makes the performance of the contract more difficult than was envisaged by the parties when the contract was made, the contract is said to be frustrated (Schmitthoff 1980: 109 – 124). When commercial frustration in the legal sense occurs, it not only provides one party with a defence in an action brought by another; it also automatically kills the contract and discharges both parties.

Factors which can produce frustration are circumstances such as import and export prohibitions and restrictions, outbreak of war, the perishing or destruction of goods, or where such a radical change of circumstances has occurred that were the parties to renegotiate it would be an entirely different contract from that originally entered into.

Very often it is a matter of degree whether an event which changes the circumstances of a contract does or does not amount to frustration. The rules of domestic law and foreign law are often at variance in this respect. This admits the possibility of one or other of the parties finding himself in a position where he is held to his contract and is exposed to claims for damages because of breach. It may then be the wiser course for the parties to introduce into their agreement a clause defining in advance their rights and obligations if certain events occur beyond their mutual control, whether or not these events result in frustration of the contract. Such clauses are used in practice and are negotiable. These are called *force majeure* clauses.

Force majeure includes all events beyond the control of the parties. The effect of the clause is sometimes to provide for automatic suspension or cancellation of the contract in the event of the occurrence of the change factor, sometimes to give each party or one party an option of suspending or cancelling the contract in that event. The best *force majeure* clauses in use these days do not provide for the immediate cancellation of the contract, but provide for the performance time of the contract to be extended by an agreed period; and if the event continues after that extended time either party is entitled to cancel the contract by notifying the other party to this effect. The worst situation is where the contract does not contain a *force majeure* clause. In that circumstance the only excuse by a party who cannot perform is to plead frustration of which is has been said 'it is a kind of last ditch defence, often pleaded but rarely successful'.

THE LAW WHICH APPLIES TO A CONTRACT

We have already seen that different legal systems have different approaches to making and performing a contract. Indeed, an international commercial contract can span a number of legal systems. Not only that, but the law that applies to the contract and the jurisdiction of the courts that have to pass judgment do not necessarily coincide. Executives negotiating sales/purchase agreements have to be aware of that branch of law known as private international law or conflict of laws which determines, in an individual case, the applicable law and the jurisdiction which will pass judgment.

It can happen that, according to the rules of the conflict of laws, a dispute has to be heard in a domestic court, but that these courts have to apply a foreign system of law. It is important for salesmen and buyers to know the law under which their contract is governed, whether by the law of the seller's country or of the buyer's country, or of that country to which the goods have ultimately to be shipped. Central to any contract spanning more than one country is the law governing that transaction. In most Arab countries and a number of developing countries, local law applies to a contract.

Methods of avoiding conflict

A number of attempts have been made to avoid a conflict of laws. The United Nations Economic Council for Europe (ECE) has devised model forms for contracts between organizations working within different legal systems. The International Chamber of Commerce, as noted above, has developed an international approach to the definition of trade terms in its 'Incoterms'. In particular, the 1980 Vienna Convention went a long way to resolving the danger of conflict of laws by establishing straightforward rules.

1 A contract for the sale of goods is regulated by the domestic law designated by the parties.
2 Failing designation by the parties, the domestic law of the country in which the seller has his habitual residence applies.
3 Rule 2 is subject to two exceptions:
(a) where the order is received by the branch office of the seller the contract is regulated by the law of the country in which the branch is situated;
(b) where the order is received by the seller or his agent in the buyer's country, the domestic law of the country in which the buyer has his habitual residence applies.

Choice of laws

It is always advisable for parties to agree the system they want to be applied, and a domestic manufacturer should, in his general conditions of sale, make provision for the application of his own law to the agreement. In other words he should include a 'choice of laws' clause into his contract. Because of the distinction which is made between conclusion and performance of a contract, the parties would be wise to state that both the conclusion and the performance of the contract be governed by domestic law. This obviates a situation arising under a more general clause that the contract be governed by the domestic law of the seller, whereby the domestic court might maintain that a buyer's right of inspection and rejection is governed by French law where, say, a United Kingdom exporter sells on free delivery terms, because the contract covered formation but not performance.

The negotiators and their opposers may agree to have their contract governed by any legal system they care to choose and are not limited to a legal system with which the circumstances surrounding the contract are connected.

Arbitration

In international contracts, arbitration is the normal method of settling disputes because it is private, cheap and speedy in relation to the legal alternative of litigation. Nevertheless, national courts exercise a supervisory jurisdiction over arbitration tribunals.

Basically, arbitrators or arbiters are men or women whose judgment and experience in their trade make them acceptable to either party. Their nomination will be by Chambers of Commerce, presidents of learned institutions, etc.

In normal circumstances a seller might try in his standard conditions of sale for arbitration by his domestic Chamber of Commerce. Such arbitration clauses are negotiable and sellers and purchasers who cannot agree to the others' local arbitration proposals may agree to arbitration by a Chamber of Commerce in a third country in whom both parties have confidence. For example, a French or German seller may try for arbitration in his own country, while a Russian purchaser may seek arbitration by the All-Union Chamber of Commerce in Moscow. If the parties fail to agree to the domestic arbitration of the other, Stockholm Chamber of Commerce may be acceptable as a compromise.

The International Chamber of Commerce has set up a Court of Arbitration which administers a code of rules especially adapted to the settlement of international commercial disputes; they recommend a standard ICC arbitration clause to parties willing to submit differences to its Court of Arbitration. Also, there are special clauses when one of the parties is resident in the USA or is of American nationality, to accommodate particular needs of the American Arbitration Association. In contracts between businessmen in the United Kingdom and the USA there is a British-American arbitration clause that should be included. In Japan there is in existence the Japanese Commercial Arbitration Association. Its role is rather different from the others in that, in accordance with Japanese culture, emphasis is not on the differences but rather on compromise between the parties concerned. Only a few cases brought before the association end in binding arbitration.

UNCITRAL published in 1976 their Arbitration Rules which are designed to fill gaps in arbitration agreements. These have to be adopted by the parties to be applicable. They provide a quasi-institutional framework for the arbitration. It is then no longer possible for an unwilling party to defeat the arbitration agreement by refusing to appoint an arbitrator. If the parties have agreed on an appointing authority, for example a Chamber of Commerce, the authority will appoint the arbitrator. If the parties fail to agree on an appointing authority, the secretary-general of the permanent Court of Arbitration in the Hague will appoint one.

The idea of arbitration is not one that fits easily into an Islamic setting. The source of Arab law, for example, is the Koran. Although some Arab countries have modified or extended Koranic Law as a result of their development of traditional international trading activities, to the extent in some countries of developing or adopting Code Law, the lawfulness of transactions is gauged by their concept of sale. To an Arab everything has a market value and all intelligent people are supposed to be aware of what it is. Consequently, there is no perceived need for arbitration, which is a concept Arabs in general find difficult to understand. The reverse side of the coin is that non-Arabs tend to see them as rigid and unwilling to accede to accepted norms. Disputes require to be taken to local courts, but it is normal for disputes to be referred to arbitration for quick settlement. This can either be at the International Court of Arbitration in Paris or locally. The local court has discretion to set aside arbitration according to certain rules.

SOME SPECIAL CONSIDERATIONS
IN DEALING WITH GOVERNMENTS

The sources of law in dealing with government customers has been investigated (Turpin 1972). In France the government has the choice of entering a business agreement by an ordinary private contract or of entering into a *contrat administratif* with a supplier. A contract is held to be administrative if the supplying company is required to discharge a public service, or if the contract contains terms that are not appropriate to ordinary contractual relationships.

Administrative contracts differ in formation and operation. For example, the public authority has the right to effect changes in the contract without requiring to obtain the agreement of the other party, if the public interest requires it. At the same time such contracts are also regulated by documents emanating from the various public authorities which apply to the purchase of a public authority or the particular classification of goods or services. These documents, known as *cahiers de charge* ensure a significant degree of uniformity in public authority contracting. They contain model contract terms for inclusion in appropriate contracts. These have the force of law. Other aspects of public procurement in France, such as the procedures for selecting contractors, are prescribed by decree summarizing legislative measures in respect of public contracts as a *Code de marchés publics*.

In the USA there is no special law related to administrative contracts, yet a body of law has evolved which regulates contracts in which government is involved. Federal common law, which applies to contracts with the Federal Government, regulates such matters as the formation of contracts. The Federal Courts have adapted the law to particular needs of government contracts. There is also a plethora of statutes and regulations concerning government purchases. These require government agencies to implement special procedures for awarding contracts, a proportion of which has to go to small firms. Standard forms of contract are used by federal agencies as the basis for negotiations, and certain clauses must be incorporated in a contract.

In the United Kingdom there are no such special laws which apply to government contracts. The private law of contract applies in so far as it regulates such aspects as formation, rights and obligations of the parties, breach and termination. In practice contractual relations are established more by the standard contract forms used. Together these applicable rules could be claimed to constitute the law of the contract.

OTHER CONTRACTUAL AND COOPERATION AGREEMENTS

The many types of agreement in which companies involve themselves in pursuit of their objectives are all aimed ultimately at creating sales, which will be the subject of negotiations between a salesman and a purchaser leading to a contract of sale. These different types of agreement have almost invariably to be negotiated, either at a distance through a sequence of correspondence, or more usually in a face-to-face situation by the representatives of the organizations involved who seek to derive advantage for their own organizations in a mutually beneficial exchange. Often the negotiation is a combination of the two.

Marketing strategies

To put these agreements in an international marketing context, it is useful to relate them to market strategies which can be classified according to the commitment of managerial and financial resources. Going from minimum to maximum commitment, strategies can be grouped into the following three broad categories, each of which can be associated with a particular class or classes of agreement (Robock and Simmonds 1983).

Licensing

Licensing-out by a company may stem from the need to develop the market for the subject of the licence, to overcome protective tariff barriers, to share the costs of further development of the product, or to capitalize on a market opportunity where alternative strategies are not feasible owing to market or resource factors.

Licensing-in is a short-cut to a competitive market position and is sometimes a deliberate policy to supplement internally generated research and development activity.

A licensing agreement is the outcome of bargaining activities which are perceived as beneficial to the parties involved. It can relate to the right to manufacture a product for sale or to use particular know-how, or both, usually supported by a patent right; or it can relate to the right to bottle, fill or package for sale the patented product, mostly in the food, chemical and pharmaceutical industries; or it can relate to the right to use without manufacture or sale; or to assemble and sell parts of a patented product, a form used particularly in the automotive, electrical and appliances industries; or it may be distribution and sale only of the patented product. Similarly, licences can be granted for trademarks and brands.

A sub-division of licensing is franchising. Franchise agreements are agreements whereby the franchising company provides a degree of finance, often by stocking, and gives training and know-how to franchisees, who, in return for a lump-sum payment and perhaps royalties to, and purchases from, the franchising company, receive the right to use the franchiser's name, share the rewards of his advertising and receive territorial protection.

Exporting

Within this category a company may have its own export department or division and engage in direct exporting. It and its customers will negotiate agreements of purchase and sale.

An alternative within this category is where an export merchant buys products in the country of origin and sells abroad at his own risk; a similar situation exists where an overseas customer has a buying office or is represented in the country of origin. Either way the resultant contract is equivalent to a domestic transaction and does not give rise to the same problems as in inter-country transactions. It can, however, expose expatriate buyers to the laws of the supplier country.

Another alternative within this category is the overseas based intermediary who can be either a distributor or agent, giving rise to (often exclusive) distributor and agency agreements. A large proportion of exports are handled through such intermediaries.

Consortium agreements and group representation are other modes of exporting which involve the cooperative action of a number of manufacturers of associated equipment or products, who jointly can obtain business which individually they could not achieve.

Direct investment alternatives

There are degrees of foreign direct investment within this category. The minimum is local warehousing, with direct sales staff, leading on to local packaging and/or assembling operations; and the maximum is direct investment with full-scale local production and marketing.

While wholly-owned subsidiaries can be established for all these operations, giving the parent company complete power of decision, the trend is more and more to the joint-venture arrangement. Such arrangements are more likely for the highest resource commitment alternatives for the reasons that the larger operations have greater exposure and place a greater need for local identification as well as financial support. If speed into the market is important, then local expertise is required and the joint venture is one way of acquiring it. It is therefore a way of gaining access to resources, capital, technology and markets by ensuring the best rate of return on investment through economies of scale and maximum use of capacity, without a firm losing its independence through full-scale merger. Because joint venture means a certain loss of direct control, the agreement forming the basis of joint operations is crucial.

The overseas joint venture may involve itself in sales and distributor/agency agreements under local law, and may enter into export activities bringing it into the area of conflict of laws and overseas sales and distributor agreements. If it wishes to use patents or other industrial property of the individual joint owners, this is likely to be the subject of a licensing agreement.

LICENSING

Licences and patents

A licensor has a strong negotiating hand if the licence subject is a granted patent. Trading blocs and tariff reduction have rendered inadequate patent cover in the country of manufacture only. The selection of markets in which patents should be sought is therefore an important marketing decision (Cropp *et al.* 1970:51).

Because patents convey a monopoly for a given period, most governments are concerned to ensure that they are not used in such a way as to act in restraint of competition. Different governments have different approaches. In the United Kingdom, there is provision for compulsory licensing if the patent is not being worked. In some countries importation of the patented goods constitutes working, but local working of the product or process is required in most industrialized countries. There is no compulsory licensing in Italy or Argentina, but failure to work is penalized by total loss of patent rights. In the USA there is no requirement for working, which is unique outside the Soviet bloc countries, with the result that a USA patent can be used as an obstructive weapon by an unprincipled licensee.

Individual businessmen concerned with the negotiation of licensing agreements must have a working knowledge of the appropriate laws of the countries of the parties to the agreement, particularly in relation to patents.[4] In addition, as noted below in relation to the European Community, supranational law has to be taken into account.

Apart from the differences indicated above, local laws and practices differ in respect of what is defined as patentable, the period of protection, the rights of third parties and the cover afforded by patenting (Cropp *et al.* 1970:38). In some countries, for example the traditional Arab countries, patent rights do not exist and confidentiality has to be written into the licence agreement.

The specifics of any agreement cover such subjects as exclusivity, licence improvements and market laws. Nowhere is this seen better than in price fixing in patent licence agreements. In American law price fixing is permissible in theory but inadvisable in practice. Under British law a licensor may not lay down a minimum resale price (this does not appear to apply to ethical drugs and medicines), although he may regulate the price at which the patent subjects are sold by the licensee. Under West German law it is perfectly legal, while in the EC the Commission of the European Community has shown itself to be opposed to clauses in patent licences which attempt to fix or recommend prices (Cawthra 1978).

The transfer of technological know-how, very often given effect by licence agreements, is viewed in some of the more rapidly developing countries in a very different perspective from that taken in the advanced industrialized countries of the West and in Japan. Environmental changes and consequent changes in philosophical, economic, political and social viewpoints have resulted in laws which are contrary to the Western business ethos. Technology transfer agreements by means of licensing are often subject to the laws of the technology receiving country, sometimes rendering irrelevant the concept of conflict of laws.

Under revised Mexican patent laws, the concept of Certificates of Invention has been adopted (Peters 1977). This is a means, favoured in the USSR, whereby processes for making mixtures of chemicals and pharmaceuticals and for making alloys, for example, not subject to the protection of patents in Mexico, can be protected. The holder is assured that users will pay royalties on the protected processes — protection is limited to ten years — but the process must be made available to anyone who signs a royalty agreement. Therefore the licensor has no say in the disposition of his inventions, which may make corporate planning and operational planning and control less effective than is desired. Also, the government agency responsible for registration of royalty agreements has the authority to set royalty fees if the parties involved cannot agree on the terms, which can compound these planning and control problems.

Trademarks, copyright and know-how

Licences can also involve trademarks and copyright. Together with patents these are the principal constituents of what is referred to as industrial or intellectual property.

Copyright is not as widely applicable for manufacturing and service firms as are patents and trademarks. Nevertheless it is of the first order of importance for organizations such as publishing and recording companies.

Patented products and processes in most cases cannot be readily manufactured or used without disclosure of 'know-how' by the licensor. This know-how may consist of secret information, drawings, formulae, technical data and the like. A licence on the patented product and the know-how connected with it are often necessary to enable the licensee to manufacture the product or use the process without difficulty.

Know-how may also be licensed in connection with a trademark. In these days of rapid technology advance, some companies prefer to communicate as know-how all or part of new inventions, processes and methods developed by their research and development departments, rather than have them patented and thereby disclosed to would-be competitors.

Combinations of the different subjects of industrial property are often incorporated within the one agreement, such as licences under patents, trademarks and know-how. Such combinations can be dangerous. For example, under the British Patents Act a licence agreement may be terminated by either party after the patent has ceased to be in force. Licences relating to several British patents or a British patent and a British trademark should therefore be granted in separate agreements.

EC LEGISLATION AND INTERNATIONAL LICENSING AGREEMENTS

Implicit in EC law is the determination of the founding fathers to ensure that, with the abolition of tariff barriers, these will not be replaced by private barriers in the form of restrictive agreements or practices which have the effect of distorting competition in the Community. Licensing agreements come within the strictures developed to maintain healthy competition in the interests of the consumer. The broad guidelines are to be found in Articles 85 and 86 of the Treaty of Rome. More specific guidelines are found in the regulations made to implement the articles of the Treaty. Most importantly, decisions of the EC Commission and judgments of the European Court in Luxembourg establish precedents which provide marketers with guides to their future actions, and licensing negotiators and their advisers with limits to their discretion and indications of the extent of their commitment of their organizations.

What patent, trademark and copyright owners and possessors of unpatented know-how and their respective licenses are permitted to do, or are prohibited from doing, in the exercise of their rights in the Common Market, have to a limited extent been established as a result of judgments of a number of significant cases in the Court of Justice. Firstly, it is not possible to call on national trademark laws in support of a licensing agreement if that agreement is in violation of Article 85 of the Treaty of Rome.[5] The Treaty guarantees only the existence of national property rights but not the exercise of these rights.

Secondly, it is not possible, by virtue of trademark right, to prevent the importation of products originating in other member states bearing the same mark because their owners have acquired the mark itself or the right to use it through licensing and trademark assignment agreements with each other or with third parties.[6]

Thirdly, import restrictions based on industrial property rights violate the Rome treaty once a product has been lawfully sold in another member country, unless a situation prevails owing to which the owner of the right concerned has no opportunity to obtain the particular benefit in his exclusive right.[7]

Fourthly, national copyright cannot be invoked to prevent imports of an item by a manufacturer who has himself sold them in another member country.[8] This rule also applies in the case of parallel patents.[9] Neither the owner of a patent nor a patent licensee can prevent the import of a patented article which another licensee of the same patent owner has sold within the other licensee's territory in another member country.

Clauses in licence agreements which provide for exclusivity of manufacturing or selling rights, or which prevent the licensee from challenging the validity of the patent which is the subject of the licence, or which contain restrictive provisions in relation to grant-back, or which prevent competition by agreeing to refrain from competing with each other in the relevant markets, or which prohibit exports, are all prohibited under Article 85(1).[10] They may be granted exemption under Article 85(3) if they are shown to contribute to the improvement of the production or distribution of goods, or promote technological or economic progress, while allowing consumers a fair share of the resulting benefit. For example, prohibition on export or exclusivity of licence could be exempt for a limited period where a licensee needs temporary protection against the licensor or other licenseees in order to reduce the risk inherent in an initial investment in a new market.

Franchising in the EC

Only recently has franchising, one of the fastest growing ways of doing business in the EC, received any legal backing. A new regulation is to be introduced which will allow franchising overall legal backing in recognition of its role as a job-creating stimulant to small business activity. It also argues that the industry can help to improve competition. Until this proposal, any kind of franchising had been subject to Article 85(1) of the Treaty of Rome and the general prohibition on restrictive agreements likely to distort free competition. It therefore gives European franchisers and franchisees guidance on how to run their business in a way that can be defended in EC law.[11]

The scope of the ruling is restricted to franchises involving the distribution of goods and services, but does not extend to industrial franchising where a manufacturing process or technology is the subject of the contract. This area is covered by separate draft regulations which provide exemption from competition restrictions on know how licensing agreements and by an existing rule giving clearance for patent licences.

US LEGISLATION AND INTERNATIONAL LICENSING AGREEMENTS

American anti-trust legislation can affect licensing agreements. In particular, exclusive agreements are more and more being considered as *per se* violations of the law. A similar view may well be taken where a restriction is placed on a licensee that he cannot sell to specified customers or in a specified area. Certainly such a policy is illegal when competition is substantially lessened, as is any other provision which has this effect.

Anti-trust is treated more fully under 'US law and agency/distributorship agreements' below.

AGENCY AND DISTRIBUTORSHIP AGREEMENTS

At the exporting level of commitment of the financial and other resources of a company, a considerable amount of business is done via agencies and distributorships. Sound agreements for these form the basis of good working relationships. It has been said, not without truth, that arbitration is better than litigation, conciliation better than arbitration, and prevention of legal disputes better than conciliation. Such prevention is very much the responsibility of executives drafting and negotiating the relevant agreements. The effectiveness of these negotiations will influence the operation and future maintenance of the agreements.

The rights and duties of each party are governed by the agency or distributorship agreement which operates when the manufacturer/principal grants the distributor/agent the sole trading rights/sole right to procure or conclude the contracts with third parties on his behalf. The contract is normally made by an exchange of letters embodying the offer and its acceptance, or by a formal contract. Where French law applies in a contract of commercial agency, a commercial agent cannot rely on a mere exchange of letters. Judgments of the Supreme Court appear to indicate that a person who cannot produce a written contract may not claim the status of a commercial agent in the event of litigation (Guyerot 1976:47).

In order to understand the differences between agency and distributorship it is necessary to get rid of misleading commercial terms and focus on their legal meanings. Common business terminology in English-speaking countries uses 'agent' to cover both distributorship and agent as distinguished by lawyers. By an agent the lawyer means a person who, acting on behalf of and for the account of another person known as the principal, constitutes a direct legal relationship, a contract between the principal and the customer. For getting the business and bringing about the contractual relationship between manufacturer and customer he is normally paid a commission, or a retainer and commission. An overseas agent very often enjoys the exclusive representation of his principal in his defined territory.

A distributor, in the legal view, is a different person. The manufacturer usually gives him sole distributing rights in a specified country and sells his goods only to appointed distributors. The distributor pays for his goods and bears the commercial risk. His payment arises from the profit he makes on reselling the goods. The extent of his profit will be a function of his business acumen.

Differences in treatment of agents and distributors

A number of countries, including Germany, France and Italy, have more protective legal provisions for some types of agents, the more so where the agent is likely to be the weaker of the parties to a negotiation, through smallness of size for example. In particular, they provide for a goodwill compensation to which the agent may be entitled after termination of an agency relationship. In some legal systems the manufacturer/ principal cannot contract out of it. There is a mistaken tendency to assume that the contractual relationship between principal and agent is governed by the law of the country in which the agent carries on business, except where the contract between the parties expressly states that the applicable law will be that of the principal's country. Some countries, like Belgium, Italy and Holland, extend to distributors also the concept that the goodwill created by agents accrues to the principal/manufacturer. A recent case in Belgium resulted in a German manufacturer being required to pay considerable compensation to a Belgian distributor despite the fact that the agreement provided for

German law and Zurich arbitration (where the arbitrators found in favour of the manufacturer). An outline is given in Reading I at the end of this chapter.

The costs of terminating both agency and distributorship agreements can be considerable and underline the need to understand the relevant laws and their application as well as the need for a working relationship based on congruence of goals, mutuality of benefits and responsibilities and timely reviews of the agreement to meet the needs of a rapidly changing environment.

Careful selection and appointment or re-appointment based on these factors are clearly crucial. Therefore, an intending agent in the USA or United Kingdom of a German, Italian or French company, for example, might find he had more protection under the law of any of these three countries than he had under the law of his own country as it presently stands. By the same token an Italian, French or German manufacturer might prefer to negotiate an agency in the United Kingdom under British law, as terminating the agency would in all probability be much less costly than under his own law since no compensation element would be involved.

The EC is currently formulating proposals for common treatment of agents in the event of termination which may eventually regularize the situation in member countries.

EC LAW AND AGENCY/DISTRIBUTORSHIP AGREEMENTS

EC law in relation to agency and distributor agreements is applicable under Article 85 of the Treaty of Rome and the regulations made in amplification. It takes precedence over domestic law only where these agreements are in a position to affect trade between states; it does not apply to purely domestic situations or to export cartels.

EC competition policy distinguishes between agents and distributors. The agent is viewed as a tool of the principal and agreements between agents and principals are not seen to come within the prohibition on restrictive agreements contained in Article 85(1). There is no competition between an agent and principal. Since a distributor operates on his own account he is in a position which can be of a competitive nature, and he therefore comes within the prohibition. Guidelines as to whether a distributorship agreement comes within the prohibition indicate that it does not apply where two conditions are met:

1 where the market share of a firm in that part of the Common Market where the agreement is effective is less than 5 per cent; and
2 where the combined turnover of the parties to the agreement is below 50 million European Currency Units, or in the case of commercial undertakings 70 million units. To take account of inflation and other factors affecting them these figures are brought up to date every few years by publication in the 'Official Journal' of the Community.

Other constraints on distributorship agreements arise from the application of the principle of parallel imports. Under this concept a manufacturer may not forbid a distributor to re-export his products to other EC countries; may not force a distributor to take action, for examply by denying sales, against third parties such as wholesalers,

138

who export his products into another distributor's exclusive sales territory in another part of the EC; may not permit the distributor to invoke patents, copyright or special trademarks for the purpose of blocking entry of the manufacturer's product into the distributor's territory when the goods come from other sources (for example, from his distributors, wholesalers and licensees in other EC countries).

Outside these constraints a manufacturer may still appoint an exclusive distributor in an EC territory, forbid him to advertise or maintain warehouses in another distributor's territory, require him to provide market information and maintain stocks, oblige him to sell under trademarks, packaging or labels specified in the agreement, and generally draw up agreements of the kind he might conclude with distributors outwith the EC.

An example of the application of the principle of parallel imports is given at Reading II at the end of this chapter.

US LAW AND AGENCY/DISTRIBUTORSHIP AGREEMENTS

In the USA, the bastion of the capitalist system, the laws enacted to defend competition in the interests of the consumer are more stringent than elsewhere in the world, including the EC. The heart of US competition policy lies in the Sherman Act, which prohibits contracts in restraint of interstate and foreign commerce and prohibits monopoly. It is supported by subsequent legislation in terms of the Clayton Anti-trust Act, which prohibits agreements where the effect is substantially to lessen competition, prohibits price discrimination in sales, exclusive dealing and tying contracts. Discriminating prices at any point in the channel of distribution, discrimination in services and promotion allowances to buyers in competition, and selling below cost are all prohibited by the Federal Trade Commission Act, the Robinson Patman Act and the Celler – Kefauver Act. The Federal Trade Commission (FTC) defines unfair competition for individual industries and prohibits unfair practices so defined.

The American fear of concentration of economic power is vividly reflected in the *doctrine of 'per se' illegality* which has evolved. Restrictive agreements are deemed to be illegal *per se*. Companies are required to show that a restrictive agreement does not significantly affect competition. In each individual case it has to be decided by the courts whether, in the light of reason, an act or agreement is anti-competitive.

Under these anti-trust laws of the USA it has been claimed that the aims and effects of a restrictive agreement account for nothing; the fact that the situation may be one in which the public interest is served by cooperation rather than competition is a fact of which account is not taken (Everton 1978). Agreements, the sole effect of which are to restrict competition, are void. In consequence of all these laws, agencies like the FTC and rules to maintain competition, it is not surprising that American firms rarely negotiate agreements without the presence of a lawyer, or at least without a lawyer on hand to advise.

Distributorship agreements must take such constraints into account.[12] The granting exclusively to a distributor of a territory or product or brand, or the requirement that a manufacturer's customers resell only to specified customers, are increasingly being viewed as outright violations of the law, irrespective of their competitive effects. Other applications of these concepts include the prohibition of discriminatory pricing as between two sellers of merchandise of like grade and quality where such a policy substantially lessens competition. Such a policy is legal only when it can be justified on the grounds of cost differentials or as being adopted 'in good faith' to meet competition. The granting by a seller to resellers of payments for services rendered in connection with processing, handling and selling of any of his products sold by them, is only legal where the payments are offered on proportionately equal terms to all resellers. Similarly, functional discounts and geographic pricing may infringe the law if their effect is substantially to lessen competition.

AGENCY/DISTRIBUTORSHIP AGREEMENTS IN THE ARAB COUNTRIES

These agreements take on a greater significance in the Arab countries in relation to licensing and direct investment alternatives. These latter alternatives are relatively less used because of the requirements in the commercial sector of local participation which stems from fear of foreign domination (Dunn 1979). Joint ventures, for example, have usually been limited to less than half ownership; employment of locals in key positions is often required; local laws mostly apply to contracts whatever choice of laws clause is included. Also, behaviour patterns in the Middle East are deeply rooted in Islamic traditions unfamiliar to Western businessmen. Islam goes beyond ritual matters, making it difficult for non-Arabs to absorb the culture. This makes communication with Arabs difficult for the average Occidental executive.

Accordingly, there is a greater need for a knowledge of the market than knowledge of the product and good communications with Head Office. This need to communicate with the market is best achieved, many people feel, through local representatives. The agent/distributor channel tends, therefore, to be perpetuated as it is a form ideally suited to the market in the perception of many organizations. Even so, the negotiator of agency/distributorship agreements must tread warily. There are commercial codes in most of the Arab countries. Provision is made for disputes to be taken before local courts, but it is normal for disputes to be referred to arbitration for a quick settlement. This can either be at the International Court of Arbitration in Paris, or locally.

As and when stability returns to the Lebanon, and the country re-assumes its place as a leading international trading centre in the Middle East, there is little likelihood that its agency law will have been revised. Under existing law, an agent, once appointed, has inalienable rights and privileges whereby satisfactory termination is extremely difficult.

JOINT-VENTURE AGREEMENTS

The concept of joint venture has been applied to every kind of economic activity undertaken jointly by two or more organizations. It may take almost any form: it may be horizontal, vertical or conglomerate; it may be owned by firms which are unrelated in business interests or created for marketing, production or research. It is chiefly used in connection with a legally independent entity under the joint control of the participants, but the term is also used to connote other undertakings which have no legal status and in which the participants are controlled by means of a committee or management team to which have been delegated the power to make decisions.[13]

Whether or not there is a truly legal form of joint venture, the negotiation of the cooperation agreement is where the working basis is determined.

Joint venture is a useful concept whichever form it takes, being used when a purely contractual arrangement is insufficient and where the drastic and irreversible solution of the merger is more than is required to achieve the desired objectives. The participants are willing to cooperate as independent operators. The venture is only workable as long as they agree and as far as they have a basis of mutual understanding.

Sometimes the joint-venture investment decision is complicated by discriminatory legislation against ethnic minorities whose business acumen might normally favour the selection of one of their number as joint venture partners.

'For some years the Malaysian government has pursued a policy of positive discrimination, favouring the majority racial group, the indigenous Malays who represent 45% of the population, against the Chinese at 35%.

Malaysia's new economic policy has concentrated on the *Bumiputras*, literally translated 'sons of the soil', providing them places at universities and awarding government contracts to *Bumiputra* companies. There are set equity targets for Malaysian companies to achieve so that 30% of medium to large companies are in Bumiputra hands. Malaysian non-*Bumiputra* companies may account for up to 40% while 30% of a company's shareholding can be held by foreign companies. Completion of equity restructuring is scheduled for 1990.' (From a report in *Export Direction*, September 1985.)

Foreign government restrictions on ownership of joint ventures have intensified in recent years, very often specifying maximum foreign participation at 50 per cent or less, forcing sophisticated management to examine means of ensuring efficiency and control. The burden of giving effect to these or achieving an acceptable compromise falls squarely on the shoulders of the negotiators. Also, there are laws in many countries against agreements and practices which are in restraint of trade. In developed, industrialized countries these usually refer to restrictions on competition between independent companies. In developing countries it is frequently viewed as limitations imposed on a locally based company by a foreign parent company.

Joint-venture agreements in the EC

In the EC, when undertakings remain economically independent following a concentration — as is usually the case with joint ventures — agreements or practices which are restrictive will come within the prohibition of Article 85(1) of the Rome Treaty. Where this economic independence no longer exists and the organizations are no longer seen to be in competition or in a position where they can compete, they are regarded as having merged and Article 86 is applied.

The essential factors in the consideration of a joint venture are its objects and effects. Where restrictive clauses are likely to have a significant effect on competition — by bringing about a change in the market structure or affecting trade between member states — exemption under Article 85(3) will depend on the economic context within which it must be examined.

As yet, there are no judicial precedents from which to derive guidance as the European Court of Justice has still to consider specific implications of joint ventures in relation to EC competition law. Nevertheless, the Commission's practices, decisions and announcements can help in giving direction to joint-venture negotiations (Ritter and Overbury 1977). The Commission, for example, can refuse exemption unless a specific non-competitive clause is dropped. Such a clause may not be indispensable to the agreement; and while the Commission cannot force parents to compete, it can insist on the removal of specific barriers which would enable one parent to prevent the other from competing if at some time it found good reason for wanting to do so.

Non-competition clauses may be accepted as dispensable and exemption granted to enable a joint venture to get started or for other compelling reasons; but they will invariably be limited in their duration to ensure that such restriction is confined to the minimum which is indispensable. Restrictive provisions such as territorial limitations and export prohibitions which are held to be in restraint of trade in purely contractual situations are equally infringements of the prohibition in Article 85(1) in joint ventures, and require consideration under Article 85(3) which allows the possibility of exemption. Where a joint-venture agreement is unlikely to have a significant effect on the pattern of trade between member states, Article 85(1) will not apply. The Commission Notice on Cases of Minor Importance, already noted in relation to distributorship agreements, gives specific guidance in terms of market share and turnover where, if the limits are not reached, Article 85(1) will not apply. Normally the Commission will just require to be notified unless there is a block exemption, as in the case of specialization agreements within certain limits.

AGREEMENTS OF MINOR SIGNIFICANCE

Other kinds of agreements exist which may require to be negotiated, among them agreements concerning information exchange, specialization, purchasing and production, as well as joint selling and consortia agreements.

SUMMARY

International businessmen make their commercial agreements within a framework of widely differing national and transnational laws. In an attempt to overcome the problem as to which country law applies in contracts between organizations in different countries, attempts have been made to establish an international trade law, as yet without real success.

Agreements of sale are formed by the offer and acceptance procedure and differences exist between common law and civil law countries. Problems arising from this are highlighted by reference to the United Nations Convention on Contracts for the International Sale of Goods. Similarly highlighted are the problems in respect of the disposal of goods concerning a contract which differ from country to country in respect of delivery, passing of property and passing of risk. In relation to non-performance or delayed performance, penalty clauses in civil law countries are penal in their purpose and readily enforceable. In common law countries they tend to be enforceable only if they are recognized liquidated damages.

Owing to the different interpretations of commercial frustration under different legal systems, *force majeure* provisions are advisable, preferably where they extend the performance time of the contract.

In order to ensure there is no dubiety about the law under which a contract is made, a seller should include a choice of laws clause in his contract to the effect that both the conclusion and performance of the contract should be governed by the law of his own country. Parties may agree, however, to have their contract governed by any legal system they care to choose.

In certain less commercially advanced countries contracts must be made under local law, whatever the intention of the parties.

Even when the law under which the contract is to be interpreted is agreed, disputes can still arise and are usually resolved by arbitration, which itself may be the subject of negotiation. Various codes or rules have been established to assist arbitration, but philosophical differences in some countries make arbitration something very local.

In dealings with government departments the law varies from specific legislation in France, to case law which has emerged in the USA, to the private law of contract together with standard contract forms which constitute applicable rules in the United Kingdom.

Other contractual and cooperation agreements can be viewed in relation to different market strategies and the extent to which resources are committed. Licensing is the strategy of least resource commitment and is usually associated with patents. Because patents convey a monopoly for a given period, governments are concerned to ensure that they are not used in a way that restricts or distorts competition. Different countries have different laws and treat patents differently in respect of whether a patent must be worked, if so what constitutes working, and what happens when it is not worked. Local laws differ in respect of what is defined as patentable, the period of protection, the rights of third parties and the cover afforded by patenting. They also differ on such subjects covered in agreements as exclusivity, licence improvements and market restrictions.

Licences can similarly involve trademarks and copyright. Most patented products and some trademarks cannot readily be used without associated know-how, which is often the subject of a separate agreement. A sub-set of licensing is franchising for which some countries including those of the European Community are only now beginning to implement legislation.

In EC competition law decisions of the Commission and judgments of the European Court provide guidelines in relation to exclusive manufacturing and selling licences, export prohibitions, grant-back provisions, the payment of royalties, duration of agreements and no-challenge clauses. If a licensing agreement is within the prohibition of Article 85(1) of the Treaty of Rome on one or more of these points, and others associated with industrial property, it may be granted exemption when the agreement is looked at under the criteria of Article 85(3).

Agency and distributorship agreements are seen from different viewpoints in different European countries. Some countries have more protective legislation for agents than do others in the event of termination, on the assumption that the goodwill created by the agent accrues to the principal and provides for substantial compensation. Some countries extend this concept to distributors and provide for their compensation under certain conditions. The EC also distinguishes between agents and distributors and gives block exemption to agents from the prohibition of Article 85(1). Distributors are only exempt under certain conditions in which their market power is considered to have no effect on competition. The principle of parallel imports has been established and certain actions which would prevent this are forbidden and may not be included in agreements. In the USA restrictive agreements are deemed to be illegal *per se*. Exclusive distributorships are increasingly viewed as outright violations, irrespective of their anti-competitive effect.

In joint-venture agreements foreign government restrictions very often limit the participation of the overseas parent. In developed industrialized countries agreements and practices in restraint of trade usually refer to restrictions on competition between independent companies. In developing countries it is frequently viewed as limitations imposed on a locally based company by a foreign parent company. In the EC, joint ventures which in object or effect are anti-competitive come within the prohibition of Article 85(1), although non-competition and other restrictive provisions may be accepted as indispensable and exempted under Article 85(3); for example, to enable a joint venture to get started or for other compelling reasons. These will be limited in duration so that the restriction is confined to the minimum period which is indispensable.

The negotiator who is aware of all these possibilities is in a position to make more effective agreements in implementation of his company's marketing strategy.

Notes

1   The Convention is given in full at Honnold (1982).
2   See Schmitthoff (1986:61). This gives a description of, and commentary on, the offer and acceptance procedure. The section on sales agreements draws heavily on Schmitthoff, who is an international authority on international sales.
3   Retention of title is examined in Parris (1982) and Pennington (1982) in relation to French, German, UK and US law.
4   Pollzien and Langen (1973) is a standard reference and updating work for licence negotiators and deals with patent, trademarks and copyright licences and combinations of these, as well as know-how agreements. The work covers the applicable law in European countries, the USA, Canada, Japan, Israel, Mexico, India, South Africa and Australia.
5   In what has become known as the Gründig Consten case, the European Court held it inconsistent with the principles and aim of the competition system of the Treaty of Rome if the rights granted under national trademark laws of the member states could be abused for purposes in conflict with the competition law of the Community. It arose from the agreement which Gründig, the German manufacturers of tape recorders etc., had made with its distributor, Consten SA in France. Having

imposed an export prohibition on its German distributors and on distributors in other countries, it created a supplementary trademark Gint which it assigned to national distributors. Gründig's pricing policy was to charge a higher price in the export market than in the domestic market. A French wholesaler, Unef, had imported tape recorders from Germany and sold them to French dealers. Unef were sued by Consten for unfair competition and trademark infringement. Unef appealed to the then designated EEC Commission, which ruled that the agreement between Gründig and Consten violated Article 85, a ruling affirmed by the European Court.

6 In the Sirena case the plaintiff invoked national trademark law to prevent import of a product from another member country. The trademark Prep was originally registered in Italy and other European countries by the American Mark Allen Company in respect of a shaving cream. It was transferred by them to the Italian company Sirena, which has since then manufactured a cream and marketed it in Italy under the same trademark. At a later date Mark Allen had allowed a German company to use its trademark in Germany. It was the sale of that cream in the Italian market that Sirena tried to prevent through the courts. The European Court of Justice, to which the Italian court had referred the question, ruled against Sirena. The judgment extended the trademark rules of the Gründig judgment in that Article 85 is not limited to licensing agreements that are part of a larger market arrangement, but also covers pure trademark assignments. Also, until this judgment, it was believed that an intention to divide markets was necessary.

7 This was established as a result of the Parke Davis case dealing with patent restrictions. The American firm Parke Davis invoked its Dutch process patents for the preparation of an antibiotic to prevent import of the same drug from Italy made by an Italian licensee of Parke Davis. In Italy there is no patent cover for pharmaceutical products. The Court of Justice ruled in favour of Parke Davis after referral by a domestic court.

8 This arose from the Deutsche Grammophon case. Under German copyright law the manufacturer of a sound recording has the exclusive right to reproduce and distribute the recording. Deutsche Grammophon invoked this right to prevent a German supermarket company from selling in Germany records made by themselves and supplied to their French subsidiary Polydor France, from where they had been re-imported by a third party. Resale price maintenance was legal in the German market and this was applied by Deutsche Grammophon at a price 100 per cent higher than charged to Polydor France. The European Court ruled against Deutsche Grammophon, thus establishing that national copyright cannot be invoked to prevent imports of an item by a manufacturer who has himself sold them in another member country.

9 The ruling in the Deutsche Grammophon case was extended to patents in the Centrafarm case. An American company, Sterling Drug, owned national patents in Holland for a drug called Negram. Another Sterling company, Sterling Winthrop, owned the trademark in Britain and Winthrop BV in Holland. Centrafarm imported into Holland, without the agreement of Sterling Drugs, products manufactured in Britain, properly put on the market there under the

trademark Negram. Such imports were profitable because of the price differential. Sterling Drug and Winthrop brought actions against Centrafarm in the Dutch courts for patent and trademark infringement, which on referral from the Dutch court was not upheld by the European Court.

10 An up-to-date commentary on the restrictive aspects of clauses is given in Cawthra (1978). This publication has the advantage of comparing, where appropriate, EC law, American law, English law and German law.

11 See Official Journal Notice No. 87/C229/03 of 22 August 1987.

12 A useful discussion of the issues and a review of key cases is given in Stern and Eovaldi (1984); the issues are also addressed in Stern and El-Ansary (1982) in which the summary and conclusions at pp. 396−399 are a particularly helpful guide to the making of distributor agreements in the USA.

13 See Mazzolini (1974:21). Mazzolini makes the point that legal, fiscal and other barriers discourage international mergers. In default of a European Company Law or other appropriate tool, companies have developed hybrid solutions which fall short of true legal mergers but the effects of which are the same. These could be construed as joint ventures, although the EC Commission has treated some of them as *de facto* mergers to which Article 86 of the Rome Treaty applies, and not Article 85.

Questions

1 You have submitted a quotation to a potential customer in West Germany for the supply of 3,000 cases of Fish Soups. The German company has written to you accepting the offer, but attached to its letter are its conditions of purchase which differ from your own on a number of important points. Your own conditions on the reverse side of your quotation stipulate your own law as the law under which the agreement of sale will be operative.
Do you (1) deliver whatever?
　　　　(2) take any other action?

2 You are agent for a French company increasing spectacularly its market share in your own territory due to a good product and the efforts of your own small organization. You operate under an exchange of letters agreement to which French law applies.
　　Could you have improved on this arrangment in your original correspondence setting up the agency or in any talks you might have had with your French principal?

3 You are Export Division Manager of Cincinatti Laundry Machines Company (CLAM) who make towel and sheet folders, ironing machines, hydro-extractors and dry cleaners for the laundry and dry cleaning industries. Electronic developments have removed much of the direct labour cost which over the last fifteen years has been responsible for a contraction in business. As a result of the economies created by these developments, new opportunities have been identified in Western Europe which, together with a favourable exchange rate, have resulted in long-term plans to set up marketing companies there to exploit the market potential. In the meantime, operation in West European countries is via agents and distributors.

Owing to the death of CLAM's Dutch agent who had covered Belgium as part of his territory, it has been decided to appoint, for the short and middle term, a sole distributor for Belgium where the market is now considered sufficiently large to justify such action. In any case your late agent had not really exploited the market there and the French-speaking southern half of Belgium was virtually untapped.

Your search for a distributor has been made and a target distributor chosen. You are actively considering the appointment of Atelier Rupin SA, with whom you have already had discussions and who have now written you asking for:

(a) an agreement, subject to Belgian law
(b) an agreement to run a minimum of five years (to give them the assurance that they can allocate resources to the distributorship without reservation)
(c) provision for arbitration in a third country.

Familiarize yourself with Reading I prior to answering the questions below.

Do you (1) agree to all the requests?
     (2) agree to one or two of them?
     (3) agree to none of them?
     (4) put forward alternatives?

4 Negotiations covering manufacture under licence between your company which makes iron dextran, a patented treatment for mastitis in cattle and sheep, and Jee Akakinci, a Turkish manufacturer of drugs, are at an advanced stage. Settlement now hinges on resolving the following issues:

(1) You wish to recommend prices in Turkey, a proposal opposed by Akakinci.
(2) You wish to restrict exports by Akakinci to the countries bordering Turkey, with the exception of Greece. They wish to be able to supply European markets.
(3) Akakinci insist they have exclusive manufacturing rights in Turkey. You wish to keep your options open as you believe that there is 1,000 per cent growth potential in southern Europe. You intend to take advantage of this growth and wish to maintain flexibility in Turkey, particularly in view of the cost advantages of manufacturing there and the possibility of Turkey's accession to the European Community which, by 1992, will have a single internal market.

Which of these issues would you be prepared to trade off in order to achieve an acceptable outcome on the other issue(s)?

5 Yours is an American-owned company which manufactures high-quality video systems in the United Kingdom for industrial use. A large claim has been made on it by an Italian purchaser in respect of warranty. Investigations have shown that the equipment was not purchased through your authorized distributor in Italy but had in fact been purchased from your distributor in Greece (where, for reasons of company policy, you sell at a cheaper relative price than in Italy). Your company's systems have patent and trademark cover in Italy and it is felt in the company that this import infringes the patent and trademark cover. There is a strong feeling in top management that the warranty claim should not be met.

Advise them.

READING I

Belgium stands by its sole agents*

The relationship between a manufacturer and his sole distributor in a foreign country is a very special one. The manufacturer puts an important market in the hands of the distributor and the distributor may stake his entire business, or large part of it, on the continuity of the relationship.

While in the UK the law applicable to such a relationship is the law of contract, as between two business enterprises, some countries have adopted legislation which provides special protection to the distributor.

The need for such protection is not immediately obvious from the present-day business scene, but in some countries, and particularly in Belgium, the idea survives that the distributor is the weaker party in the relationship and must be protected as a matter of public policy.

This approach of the Belgian law, which is partly shared in France and Germany, is also the inspiration of a project of the EEC Commission which proposed a directive for the harmonization of the member states' law concerning commercial agencies. This proposal caused quite a shock to those accustomed to view the agency agreement as a purely commercial relation in which the agent is often equal and sometimes financially and commercially stronger than the manufacturer.

A recent decision of the Belgian Court of Cassation in the dispute between Audi-NSU, a member of the Volkswagen Group, and its Belgian sole distributor, S. A. Adelin Petit & Cie, is therefore not only of interest to companies with agents in Belgium but also throws some light on the shape of things that would come throughout the Community should the commission's draft on commercial agents be adopted.

The relationship between Audi and Petit was of long standing. Petit was the exclusive distributor of the German car manufacturer since 1937. Its territory covered Belgium and Luxembourg. The agency agreement had been renewed several times. A renewal agreed in 1962 extended the agreement until 1968 and it was then renewed annually until the end of 1970.

Before the end of that year, Audi gave notice that it wished to terminate the agreement, but when Petit claimed damages, the parties agreed to extend the agency until the end of 1973.

* Source: A. H. Hermann, *Financial Times*, London, 4 October 1979. Reproduced with permission. The case is also discussed by the author on p.234 in *Judges, Law & Businessmen*, Kluwer, 1983.

As early as 9 December 1972, Audi informed Petit that it would not further extend the agreement and that Petit would cease to be Audi's sole agent by the end of the following year. As Petit was not willing to accept such termination without a substantial compensation, Audi started arbitration in Zurich on 15 May 1973, relying on an arbitral clause in the agency agreement which provided also for the application of German law.

The reason why Audi wanted the contract to be governed by German law is obvious. It wanted to avoid the very onerous provisions of the Belgian law of 27 July 1961, on the Unilateral Termination of Exclusive Distributorship Concluded for Indefinite Time. This law provides that such a distributorship cannot be terminated (except when one of the parties seriously defaults in its duties) without giving a notice of reasonable length or an equitable compensation and additional compensation under certain circumstances.

If the parties cannot agree a court of law can determine the amount of fair compensation in accordance with business custom. Any agency agreement concluded for a definite period of time and renewed twice is deemed to be an agreement concluded for an indeterminate period, even if the renewals include substantial modifications of the original agreement.

However, the precautions taken by Audi by providing for German law and Zurich arbitration did not bring it much luck, though it made a good start in Switzerland. Petit appeared before the Zurich arbitrators only to contest their competence (jurisdiction) to deal with the dispute. But the arbitral tribunal declared itself to be competent and its decision was confirmed by the Superior Court of Zurich on 1 July 1974. The tribunal then made an award in favour of Audi, holding that the agreement was terminated at the end of 1973 and that its termination did not give Petit any right to compensation.

In the meantime, Petit started a parallel procedure in Belgium, asking the Commercial Court of Liège to make a declaration that it had jurisdiction to deal with the dispute and to refuse recognition and enforcement of any Swiss award. This was granted and Audi appealed, first to the Court of Appeal and when this decided against it, to the Court of Cassation.

All three Belgian courts held that the agreement came under the Law of 27 July 1961, because the repeated extensions of the distributorship transformed the agreement into one concluded for an indeterminate period. This in itself was sufficient to give the distributor a right to compensate on termination.

The next question to be decided was whether the arbitration clause of the agreement was valid. The lower courts held, and the Court of Cassation confirmed, that jurisdiction over any disputes must not be withdrawn from Belgian courts and transferred to an arbitration tribunal during the validity of the agency agreement.

When dealing with this issue, the Belgian courts considered the applicability of the New York Arbitration Convention of 1958, the Belgian/Swiss Convention on the Recognition and Enforcement of Judgements and Arbitral Awards of 1959, and the European Judgements Convention of 1968.

The Court of Cassation concluded that none of these conventions calls for enforcement of arbitral awards in disputes which are reserved for courts by the law of the land. They also exempt from enforcement awards which are contrary to public policy. As the provisions of the law for the protection of the distributors was a matter of Belgian public policy, and moreover specifically prohibited the conclusion of arbitration agreements before the termination of such an agency agreement, the Swiss award could not be recognized and enforced in Belgium.

After deciding that under Belgian law arbitration was inadmissible, the Court of Cassation had to deal with the question whether the agreement between Audi and Petit was governed by Belgian or by German law. The agreement provided for German law, and to justify its choice, stated that the contract would be performed in Germany.

The Court of Appeal held and the Court of Cassation accepted that this assertion made in the contract was not true; that in fact the agency agreement was to be performed on Belgian territory. The assertion that it would be performed in Germany was, said the Court, only an artifice inspired by the desire to escape from the application of Belgian law.

The decision reaffirmed the protection provided by Belgian legislation to Belgian sole-agents of foreign manufacturers. It brushed away any possibility of softening the impact of the Belgian law by reference to any of the international conventions concerning either arbitration or jurisdiction and the enforcement of judgements. It made it quite clear that arbitration clauses in such agency agreements are invalid and that the application of foreign law will be firmly resisted, even if agreed to by the two parties when concluding the agency agreement.

It was emphasized that the mandatory provisions of the Belgian law are a matter of public policy and that consequently the parties to the agreement have only a limited possibility of changing them. The door seems to have been firmly closed to all attempts to take such disputes out of the jurisdiction of Belgian law.

READING II

Application of the
principle of parallel imports*

The Distillers Company Ltd (DCL) is a group which supplies Scotch whisky, gin, vodka and Pimm's to trade customers in the United Kingdom. It is the world's largest supplier of Scotch whisky, accounting for 40−50 per cent of market share in production and sales in the United Kingdom.

Distribution and marketing is the responsibility of each of the thirty eight subsidiary companies which comprise the group. Distribution channels in the United Kingdom are mostly via wholesalers, of whom there are about 1,000. In the other EEC countries most of the DCL companies each have their own sole distributors who, within their own areas, import and distribute for resale one or several brands of DCL subsidiaries' spirits. The brands thus sold to distributors are resold to wholesalers. There are about 200 sole distributors within the EEC.

DCL sought, under Article 85(3) of the Treaty of Rome, exemption for the special conditions of sale applied by each of its subsidiaries to its United Kingdom trade customers only from the prohibition on restrictive agreements in Article 85(1). These conditions included a clause which stated: 'If the goods are sold by the seller in bottles for delivery in the United Kingdom, they will not be resold for delivery outside the territories of the EEC. This condition must be incorporated in all subsales.'

In a circular to UK trade customers, 'Home Trade Conditions of Sale and Price Terms', DCL on behalf of its subsidiary companies included conditions of sale which confirmed UK customers could now export to EEC countries, as required by EEC law. Prior to Britain's accession to the EEC and up to 24 June 1975, trade customers were prohibited from exporting. However, it was made clear that the various allowances, rebates and discounts were designed to meet the particular requirements of the home trade, and customers would only be entitled to them when the goods were consumed within the UK. Customers wishing to purchase for export to other common market countries were required to indicate this in their orders and purchase had to be made at the gross price. These provisions were to be part of every contract made between a customer and DCL subsidiary. Any DCL company would be entitled to charge the gross price without allowances if it had reason to believe that any quantity bought by the customer from a DCL subsidiary had been consumed outside the UK, even if exported by a subsequent purchaser. That situation would continue regardless of the

---

* Condensed from the Official Journal of the European Communities, Commission Decision of 20 December 1977; and, the Official Journal of 14 September 1983, Notice of notification of Distillers Company Ltd's application for exemption. References to the EEC reflect the situation prior to the incorporation of the three original communities within the single European Community.

quantity ordered until the purchaser provided evidence satisfactory to the DCL subsidiary concerned that the goods would be consumed in the United Kingdom. The gross price mentioned was changed to 'gross EEC export price' in a subsequent circular to UK trade customers. This would be the gross EEC export price charged to sole distributors in other EEC countries before deduction of any allowance granted to them.

These price terms resulted in a complaint to the Commission of the European Communities by related companies established in the Glasgow area of Scotland following the application of these terms, after discovery that whisky bought by them at the home trade price and sold to another whisky dealer in the UK had later been found in supermarkets in France and Belgium by DCL representatives. The price paid by UK customers for consumption in the UK was about £7.00 for a case of twelve bottles of Johnnie Walker Red Label (VAT and excise duty excluded), as against a gross EEC export price of about £13.50. The price allowances to UK customers in this differential included a wholesale allowance to purchasers buying a minimum of 1000 cases per year, a rebate in respect of spirits bought from DCL subsidiaries, a 'loyalty' rebate, an occasional promotional allowance for special promotions, a performance bonus and a cash discount for cash with order.

In support of an exemption of the price terms, DCL raised the benefits of the sole distribution system, of which consumers received a fair share. The price terms tended to ensure that competition between sole distributors and parallel importers was fair, having regard to their different obligations and different market conditions within the other EEC countries. In the UK market whisky was a traditional drink and competition was on price. The retail trade was highly concentrated, 40 per cent of total sales coming from brewery customers with tied outlets, placing them in a position to obtain important price advantages.

In other EEC countries whisky has only a very small share of the spirits market. Furthermore competition between Scotch whisky and other spirits in these member EEC States was made more difficult by discriminatory taxes and other protectionist legislation. As an example, excise duties on Scotch whisky in France were nearly double those on rum. Sole distributors were necessary, it was maintained, to ensure penetration of markets and the necessary promotion of DCL spirits. They ensured orderly marketing and had, unlike UK wholesalers, to invest in the long-term interest of the brand. Their promotional activities cost distributors on average £5 per case. The price structure within the EEC had to be such as to enable them to bear this cost without being undercut by parallel importers. That was why the various discounts would not be payable in respect of UK wholesalers exporting to other EEC countries.

The Commission dismissed the claim for exemption under Article 85(3). It also held that the price terms tended to restrict competition in the EEC countries other than the United Kingdom, amounted to an indirect export prohibition and came within the prohibition of Article 85(1). It was further held that, as the price terms clearly had as their object the restriction and distortion of competition within the common market, it was not necessary to show their effects. With regard to the claim that their price terms were intended to protect sole distributors from unfair competition arising from traders purchasing from DCL trade customers in the UK and reselling for consumption in the sole distributors' territories, the Commission held to the contrary. It took the view that the non-applicability of price allowances on spirits for export and the application to the same customers of different prices for spirits for export and for spirits for UK consumption are clearly an attempt to impede parallel imports from the UK into EEC countries other than the UK, with the same object as a formal export prohibition, and can be regarded as a more efficient way to discourage export.

The decision affirmed the refusal for exemption under Article 85(3), stated that the price terms adopted were an infringement of Article 85(1), and required DCL to bring the infringement to an end forthwith. DCL withdrew Johnnie Walker Red Label from the UK market in 1978. They appealed against the decision of the Commission, but this appeal was dismissed by the Court of Justice in 1980.

Subsequent developments

Subsequent to the Court's judgment, DCL has proposed UK conditions of sale and price and also a standard-form distributor contract in respect of Johnnie Walker Red Label (JWRL). The agreements proposed provide for the institution of a 'promotion equalization charge' (PEC) for JWRL. The PEC is an amount calculated on the basis of the weighted average of expenditure on promotion and the administrative and overhead costs related to such expenditure by the DCL's sole distributors in EEC countries other than the UK, less an amount corresponding to a parallel trader's own marketing expenditure. The PEC would be levied by DCL on purchases of JWRL in the UK for export to other EEC countries. It would be added to whichever was the lower of the price charged by DCL in the UK and the price charged by DCL to distributors elsewhere in the EEC.

DCL applied for exemption under Article 85(3) of the EEC Treaty on the grounds that it was not possible for JWRL to be reintroduced to the UK market at the price at which it is sold in the EEC because it could well encourage parallel transactions which might disrupt DCL's existing distribution network in the EEC.

In order to take account of the exceptional circumstances in the light of the Community's competition policy, the Commission has expressed itself ready to consider DCL's notification requesting exemption, subject to comments of interested third parties. A proposed condition on DCL would be that the exemption would be subject to the progressive reduction of the PEC during the short time necessary to allow for the adaptation of marketing conditions for JWRL in the Common Market to the consequences of its large-scale reintroduction in one member state. It is also envisaged as a further condition that no similar arrangement could be applied to DCL's other brands.

In any case, the arrangement in respect of the notified conditions of sale and the standard-form distributor agreement for JWRL would be limited to three years. The intention would be that at the end of the three-year period all DCL's products would move freely within the Common Market. DCL launched JWRL on the UK market in November 1983 where it had been an established whisky since 1820 until its withdrawal in 1978.

READING III

Eurocrats seek wider shopping
Jonathan Todd

More than £14 billion a year could be saved by the British and other European Community governments if they agreed to end their protectionist public procurement policies, according to the European Commission.

It estimates that if the UK, for example, were to open up more procurement contracts to bids from other EC countries, it could cut spending on telephone switching equipment by 50 per cent on pharmaceuticals by 40 per cent and coal by 25 per cent.

'The importance of public procurement — and the deleterious effects of EC member states' success in keeping contracts in this field largely for the benefit of their own nationals — cannot be exaggerated,' says Lord Cockfield the European Commissioner who drafted the EC plan to create a genuine common market by the end of 1992.

As a result, public procurement is one of the programme's top priorities.

Cockfield announced Commission proposals, due out in June, to extend EC rules to telecommunications, energy, transport and water supply, which now fall outside community rules because EC governments consider them strategically important.

Cockfield stressed that the Commission is not trying to impose bureaucracy, compel public bodies to 'buy foreign' or push a particular view of the best structure for European industry. As far as he is concerned, EC procurement rules should ensure that big purchasers can use their commercial judgement, without being pressed by their governments into 'buying national' for its own sake.

Procurement decisions must be transparent, so that they can be seen to be fair.

In 1986, public sector purchasing in the EC (including central and local government, their agencies and companies with monopoly-type concessions) totalled £350 billion — no less than 15 per cent of the Community's GDP. Of this, between a half and two-thirds was subject to tendering procedures. Yet only a tiny fraction of these contracts (accounting for 0.14 per cent of GDP) was awarded to companies from other community countries.

But the Commission's efforts to force governments to open up procurement practices offer a perfect example of the sort of hypocrisy by EC governments that could mean the whole 1992 programme ends up as no more than a fairy-tale.

EC rules requiring procurement contracts to be opened up have existed since the 1970s. But while prime ministers have made declarations of good intent to end discrimination, public purchasing bureaucracies have found loopholes or simply ignored the rules to protect 'national champions'.

* Originally published in the *Sunday Times*, 15 May 1988, and reproduced with permission.

The situation could now be changing. EC ministers recently agreed to tighten up the rules requiring public supply contracts (for anything from pencil sharpeners to Mrs Thatcher's limousine) to be open to companies from all community countries. A similar strengthening of the rules on public-works contracts (such as hospital building) should be approved this year.

A 1987 Commission proposal would give unfairly excluded companies the right to complain directly to national courts instead of the EC court in Luxembourg. However, EC governments have objected to a provision giving the Commission power to suspend tenders pending inquiries into complaints.

The Commission proposals to extend existing rules to telecommunications energy, transport and water — which account for 80 per cent of procurement contracts — would apply to private companies to which government grant exclusive rights, such as British Telecom and a future-privatized UK electricity industry, as well as public authorities. This is because private bodies can come under pressure from governments to follow a 'buy national' policy.

The Commission is taking particular care to ensure the rules are flexible and correspond to commercial realities. But the proposals are bound to run into bitter opposition from governments.

The Commission hopes this opposition will be attenuated by the findings of an extensive study published in the UK last week. It says that huge public procurement costs arise from paying over the odds instead of buying from the cheapest suppliers, the lack of competition, and the fact that protectionist policies support the existence of too many inefficient companies.

It is no coincidence that sectors such as telecommunications equipment, power generation, railways and defence are dominated by American and Japanese firms. EC manufacturers, restricted to their own small national markets, are denied the US and Japanese economies of scale.

In the EC boiler-making industry there is virtually no trade within the community, and only 20 per cent of production capacity is used. The Commission thinks open procurement would result in the number of EC manufacturers falling from fifteen to around four, with a 20 per cent fall in prices.

Similarly, only 60 per cent of capacity in the turbine generator industry is utilized. Open procurement would encourage mergers and rationalization, reducing unit costs by some 12 per cent without major closures, according to the Commission.

In locomotives, where the EC's sixteen main manufacturers use only 50 per cent to 80 per cent of capacity, the Commission envisages rationalization down to three or four and a 13 per cent cut in costs.

In the case of telephone exchange switching equipment, seven different digital systems are now being installed, including the UK's System X. Prices per phone line in the EC stand at between £120 and £265 (compared with £53 in America). The Commission estimates that open procurement would bring the price per line down to some £80 and reduce the number of community suppliers to two.

PART II

NEGOTIATING MARKETING AGREEMENTS

This part develops the conceptual material of Part I and relates it to the reality of sales/purchase agreements in Chapters 7 and 8. Chapter 7 links organizational selling and organizational buying to the interaction and negotiation theme, and presents an escape from the limiting views of selling as a multi-stage influence process and buying as a multi-stage decision process. As in all the Part II chapters, Chapter 8 views the negotiation process in relation to the 'negotiation skills model'. At the same time it draws on concepts of dependence, conflict and power not usually touched on in selling and only rarely in organizational buying.

After relating agency/distribution agreements to marketing channels, Chapter 9 builds on the Part I conceptual material to provide insights into the process of negotiating original agreements, negotiating operational aspects of agreements made, as well as the revision and discontinuance of agreements. Chapters 10 and 11 perform a similar function for licensing and joint-venture arrangements. Relationships are seen to have an increasingly important role in such agreements.

Chapter 12 is a review of the management of negotiations and seeks to draw together the threads connecting sales, intermediary, licensing and joint venture agreements.

CHAPTER 7

The sales/purchase agreement I

Organizational selling: some antecedents.. 157
   The stimulus – response model.. 157
   The formula model... 157
   The needs satisfaction model... 158
   The problem-solving model... 158
   The traditional selling process.. 159
Contingency approaches to selling.. 159
   Failure to identify universals... 159
   Matching buyer and seller styles... 159
   'Hard' and 'soft' selling approaches... 159
   The Weitz contingency model... 160
   Selling and negotiation... 161
Organizational buying.. 161
   Buying stages... 161
   The buying centre concept... 161
   Factors affecting buying behaviour... 162
   The interactive dimension... 163
   Interaction variables... 163
Negotiation as a focus for buying and selling..................................... 165
   Negotiation as the critical link... 165
   Centrality of relationships to negotiation................................... 166
   Intercultural aspects of relationships....................................... 166
   Mutual role-taking 168
Organizational perspectives.. 169
   Mutual interest and conflict... 169
   The need for standard conditions... 170
   Various kinds of standard conditions... 170
   The role of the tender.. 170
   Setting aside offer and acceptance... 171
Main areas to be covered by standard conditions................................... 172
   Scope of the contract... 172
   Price... 172
   Payment... 172

Delivery.. 174
Performance.. 174
Patents, trademarks, copyright, designs.. 174
Arbitration.. 175
Towards specific agreements... 175
Negotiation and company objectives... 175
Evaluating target objectives... 176
The power balance.. 177
Setting the level of first offer.. 177
The bargaining framework... 180
The bargaining area.. 180
The settlement range... 180
Varying the bargaining area and settlement range.......................... 181
Summary 182

ORGANIZATIONAL SELLING: SOME ANTECEDENTS

There can be no sale without a purchase. The interaction of buyer and seller is an important factor in the buying – selling process. The selling and buying purpose is served by the communication that takes place during the interchange. When we consider past approaches to selling it becomes clear that they have not all viewed buying as equally active and participative. An examination of these past approaches is useful as an illustration of the developments that have taken place.

The stimulus – response model

The simplest approach is the stimulus – response model which has its origins in early experiments with animals. This postulates that if the salesman says the appropriate things the prospective customer will buy. It assumes that what works in selling to one wholesaler, for example, will work for another.

The model can be useful in situations where the value of the unit sale is low and the time allotted to the selling effort is short. It has the weakness that it does not take account of individual differences among buyers and prospective buyers, who may not react in a similar way to the same stimulus or in a similar way in varying circumstances. Also it ignores buyers' feelings and attitudes and eliminates choice as a consideration. As far as the salesman is concerned there is no feedback by which he can improve his performance on the basis of experience.

The formula model

This takes the prospective buyer through a series of steps in which the salesman makes statements designed to attract attention, arouse interest, create desire and obtain action. (This is the well-known AIDA formula.) The salesman does most of the talking and controls the conversation by taking one step at a time.

Such formula selling treats all customers alike by assuming that the salesman knows about his customers' preferences. It can be of some advantage where customers have similar needs and where the salesman lacks the ability to develop an approach based on the needs of each individual buyer.

Like the stimulus — response approach, the formula approach assumes a similarity of reaction among buyers that does not exist. The little investment in training which this approach involves is likely to be exposed when the salesman, whose presentation does not prepare him to interact with buyers, is asked to answer a specific question. The approach encourages the use of 'canned' presentations and discourages questioning.

The needs satisfaction model

This approach allows the customer to do most of the talking and is a more interactive approach than the two previous ones. It starts with the establishment of the prospective buyer's needs, which presupposes the ability of the salesman to ask questions which cause the buyer to question his satisfaction with the existing supply. By questions and observations the salesman seeks to establish how the buyer's needs are currently being met. He follows this with the particular benefits which his product or service can bring to the buying company in meeting identified needs. When the salesman does this he is striving to induce the buyer to make a purchase, that is to perceive himself as making his own decision.

The problem-solving model

This model provides the opportunity to analyse buyer problems and come up with a solution after evaluating possible alternatives. It presupposes prior study of the prospective buyer's business, the industrial sector he operates in and the existing economic and competitive conditions affecting the buyer's problem. By doing this the salesman goes beyond the needs satisfaction approach and puts himself in a better position to obtain an order for his company's products or services.

Both this approach and the needs satisfaction approach have advantages and limitations. They take account of both selling and buying elements in the selling/buying process by focusing on needs, attitudes and values. There is some accounting for individual differences and an implicit prescription to match presentation to identified feelings and views. Both approaches are considered appropriate where there is a diversity of needs to be met, where products or services are complex, either in level of technology or breadth of application, where skill and knowledge of the salespeople is high and the unit transaction is large. The effective use requires fairly sophisticated and highly trained personnel.

They do not reflect the buyer's definition of the situation in seeking to be able to take the seller's role and in understanding the implications of it for himself just as, in turn, the salesman must define the buyer's behaviour and intentions. Such mutual role-taking is a necessary prerequisite for effective communication and successful interaction.

The traditional selling process

Most sales-training programmes are based on one or more of these models. All are aimed at converting a salesman from being a passive order-taker to being an active order-getter. Most view the selling process as consisting of a series of steps which the salesman has to carry out, each involving certain skills indicated in the discussion on the models. The major steps usually identified in the sales literature are identifying prospects, identifying influences, making an appropriate approach, selling benefits and using influence strategies, handling objections, closing the sale and following-up.

CONTINGENCY APPROACHES TO SELLING

Failure to identify universals

Researchers have attempted to relate salesmen's performance to variables that can be assessed with some accuracy, for example, age, intelligence, education and sales experience. Results have been so inconsistent that a growing interest in dyadic research approaches has been exhibited. This has related salesman characteristics to those of the buyer.

The approach suggests that effectiveness in sales interactions is dependent on characteristics of both salesman and buyer. In other words the outcome depends on the match of buyer and seller characteristics. What matters is the perceived similarity more than the actual similarity. The implication for salesmen is that, if they can adapt their behaviour to create a perceived similarity, the likelihood of a sale is increased. However, studies in dyadic similarity have either not shown a meaningful relationship between similarity and effectiveness or have shown a relatively low correlation.

Matching buyer and seller styles

Blake and Mouton (1977) see the problem of selling along two dimensions. One is the salesman's concern for the sale and the other his concern for the customer. They have developed a 'customer grid' based on these dimensions, which identifies different styles of selling depending on the levels of interaction along the two dimensions. Because a buyer's style is just as varied as the salesman's, no one style of selling is going to work with all buyers. The variability in natural styles underlines the low probability of achieving compatibility between buyer and seller. The purpose of the grid is to provide diagnostics to the salesman for analysing a particular buyer and determining the best selling style to use. It suggests that the buyer plays an active role in determining the outcome.

'Hard' and 'soft' selling approaches

The distinction between 'hard' and 'soft' sell is one which has been made on a number of occasions (see also p.44). A contingency model developed by Poppleton (1981) views the favourability of the situation for the salesman as being affected by three variables. These are the acceptability of the salesman to the buyer or the potential buyer, the power of the salesman as reflected in his referent value and his expertness, and the complexity of the task. Under clearly favourable or unfavourable conditions, the more effective approach will be the 'hard' sell. Under conditions of moderate favourability, the 'soft' sell will be the more effective.

The Weitz contingency model

The approach which relates effectiveness to the characteristics of the parties to a sale has been extended by Weitz (1981), to provide a contingency framework for sales effectiveness across interactions. His model has as its basic elements the salesman's resources, the customer's buying task, the behaviour of the salesman in interactions with buyers, and the salesman/buyer relationship. The effectiveness of a salesman's behaviour across his interactions with a buyer is moderated by the relationship with these factors.

Weitz defines effectiveness from the point of view of the salesman rather than that of the salesman/buyer. This perspective differs from those which conceptualize salesman/buyer interaction as a joint problem-solving activity in which two parties seek to reach a mutually beneficial conclusion. The problem-solving perspective is not used because it does not take into account the advocacy nature of the salesman's activities — a subject to which we shall return when looking at negotiation frameworks.

While effectiveness of sales behaviour across buyer interactions is seen to be contingent on the above-mentioned variables, Weitz sees little evidence of identifying dimensions in which a salesman's behaviour can be assessed. He sees the behaviour of salesmen as being characterized by the degree to which they can adapt their behaviour to the interaction. At one extreme, salesmen are not adaptive in the stimulus — response and formula selling models. Measures of adaptivity in sales behaviour have not been developed, but there are some personality measures that indicate a predisposition to indulge in adaptive behaviour. One dispositional measure that appears to be related to adaptive behaviour is self-monitoring. One would expect salesmen who are self-monitors to be more adaptive in sales situations (Snyder 1974).

Another dimension of salesman behaviour is trying to establish a base of influence. The armoury of the salesman includes his personal skills and abilities which harness the appropriate power bases for the particular situation. His power is reinforced by company derived resources such as reputation, the authority invested in the salesman to vary price and delivery terms, and the time available to him. The more important a buyer's problem, the more power a salesman possesses. By the same token, if a salesman's rewards are dependent on obtaining the buyer's business, the boot is on the other foot. From this it can be seen that it is possible for the relative power in an interaction to be measured in terms of the importance of each party's goals related to the purchase decision, and the extent to which each affects the other's achievement of these goals. Like relative power, conflict has not been considered in personal selling research, and yet there is a conflict element in most sale/purchase situations and power is one of a number of variables brought to the conflict situation.

Selling and negotiation

It has been argued by Lidstone (1977) among others that a number of major changes have affected the role and importance of the sales force. Companies have become larger in size and fewer in number. Many have developed multinational interests. Because of concentration of strength, buyers in manufacturing companies, retail distribution chains and even local authorities are becoming increasingly powerful. Many centralize the buying function and eventually develop increased power from greater knowledge of suppliers' products, processes and capabilities. Forward vertical integration by large companies has reduced the actual market available to suppliers and further increased competition.

This limited availability of markets and supply has led to a greater interdependence of seller and buyer. Under conditions of a good product/service and sustained salesmanship, the question is not so much convincing the buyer whether he should buy, but rather establishing on what basis he should buy. This, it is claimed, is where negotiation comes into its own and presents the salesman with a challenge for which the traditional multi-stage influence training process ill prepares him. The negotiation process takes account of the differences that can arise within a situation of mutual dependence, and hinges on an exchange of resources related to such items as specification, promotional support, service, technical advice and price.

ORGANIZATIONAL BUYING

Buying stages

If approaches to selling have in the past been based on multi-stage influence processes, equally approaches to organizational buying have largely focused on multi-stage decision processes. Perhaps the most widely used of the many classifications for stages or phases in the buying process is the Robinson and Faris (1967) buy-phases model, which includes eight stages or activities. Each phase is related to three types of buying situation: (1) the new buy, where the need for the product/service has not previously arisen, so there is no experience in the buying company and a great deal of information is required; (2); the modified rebuy, where a regular requirement for the type of product exists and the buying requirements are known, but sufficient change has occurred to require some alteration to the normal supply procedure; (3) the straight rebuy, where a routine procedure exists and there is an approved list of suppliers. While indicating critical points in the buying process and suggesting that the process is incremental, the phases tend to imply a static situation rather than a dynamic one.

The buying centre concept

In order to identify people who make and influence decisions in the buying process, it is useful to think of the concept of a buying centre. This includes all those people who have a significant involvement in a purchase. It reflects the diffused nature of the buying process which is spread across functions. Individuals from different 'home' work groups or departments or sections are brought together in different combinations to make decisions or recommendations which bear on the ultimate purchasing decision. The roles of these different individuals affecting the decision have been classified by Webster and Wind (1972) as users, deciders, influencers and gatekeepers. Approaches have been developed which assist in identifying under certain circumstances where the buying influences lie (Bonoma 1982). Identification of buying influences has been shown to be much more difficult in matrix-type organization structures (Robles 1984).

Hill and Hillier (1977) have established a relationship between the buying process and the buying centre. They have viewed the process as key decision points which consist of four stages:

1 the precipitation decision stage;
2 the product specification stage;
3 the supplier selection stage;
4 the commitment decision stage.

As the process moves through each of the stages, so there is increasing restriction on the freedom of decision-making activities. Each stage has its buying centre, comprising individuals most of whom are unlikely to be included at all stages. The buying centre activities focus on the decision-making unit which is influenced on the one hand by those individuals who, although not necessarily involved in a purchase, may in fact take policy decisions which can limit and affect later decisions, including the purchase decision. Examples of this can relate to such factors as reciprocal buying, extent of alternative sourcing and degree of financial responsibility delegated downwards. On the other hand, individuals who act in a specialist capacity in the buying organization can influence the decision-making unit by the provision of specialist information held only by them.

There is evidence to show that the buying process will be longer and more complicated if the purchase items are buyer rather than supplier specified, if they are new and custom-built purchases rather than routine, and if they are of complex high technology rather than simple and cheap.

Factors affecting buying behaviour

In most studies of the way buying organizations behave, attention is fixed on the overt behaviour of the buying participants — for example, search activities, buying techniques and source loyalty. These task activities do not take account of how participants' beliefs, values, feelings, attitudes and perceptions affect overt behaviour. These non-task behaviours bear on the purchase process through the individuals present for such needs as ego enhancement, personal risk reduction and the maintenance of status. Such behaviour is interlinked with departmental politics and the conflicts associated with lateral relationships.

Webster and Wind (1972) have identified a number of factors bearing on the buying decision. Environmental factors, for example an over-valued national currency, may force buyers to give preference to cheaper suppliers from another country, or at least to give consideration where it had not been given before. Organizational influences can have an important effect because they reflect the way in which buying is structured and processed. The decision-making unit is a temporary physical group, as distinct from the perceived group represented by the people in the functional areas or departments. It usually consists of individuals who have varying degrees of affiliation with other groups in the organization. Conflict in such situations is inevitable and lends itself to non-task behaviour.

The mix of people involved, the nature of the buying process, the nature of the product and its use, the reason for its purchase and the behavioural characteristics of participants all combine with the above factors to determine buying behaviour and to underline its complexity.

The interactive dimension

More recently, research undertaken and concepts and models developed have viewed organizational buying behaviour as a more interactive process between buyer and seller. Webster's definition (1984) of the product in industrial markets as 'an array of economic, technical and personal relationships between buyer and seller' points to the interdependence of buyer and seller as a basis for continuing interaction.

The interactive view has received very considerable support from the work of the IMP Group. This is a stimulating piece of research in which the separation which has occurred in analysing industrial marketing and purchasing is challenged. Based on a research project carried out in five European countries, it presents a theoretical approach to industrial marketing and purchasing which identifies a need to examine the interaction between buying and selling firms. This is viewed as a more productive approach than one which views industrial marketing as the manipulation of marketing mix variables to strike a response from a generalized, and by implication, passive market. There is a focus on relationships between buyers and sellers which are often close and involve a complex pattern of interaction between two companies which have a mutual dependence not always recognized in the literature (Hakansson 1982).

There is some evidence, too, that the kinds of developments taking place in industrial markets equally affect consumer markets, in that suppliers have to deal with increasingly smaller numbers of resellers and, by the same token, resellers require to buy from a smaller number of suppliers. Dependence on each other has grown as firms have sought to protect markets and defend sources of supply. There have also been interactive developments in supplying to governments at national and local level, whereby changes such as central purchasing and co-operation among smaller units have been brought about by the need for more cost-effective approaches.

Interaction variables

The IMP Group researchers identified four groups of variables in relation to the buyer/seller interaction which they have incorporated into their interaction model (277–287). These are as follows.

Interaction processes

These can be looked at in terms of a matrix of relationships and episodes. Relationships are either limited or extensive, and episodes which are short-term aspects of an interaction — for example, transactions — are either simple or complex.

Simple episodes within limited relationships correspond to the 'classical' model of exchange situations. The buying firm can freely choose among available alternatives and the decision variables are few. Open channels of distribution tend to be used.

Complex episodes with limited relationships are characterized by being complete business transactions in themselves. The relationship is limited because in most instances the parties are meeting for the first time or for the purpose of a sale/purchase of a piece of capital equipment unlikely to be repeated in the foreseeable future. The organizations have no common routine to follow for problem-solving and have to demonstrate their trustworthiness to each other.

Simple episodes with extensive relationships reduce the risk for the parties concerned. The companies need not solve all the problems within the episodes because the relationship is used as an insurance.

In complex episodes with extensive relationships, need for change is typically perceived within the relationship — for example, when the buying firm requires product development or the selling firm has suggestions in relation to it.

The main difference between limited and extensive relationships is that episodes in the relationship must be viewed and handled as part of the relationship, and not in an isolated way. In the limited relationship the episode must be treated as a totality in itself, and the parties cannot rely on implied agreements. The main difference between complex and simple episodes is that, when there are complex problems that must be solved within the episode, there is a clear requirement for both parties to organize the problem-solving process in an efficient way.

Interacting parties

Because technical and social differences as well as marketing and purchasing strategies can affect the relationship, the IMP Group have developed another matrix to assist interacting parties to identify different situations.

The parties' knowledge of each other is classified as familiar and unfamiliar and the structural fit between them as matching and not matching. The extent to which the parties get to know each other is related to the episodes which reflect the characteristics of the exchange. The more complex the problems the greater the need for mutual knowledge. Differences between the parties make the interaction more difficult, and hence more resources must be applied if the parties are to make effective use of each other.

Interaction environment

Using yet another matrix which takes account of degree of market homogeneity or heterogeneity and relates it to the degree of stability or dynamism in the market, the

IMP Group describe an approach which simplifies the issues in the environment which may influence the relationships and episodes. A dynamic environment makes it necessary to develop the relationship or to be prepared to switch to another counterpart. A heterogeneous environment makes it more important to choose the right counterpart, as well as making it more difficult to change from one counterpart to another.

Atmosphere

Affecting and affected by the other three variables, 'atmosphere' is best described in terms of the power-dependence relationship which exists between companies, the state of conflict or cooperation in the relationship, and the mutual expectations of the companies who are party to the relationship. Close relationships are established and used to give economic benefits, lower costs, higher profits and/or to improve the organization's control of some part of its environment.

A critical aspect of the management of these relationships is the extent to which the firm can balance its interdependence with others. It must seek to balance the advantages of a close relationship, perhaps in terms of cost reduction and ease of speed and interaction, against the opportunity costs of that simple relationship and the dependence which it involves.

NEGOTIATION AS A FOCUS FOR BUYING AND SELLING

Negotiation as the critical link

Selling and organizational buying fit readily into the framework of the interrelated factors influencing negotiations and their outcomes shown at Figure 2.1, and the negotiation skills model at Figure 2.4 which accommodates these interrelationships.

Selling and negotiation are not discrete areas in which different actors play out different roles. Every sale involving some form of conflict has its negotiation aspect, and every negotiation presents opportunities for the seller to emphasize benefits. Indeed, there are often situations where selling and negotiation take place simultaneously, as in many simple episode types of transaction in which decision variables are few and negotiation is correspondingly uncomplicated. While there will always be open channels of distribution in which buyers can shop around and chop and change their suppliers according to the current advantage, developments are very much in the direction of contractual or closed arrangements which foster mutual dependence. The view of negotiation as a broader concept than bargaining makes it particularly easy to embrace the idea of buying and selling in terms of relationships and episodes. The salesman links negotiating episodes in his relationships with buyers.

The skills of the negotiating task are in no way vitiated by traditional selling skills. The prime task of a negotiator is to convince an opposer that his organization controls resources, that the opposer needs these resources and that he may be willing to use the power which his organization wields in a sanctioning manner if mutual dependence is present.

The Weitz model appears to fall short of its potential by not accepting the cooperative possibilities in salesman/buyer interactions for fear of compromising the advocacy role of the salesman. It can fit into the interrelationships framework and the negotiation skills model because there is provision for matching behaviour on the part of the seller without moving to a cooperative mode. Similarly fitted are the needs satisfaction and problem-solving models, as well as the Blake and Mouton consideration of selling and buying styles.

Organizational buying as a multi-stage decision process has been seen to provide an inadequate view of what is essentially a dynamic practice. The interactive dimension represented by the IMP Group interaction model can be accommodated alongside the negotiation perspective for the reason that personal interactions and the negotiations which accompany them are central to interaction between organizations.

Neither power and dependence nor conflict has been considered in personal selling research, and again negotiation embraces these aspects. The importance of relationships and role in buying and selling activities is likewise embedded in the negotiation literature and is examined further below, as is a further consideration of intercultural factors.

Centrality of relationships to negotiation

Personal contacts are at the heart of interaction between organizations (Hakansson 1982:314). Apart from their function of information exchange they facilitate other aspects of the interaction, such as the adaptation of products, delivery scheduling, establishment of mutually compatible accounting procedures and after-sales service. The salesman is almost invariably the first person in the supplying organization that a buyer meets. Their contact, both formally and informally, provides the buyer with a means by which risk may be reduced in choice of supplier. They provide the focal points from which others in their organizations may be introduced to reduce the uncertainty in complex episodes. The marketing and purchasing functions have the job to ensure that contacts so introduced and the relationships developed are coordinated and controlled.

The salesman has to depend largely on his own skills to develop relationships with buyers and, in the case of major sales and complex episodes, key individuals in the decision-making units of a customer organization. He is constrained by previous transactions in his relationships with the principle influencers, just as he is constrained by environmental and situational influences. Future episodes and relationships will be affected by current episodes.

Intercultural aspects of relationships

We have seen in Chapter 3 that relationships between individual negotiators of different cultural backgrounds can be assisted by communications which involve a number of parallel channels. Language, which becomes more expressive and meaningful in the negotiation by the use of paralanguage, is assisted by other non-verbal aspects, and is in turn mediated by the particular situation of the interaction and further mediated by the social context and social structure constraints which abound in any culture. Such a combination of features is necessary to convey meaning and is the communicative aspect of behaviour. In turn it requires an appropriate behaviour response and a corresponding multi-channel communicative act. Hence a sensitivity to culture as an important component of communication is a prerequisite for company officers whose fulfilment of their roles exposes them to negotiations in other cultures.

But even within national cultures there are rules and conventions which, while deriving from the culture, have to be learnt. These rules emerge to regulate behaviour so that goods can be obtained and needs satisfied. However, different sets of rules can develop to do the same job (Argyle 1981).

A sales/buying interaction takes place in a particular physical and social setting. Any setting has such rules and procedures and conventions that are culture bound. If these are transgressed it is not unusual for an unfavourable view of the transgressing party to be taken. The salesman whose work takes him round the world, or the sales manager or managing director receiving foreign visitors, will create a better atmosphere for developing relationships if he has taken trouble to master the rules. They can relate to time, eating and drinking, gifts or bribery or to status rules as in the seating of guests and the effecting of introductions.

A specific example could relate to the Arab characteristic of hospitality which is immediate, a characteristic which an Occidental might copy if he wished to initiate or seal a relationship. The implication is that if that immediacy is not evident, the relationship might never begin.

Another example might relate to the determination of the distribution of deference which is a crucial understanding in those cultures which are more than usually pre-occupied with the establishment of relative status, e.g. Western Europe, East Asia and the Americas. When introductions are being made in Denmark, for instance, both the person being introduced and the person to whom the introduction is made, are described by the sponsor in sufficient detail for the proper relations to be made quite clear. This occurs in Danish ritual before either of the people being introduced have spoken. This is more elaborate than in other West European countries where introduction sequences are such that the determination of identity is achieved by the participants themselves.

In so far as initial contacts in Sweden have a hidden agenda, it is to establish the competence of the various parties, not their relative status (Lawrence 1982). Sweden is characterized by a low differentiation between individuals, groups and classes. It has a strong commitment to egalitarianism with consequent disapproval of people who set themselves apart from others.

Arabs have developed a value for qualities of character such as generosity, fellowship and a certain ability to spend:

'Even when it is inconvenient, one is under a compulsion to accept another's hospitality. Just as an Arab is more than willing to extend hospitality to others, he expects them to be hospitable to him also. For example, when an Arab businessman goes to the United States and calls on an American executive he expects considerable hospitality. If the American says "I'm free for lunch next Wednesday" or "I'll be free for thirty minutes in the office tomorrow", he might just have done himself a bad turn. To an Arab hospitality should be immediate.' (Adapted from Almeney 1981.)

In Japan there is a widespread custom of gift-giving, both in society in general and in business. The experience of those who have lived in Japan makes it clear that a gift received should not be opened in the presence of the donor.

Mutual role-taking

If the processes of interaction, which are inherent in all relationships and episodes, are key factors in the behaviour of buyers and sellers, it is relevant to examine what is known about social interaction between pairs of individuals. The point is made by Mangham (1978) that, in any situation, what others do or are perceived to be doing are important clues to the definition of the situation. If a negotiator takes up a particular position and puts together a set of behaviours which can be inferred to be the expression of his preferred goal or goals, he is presenting himself and creates a part for his opposer in the developing interaction. What he is saying in effect is: 'This is who I want to be taken for and this is who I take you to be'.

The opposer's interpretation of the situation consists in attempting to take the negotiator's role and in understanding the implications of it for himself just as, in his turn, the negotiator has to define the opposer's behaviour and intentions. The significance of the process of definition is that it involves trying to understand the implications of the actions of each of the parties for the other. From this stems patterns of behaviour and the imputation of roles for the negotiator and his opposer. Such mutual role-taking is a necessary preliminary for effective communication and successful interaction.

The opposer seeks to determine the meaning of the negotiator and the situation he finds himself in. In making this interpretation the opposer imputes a role to the negotiator and, by inference, to himself. If in the process of considering the implications for himself he then dramatizes and acts out what he takes to be his part in the unfolding interaction, this becomes part of the situation for the negotiator, and thus begins another cycle which repeats until the interaction comes to an end.

Mangham (1979) views the process of effective interaction as dependent on the implementation of the following three core interpersonal skills which can be developed.

The definitional dimension

This includes the ability to perceive what is appropriate in any given situation. Factors determining the depths of insights into situations are those related to past experiences, familiarity with the other party to the negotiation, and conversancy with the culture of similar people and interactions with them.

The technical competence dimension

This relates to consideration of the other party's behaviour for oneself. If a buyer strings together behaviours which are perceived as an attempt to dominate, the seller may wish to adopt a matching behaviour which inclines to the submissive in the interest of the relationship. On the other hand he might well wish, in the distributive stage of the negotiation, to take a much more aggressive stance to lower the expectations of the buyer. Unless the seller understands how to match his behaviour to the needs of the situation, his subsequent actions may not have the desired effect.

The performing dimension

This is the skill to put into action one's definitions and technical ability. It is seen as a function of training which can widen the negotiator's repertoire of suitable behaviour.

In the negotiation of international agreements for purchase and sale, there is very considerable scope for misinterpreting roles, brought about by differing national cultures. Examples of these have been given in Chapter 3. English suppliers and French customers, because of lack of understanding of differing cultural approaches to negotiation, may not be keyed into the cues which might help them to interpret the situation and formulate appropriate responses. Relationships between multinational companies with objectives arising from the planning process, and national governments with a broader pattern of objectives which can be largely non-economic, were seen to contain the germ of role misperception. Advertising agency executives who failed to relate their own behaviours to the linguistic behaviours of potential clients in a large soap company were unable to define the situation, and were excluded from consideration because they were unable to develop any interaction in which a soap company's executives could create a part for themselves. It is no coincidence that a thrust of this book is towards understanding the cultural implications of behaviour in business encounters.

ORGANIZATIONAL PERSPECTIVES

Mutual interest and conflict

Companies normally prepare themselves for working within negotiation frameworks. Organizational philosophies and perceptions are conditioned by national cultural perspectives and philosophies. The philosophy underlying business can be different as between countries at different stages of economic development, of differing culture and history and of differing political and/or religious persuasion. Such differences tend to be written into the laws of the respective countries and into the terms and conditions under which companies in these countries would prefer to trade.

If we add to this the different approaches that buyers and sellers take towards a basic trading situation, then it is possible to understand individuals who identify items of potential conflict for negotiation within the mutual interest that can exist in a sales/ purchase episode. A buyer might be interested in the purchase of a particular product but prefer post-shipment payment in the currency of his own country, whereas a seller in another country might try for pre-shipment payment in his own currency. There is a host of other issues related to product, delivery, price, support levels, insurance and other matters on which genuine conflict can arise within an overall requirement to procure a particular product.

In order to make clear exactly where they stand both sellers and buyers have their own standard conditions of sale or purchase. A quotation or offer made by the seller in which commercial, technical and financial conditions are spelt out, together with the terms and conditions of contract, represent the area covered by any contract negotiation.

The need for standard conditions

Parties to a sales/purchase negotiation may wish to vary the terms of delivery, or the terms under which risk passes, or they may wish to make provision for different remedies for, say, late delivery. This is because the German Commercial Code or the Uniform Commercial Code in the USA or the Sale of Goods Act in the United Kingdom, for example, may be too imprecise for a given situation, or it may be too rigid or too difficult in its application.

Since both buyers and sellers operate against a background of urgency they are quite ready to accept the principle of standard conditions to avoid the negotiation of specific terms for each transaction. When they know that every contract will be regulated by known conditions they can apply themselves to the negotiation of what the parties view as important, such as specification, delivery, price or service.

Various kinds of standard conditions

It is unlikely that buyers and sellers will adopt a single set only of standard conditions. Different conditions apply to complete projects, units of equipment and to components. Conditions differ depending on whether there is patent protection or not, whether the goods are mass-produced, made to a standard pattern or 'one-off' specification, or whether the purchaser is buying as ultimate user or intermediary. In the case of engineering products or products of high technology in particular, different standard conditions may apply depending on whether the agreement is for supply only, for supply and installation, or whether it is for the home or overseas market.

The role of the tender

Estimates or quotations given by sellers do not have implications as wide as the tender, sometimes referred to as an offer or bid. They are associated with the price today but not necessarily the price in three months' or six months' time. The term 'tender' reflects a more complex situation. It subsumes 'quotation' and 'estimate' and goes beyond these to encompass such subjects as credit terms in international transactions, guarantees on delivery and performance, limitations of supplier liability, proving tests where appropriate, contingency arrangements in respect of loss, liability for defects, and settlement arrangements in relation to possible disputes. In its most extreme form it covers all possible situations.

The tender fulfils three principal roles:

1 it is a presentation by the seller which, in the view of the buyer, represents the seller's basis for negotiations;

2 it provides the seller with the opportunity to capitalize on previous discussions in relation to the customer's needs by encapsulating these in a convincing submission;

3 it is the formal expression of the aspiration level of the seller; any trade-offs in bargaining will attempt to maintain that level.

Together with the conditions of sale, the tender embraces the terms of contract which will result if the buyer accepts, and the applicable law is that of the seller's country. A buyer may seek to obtain agreement to his own terms, which are certain to be different from those of the seller. In the event of a dispute the rules or the conflicts of laws will determine whether the law of the buyer's or seller's country will apply. Foreign government departments and organizations sometimes put out 'calls for tenders'. To obtain the appropriate documents and have a subsequent tender considered, a tendering firm is occasionally required to take out a *bid bond* or 'tender bond'. This is the foreign institution's guarantee of good faith on the part of the tender. It is often converted to a *performance bond* (see p. 174), if the tenderer is successful.

If the contract is governed by foreign law, rules in relation to offer and acceptance, delivery, passing of property and title may differ from those of the home country, see Chapter 6.

Setting aside offer and acceptance

Large and powerful buyers such as multinational companies, main contractors of construction works, national governments and government agencies, who are involved in buying a widely varied range of products or services from fast-moving consumer goods to standard capital units and complex systems, have developed their own conditions of purchase. This is because there would be a perceived lack of control if suppliers' own terms were to be used or if all items had to be negotiated in each instance.

These standard conditions usually take the form of a contract to be signed by buyers and sellers. This contract almost invariably includes a clause which excludes any previous correspondence or dealings, effectively invalidating any procedures previously initiated based on concepts of offer and acceptance. It is these contract forms incorporating standard conditions which form the basis of any negotiated variation of the contract.

Standard conditions of this kind have been drawn up by officers of such institutions as the United Nations Economic Council for Europe (ECE) for contracts between suppliers and customers in countries having different legal systems. The International Chamber of Commerce booklet *Incoterms 1980* attempts to define terms used in such a way that there can be no doubt as to interpretation. If Incoterms are incorporated in contracts, then the possibility of misunderstanding is likely to be removed and will certainly be reduced. These can be adapted to the needs of the particular sales/purchase situation.

MAIN AREAS TO BE COVERED BY STANDARD CONDITIONS

Whether a contract emerges from the process of offer and acceptance, or results from the signing by the parties of a formal contract document which normally supersedes that process, there are certain main areas that must be addressed by any standard conditions, supplemented as necessary by financial, technical and commercial conditions.

Scope of the contract

The scope includes the specification of the goods or services involved, and should be defined in such a way that it cannot be interpreted differently by the parties. The seller may be concerned, if the buyer is a wholesaler buying on long-term contract, for example, to establish who will warehouse stocks, whether the wholesaler can accommodate electronic data-processing of procedures and payments and maximum/minimum take-offs in given periods. In the industrial market he may be concerned with exclusions or purchaser's responsibilities.

For example, an air compressor may be ordered which includes the compressor unit with driving motor. But a compressor requires a starter; it has to be connected by electric cable from the starter to the motor and from the motor to the customer's distribution board. If the starter is to be included it should be stated specifically; similarly with the cable.

The buyer will be concerned to reserve the right to inspect or witness appropriate tests, to stipulate a particular manufacturer's supply of electric motors, for example, on which he may have standardized, or to specify crate sizes and packing requirements.

Price

All buyers would ideally like to agree to contract prices which are fixed, because this facilitates forward planning, administration and costing. Sellers, on the other hand, take the view that prices quoted outside the immediate short term should incorporate some form of variable pricing to cover the possibility of increases in material prices and labour rates. Under inflationary conditions the duration of fixed price contracts tends to shorten. Buyers who push for an unrealistic duration of a fixed price contract are inviting it to be loaded generously to meet all possible contingencies.

In these circumstances the seller's terms have to be clearly agreed so that the basis of negotiation can be seen clearly by both parties. For example, it should be made clear what the basis is of any escalation or price adjustment clause.[1] If no suitable formula can be found, the question of variations is one which buyer and seller can cooperate to their mutual benefit. In the end the basis of price variation has to be acceptable to both parties.

Payment

The terms under which payment is usually made are for settlement within a certain period after delivery. Sometimes, in contracts for construction engineering works, for instance, progress payments are agreed and/or a percentage of the contract value is withheld until such time as commissioning or performance tests have been completed. The buyer seeks to write safeguards into his conditions if he has advanced money against stages of work completed, while the seller will be concerned to ensure that where he has carried out his part of the contract he will receive the price for the work done.

If payments are related to erection or commissioning, or to performance tests, the seller would be wise to seek payment within a fixed period from, say, delivery or completion of erection. This avoids circumstances which prevent or delay commissioning, for example by another contractor's work being delayed through technical difficulties.

The seller is equally concerned to ensure that tardy payment on the part of the buyer is not encouraged. He may wish to include a clause in his conditions whereby the buyer would pay interest on delayed payments. The seller may terminate a contract if the buyer fails to make payment or becomes insolvent. It will depend largely on the individual circumstances whether or not this would be an advantageous course of action.

Below is the contract price adjustment formula agreed by Rolls Royce and Lockheed for the RB211 engines to power the Lockheed Tristar jetliner:

$$P = P_0 \left[(0.10 + 0.55 \frac{L}{L_0} + 0.35 \frac{M}{M_0}) - 0.6121 \right]$$

All the formula means is that the final contract price P would be made up of:

10 per cent of the original contract price P_0

55 per cent of a factor L/L_0 which allowed for increases in labour costs since signing of the contract

35 per cent of a factor M/M_0 which allowed for increases in material costs since signing of the contract less 6 per cent so that Rolls Royce would not get the benefit of inflation in their profit margin as well; figures for labour L and materials M were from national cost indices.

However good is a contract price adjustment clause, it will not be a sufficient protection if the starting price is too low. At the time of the Rolls Royce 'collapse' there were three factors which made a nonsense of their calculations:

1 Lockheed failed to sell as many Tristars as was hoped for. In any case Rolls Royce were optimistic in assuming they could recover their development costs over the number of aircraft which Lockheed expected to sell.
2 Carbon fibre blades which were to give the engine a vital technical edge failed to stand up to requirements in practice. More costly material was incorporated which gave poorer power/weight ratios and exposed the company to performance penalties.
3 Rolls Royce engineers failed to solve the problems of an entirely new engine design in the almost impossibly short time agreed in the contract. They therefore failed to meet delivery commitments as well as exposing the company to liquidated damages.

The formula was originally published in the *Sunday Times* of 7 February 1971 and is reproduced with permission.

Delivery

It is usual to define unequivocally the place of delivery, in what situations delivery may be deemed to take place, and who arranges for carriage and for items incidental to delivery. In the event of goods being sent on consignment, for instance to distributors, arrangements must be made about who looks after the goods until they are sold and who bears the risk of loss or damage before use.

Very often buyers are operating on a tight programme and may require the seller to give an undertaking that delivery will be carried out within a given time, in which case time becomes the essence of the contract. Breach of this gives the buyer remedies at law which may be unlimited, usually taking the form of damages. It is possible for consequential losses to arise which are far in excess of the contract value, for example where loss of profits arise as a result of delay in delivery. The seller therefore tries to limit the extent of his liability within his contract conditions. This he often does in some common law countries by making provision for compensating the buyer for delays by means of liquidated damages. In the United Kingdom the law requires that this should be a genuine pre-estimate. In civil code countries in general, penalty clauses are included for delay in delivery.

Sometimes the seller may require an extension to his delivery time because of *force majeure*. The seller requires protection against causes of delay which are beyond his control.

Performance

Buyers seek guarantees of performance to reduce risk, and sellers normally provide these. Failure to reach guaranteed performance is normally a breach of contract entitling the buyer to claim damages. The buyer will often reserve the right to witness performance tests at the supplier's works, if this is relevant, or any other inspection to ensure the goods conform to description. The supplier will take care to write into his conditions adequate opportunity to correct faults or make modifications. As in the case of delivery, liquidated damages can be applied to ensure compliance with performance, as can retention of a percentage of the contract value until satisfactory completion of the contract.

Performance bonds, sometimes called contract guarantees, are sometimes required of the seller by the buyer, to ensure that the seller will do what he has said he will do in the contract. The amount can vary from 5 per cent to 100 per cent according to the nature of the work. 30 per cent is usual.

Patents, trademarks, copyright, designs

The buyer, to protect his interests, may seek to obtain indemnification against any claim for infringement of patents, registered designs, trademarks or copyright, resulting from the purchase of any article or material supplied by the seller. The seller will normally include this in his own standard terms, and he will seek his own protection against a buyer's instruction or design leading to infringements, as well as making any claim conditional upon the buyer notifying him as soon as possible after any action has been brought or threatened.

Arbitration

A seller will usually provide that a contract will be referred to an arbitrator in the event of a dispute, the arbitrator(s) to be appointed by agreement between the parties. Failing agreement on this the seller may provide that the dispute be referred to the president of a professional institution, a trade association or a Chamber of Commerce. In international contracts the seller usually provides that the contract should be regulated by the law of his own country and tries for arbitration in his own country. Buyers in another country are most at home with their own institutions and will normally try for arbitration at home, and sometimes insist that the law of their own country should apply.

TOWARDS SPECIFIC AGREEMENTS

Negotiation and company objectives

The negotiation process is a result of the need for resolution of conflict on such issues as the differing views represented by buyers' and sellers' terms and conditions and the financial, technical and commercial differences on which they seek agreement. These in turn are linked to the overall company objectives.

Marketing objectives, and hence sales negotiation objectives, must be consistent with company objectives which might lay down a given overall return on investment. Purchasing objectives must be consistent with a company strategic plan based on the need, say, to purchase a given quantity of items at regular intervals within a given price ceiling.

Sometimes selling or purchasing objectives may not be achievable. For example, a selling company may be using an outmoded technology which forces costs too high; or a company in the market for items which have become limited in supply may find that objectives, which have been included in a budget of planned profit, are not reachable. Such conclusions stem from assessments made by the negotiating team of the feasibility of achieving objectives in line with company and marketing/purchasing objectives.

The need to modify objectives requires internal bargaining within the supplying and procuring organizations. In the modern organization decision-making is diffused. Thus intra-organizational bargaining is necessary to ensure that both negotiators and the management group responsible for operations have a clear understanding of their terms of reference. The negotiators of both buying and selling parties will wish to establish the target objective and their authority limits in relation to departures from the objective it might be necessary to follow during across-the-table discussions. The management group will require to accept any commitments necessary to achieve the negotiating objective in terms of such aspects as early ordering of long-lead items to support any improved delivery requirement, specific allocation of duties in respect of critical paths in supply, and likely technical modifications.

Modification of objectives may require pre-negotiation contact between buyer and seller to ascertain there is mutual benefit to be obtained from the exchange. There is research evidence to support the view that where pre-negotiation contact takes place, agreement is more easily reached. At this stage the target negotiating objective can lie within a range. This will vary between a maximum which is considered feasible and an agreed acceptable minimum. Only where a first offer is a final one must a seller choose a single figure from within this range.

Evaluating target objectives[2]

The seller

The price level at which the seller makes an offer or bid is crucial. If the level of the bid is increased — that is, the target profitability is increased — the bid becomes more desirable in relation to alternative possibilities. Conversely, the probability of success is reduced. Both desirability and probability of success can be affected by the extent to which resources are required and allocated to bidding and the execution of an agreement. Non-task factors tend to be identified in the face-to-face negotiation, unless there is prior knowledge of the opposer, and these are the subject of on-the-spot judgment.

The buyer

A buyer looks ideally for a competitive market in which price is established by the supply — demand mechanism. Perfect competition is, however, a concept rather than a reality. The buyer therefore seeks, or should seek, to increase the competitiveness of the market and so strengthen his negotiating position. To this end he has the ability to increase the competitiveness of the market:

1 He may aim to buy in the widest possible market. To achieve this he can, for example, avoid 'one-offs' by ordering or redesigning his product to accommodate standard industrial items. Alternatives can be to specify requirements in general terms or in terms of performance. For example, he can specify animal feedstuffs in terms of its value in calories or process equipment in terms of the throughput to be handled for a given quality, or within given limits.
2 He may select the best potential sellers. Within the buyer's requirements for quality, reliability, service and delivery, the purchasing officer's up-to-date knowledge of suppliers' capabilities and weaknesses and the operation of a vendor rating system can help to identify the most likely sellers. By these means he can select a short list of firms most likely to submit low-price bids. He will only be constrained in the application of such a system by the measure of dependence and trust that has been built up with particular suppliers.

Modification of the buyer's target objectives will always be associated with company plans, as will the seller's. A company will not always opt for the lowest price. Where it is a sole purchaser it may wish to ensure that certain smaller supplying firms do not go out of business as a result of its policies, as it will wish to maintain long-run competitiveness among suppliers. This can be particularly true where the purchaser seeks to maintain certain research and development capabilities which such companies may have. Similarly, a buying company may lower its target objective in terms of price where there is a requirement to meet a seasonal marketing programme and the lead times, for whatever reason, are less than optimal.

The power balance

The relative power balance between the parties will have a bearing on the level of first offer. The objective distribution of power between the parties is only important to the degree that it is interpreted and used at the bargaining table. Negotiators seek to manipulate their opposers' perception of the power distribution situation. Through tactics such as bluffing and argumentation they attempt to create a mutually acceptable definition of the power relationship that is of some advantage to themselves (Bacharach and Lawler 1981). The negotiator's task is to convince his opposer that he controls resources, that the opposer needs these resources, and that he, the negotiator, is willing to use the power that comes from possessing these resources. By managing impressions of bargaining power, parties can use uncertainties and ambiguities to their own advantage.

Where companies interact with each other in the course of their transactions as buyers and sellers, so the objective distribution of power becomes more specific. The negotiators become aware of the resources which each controls, and uncertainties and ambiguities are reduced, diminishing the importance of managing impressions of bargaining power, although never eliminating the need for it which has to be ongoing. The true power balance emerges and is seen at its most extreme in cases of what has been termed 'vertical quasi-integration' (Blois 1972). A major characteristic of this type of relationship is customer influence over the supplier by the exercise of economic power. A large customer is able to exercise power over a small supplier because the latter is heavily dependent on it for output absorption. This type of relationship has been extended to include all vertical inter-firm alignments described by independent ownership of the transacting units and a transaction mechanism based on the loss of power and exercise of control (Diamantopoulos 1987).

Setting the level of first offer

In arriving at a decision about the level at which to make an offer, suppliers and purchasers are confronted with the same basic problems.

In relation to the level at which any offer is made, there is some evidence to show that the higher an offer is pitched, whether as seller or negatively as buyer, the higher is the level of settlement likely to be. This is usually associated with conceding little slowly to obtain the best of a bargain. The corollary is also true that the higher the level of offer, the less likely it is that an agreement will ensue at all. There has therefore to be a reasonable level at which an opposer will settle, or at least be prepared to talk (Chertkoff and Esser 1976).

High first offers have been observed on the part of Japanese sellers. This stems from the status relationships that exist in Japan. There the buyer has the superior position and research has shown that outcomes favour Japanese buyers, although he has an implicit responsibility not to exploit the seller. Sellers realize that their subordinate position prevents them from disagreeing strongly with the buyer, and the easiest solution is to put in a high offer in the first place. The situation for foreign sellers is somewhat different in that they are accorded a higher position than the native Japanese seller, but the tradition of high initial offers appear to persist.

On the other hand there are countries where a high level of initial offer will be unacceptable if perceived to be so either in comparison with other offers or by evidence of willingness to reduce the price in the course of negotiation. Finns and Norwegians come into this category, believing that an opposer who has built in a high concession factor is indulging in sharp practice. Germans tend to make first offers based on extensive preparation and are not noticeably open to compromise. Arabs believe there is a market price for everything and provision for a high concession rate if perceived by them may be interpreted as irresponsible and unprincipled.

The seller

There are two strategies affecting level of offer which can be employed. These are 'final offer first' (FOF) or 'hold off' (HO).

In FOF the seller selects the level which it is anticipated the recipient will accept without further negotiation. In HO he selects a level which is felt to be sufficiently attractive to encourage the recipient to pursue it further and which has a margin for negotiation built in. FOF is used when responding to a call for tenders from a public authority, where choice is usually made on the basis of the lowest price and negotiation is possible only with some authorities and only after the choice has been made. The level of bid is normally related to resource requirements and availability and can often be quantified by allocating probabilities to the different levels considered (Marsh 1984: 145 – 149).

HO is much more widely used. The level of offer will, depending on circumstances, be determined by an amalgam of some of the following factors. These will interact with non-task factors such as a manager's achievement of sales, profit or contribution objectives or his propensity to take risks:

1 the need to cover fixed costs and retain key staff in conditions of poorly filled order books, and to maintain as far as possible advantageous cost/volume/profit relationships;
2 long-term aspirations, such as obtaining entry to a new market, or acquiring a base in an overseas market to retain the account of a major customer who has already moved there, or obtaining recognition as an international supplier;
3 contractual risks involved, such as the risk of incurring a penalty for delay, risks of late or non-payment, or disputes which cannot be referred to a truly independent arbitration or court;

4 the need to recover expenditures such as special research and development effort not recoverable over the product volume to which the customers would be contracted;
5 competitors' likely price levels, computed on the basis of past experience, including factors affecting price levels like time-scale of extended credit, interest charges of overseas competitors, and time costs and discount rates;
6 the relationship between the parties and the dependence and relative power that exists within the relationship;
7 any knowledge which the seller has, or can imply from past behaviour, of the customer in relation to the concessions he has built into the price he will pay.

Level of first offer to enter a market

A European manufacturer of capital goods for the sugar industry adapted his product to 60 Hz electricity supply and identified Hawaii as a potential market, not only in its own right, but as a means of entry to the wider US market. On an initial visit to the islands the sales manager made contact with a number of technical and commercial staff at various sugar estates of one of the main groups of producers. He was able to establish that it was the policy of the group not to buy outside the USA unless there was a substantial price advantage, variously estimated at between 12 and 15 per cent at least below the US price for similar equipment.

The manufacturer estimated his machine to be 17 per cent cheaper than the rival American model. There was an import duty of 12½ per cent on all such equipment entering Hawaii from outside the USA, which reduced the advantage. The sales manager also discovered there was a strong lobby among Hawaiian producers to have the duty reduced in line with other agriculture associated equipment.

The manufacturer was reluctant to price at more than 8 per cent below the American rival, owing to the difficulty of making future sales in a closely knit industry where information was freely exchanged. He eventually submitted a quotation as the basis for negotiation which took account of the following factors:

1 a first offer 10 per cent less (after duty) than the estimated US price, with an indication of a willingness to visit to discuss it;
2 readiness to promise regular visits by technical staff during familiarization of factory staff with the equipment (service engineers and other personnel were already visiting a subsidiary company in South East Asia on a regular basis—it was a simple matter to route them via Hawaii);
3 technical specifications which could be varied to reduce the cost, subject to negotiations;
4 the availability of the standard agency commission if a sale was concluded before the appointment of an agent;
5 the long-term possibility of tariff aboliton.

The buyer

A purchaser usually elects to bargain directly on price or indirectly through bargaining on the terms of contract which significantly affect risk such as penalties in respect of delivery or performance and terms of payment. In reaching his decision he has to take into account, as has the seller, that the more favourable the terms he demands within the range that retains his interest in the negotiation, the longer the negotiations will take and the higher the time costs may be. The costs will largely be the loss of revenue or additional expenditure due to the delay in starting work and hence in its completion. In times of inflation escalation costs result from work being completed later rather than earlier.

THE BARGAINING FRAMEWORK

The bargaining area

The initial position which the parties adopt should take into consideration the expectation of a pattern of responsive concessions occurring over the bargaining period. These can include real concessions built into the first offer, and 'straw issues' which are very minor points used in the negotiation as bargaining counters. The bargaining outcomes rest between what the seller initially asks for and the buyer specifies as the top limit of what he will pay. As has been illustrated above, the initial position adopted will depend on the actual or perceived relative power position of the parties. There is no absolute datum line like a target margin on sales because the power balance may not allow it.

A seller who gets what he asks for receives a bonus in terms of the concessions or contingency features built into his price which do not have to be traded away after all. In the event, he has at best misread the situation and may have failed to involve himself with the potential buyer in pre-negotiation planning. This bonus is everything in excess of his target objective. A wise seller will have planned also a minimum below which he is not prepared to go, just as a buyer will have planned a maximum amount over which he cannot or will not pay.

The area between the two sides is described as the bargaining area and is illustrated in Figure 7.1. Where what the seller wants is well in excess of what the buyer is willing to give, no agreement will follow until both parties have altered the expectations of the other. Where the overlap between the buyer's and seller's limits is small, neither will see possible outcomes as a fair deal to himself unless he can, again by altering the other's expectations or by cooperation, enlarge the bargaining overlap. Where there is a large measure of congruence—that is, where there is sufficient bargaining room for each to go away satisfied that he has made an advantageous agreement—agreement will be easily reached.

The settlement range

While the bargaining area may well be the difference between the minimum a seller will accept and the maximum a buyer will pay, the settlement range is based on both parties' perceptions of that situation. One writer has defined the settlement range as 'the buyer's estimate of the seller's minimum and the seller's estimate of the buyer's maximum' (Karrass 1974). In theory the smaller the difference between the bargaining area and the settlement range, the more effective the negotiation and the greater the likelihood of mutual satisfaction in the exchange. In effect the notion of the bargaining or contract area is useful if it is remembered that this is not absolute, but determined by how the parties see it.

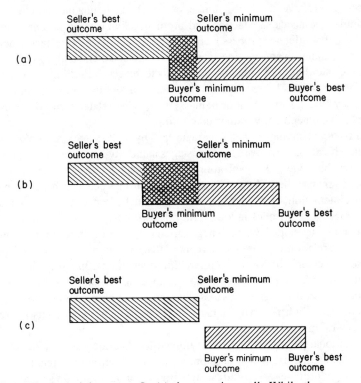

Figure 7.1 The bargaining zone. In (a) the zone is small. While there may well be agreement, neither party will perceive the outcome as satisfactory unless either an alteration in the parties' approach can enlarge the bargaining area. Whether the buyer persists will depend on available alternatives and opportunity costs. Negotiations are extended.

(b) The zone is wide. Either party can take a larger piece of the joint outcome and the other party can still leave satisfied. This situation presents the negotiator with an opportunity to cement relationships with his opposer and simultaneously sustain a good self-image.

(c) There is no overlap for bargaining. No agreement is likely unless parties' expectations can be considerably altered. Negotiations are extended, or break down.

Varying the bargaining area and settlement range

The strategic nub of the negotiation process is the information which the parties can extract from each other during their interaction and use for mutual influence. The negotiator who obtains information emphasizing the seller's need for a sale or the buyer's need for his product or service is then in a position to increase his demands, so altering the bargaining and settlement areas. The seller's and buyer's minimum outcomes are therefore not fixed, and Figure 7.1 should be read accordingly. Establishing these minimum outcomes is a function of the face-to-face situation addressed in the next chapter.

SUMMARY

The traditional approach to selling has been characterized by multi-stage influence processes. These have included a number of models, including the stimulus response, the formula, the needs satisfaction and problem solving models. The major steps constituting the influence process were seen to be identifying prospects, identifying influences, making an appropriate approach, selling benefits, handling objections and closing the sale. Failure to identify universals in successful selling has resulted in a more adaptive approach, witnessed by the Blake and Mouton sales grid and the Weitz contingency model. Concentration of markets and other related factors have increased the emphasis on negotiation rather than selling.

Organizational buying has been characterized by multi-stage decision processes in which classifications have been made of stages in the buying process. Recent research and theories have viewed organizational buying behaviour as an interactive process between buyer and seller. There is a focus on relationships between them which involve a complex interaction, of which a feature is the mutual dependence of buyer and seller, viewed in terms of episodes in long-term relationships.

The theme is developed whereby negotiation is seen as the focus for buying/selling activities and relationships are seen as central to negotiation activities. Such relationships are particularly important in intercultural situations, in which the concept of communication as a multi-channel process developed in Chapter 3 is seen as paramount. Some consideration was given to rules stemming from particular cultures. Relationships were seen to be affected by mutual role-taking, which is a necessary pre requisite of a successful interaction.

Organizational perspectives were examined to illustrate how buying and selling organizations see mutual interest and conflict in inter-organizational relations. Conflict is rooted in philosophies and cultures, and differing organizational views are reflected in the way organizations try to regulate their business by conditions of sale and purchase. The role of the tender is to present conditions of sale together with financial, technical and commercial conditions in a way which presents the situation to the buyer as a response to his needs and provides the statement of the seller's position. A buyer may try to obtain agreement on his own terms. Powerful buyers use their own standard conditions as the basis for negotiations. Main areas to be considered in standard conditions are scope of contract, price, payment, delivery, performance, patents and arbitration.

Negotiation objectives are related to company objectives through marketing and purchasing objectives. Planning negotiation objectives involves internal negotiations in the organization, the outcome of which may be a modification of policy guidelines. Target objectives are evaluated in the light of the circumstances in which negotiation takes place and the factors likely to influence these circumstances. The level of the first offer will in the first place be affected by the strategy adopted, which will be either 'final offer first' or 'hold off'. The former is used in formal tendering to public authorities, but the latter is much more common.

A seller's level of first offer will be affected by non-task factors in relation to such factors as need to cover fixed costs, maintain cost/profit/volume advantages, long-term aspirations, contractual risk, contingency amounts including negotiation contingency, and relationship between the parties. The buyer has to consider his level of first offer in relation to time costs, as any delay occasioned by extended negotiating times, brought about by asking for more favourable terms, may result in his increasing escalation costs or causing delay in completion.

The bargaining area is represented by the overlap between what the seller wants and what the buyer is prepared to pay. The settlement range is the difference between the buyer's estimate of the seller's minimum and the seller's estimte of the buyer's maximum. The bargaining and settlement areas can be altered as a result of information elicited during the interaction. That is the strategic function of the face-to-face situation, addressed in the next chapter.

Notes

1 For a practical example of contract price adjustment, see Flynn and Kynoch (1983).
2 This section draws heavily on Marsh (1984), which has become the standard reference work on negotiation of contracts of purchase and sale.

Questions

1 What do you understand by contingency approaches to selling?
2 Why is it inadequate to regard selling as a multiple-influence process and buying as a multiple-decision process?
3 Give examples of cultural rules or conventions which, in your own experience, have had to be learnt.
4 What is the purpose and content of standard conditions of sale and purchase?
5 Justify to a potential purchaser your inclusion of a contract price adjustment clause in a proposed agreement.
6 Justify to a would-be seller your refusal to agree to meet in full a contract price adjustment clause with the settlement price tied to his/her country's indices for labour and materials.
7 Indicate the factors that affect the level of the initial offer by
   (a) a seller
   (b) a buyer.
8 Distinguish between the bargaining range and the settlement range and isolate the circumstances in which these might be varied.

CHAPTER 8

The sales/purchase agreement II

Pre-negotiation stage.. 185
Relative power of parties... 185
Environmental forces of power.. 185
Situational forces of power.. 186
Building in power.. 186
Getting to the negotiating table... 187
Availability of information... 187
Quality of presentation... 188
Influence channels.. 188
Face-to-face.. 189
Negotiating rules for the meeting... 189
Using the agenda to influence outcomes.. 190
Setting of time limits... 191
Distributive bargaining stage.. 192
Exploring the negotiating range... 192
Taking the initiative... 192
Probing.. 193
Anticipating form of ultimate agreement.. 193
Some cultural snares... 195
Getting movement.. 196
The dilemma of buyer and seller.. 196
Sending and receiving signals... 196
Conditional movement.. 197
Integrative bargaining stage...197
Testing commitment to issues.. 197
Relative strength of commitment and concession rates.......................... 198
Development of the interaction.. 199
Maintaining flexibility.. 200
Commitment and constraints... 201
The interpersonal dimension... 202
Bargaining away the unacceptable.. 203
Narrowing the gap.. 203
Price and worth.. 203
Trading-off... 204
Face-saving.. 206

Decision-making and action stage... 207
Assessing what is acceptable.. 207
Testing understanding... 207
Memorandum of agreement... 208
Governments and government sponsored agencies............................. 209
Negotiating with government departments.. 209
Public corporations and services... 212
Local authorities... 213
Negotiations arising from agreements... 213
Parallel agreements.. 213
Disputes... 214
Philosophy of negotiation... 214
Summary 215
Reading I... 218
Reading II.. 219
Reading III... 222

PRE-NEGOTIATION STAGE

Relative power of parties

As indicated in the previous chapter there is a close link between company objectives and sales/purchasing objectives developed and the parties' levels of first offer. One important factor which arises from the mutual dependence inherent in a voluntary relationship is the relative power that exists between companies. If there is a preponderant dependence of one party on another, that party is in a position of relative weakness *vis-à-vis* the other party. This will have a bearing on the negotiation objectives, but only if there is an awareness of the position of strength or weakness. In the absence of the awareness of the weaker party, it will affect outcomes if the stronger party decides to exercise his power.

Environmental forces of power

From time to time companies are blind to changes taking place in their environment, often because they have become locked into policies, procedures and controls derived from an earlier situation which is no longer relevant. Such changes usually come from an extension of competition through the appearance of such factors as new or substitutable products, changing market structures, new selling support activities, adverse exchange rates, new perspectives on payment terms, or changes in consumer preferences.

The whisky industry is currently sharing, with other brown spirit manufacturers, a worldwide downturn in consumer demand in the face of growing competition from clear spirits. Whisky distributors and wholesalers have therefore been in a relatively strong position to negotiate as distillers have experienced a need to generate the necessary cash flows to finance operations. Distillers who are still using marketing and negotiating strategies developed in an era of growing demand are likely to find themselves short of orders.

Manufacturers of earth-moving equipment with potential customers in countries which have become short of foreign exchange, for example Mexico and Brazil, find they are losing out to competitors, and losing relative power to their distributors, unless they embrace strategies which call on the support of Eurodollar financing.

An exporter whose house rules require all overseas quotations to include whole or part payment by confirmed irrevocable Letter of Credit when the market is becoming noticeably tighter, is likely to cut himself off from potential sales.

On the other hand, a firm which monitors closely its environment is less likely to suffer such traumas if it as a result, identifies the problem and takes appropriate action. Relative power can change quickly with changes in the environment of interacting organizations.

Situational forces of power

Within the framework of relative power created by circumstances in the environment there will be variations brought about by the negotiation situation. Buyer and seller are dealing with incomplete information about each other. The strategic function of negotiators is to fill out as much information as they can about each other to enable them to revise their objectives and strategy as the information obtained dictates. A seller who finds out from, say, an engineer in the buying organization that his is the only quotation that meets the specification, has immediately widened his power-base. When a purchaser establishes that a supplier is short of work, he increases his power. So the relative power between the parties can change during the course of negotiation. Whenever a concession is made without reciprocation, the conceder yields some of his bargaining power.

If there is prior experience of the opposer's true preferences, that too represents power. If the buyer is known to be a person who is concerned with his own image among his own management team, then there can be built into the original proposal the means by which he can sustain this image. For example, a buyer may be known to have a certain concession threshold which can be allowed for in the proposal.

The credibility of the selling company has been found to be a factor which can clinch a sale; hence the importance of a history of good relationships, particularly in connection with recent dealings. The credibility of the negotiator, if he has had prior contact, is another factor. If before the actual negotiation a climate of confidence has already been established by salesmen or other company officers, giving the impression of reliability, that too can affect the relative power situation.

Building in power

Apart from the protection of its own bargaining position which a buying or selling company achieves by defining its negotiating objectives and determining the level of first offer, there are forecastable events which can on occasion be harnessed to advantage. When tariffs are being, or are likely to be, dismantled over a period — Portugal and Spain's accession to the European Community are recent examples — it is possible for seller or buyer to take advantage of this if the other party is unaware of it. The decision as to whether or not this should be done is a question which relates to company values.

When Denmark joined the EC a Danish supplier of specialist electronic equipment elected to incur a penalty for delay in delivery to a German company because the cost of the penalty was less than the reduction in tariff which would be applicable as a result of the delayed delivery. The basis of the agreement was 'delivery to customer's factory', and therefore the responsibility for paying the tariff was the selling company's.

When a small US supplier quoted a large European electrical company in the European currency and was asked in negotiations to agree payment in dollars, he did so with alacrity. What the US supplier did not know was that the European company was in possession of currency fluctuation projections which indicated that over the period between agreement and payment there would be a considerable weakening of the dollar in relation to the European currency. Had the US company been in possession of this information, it would not have agreed to payment in dollars at the going rate at the time of contract. Its sales executives' perception of the European company's negotiating position would have been different, and therefore its expected outcome would also have been different. It would have wanted some share of the benefit to the European company by asking for a substantial concession in return.

When a supplier in the United Kingdom quoted in the currency of an overseas customer's country, he wished to protect himself from unforeseeable variations in the exchange rate. This he did by insisting on payment by a claused Bill of Exchange in which the stipulation was incorporated that variations from the agreed rate, namely the rate obtaining at the time a quotation was submitted, would be for the customer's account. This is particularly useful for a seller who does not wish to incur the possibility of loss due to an unfavourable shift in the exchange rates or, by implication, take advantage of a favourable one. Information is power, and thorough collection and analysis of all relevant information strengthens the negotiator's armoury.

GETTING TO THE NEGOTIATING TABLE

Availability of information

Given that the seller and the buyer have taken appropriate steps to identify target objectives for a sales/purchase interaction, have calculated their level of first offer and have taken requisite pre-negotiation action, there remains the problem of getting to the negotiating table. The showing of interest on the part of the buyer is no guarantee that the salesman or other company representatives nominated to negotiate a sale will get to the face-to-face situation where agreement can be reached. Adequate information has to be available to the seller as to the possibility of a successful sale.

When a British manufacturer with inadequate representation in Pakistan received an enquiry from that country for special filtration equipment, he followed up his quotation with a sales visit in which it was hoped to finalize a sale. His consternation was unbounded when he eventually found out that the reason for asking for the quotation was to establish whether a Soviet bloc country quotation for equipment to be supplied against a tied loan was value for money. There was no way in which a successful conclusion could have been reached. This is just a variation of the technique used by some buyers who look for a proposal from a salesman so that they can use it to exert pressure on a chosen supplier. In either case withdrawal at the earliest possible moment is the counter to it.

Quality of presentation

The vast majority of negotiations take place as the result of a bid or quotation being submitted by the supplier. In some cases there may be little or no discussion between the parties, either because an established course of dealing has eliminated problems over an extended period and developed trust, or the parties' countries are so distant geographically that face-to-face discussion is not readily possible.

If there is no barrier to communication and there is a great deal of power in the system — for example, where a major purchase is to be made in circumstances of considerable mutual experience and dependence — then it is certain that a tender/quotation/bid will be supplemented by discussion. Most conscientious buyers and sellers will in any case want to hold such discussions. Buyers will not necessarily see the same set of circumstances in the same way as the seller and will probably wish clarification on a number of issues; sellers will want to get close to buyers, particularly if their own case is not a strong one. It has been found that the stronger a party's case, the more likely is the outcome to be adjudged on the strength of the case if communications are kept formal (Morley and Stephenson 1977). If the case is weak then the strength of a buyer's position is weakened if the parties move closer together in an interpersonal relationship which is promoted by informal communications. Either way, the quality of the written presentation made to a potential buyer, plus the prior experience the buyer has had with the seller company and its salesmen, will be powerful factors in getting the seller to the table.

Influence channels

Different people within an organization will have different views on what ought to be done in relation to decisions that must be taken. Political processes have never been given the importance they deserve in the marketing and purchasing literature. In coming to a buying decision a much more subtle process takes place than is normally portrayed in the organizational buying behaviour literature; specific interest groups and coalitions develop and interact not only with other interest groups and coalitions within the organization, but also with external agencies such as consultants, suppliers and customers. Studies have varied from the circumstances giving rise to the first export order (Simmonds and Smith 1968) to a buyer purchasing a second generation computer for a department store (Pettigrew 1973).

Figure 8.1 shows some possible channels through which influence can be exerted to effect a meeting between buyer and seller.

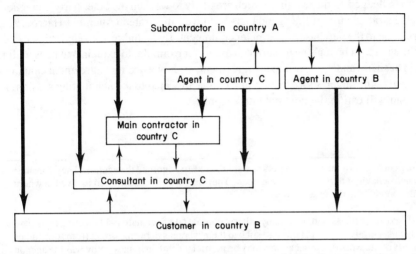

Figure 8.1   Channels of influence (heavy arrows) for a would-be subcontractor in country A for supply to a customer in a second country B, through a main contractor in a third country C to the specification of a consultant in country C.
Some coordination of the influencing processes could be expected via the subcontractor/agent relationships. This could possibly influence the ongoing customer/consultant or main contractor/consultant dialogue to effect a meeting.

FACE-TO-FACE

Negotiating rules for the meeting

While it is not the intention here to go into details of the physical components of bargaining structure, research shows it to be a variable affecting outcomes. Home teams tend to have an advantage, and there is a literature to support the view that bargaining on his own territory is likely to increase the assertiveness of, and the outcomes obtained by, the negotiator. Seating arrangements can affect proximity and bodily orientation, which in turn can affect the participant's reaction to a situation. There is, for example, some evidence to show that in certain competitive situations proximity and eye contact, which can be promoted by seating arrangements, can be stressful and should be avoided. Side-by-side or corner-to-corner seating tends to encourage cooperative relationships which would be discouraged by seating negotiators and opposers far apart or opposite each other. These physical factors form part of the situational influences on negotiating parties (see Figure 2.1).

Other rules which may help a party control negotiations can relate to such items as order of speaking, who may speak, making of telephone calls and eating times. If a negotiator feels these are against his interest, the best policy is to question why the rule was made.

Using the agenda to influence outcomes

Control over decisions is exercised by the negotiator who arranges the agenda, unless he is challenged on those points which are likely to weaken the other party's position. Such a strategic use of the agenda has been well illustrated (Auer and Harris 1981) in relation to the purchase of computer equipment. By including a ground rules section in the agenda, a buyer's negotiator can use it, for example, to explain that he is willing to do business and to enter into an agreement. If, however, that agreement cannot be reached to the buyer's satisfaction in the time allocated to the negotiating session, he can and will call in the next potential supplier.

In many parts of the world buyers and sellers like to negotiate the agenda. They consider such behaviour to be effective and open. They may well be discomfited in Sweden where the opposite is the case.

'Swedish businessmen, like many others, consider it efficient to hold meetings, prepare agendas in advance, and honest to stick to them whereas to businessmen from some other parts of the world their behaviour may be inefficient and dishonest. Why was the agenda prepared in such detail in advance? — It is inefficient to leave no room for initiative and creative ideas. Why did they insist on sticking so feverishly to it? They are obviously trying to impose their conditions on us, pull the wool over our eyes and leave no room for negotiation. It's dishonest. Why hold a meeting at all. We could have worked out these details together, once we had become friends.' (From Phillips Martinsson, 1981.)

An agenda can be used to 'position' a seller. It may require him to present his commitments. If at the end of negotiation the seller refuses to meet these commitments because of pressures exerted, he will be seen to be backing off from earlier commitments, and thus in a position of weakness.

French negotiators brought up in a bureaucratic, administrative tradition believe that negotiations should start with agreements in principle. Once these principles have been determined the conflict with regard to details can be fitted into the broad framework. Trade-offs become related to overall performance, rather than points of detail. Very similar is the approach in the People's Republic of China, in which the personal relationship and the underlying principles which the relationship cements are important. Negotiations with USSR officials are often characterized by agreement in principle in the first instance (Brislin 1982).

Step-by-step bargaining isolates high-risk issues and enables agreement to be achieved on low-risk issues. It gives the parties an overall flavour of the issues at stake and helps in the gradual building up of trust.

The negotiator must therefore be flexible to accommodate these different approaches, or combinations of them. He should, however, be aware of the differences between the two, for each has advantages and disadvantages. Whichever approach is adopted can influence the result. If he feels that the rules of negotiation shaped by the agenda seriously prejudice his interests, then he should challenge them.

> The order in which issues are negotiated can provide useful signals for negotiators.
>
> 'Suppose that suppliers have established from prior experience or pre-negotiation contact that potential purchasers put a premium on performance guarantees and that suppliers want to use their leverage on performance to lever out a better price. If they can arrange to have performance guarantees placed ahead of price on the agenda, then they can put up very strong resistance in discussion of the guarantees. After this resistance has been going on for some time they can suggest that it looks as though nothing can be done at this stage and so it might be better to return to the issue after price has been discussed. The implications are that if the customer gives on price, they might be prepared to give on performance guarantees.' (Adapted from MacMillan, 1978.)

Setting of time limits

When time limits are set on the negotiation at the outset, there is an implication that the higher the initial concession rate of either party in relation to time, the less advantageous bargain will the party obtain. If concessions are to be made at all these should be minimal. There is also the requirement that at some time before the expiry of the time period both parties should make some moves to identify a mutually acceptable outcome. Whether these moves are concessionary or a repetition of earlier offers will depend on the bargaining strengths of the parties. If the time period is not long enough because neither side has moved soon enough from their initial positions, the party with the weaker relative bargaining power will be exposed to the threat implied in the time limitation of accepting the other party's initial offer or run the risk of no bargain. Where the time limit is perceived by the weaker of the two parties, very often the seller, to be too short to reach agreement, because of difficulties of communication and the corresponding time taken up testing understanding, then he should try to negotiate a longer duration.

Time limits may be implicit, yet different, in the perceptions of the parties. In Japan, and to a degree in South Korea, the normal time for negotiating, from the viewpoint of the Western businessman, can be far exceeded. Understanding the system of consensus in Japan is a prerequisite for patience, and therefore for escaping the temptation to attribute delay to lack of interest or etiquette. In China the bureaucratic overlay on the social structure, which compels officials to procrastinate until a higher official sees himself as having the authority of a committee to communicate a decision downwards, is another factor counselling patience in the face of delays. Where price is the critical factor, as in negotiations with Eastern bloc countries and other countries short of the currency necessary for the import of specific equipment or materials, negotiations are frequently delayed in the hope of extracting price concessions. In these cases Western negotiators should be aware of the need to hold back a concession which may be needed to effect agreement.

There are occasions when the setting of time limits is to be avoided. In Arab countries to set a deadline for transactions is considered ill-mannered. In Ethiopia the time required for a decision to emerge is directly proportioned to its perceived importance.

DISTRIBUTIVE BARGAINING STAGE

Exploring the negotiating range

In taking up the extreme positions outlined in Chapter 2 in relation to those aspects of the negotiation about which they see themselves in conflict, buyers sometimes and sellers usually define these issues in advance. This is achieved by the submission of prior written proposals, usually those of the seller. Such proposals give buyers an opportunity to prepare their own plans with some knowledge of the line the seller intends to follow. These proposals do, in fact, help to define the agenda.

The kind of questions asked and statements made will be conditioned by attitudes created by prior knowledge the participants have of each other and experience of prior negotiations with their companies.

The language used will reflect these attitudes. Where the relationship has been characterized by mutual respect and the negotiating episodes by mutually satisfactory outcomes, the negotiator could be expected to make appropriate opening approaches. These might be aimed at reinforcing common business interests: 'How are your plans going for computerizing your stock control system?', or 'Have you made any further progress in the direction of continuous operation?'. Others might have the purpose of reinforcing the personal relationship, as in 'How is that boy of yours who had the motoring accident?' If the most recent transaction had not satisfied the buyer, he might say something like 'I must say at the outset that we can't have a repetition of your failure to delivery on schedule. I know you eventually made some recompense to us, but really I stuck my neck out on the grounds that you had never failed to deliver on time'.

Where there is no previous relationship, a seller might seek to uncover points of common interest. Where there is neither a history of relationship nor of dealings between the companies, questions will be directed to identifying strong commitments of the other party. Where social opportunity presents itself or is created, points of common interest can be established.

At the opening stage of the discussions, negotiator and opposer seek to explore the entire area covered by the negotiations through the taking up of their extreme positions, which include their hopes for outcomes plus the concession factors built into their first offer levels. The aim is to sound out the strength of the opposer's view on each point so that, later in the proceedings, it might be possible to assess the probability of the opposer sticking to his position under pressure.

Taking the initiative

The parties use tactics which are aimed at taking the initiative in the interaction. The negotiator examines the defences of his opposer by asking questions. When a buyer has analysed a seller's quotation or bid, he might well initiate the dialogue by trying to find out more about what appears to be a weak point by saying 'We have looked at your quotation, but before we go any further perhaps you can tell us more about how you have arrived at the increase in price compared with the last order?' Such a general question does not tell the seller anything about the buyer's actual views. Any general response could well provide the buyer with points which he can use as the focus of an attack. The seller will therefore wish to limit the scope of the buyer's probe. This he can do and at the same time get the buyer to reveal more about his own position by replying in such terms as 'I'm sorry if you feel the position isn't clear. I was under the impression we had stated it in our offer. It is certainly not our intention to confuse any issues. What is it exactly that is troubling you about our quotation?' Such a reply in the form of a question requires the buyer to be more specific and implies that he must be dissatisfied with some particular aspect of the quotations. The seller has regained the initiative for the time being.

Probing

As the stage proceeds suspected weak points are either exposed or explained. In the process of probing the issues become more specific and the language more pointed: 'Why have you lumped together the price of the vacuum pans and the filtration equipment?' or 'You have shown interest payable on the reducing balace at 13 per cent. What are the actual amounts we would be required to pay?'

The language is strongest as a weakness is found and an attack is mounted. If the buyer is sure of his facts he might ask a question in such a way that the seller can only answer 'Yes' or 'No': 'Our information from your competitors is that vacuum pans of the capacity quoted cost x Guilders. Do you really mean to tell us that the filtration equipment cannot be supplied for less than y Guilders?' or 'Are you saying that interest of 13 per cent represents the keenest rates you can offer?' If the buyer is uncertain of his facts, the language can be equally strong, but the question allows the respondent scope for an explanation: 'How can you justify such a price level when competitors can supply at as much as $120 less per case?'

The problem for the negotiator in these skirmishes is to identify if there is a gap between what his opposer says and what he is prepared to do. If the opposer's language is strong and simple, then there is a presumption that his commitment is considerable. The less ambiguity there is in his statements, the greater can his commitment to his position be taken to be.

When the parties have completed their exploration of the negotiation range, satisfied themselves that they know the extent of their differences, and identified the strength of the other's resistance on perceived key issues, they are in a position to envisage the form of the ultimate agreement.

Anticipating form of ultimate agreement

Where there is considerable overlap in the bargaining zone and a consequent narrow gap between his own and his opposer's position, the negotiator may be tempted to make proposals for an immediate settlement. There is a number of good reasons why he should not do so:

1 A proposal for final settlement will be seen as a move from the negotiator's level of first offer and could lead his opposer to prolong negotiations to see if he can

      get further concessions.

2 Businessmen like to see themselves as strong negotiators. Such self-image is best sustained where they feel they have had to work for their concessions.

3 A negotiator who makes an immediate final settlement proposal can only be disadvantaged, as has been cogently illustrated:

> 'Suppose that Party has made an initial offer of 100 to which Opponent has responded with a counter of 90. If asked separately their belief as to a settlement figure it is highly probable they would both reply 95. If Party makes an offer of 95, it is likely that Opponent . . . will respond with an offer to split the difference at 97.5.
>
>   On the other hand, if Party's first negotiating proposal is 92.5, to which Opponent responds with 97.5, thus establishing a pattern of mutual concessions, Party can then propose a further mutual concession of 2.5, so arriving at a final bargain of 95.'*

Where there is an overlap in the bargaining zone sufficient to maintain interest but insufficient for settlement without further negotiation and extension of the bargaining zone by cooperation or compromise, the negotiator should be able to identify the totality of individual elements which comprise the negotiating area. Different delivery conditions, for example, may be balanced against quantifiable items such as price and terms of payment, and non-quantifiable items such as warranty and liquidated damages which have to be estimated. The success of the negotiator arises as much from his preparation to anticipate and put a value on possible trade-offs before getting to the negotiation table, as on his ability to relate these to the overall position in the face-to-face situation. In this circumstance of a foreseeable bargain, much depends on the negotiator not only having the facility to estimate the worth of an overall bargain as it unfolds, but also having the firmness to reduce the aspirations of his opposer. He should in any case be in a position to revise any predictions he has made of the likely form of the final bargain and estimate the likely duration of the negotiation.

Where there is no overlap in the bargaining zone, the lowering of aspirations is of critical importance. Because the maximum the buyer will pay or the minimum the seller will settle for usually represents the limits of the negotiator's authority, lowering of aspirations cannot happen on the spot. If either of the parties is convinced that the degree of movement needed can be achieved, he may do this by negotiating with his own management for a revision of his authority which will facilitate this, or seek to get his opposer to obtain revised authority. To achieve this may entail the breaking off of negotiations if that is seen to be the only way to convince an opposer to change his mind. It is not unusual for a buyer, for example, to break off negotiations in order to influence the seller to reconsider his position, and at the same time to negotiate with his own management for revised authority.

* From P. D. V. Marsh, *Contract Negotiation Handbook,* Aldershot, Gower, 1984. Reproduced by permission of Gower Publishing Co.

Some cultural snares

While the negotiation skills model (Figure 2.4) has universal applicability, it has to be remembered that it is a conceptualization of the real thing. The classification into stages and the steps to effect movement between stages are means of drawing attention to the behaviours that are most appropriate at a given point in the negotiation. Users have to relate it to their own particular needs.

Where organizational structures permit the development of a close relationship between a salesman and a buyer, the parties can sometimes have such open communications that they can state their positions and move straight into the 'integrative bargaining' stage.

The hard-line 'distributive bargaining' stage is de-emphasized in many other cultural environments. In large areas of East Asia, which numbers one-third of mankind, there is a strong emphasis on relationships in the social structure. The same is true of the Arab countries where man is not analysable separately from these relationships. Indeed the view has been put forward that the Arab buyer often bases his buying decision on the personality of the salesman, rather than on the quality of the product (Muna 1980:30). Relationships are important for Latin Americans. No one rushes into business, but rather spends time in pleasantries which assist in the creation of a suitable climate for the interaction. Brazilian negotiators like relationships to be continuing ones and dislike opposers who are in their view over highly task-oriented. West Africans see friendship as an element of the business relationship. Indeed they tend to treat a foreigner's motive as suspect if they feel they are being hurried through negotiations without regard to the local custom. The Chinese have developed sensitive feelings of pride, the wounding of which, or the threat to which, controls conformity. It is the same pride which is the basis of so-called 'face'. Few Chinese feel comfortable when exposed to a situation of confrontation which carries with it the implication of loss of face.

The stage of distributive bargaining is therefore unimportant in relations with the Chinese. The integrative stage assumes for the Chinese a greater importance for the development of relationships and the assimilation of information which appears to be a prerequisite of the intuitive understanding of a particular issue. Likewise the Japanese, with a social structure supporting unequal vertical relationships, are reluctant to give offence by deed or word. By the same token they suffer discomfort where confrontation is threatened. Both Chinese and Japanese have a need for time to assimilate information and to come to the kind of consensus which typifies decision-making in these countries. Such tactics as trying to impose a time limit for the negotiation will place intolerable constraints on them. The use of strong language associated in the West with the early stages of bargaining can only make negotiation more difficult.

Arabs believe there is a market price for everything. The concept of the 'just price' is one to which they give ready acceptance. In consequence, any attempt to inflate the asking price to lower an Arab opposer's aspirations may well result in the Arab considering the proposal to be not serious. Because of the limitations of his own language he requires to exaggerate to be definite. 'No' may be a word which he uses in his negotiation dialogue, but unless it is used strongly and repeatedly it will not have the effect of a direct negative unless he has spent a longish period abroad or has otherwise learnt how to accommodate to Western cultures.

GETTING MOVEMENT

The dilemma of buyer and seller

Playing the strong negotiator can be overdone in that it can lead to deadlock. The purpose of being firm is to convince the opposer of the strength of the negotiator's commitment to the position he has taken up. If he is firm it is likely to make his opposer think again about his own estimate of success on the particular issue involved, and may possibly cause him to reduce his commitment to his own demands. If, on the other hand, the negotiator is compelled to withdraw from a position of extreme firmness in the face of an opposer's pressures, his loss of image will be carried forward to other issues and subsequent negotiations.

A buyer or seller therefore has to strike a balance between firmness and credibility, and has to define clearly for himself those issues on which he is resolved to remain firm. If he is successful in demonstrating the firmness of his position on these defined issues, his opposer is likely either to concede immediately or increase the value of any concession he makes in exchange. But bluffing in Western business cultures is frequently practised, and bluffs can be called. How does a buyer or seller extricate himself from a position on which he has been firm and from which he now wishes to withdraw without losing credibility as a negotiator? If a concession is contemplated it may be stifled by fear that there will be no reciprocation, and the negotiator's position is weakened in consequence.

Sending and receiving signals

To get out of this impasse skilled buyers and sellers in negotiation give signals to convey that they are prepared to move from the initial stances they have taken up. Equally an experienced negotiator can always pick out inflexions in speech, variations in pitch and stress and non-verbal accompaniments which emphasize key words indicating movement in the other's position, and actions arising out of the negotiation itself. He is attentive to cues and signals coming from his opposer. Negotiators who have wide experience of each other can often develop their own conventions which can go unnoticed by outside observers. When an opposer's style is known, for example, to be one in which he makes only a slight move from a declared position, then the negotiator can interpret the moves with greater accuracy and make appropriate responses. But not all negotiators behave so consistently. In these circumstances the possibility of making a mistake is introduced because of misinterpretation of the situation.

One of the problems a sales/purchase negotiator faces is when to make the move. Both parties will not necessarily have taken stock of the negotiation range at the same time, for the reason that they may have different negotiating styles. A negotiator may be competitive in his style and dominant in his manner, giving little away by way of information and trying to get his opposer to accede to his demands. Without any commitment on his part to moving towards the opposer, he may start with the most important concession he wants and work through his points to the least important seeking agreement on each point in turn. This problem can be compounded when the negotiator is of higher status, for he will tend to behave exploitatively. The counter to this is either to be non-committal or to ask directly for the complete requirements of the other party on the grounds that it is only when the overall position is known that a reasoned judgment can be made. The over-demand can be emphasized as in 'Let's summarize what you are asking for'.

Conditional movement

It is only when both parties are satisfied they know the extent of the issues over which they are in conflict that they can, with confidence, get down to the question of getting movement. The essence of the signal is that it should convey intention without committing the speaker. It may be to indicate disagreement with an issue. A buyer might say 'We can't see our way to agreeing to what you are proposing *as it stands*'. This is an invitation from the buyer to the seller to respond by enquiring what kinds of amendments would be needed to make his proposals acceptable.

The ensuing enquiry might result in further information being conveyed: 'My company would be much happier if we could *get the price down to the level of the last order*'. A seller might reply to this: 'As I think you will know, we have already provided trade discount on the quoted price. We don't *normally* negotiate below the discounted price'. The buyer might react by: 'Can you help me? Perhaps you can suggest how I might go back to my management *with a lower price*'. This is the opening that the seller can take advantage of in order to try to balance the effect of the buyer's pressure: '*If you were prepared* to place an order on a regular basis, *we might consider* a reduction'. The possibility of agreement has been created without the parties yet committing themselves.

Where one of the parties has a different culture, language or political ideology, then the time taken is likely to be much longer. Cues are likely to be much more specific, unless one of the parties is skilled in the culture of the other. Where a specific one is needed this can often be indicated by conceding a 'straw issue'. Signalling by means of third-party case histories can be often employed as a means of conveying possible movement without commitment.

An example of signalling behaviour at the stage of negotiating the agenda is given at p. 191 where hints of a concession have been made but no promises have in fact been given.

INTEGRATIVE BARGAINING STAGE

Testing commitment to issues

Once movement has been initiated, both seller and buyer can apply themselves to ensuring that the commitment to the issues that matter most to them is maintained. By the same token they will seek to establish just how firm the commitment of the other party is on these particular issues.

Further information is sought on issues to probe further the other's commitment to them: 'How reliable are your new drive motors in high ambient temperatures?' Here the buyer is asking an apparently innocuous question. If the reply is a general one about the high quality, a supplementary question might be asked: 'Have you had any problems with them in installations similar to ours?' The question is now more specific. If the questioner possesses information about problems at such installations, then the question is loaded. It is designed to force an admission.

A wise seller would assume knowledge by the buyer and perhaps turn it to advantage by demonstrating a cooperative and open attitude: 'We did have problems at the plant of X Company. That was a fabrication problem which we have now overcome'. He might go on to emphasize the lengths to which his company had gone to resolve the problems, so demonstrating commitment to the customer's interest: 'The problem was one of breaking rotor bars which tore the windings of the stators. What we did was re-check our designs and ask the National Engineering Laboratories to perform a similar exercise in parallel. Having confirmed that there was no design fault, we then checked our construction methods and found that a new machine being used to fit the rotor bars to the rings was leaving a certain play in operation which led to breakdown. Our current methods positively preclude this'. The seller's position may have been slightly weakened, but nothing like the extent to which is would have been had he denied the existence of a problem.

In that case the buyer might have come back: 'Do you deny that you have had problems at X Company?' The question is now a pointed one, framed in a way that requires a simple 'Yes' or 'No' as an answer. These are perhaps the words which best show how great the commitment is. The buyer was reasonably sure, or should have been, before putting the question in that way, of the answer he was going to receive. From a position in which he was seeking information he has moved to a position where he has forced an admission, and is now poised to use this to exact a concession: 'In our business down-time of any equipment is revenue lost. You are asking us to pay these prices for equipment which we would have to take largely on trust?'

If the seller in the above exchange denies that a problem exists or has existed until recently, he loses credibility as a negotiator on this and any other issues in conflict. He has been caught out because of the information possessed by the buyer and his bargaining position has been weakened. All things being equal, he cannot expect to obtain the overall outcome he had been hoping for if the buyer now follows up and extracts a concession. On the other hand, if the buyer's information is erroneous or out-of-date, then the seller can use that to illustrate the kind of service his company provides. Alternatively, the buyer's actions could have been intended to confirm a position which he found generally acceptable.

Relative strength of commitment and concession rates

If, in the foregoing example, the seller concedes more or faster than the buyer had expected, this has to mean that the concessions the seller will make will be even greater. The buyer takes this as an indication that he should increase his objectives for the meeting in line with the maximum he now perceives the seller is likely to concede. The higher the initial rate of concession of either party in relation to time, the less favourable the bargain he will obtain (Bass 1966).

The lesson to be drawn from this is that negotiators should make only token concessions, or none at all, in the early stages. The weaker of the parties is the one with more to lose if the end result is no bargain.

When one party is in a position of weakness he will hope to create a better climate for negotiation of major issues by first negotiating agreement on those issues which are peripheral to the overall outcome. By progressive agreement on minor points he hopes to build up trust, which will facilitate and perhaps create a greater possibility of agreement on major issues. At the same time he will attempt to have the communication medium as informal as possible. In these circumstances negotiators are in a face-to-face problem-solving situation in which it is less easy for the stronger party to maintain his hard line and refuse concessions. In such eventualities the negotiators would be chosen for their existing relationships with opposers (Morley and Stephenson 1977).

Conversely, where a negotiator is in a strong negotiating position, he can prevent that position from being undermined by keeping a social distance between himself and his opposer, or by introducing someone more senior to the proceedings.

Development of the interaction

The negotiation progressively seeks to separate out those issues on which the parties are obdurate and those on which they are prepared to concede provided there is the equivalent conceded in the eventual overall package agreed.

It may not be possible to find concessions of equal worth on individual issues, but the possibility of equivalence of concessions is enhanced by relating them to the overall agreement. This means that the negotiator will continue to try to influence the issues by argument, emotion and by the exercise of the range of interpersonal skills which involve the shaping of predictable reactions as outlined in Chapter 3. The attempt to reduce the opposer's level of aspiration is not confined to the stage of distributive bargaining and the levels of first offer. At the same time he will wish to ensure that, as far as he possibly can, his own position on any issues is not eroded. To that extent he can attempt to persuade his opposer to give away as much information as possible by compelling him to go on talking and possibly weaken any claimed resistance points.

The more simple and direct the language, the stronger is the commitment of an opposer likely to be. In Western Europe and the USA in particular, the more precisely a position is defined, the stronger is the definer's commitment likely to be to it. If an Arab opposer behaves like an American or West European, he would either be attuned to the Western culture or his commitment is not great. Elaboration is a necessary adjustment of the Arabs to the spoken word because it lends emphasis to a statement which cannot otherwise be taken at its face value. A Japanese is likely to be characterized by ambiguous statements, for the reason that his social structure is such that logical argument, as we know it in the West, is not exercised. Because the steps of reasoning which Westerners use — namely thesis, antithesis and synthesis — are unfamiliar in Japan, such concepts are difficult for the Japanese to handle. To be given effect, the logical process or dialectic requires equality and confrontation, neither of which is supported by the vertical structure of Japanese society (Nakane 1973).

If a public statement is made in the West it is more binding than a private statement. In Japan, on the other hand, openness of communication is the norm, the Japanese tending to eschew all dissimulation and to value highly sincerity in relationships, although openness is not exercised to the extent that offence might be taken. It is therefore incumbent on the negotiator to avoid transferring the norms of his own society to the interpretation of the words and actions of an opposer of a different national, cultural and linguistic background.

Maintaining flexibility

In the face of suggestions, proposals and counter-proposals, requests for further information and clarification, disagreeing and supportive behaviour, all of which can lead to isolation of issues not immediately soluble, the negotiator would do well to maintain his flexibility of action. This he does by keeping issues linked. If he makes concessions on the way, they should not be such that they leave him concessionless when the final agreement is in view.

Sometimes the element of surprise is introduced. For people who rely on preparation of a particular approach as the touchstone of negotiation performance, the element of surprise can create distrust and fear. Sometimes it is introduced deliberately, as in the example given above where the buyer was privy to information the seller elected not to disclose. This can be unhelpful to relationships where breach of the implied obligations in the relationship might be perceived, although this might not be important where little likelihood of repeat business exists.

Sometimes it can arise from lack of knowledge of another culture and the institutions and commercial customs that exist in it. A German company, noted for its thoroughness but not its flexibility, found it difficult to cope with a Mexican commodity processor who, to overcome difficulties in payment, proposed a *cesión de centavos* whereby the association which marketed the processed commodity, both locally and abroad, guaranteed payment on a basis of so many centavos for each kilo of the commodity sold to the association. Such an arrangement was not within the experience of the German company and its credit insurers. The Germans prevaricated so much that the Mexicans eventually withdrew from the negotiations, which were re-opened with an American company which found the arrangement a very profitable one.

Flexibility is only as good as the terms of reference which a seller or buyer, a sales or purchasing team, has negotiated with its own management, and the quality of the communications between them when reporting back for support activity or revised authority. A quick turn-round of information or speedy decisions are absolutely necessary to maintain the salesman's or buyer's position in the negotiation.

Commitment and constraints

Constraints on flexibility are imposed by overriding opposer commitments with which the negotiator has no option but to comply. These can arise from various kinds of authority. In most Arab countries and a number of developing countries, the law that applies to a contract is the local law, that is the law of the country where it is to be performed. A negotiator has no alternative but to accept its authority if he wishes to continue his negotiations.

Sometimes government regulations have to be complied with — as in Turkey in recent years where payment conditions have been cash against documents, but the Turkish organization dealing with an overseas supplier has had no control over the delayed release of foreign exchange to make payment.

At other times standard procedures of the firm bind its negotiators to them. If a negotiator wants them changed, then the opposer has to obtain the approval of someone at a higher level in the organizational hierarchy before any agreement to the negotiator's proposals can be given. In these circumstances the negotiator is likely to be reluctant to ask for the approval of a Head Office or Managing Director, for fear of the order going to a competitor who is prepared to go along with the procedure concerned.

It has already been shown that previous dealings can have an effect on negotiation outcomes. Where there is a departure from terms agreed on previous occasions, this might show one's opposer as weaker than others who had been involved in earlier agreements. It is therefore up to the negotiator to provide his opposer with cogent reasons to justify to his management acceptance of the negotiator's arguments.

In defence of his position a negotiator can plead limited authority. One of the difficulties confronting high-level negotiators is that, while there is more discretion which they can exercise, they are less able to appeal to limited authority as a source of bargaining power. A buyer who cannot approve an order over a certain value, or a salesman who does not have the authority to vary terms, is more difficult to deal with than someone who has. Restrictions on authority — like budget limits, credit limits, cash discount limits, house rules against divulging costs, fair trading laws, specification changes — all give their user negotiation strength. Like any strength, if it is played too hard it may result in no bargain. Used with judgment, authority limits provide the negotiator with a face-saving way of testing the firmness of an opposer's stance and provide him with a face-saving way of giving in. The Chinese, because of their bureaucratic need to diffuse responsibility, and social need to avoid loss of face, use such behaviours widely, and the Russians often use it deliberately to exert pressure for price concessions because of their need to conserve their hard currency earnings as far as they can.

There are markets and occasions when the sales negotiator, or at least the chief sales negotiator where there is a team, is expected to be of sufficient seniority to undertake the complete negotiations on his own authority — for example, when treating with high officials in a government buying organization. When officials of foreign trade organizations in planned economy countries decide that a purchase is to be made, the sales negotiator who has to telephone home for further instructions or extended authority should never have made the journey.

The interpersonal dimension

Interaction between individuals is a key factor in determining negotiation outcomes. Each party can only learn from the other as much as the other conveys deliberately or unknowingly. In the last analysis the negotiator can only make assumptions about an opposer's preferences and expectations, both for his company and for himself. An important function of negotiation is to test those assumptions. An opposer's real intentions can only be uncovered by a process of vigorous probing, because he himself may be only vaguely aware of them.

By the time the integrative stage has been arrived at the negotiator has an idea of his opposer's style of behaviour — whether he is cooperative or competitive in his approach. If he wishes, he can try out a cooperative behaviour, as when he makes a token concession to see the kind of response he gets. Cooperation tends to beget cooperation. If the negotiator finds that his opposer intends to be competitive in his behaviour, he can adopt appropriate behaviour. This has sometimes been observed to be a mixture of cooperative and aggressive behaviours. Most negotiators strive for greater gain. This is apparently not the case with Koreans. Seemingly they will not cooperate. Depriving the opposer would appear to be more important in contrast to attitudes in Western culture (Webber 1977).

The effect on the negotiation of competitive behaviour will be hard bargaining by the parties to share the settlement range between them. The better bargainer or stronger party will get more at the expense of the other. Cooperative behaviour between buyer and seller lends itself to the problem-solving process in which each understands the problems of the other. The assumption is that both can benefit from the process. If a seller's data-processing system is geared to providing data on a monthly basis, a buyer might well accommodate to that, although his normal procedures might require more frequent reports. If a buyer is concerned with the supply of key parts for his own product, a seller can often find a solution by providing higher stockholding facilities or advantageous credit terms not covered in his proposal because he did not know the problem. It does not mean there are no conflict issues, merely that these are handled by a different mode of behaviour. Such an approach requires behaviour consistent with the trust implied. If there is any perceived violation of that trust, this can be accompanied by a sharp decrease in joint outcomes.

Behaviours which are acceptable at the distributive stage may be entirely unacceptable as the integrative stage progresses. By the time the integrative stage has developed, negotiators have committed themselves to courses of action. They have divulged deliberately or otherwise more and more of their hands and probably become more truthful. A return to the situation of hard talk and attacking language by one of the parties can be perceived by the other as a breach of form. Outright disagreement is replaced by language which is less pointed, often taking the form of an explanation leading to a statement of disagreement in the least contentious terms: 'Yes, but because of our commitment to our Financial Authority which requires us to have a downpayment of 10 per cent of the contract value, we are not in a position to accept your terms in that form'.

This is more the kind of behaviour which is suited to dealing at all stages with Chinese and Japanese, not the kind of language which seeks maximum commitment in terms of 'Yes' or 'No'. Gentle pressure in terms of flattery might seem normal behaviour to an Arab.

The kinds of shaping behaviours discussed in Chapter 3 may be used to influence the opposer's reactions. If the negotiator finds that his opposer is, in his view, making unfair demands of him, he may make appeal to some form of legitimate power or moral rules related to social norms of equity, equality, need, opportunities, equal concessions and historical precedent (Magenau and Pruitt 1979). Such appeals are emotional and may have some effect if the interpersonal relationship is a close one.

Eventually, the number of issues in conflict is reduced and the remaining ones are those on which agreement will now have to be sought. Issues on which agreement is made are usually checked out for ambiguity, before proceeding to those which are outstanding.

BARGAINING AWAY THE UNACCEPTABLE

Narrowing the gap

Once commitments have been demonstrated and tested, trading-off may begin on terms which will provide each side with the satisfaction that they have achieved their objectives, while giving recognition at the same time to the other's view. A seller might agree to a shortened delivery period provided the buying company agrees to make available by an earlier date site drawings which would enable engineering and manufacture to proceed. Thus the gap is gradually narrowed, and further movement can only take place when the parties identify and reach the ultimate bargain.

Muslims might well be prepared more than others to make concessions on aspects of warranties or safety. This derives from the concept of fair dealing inherent in the faith which is strong and often mistakenly dubbed as fatalism.

Price and worth

In order to come to his ultimate bargain the negotiator has first to ensure that any minor issues on which agreement has been reached have resulted from reasonably equitable bargaining. It is in the overall bargain that equitability can be perceived, subject to the relative negotiating power of the parties. If the negotiator has not agreed on all minor issues, but has decided that they should be part of an overall package, then the judgment has to be made on the spot.

Such approaches to the negotiation hang on earlier preparation, both in relation to costs of possible trade-offs and the communication arrangements between the negotiators and their managements for quick handling of queries on such items as delivery and specification amendments. A good negotiator has those facts at his fingertips. Without them he can only guess. If his opposer seems to prefer to agree to a reduced quality or minimal packaging, or to provide his own electric cable or to prefer FOB delivery to CIF, then the negotiator has to know exactly the implications for his company.

Some elements which are traded-off are worth less than, or more than, any figure determined by an accounting convention. If a seller is less interested in immediate profit than in a long-range goal — like establishing a foothold in a market of considerable growth potential — then he may be prepared to trade it off for a value much less than cost. If a buyer in Germany urgently requires a part costing DM5000 for a process producing a single product, and a week's delay costs DM50,000 he might feel justified in paying up to ten times the cost of the product if he could save a week's production. The seller might realize he could capitalize on such a possibility, but that would be at a cost of any long-term relationship that had been built up. Nevertheless, in any assessment he made of its worth in relation to an overall settlement, he might just calculate it at something in excess of the going rate.

The problem of setting a value on concessions is made more difficult by the fact that some aspects of a concession are not measurable directly in money terms. There is the element represented by such factors as performance, delivery and arbitration in which there will only be a financial element should the contingency happen. What is the value that is to be put on these risks in the trade-off situation? With liquidated damages, for example, these should 'bite into the potential profits of the seller' to encourage him to maintain promised delivery or performance. But if the rates normally used are 3 per cent per month up to 15 per cent or more, and what is asked is well in excess of what is normal, then this combined with the probability of liquidated damages being incurred may raise the monetary equivalent value.

There has also to be an awareness of what value the opposing party puts on its non-quantifiable factors. A Saudi buyer will tend to put high value on contract disputes being determined by local courts, and will resist strongly arbitration either in the seller's country or under the rules of the International Chamber of Commerce. A buyer from an organization in a developing country may be adamant in maintaining a resistance on political grounds to indemnifying the seller against patent infringement stemming from the buyer's instructions. Japanese buyers may have good sociological reasons for holding to an outcome which is more likely to increase their turnover than their profitability.

Trading-off

Time is not a function of the bargaining process. It is not at all unusual in commercial negotiations for limits to be placed on the time available. This can arise from rules agreed before the negotiation starts, or from a time framework which one of the parties imposes in the course of bargaining. A buyer may so limit the duration, possibly issuing a statement of the terms on which he wants agreement.

At some time before any deadline both seller and buyer should make a series of moves so that the exact nature of the ultimate bargain can be identified. If one of the parties is in a position of relative power advantage, he may repeat earlier offers. Where there is more balance to the relative power, and hence the possibility of more effective bargaining, concessionary moves may be made by seller and buyer to bridge the remaining issues which separate them. The more even this balance, the later they can leave it before making their moves. Seller and buyer will both know that the other prefers agreement to no bargain, and that sooner or later they will come to terms. If the move to bridge the issues is made too late in relation to the time available, the weaker of the parties will have failed to achieve compromise and will be left with the alternative of accepting the other's offer or failing to agree. If the move is made too early this could be interpreted by the other party as a sign of weakness and encourage him to seek further concessions, so reducing the possibility of agreement.

Neither buyer nor seller knows exactly how far he can maximize his advantages. A negotiator can only make assumptions about an opposer's preferences, expectations and goals. It is the testing of these assumptions that is an important function of negotiation, and the interpretation made will vary with the experience and perception of the tester.

There are, therefore, two forces at work on the seller and the buyer. One is the esteem motivation that drives them to strike the best possible bargain and provide the satisfaction of a job well done, perhaps establishing a precedent for future negotiations. The other is the security motivation to settle when a reasonable bargain is identified, rather than seek a more advantageous outcome at the possible risk of the loss of agreement.

It is against this background that buyers and sellers convey to each other, by the moves and counter-moves they made, how they see a resolution of the differences. This is the time when they have to bring together all those items which they have promised to 'consider', 'bear in mind', 'take account of' — and all the other phrases used when waiting to establish the full negotiating range before making a commitment on issues — and put forward a package for consideration of the other party.

At this point it is important to see with what commitment an opposer makes his moves and how he responds to those of the negotiator. He may put forward a proposed solution and show absolute support for the position he has taken up by putting papers in order or sitting back with arms folded when a countermove is being put forward. There is a need on both sides to communicate the true position in the later stages without deception. To this end negotiators have developed certain words, expressions and gestures which convey this. Tone of voice may be one of complete finality and the words, those which indicate the absence of bluff, such as 'That is the best I can do. Now it's up to you'. If his proposals have no loose ends, that reinforces the finality.

In Western cultures the negotiator may look his opposer straight in the eye as he speaks and treat the statement with a corresponding seriousness. His language is likely to be terse and to the point, confirming the finality. He may, during a break, have signalled his intentions by treating his opposer with a greater degree of familiarity, using a cordial mode of speech, referring to mutual links or indulging in other forms of intimate behaviour. But perhaps the most convincing of these parallel indications of pending agreement is repetition of an offer with no apparent fall-back position. His opposer is then in a position to know that he has gone about as far as he is willing to go, for he has signalled that he is now willing to risk no bargain. The opposer may reassure himself by summarizing what the other has told him in order to ascertain that he has a correct understanding of what has been said.

206

In Eastern cultures signals may not be so apparent. One authority has reported that Chinese negotiators never telegraph their next move through a show of emotions. The level of friendliness or impersonality remains the same whether negotiations are approaching agreement or failure. Consequently there seems to be a considerable element of surprise in negotiating with the Chinese (Pye 1982).

Face-saving

It is often at this stage that an opposer's obduracy over an apparently straight-forward or simple issue is an indication that for him the issue is an important one. Marsh gives the following example:

> 'An exporter had been arguing with an overseas buyer that acceptance of certain high technology equipment should be at the exporter's works; the buyer had been arguing that he only ever accepted goods on delivery to site. There were three remote sites involved.
> 'The exporter finally proposed provisional acceptance at his works and final acceptance at the buyer's central depot, with the buyer having the right only to repeat the exporter's factory tests according to the exporters tests procedures and specifications. If the tests were not carried out within thirty days of the equipment's arrival at the depot, acceptance would be deemed to have been given.
> 'The proposal was accepted by the negotiator for the buyer although he knew they had no intention of carrying out tests, since to do so would have meant purchasing additional and expensive test equipment. However, the proposal satisfied the negotiator's aspiration level in that:
>
> 1 it appeared on paper to be an improvement of the exporter's original proposal;
> 2 it retained the principal of final acceptance only being given after the equipment had been delivered to the buyer's country;
> 3 it satisfied the objection of the buyer's legal department since it followed closely enough past precedents for other contracts. (They were of course unaware that the right existed only on paper and the negotiator for the buyer had no intention of telling them.)' *

Where an opposer has agreed to reconsider his position on an issue holding up agreement, it is a sensible tactic to seek an adjournment on any pretext to enable him to contact his management should he be at the limit of his authority. Equally, it is unrealistic to expect concessions across the table from negotiators in societies where consensus decision-making is the norm and/or bureaucratic structures prevent this, as in the People's Republic of China. Therefore adjournment again is an appropriate tactic to enable normal negotiation processes to go on.

* From P. D. V. Marsh, *Contract Negotiation Handbook,* Aldershot, Gower, 1984. Reproduced by permission of Gower Publishing Co.

'The Japanese like to use a "let us consider this" approach. In contrast, the US management style is typically "All right, give me three alternatives and I will choose among them today". This difference could be attributed to the Japanese preference for avoiding direct confrontation and saving face. Through the "let us consider it" approach, the Japanese would not have to reject a proposal outright, and thus could save the face of everybody concerned.' (T.J. Bacher, quoted in Tung 1984).

DECISION-MAKING AND ACTION STAGE

Assessing what is acceptable

The moves and countermoves of the buyer and seller have now reduced the area of conflict to the point where they are in a position to assess the possibilities of early agreement. These moves and countermoves have also drawn the parameters describing available possibilities. The parties seek to evaluate all these factors bearing on the outcome and now have to make a judgment of what is or is not acceptable. One or the other will put forward his proposal for the final bargin. This will normally be in the form of a package because issues have been kept linked while all the issues on which there would be conflict have been established. In major sales/purchase agreements which are characterized by some complexity, more than one package may be proposed.

The bringing of a negotiation to a conclusion can be tried by summarizing the position. This may be a recapitulation of the concessions exchanged and proposals made which a weaker party might accept in their totality. Often it is achieved by means of a final concession. Its magnitude should be sufficient in that it is not considered trivial, but small enough to convince an opposer that it represents the negotiator's last word. The negotiator wants a response from his opposer, and usually indicates as much in the course of making the concession, for he wants to make sure that the final concession is linked to a concession on the part of the opposer. He can signal to his opposer by various means that he expects some reciprocation: 'I think we may be able to accommodate you on your proposal for payment provided you are prepared to accept our standard model of motor'. Such phrases as 'I think we may be able to accommodate . . .' or 'I don't see much difficulty in . . .' have come to be standard signals for conveying that the negotiator is willing to come to an agreement provided there is reciprocal concession.

Testing understanding

Perceptions of an agreement can differ with the parties to it. It is important that the interpreted meaning of the proposals for final agreement are identical to the intention of the proposer. Difference in terminology, even within the same language, can lead to misunderstanding. The American term FOB is different from the definition of FOB given by the International Chamber of Commerce, to which most of the rest of the industrialized world subscribes. Differences between languages and the cultures they reflect can contribute to misunderstandings. East Asians are more concerned with the spirit of an agreement than with its observation to the letter, which is more or less the view in many Western countries and which is evidenced at its extreme in France although that may well be changing. It is therefore of the essence that every effort is made to ensure that the parties do not leave the negotiating table with differing ideas of what they believe they have agreed. Failure to test understanding is a recipe for further negotiations arising from differing interpretations of the agreement.

The French will not regard a deal as valid unless it has been drawn up in meticulous legal detail.

'They have little understanding of the British "gentleman's agreement" since each party to a deal fears, as one manager put it, "that the other will slyly introduce a fatal comma". But, having codified their elaborate agreement, their attitude to it then is very ambivalent. They will continually refer back to these written texts: but they will also feel the need to keep on questioning them or re-interpreting them, or finding ways of getting round them. The British are content with a much simpler set of rules which they then stick to without worrying: it is all the difference between a nation with a strict written constitution and one with none at all. So in France there are always two sets of rules, the written ones and the real ones. It is a system that is workable in practice and it is not nearly as dishonest as it sounds. However, this byzantine legalism is now increasingly contested by a younger generation. In recent years the old legalistc spirit has been gently in decline, as the new pragmatic values have gained ground. The lawyer, whose prestige in France used to be paramount, has been losing position to the planner and technocrat; and it is significant that ENA (the influential postgraduate civil service college) puts more emphasis on economics rather than law, whereas older generations of public executives received an essentially law-based training. A new generation, especially the élites adopting American techniques, is moving to a new approach: but it is not easy, for the actual texts and regulations that govern French life have not been sufficiently altered.' (John Ardagh in *France in the 1980's,* Penguin Books, Harmondsworth, 1982. Reprinted by permission of Martin Secker & Warburg Limited.)

Memorandum of agreement

'Memorandum of agreement' is a common term for the recorded bargain. Very often it takes the form of notes of the discussion, prepared by one side and presented to the other side for approval and initialling when the negotiations are complete.

The negotiator who records the agreement can interpret meanings and shape the phrasing to reflect the understanding as checked by him. The memorandum emphasizes intent rather than the special language of lawyers. If it is written by the other party, the negotiator would be wise to rewrite the wording as he sees it and get agreement on that. It is usually qualified as 'subject to contract'.

Sometimes in protracted negotiations one side keeps a note of the discussions of the day, and these are considered as the first item on the agenda on the following day. Sometimes these minutes can be manipulated, or at the very best written according to the perceptions of the party writing them; and they have to be examined and, if necessary, challenged prior to a resumption of negotiations. This is a bureaucratic device sometimes used in East European countries.

When negotiations are concerned with the clauses, specifications, payment terms and special conditions of a complete contract, as in negotiations with the Communist bloc countries, the negotiator has to have a facility for legal-type drafting in order to influence the final version in the way which has been agreed. Some large firms may have lawyers who are involved in the negotiations. Nevertheless it is businessmen in their capacities as customers and suppliers who have to negotiate these agreements within legal frameworks.

GOVERNMENTS AND GOVERNMENT SPONSORED AGENCIES

Negotiating with government departments

When a seller negotiates with a government contracts or purchasing officer he has an opposer who operates against a background of decision rules which differ in many ways from those of the buyer in private business. These differences have important implications for sellers.

Pre-negotiation stage

At the stage which precedes the face-to-face interaction, environment and situational factors have a number of characteristics which differentiate them from normal commercial negotiations. 'Value for money' is the principal criterion in deciding to whom a contract should be awarded. This rule arises from political pressures which require that officials should be accountable for the actions they take which bear on the public purse. Price is not, therefore, an overriding factor. It will certainly be of prime significance for government stores or stock items in small contracts when a discount appropriate to the volume of purchases may be negotiated. Often more important are procurement considerations which stem from the implementation of government policy. A particular firm may be awarded a contract because the government wishes to maintain that firm's capacity for government work, or to maintain competition, or to provide a base for development of the export market for a product, assist the balance of payments situation, or promote other policy objectives such as keeping down overheads on future contracts.

Work at the preparatory stage will be dictated by the kind of contract envisaged. This will normally be either by competitive tender or by negotiated contract. Competition by tender may from time to time resemble the process of simultaneous negotiation with several firms. By the same token, where a negotiated contract is intended, governments may seek to introduce an element of competition by negotiating independently with prospective suppliers. The kinds of situation which would indicate a negotiated contract rather than a competitive tender might be associated with national security as in defence contracts, urgency as in computerizing departmental procedures or in coping with some emergency, or in research and development contracts where the specification may be too imprecise for competitive tender.

Price negotiation is restricted by a number of factors. The evolved philosophy of a 'fair and reasonable price' is subscribed to by most governments as a basic tenet of any settlement. A contract may be made but provide for future agreement on price, with provision for arbitration in the event of failure to agree. Sometimes government

210

departments have special arrangements with associations of suppliers or with groups of suppliers.

The implications of these differences for pre-negotiation activities are far-reaching. The level of first offer which one might expect to set in a private negotiated contract, is constrained by the procedures, methods, rules and different kinds of contracts to which the government negotiator is tied.

Getting to the negotiating table

A high quality of presentation to obtain an invitation to negotiate is a normal objective in commercial sector negotiations. In negotiating with governments the implementation of selective competitive tendering is usual. Firms on approved lists are deemed to have the experience, capability and financial standing to satisfy government requirements. This promotes closer relationships and transcends the individual contract.

The quality of the presentation in negotiating with government should not be confined to the present business. There will be no present business unless a company's strategy is to get on an approved list, whether that is a list which is available to the public, or can be inferred from the actions of the buyer. One of the ways by which suppliers become acceptable to Russian and Chinese buyers, apart from their record, is first to exhibit at the Moscow or Peking Fairs, perhaps followed by presentations at technical seminars. Other countries may have other criteria by which they adjudge the commitment and capability of would-be suppliers. Very often a demonstration of good faith and commitment is required in the form of a bid bond convertible to a performance bond when the tenderer wins a contract.

Distributive bargaining stage

This stage is usually used by the parties to explore the negotiating range and establish the limits of their offers and demands. In government negotiating the measure of profit is normally known, either as a given amount or as a margin over cost. What becomes more important is the nature of the costs which may present greater opportunities for reducing expenditure than profits. These may well involve discussions at the pre-negotiation stage. Because a relationship is being or has been established by the nature of government contracting, the cooperative mode is particularly relevant to this activity. While there will tend always to be conflicts for resolution, these can be resolved within a cooperative framework. In negotiations with government this stage is de-emphasized and moves readily into the integrative bargaining stage.

Moving from entrenched positions

Because of the cooperative mode induced by government procurement principles and procedures, the extreme positions often evident in negotiations between commercial firms are not taken up. Image loss is largely avoided, and position loss does not happen because profit margins are largely predetermined.

Integrative bargaining stage

One of the skills in commercial negotiations is maintaining flexibility by keeping issues linked in the face of proposals and counter-proposals. Because government purchasing is circumscribed by rules and procedures which reduce the need for such proposals to bridge the gap between opposing viewpoints, flexibility is not a question of keeping linked issues like specification, delivery, price and service levels. These all relate to the settlement price and the estimated profit margins achieved. As profit margins are established by formulae in the main, these will vary with the type of contract entered into.

In addition to fixed-price contracts, which most government organizations like to agree for small-value and short-term contracts and contracts entered into at a price to be agreed, there are also cost-plus, fixed-fee and cost-plus-percentage-of-cost contracts. Further refinements are cost-plus-incentive contracts which seek to dampen down the tendency for costs to increase in cost-plus contracts; there are maximum-price contracts which set limits on eventual contract price and encourage contractors to keep prices under control; there are also target-cost contracts which provide financial incentives to reduce costs below target.

In commercial transactions the essence of negotiating strategy is to elicit information from the other party which can be used to obtain a more advantageous outcome. In government negotiations, openness of communications and the willing divulgence of information are key inputs to the relationship. If the public interest requires emphasis on costs and their control, this must be so. The principle of equality of information is considered paramount in a number of countries. In the United Kingdom, the would-be supplier must produce such cost information as can reasonably be extracted from the company's accounting system. In the USA, the principle is enshrined in the Truth in Negotiations Act, which stipulates that for a contract price in excess of a given relatively low sum, the intending supplier has to submit cost data prior to negotiation.

The fact that such differences exist between commercial and public sectors does not mean that no negotiation takes place. There is still a need for negotiation. What happens is a shift in emphasis from the normal resources exchanged in commercial negotiations — like delivery, service and technical aspects — to such items as cost, the conventions to be adopted, formulae for operation if no departmental guidelines exist, or where guidelines permit a flexible approach for exploring and negotiating acceptable alternatives. There is always room for identifying and responding to non-task behaviours and for exercising of interpersonal skills in influencing and communicating. The checking out of ambiguities can be important for the kinds of standard contract conditions used by government negotiators, which can lend themselves to differing interpretations if they have a general rather than a specific application.

While these differences exist in negotiations with the commercial and public sectors, there will be variations as between different countries in negotiations with government buyers for reasons of history, culture, organization structures and local rules. In major projects in India and Nigeria, a Swedish manufacturer found that negotiators for the buyers were civil servants and engineers from different departments who had little autonomy and who had to consult higher authority for each issue that fell outside the scope of official rules and regulations (Ghauri 1985). Appeals to limited authority were part and parcel of the process. Such factors tend to lengthen the time for negotiation and make packages more complex to draw up and agreement more difficult to achieve.

Bargaining away the unacceptable

While this step will ordinarily aim to point the way to agreement by indicating possible trade-offs and packages, this does not happen to the same degree in government negotiations, where concessions are often subject to compensation. The effect is the same, but much more has to be taken on trust; hence the importance of relationships linking the transactions.

Decision-making and action stage

There is not the same need in government negotiations for closing concessions and summaries because the basis of the agreement is the standard contract form. There is the need for testing for understanding, particularly where complex negotiations take place.

The standard contract forms themselves are frequently the product of agreement between government and industry. As a result the likelihood of dispute is diminished. When an agreement is signed there are processes, not necessarily included in the agreement, which makes recompense for losses which are not the fault of the supplier.

A continuing relationship can result in increasing trust. Some firms may have broken that trust from time to time and government contracts officers may have applied such excessive zeal that profits consistent with the kind of risk and commitment involved have not been earned as a result. However, as long as our present economic system endures and governments rely on private firms for most of their needs, a relationship of partnership is best defined and regulated by contract (Turpin 1972).

Public corporations and services

In many countries the public corporation is an instrument of public enterprise for the management of various undertakings and services for which the organization of an ordinary government department is not considered suitable. They are usually corporate bodies endowed with legal personality, among the attributes of which is the capacity to enter into binding contracts. They have evolved practices which reflect the hybrid nature of their origins.

They are commercial in so far as most of them are expected to pay their way. They resemble government departments in their operations in that some of them may be obliged to pursue uneconomic social objectives. While they are often independent in their day-to-day procurement, they were not put into public ownership to put them beyond the influence of government policy. Ministerial approval is often required for investment programmes. Treasury departments often exercise influence indirectly on departments which sponsor the corporations.

It is not surprising that government practices impinge on the commercial decisions these corporations make. Price determination is seen to allow a contractor to make a profit appropriate for agreements with public corporations which are, after all, funded in the first instance from the public purse. It should allow for investment needs, research expenditure, export potential and like considerations affecting the general welfare of the contracting firm.

They differ under the law in that in many instances government departments are immune from taxation and from such legislation as that which applies to restrictive trade practices in respect of arrangements with associations or contractor groups. Sellers have to adjust accordingly.

Local authorities

Government controls over local authorities are more tenuous. In many cases governments provide some support to local authorities from public funds and can exercise control over the level of spending or its direction by the allocation or withholding of funds.

Sometimes guidelines are provided for the authorities as part of the process of diffusion of procurement techniques and controls. Otherwise they have their own forms of accountability, control and procedures which stem, as in central/federal/state government purchasing, from the need for openness in the disbursement of public funds. There is a tendency towards larger units and towards cooperation in buying. Hence there is a growing specialization and professionalism in the purchasing function and consequent consolidation of negotiating power. Sellers have to respond in a way which matches these patterns of purchase.

NEGOTIATIONS ARISING FROM AGREEMENTS

Parallel agreements

Some products require specialist maintenance or service because of their nature. Such service can also be negotiated by agreement. If these agreements are negotiated after the conclusion of the agreement for the product/plant/equipment/service, the user has little bargaining leverage with which to influence changes in a seller's maintenance or service contract. Such contracts are often standard and can fail to provide adequate protection for the user in such critical areas as price, level of service and parts availability.

In systems selling, a supplying organization helps to identify a customer's problem and comes up with a solution, not only in terms of product or products, but also ancillary equipment and consumables. The temptation is considerable to focus on the negotation of the product agreement at the expense of supporting supply agreements.

In the supply of computer systems there has been a major shift in the relative pricing for hardware and software (Auer and Harris 1981). Major mainframe processing capability has become relatively inexpensive and compact, while the software to operate and link these new control processing units has become more sophisticated and expensive. The increasing importance of software means that users have to become more skilful in optimizing the software selection and negotiation processes, particularly in combining the quality and performance of software packages to the mainframe agreement. This is particularly true in a fluid situation of continuous development, where the software packages are custom made to the buyer's requirements and are supplied by the hardware manufacturer.

If, on the other hand, a buyer is in negotiation with a major computer manufacturer for software to operate with a proven computer system being acquired, the quality of the software may be secondary to the terms and conditions of use, including the seller's ability to impose additional or increased fees or restrict in the future the transfer of the software.

Disputes

While a good agreement, in which the understanding of the parties has been tested, recorded and been given contractual status, will reduce the possibility of later dispute, it will not eliminate it. Separate negotiations may take place arising from any failure to implement the agreement in such items as delivery, performance and levels of service. See Reading II for an example of preparing an initial offer for negotiations arising out of failure to complete a contract on time.

There are many variables which can cause delay in completing a contract, problems which can cause delay in the achievement of the promised performance, and different perceptions when new variables intervene. Nevertheless, these are disputes which can be submitted to the same negotiation processes which we have examined and lend themselves to resolution by these same processes. The purchaser may seek to obtain a reduction in the contract price for a particular failure to meet the contract terms. For his part the seller will seek to minimize any such reduction. If reliability of a particular system is the buyer's primary concern, then guarantees may be valued more highly by him than a reduction in price.

Changes in the buyer's specifications are not unusual in commercial contracts for certain aspects of engineering work. The oil and chemical industries, for example, are noted for multiple changes in pipework after the contract has been made. Specification changes warrant as much consideration as did the negotiation of the original agreement, since the possibilities of loss are considerable. Again, the negotiation processes are the same.

PHILOSOPHY OF NEGOTIATION

Throughout this chapter the possibilities of the cooperative mode have been stressed as a possible style of negotiating behaviour. The advantages to parties of a similar view have been shown. However, this approach tends to be practised largely in Western business cultures and, in a somewhat different way, in East Asian business transactions. Many countries and cultures have a much more competitive approach. Indeed many individuals within these Western cultures mentioned also adopt competitive postures.

There will always be those within a group who advocate the preservation of supplier/buyer relationships by avoidance of aggressive tactics. Others will take the opposite view which inclines them to a hard-line position. It is certain that the same approach will not be appropriate for all transactions and issues. In the final analysis each negotiating team must formulate its own philosophy in relation to the pending negotiation. It will be evident from the foregoing chapter that, irrespective of whether a general cooperative or competitive approach is embraced, there will be occasions during the interaction when a cooperative or competitive mode will be required to achieve agreement within the negotiating objectives set. The good negotiator has to be sufficiently flexible and sensitive to the situation to be able to adapt as the action unfolds. Training approaches which rely on a given pattern of behaviour or pre-determined steps can place a negotiator at a disadvantage.

Reading III at the end of the chapter represents a philosophy which might be seen as the ideal one for professional negotiators. If it is not adopted by an opposer who prefers a more aggressive style, the approach outlined here gives him an indication of how the situation can be handled without loss of negotiating position.

SUMMARY

One factor bearing on negotiation objectives is the relative power of the parties which arises from the mutual dependence inherent in a voluntary relationship. Environmental and situational forces of power were examined, and how power arising from these can be built into the negotiation preparations. Prerequisites in arriving at the face-to-face situation are information as to possibilities, a presentation of quality, and the use of influence channels.

In the actual face-to-face situation rules for the meeting can be negotiated, as they can influence outcomes, as can use of the agenda and setting of time limits. At the distributive bargaining stage the parties explore the negotiating range in an attempt to sound out the strength of the opposer's view on different issues. Methods of taking the initiative were discussed and examples given of the language used to initiate the interaction and probe the positions taken up to anticipate the form of the ultimate agreement. Some cultural snares at this stage were uncovered.

The dilemma of buyer and seller rests on deciding whether or not to hold out for better terms by maintaining a firm position and risking no bargain. The strong negotiator risks position and image loss if an opposer's pressure compels him to retract from that position. Good negotiators therefore seek to send signals which indicate, without commitment, that they are prepared to move provided some movement is made by the other party in return.

This leads to movement which takes the parties to the integrative bargaining stage. Here, the negotiators test the commitment of their opposers to issues on which they have taken a given stand. When the relative strength of commitment of the parties has been established, the negotiation seeks progressively to separate out these issues on which the parties maintain their position and those on which they are prepared to concede provided there is some equivalent concession on the eventual agreement.

Flexibility is maintained by keeping issues linked. Constraints on flexibility are imposed by overriding commitments with which the negotiator has no option but to comply. These can arise from the authority of the local law, government regulations and company procedures. In defence of his position, a negotiator can plead limited authority on various grounds which provide the negotiator with a face-saving way of testing his opposer's firmness and provide him with a face-saving way of giving in.

The interaction of individuals involved in negotiations is a key factor in determining outcomes. As the stage progresses the parties divulge more and more. Behaviours which are acceptable at the distributive stage may be entirely unacceptable when positions have become more defined. Outright disagreement is replaced by language which is less pointed, taking the form of an explanation leading to a statement of disagreement in the least contentious terms.

Once commitments have been demonstrated and tested, trading-off begins to narrow the gap further to the point where the parties identify and reach the ultimate bargain. In order to come to the ultimate bargain the negotiator has to know not only the costs involved in trading-off, but also the worth to each party of non-quantifiable concessions such as risk elements like performance, delivery and arbitration.

Neither seller nor buyer knows how far he can maximize his advantage. A negotiator can only make assumptions about his opposer's expectations and goals. It is the testing of these assumptions that is an important function of negotiations.

There are therefore two forces at work on the parties. One is the esteem motivation that drives them to strike the best possible bargain. The other is the security motivation to settle when a reasonable bargain is identified, rather than seek a more advantageous outcome at the risk of no bargain.

It is against this background that buyers and sellers convey to each other, by moves and countermoves, how they see a resolution of their differences. One party may put forward a proposed solution. The strength of his commitment is confirmed by non-verbal postures, by tone of voice and language, by the use of words which indicate the absence of bluff, greater familiarity and a position of no apparent fall-back. Experienced negotiators provide opposers with face-saving means of maintaining position.

The decision-making and action stage is characterized by an evaluation by the parties of the various possibilities on offer. One or the other will put forward a final package, which may be accepted as it stands or linked to a conditional concession. Certain phrases have come to be standard signals for conveying that the negotiator is willing to come to an agreement provided there is reciprocal concession. Testing of understanding and recording of that understanding complete the agreement.

In negotiating with governments and public corporations, the government purchasing agents or contracts officers operate under decision rules different from those of business firms. Profit margins tend to be set by rules. Negotiation emphasis is more on costs, conventions to be adopted and formulae used, rather than on items like delivery, service and specification which form the basis of commercial exchange. Open communication and full exchange of information, rather than the extraction of information for mutual influence, is the norm. The strategic function is the building or reinforcing of relationships, rather than the revision of objectives from the information obtained.

Some products are negotiated in parallel with maintenance agreements and agreements for ancillary products and services. Further negotiations take place from perceived failure to implement the terms of an agreement or changes in specifications asked for by the buyer.

Questions

1 Identify in relation to other similar organizations, the sources of power in your own organization or business school deriving from factors in the environment.
2 What is probing language? Give examples in relation to a buyer seeking to elicit from a seller, information on what has been claimed as a cost-saving paper-making machine.
3 Why should agreement to split the difference on their initial bargaining stances disadvantage the proposer?
4 To escape from an entrenched position, it is necessary to convey without commitment. Give examples of how this can be done.
5 Distinguish between price and worth in coming to an ultimate bargain.
6 Show how negotiating agreements can differ as between private and public sector organizations.
7 Give some examples of the kinds of limited authority which a seller or buyer can plead in defence of his/her position.

READING I

Using alternative credit plans for concession advantage*

One company has identified three alternative schemes for extending credit to overseas customers which combine the skills of the accountant, the banker and the credit insurer:

Plan A

A lump-sum plan in which the buyer pays the financing charges incurred in negotiating the credit as a composite figure added on to the Bill of Exchange at despatch, with interest on the reducing principal being charged to the remaining Bills.

Plan B

An equal-instalments plan which spreads the financing and interest charges equally among the Bills due after despatch.

Plan C

An equivalent rate of interest plan which consolidates the financing and interest charges into a single rate of interest to be applied to the reducing principal.

Plan A is cheaper by up to 1 per cent of the contract value than Plan B or C. Plan C is cheaper than Plan B. If Plan B or Plan C is put forward, then any change to Plan A at a subsequent stage means that the sales negotiator has the difference between the cost of Plan A and either B or C with which to make conditional concessions without eroding his own position. If Plan B is put forward and subsequent negotiations elicit the fact that the buyer's cost of overdraft is greater than the interest rate quoted under Plan C, acceptance by the buyer of Plan C means the seller retains for his company the difference in costs between the two plans.

Alternatively he can freely discuss the different plans where the relationship is a cooperative one with open communication.

Where the seller's bargaining postion is weak, one advantage of not divulging the differences is that he is not seen to be conceding on price and perhaps establishing a precedent for future negotiations.

* Condensed from Case Study, *Scotpack Developments Ltd. (A)* by P. J. Flynn and W. S. Kynoch, Case Clearing House of Great Britain and Ireland, Cranfield, England, No. 583-011-1.

READING II

Negotiations arising out of a contract*

DETERMINATION OF THE LEVEL OF THE INITIAL OFFER

The basic approach to the establishment of the initial demand in a contract dispute is similar to that adopted for bidding and procurement. Party assesses what he believes the outcome will be, based on judgement of Opponent's range of negotiating objectives and his concession factor, and selects the demand which he believes will lead to the optimal outcome. It has been seen that these objectives are not as clear-cut as in bidding/procurement and that the value which one side puts on a particular issue may differ widely from the value which it possesses for the other.

Time costs will only be significant where the dispute concerns a major financial claim or the payment of other money is dependent on the issue being settled, e.g. release of retention money dependent on the settlement of a dispute relating to spares.

More so, however, than in bid/procurement negotiations Party must consider the effect which any concession will have on the future and that it is the ultimate not the immediate cost associated with any action which is significant. The right little concession made at the right time can be very useful in avoiding future difficulties. The wrong little concession made at the wrong time can be very costly to Party in the encouragement which it gives to Opponent to ask for more, and the precedent it gives him on which to base future demands.

Because there will normally be a number of issues involved, the importance of which will vary, it is essential that in formulating his initial demand and his belief as to Opponent's concession factor, Party assesses the worth of him of each issue in terms of money (or utility values if the amounts involved are of sufficient significance). The importance of each issue can then be compared and the demand structured so as to achieve the optimal outcome.

Such comparison will also indicate any anxiety issues which the form of Party's initial demand should be designed to protect. Party's initial demand is a function of a total negotiating plan which foresees a particular outcome based on Party's judgement of Opponent's concession factor and the concessions which Party considers will be necessary for him to make.

This process of formulating the initial demand is illustrated with the following simple example.

* From P.D.V. Marsh, *Contract Negotiations Handbook*, Aldershot, Gower, 1984. Reproduced by permission of Gower Publishing Co.

Party is five months late in completing a contract for Opponent. Responsibility for the delay is disputed since neither side is wholly to blame. The defects liability period runs for twelve months from the original date for completion, extended by any period for which Party is in default. During the period of delay spares to the value of £500 have been used on maintaining the plant which Opponent considers should be paid for by Party, as free replacement of defects, and Party asserts should be paid for by Opponent since their use only became necessary through maloperation of the plant by Opponent's staff. Liquidated damages for delay are at the rate of £1,000 per month and Party assesses the cost of extending the defects liability period at £200 per month.

Party prepares the following analysis of the position:

1 Negotiating area. Liquidated damages: £1,000 per month to a maximum of £5,000. Defects liability period: £200 per month to a maximum of £1,000. Spares: £500.
2 Negotiating objective. Party's preferred objective £3,000; minimum acceptable £4,500. Opponent's expected minimum objective £2,500; expected preferred objective £5,000.
3 The anxiety factor. This is clearly the penalty. If the preferred negotiating objective is to be achieved then the penalty payment must not exceed £2,000 on the basis that at least £1,000 will have to be conceded on the other two points. If the minimum negotiating objective is to be achieved then assuming the other two points have to be conceded completely, the penalty payments must not exceed £3,000.

  Additionally, a concession on the period of delay will automatically involve a similar concession on defects liability. However, the converse is not necessarily true. A concession on a longer defects period could be traded for a lesser penalty.

In deciding on his initial offer, Party has the choice of either:

1 Offering the limit to which he is prepared to go on penalty, making it clear that this issue is not a matter for further negotiation, whilst at the same time indicating a greater flexibility on defects liability.
2 Saying nothing, or reserving his position on penalty and making an offer only on spares and defects liability.
3 Making some offer on each issue but indicating on which he would prefer the initial negotiations to be concentrated.

Unless the negotiating position on penalty is considered to be very strong, so that the offer could be kept down to say £2,000 as a maximum, the preference would be for alternative 3. The penalty is a major issue for both sides and as such must form an important part of the negotiations. On the other hand, unless his position is very strong Party would not wish to commit himself to too firm a position too early. The negotiating plan would therefore be:

1 An initial offer of:
  (a) The minimum penalty thought to be acceptable and not regarded as insulting, say, £1,000.

(b) Acceptance of defects liability for half the disputed period which would cost £500.

(c) Half the value of the disputed spares which would cost £250.

2 To concentrate the subsequent negotiations first on the penalty issue, conceding slowly and reluctantly to £2,000. At that point make no further concessions on penalty but offer the balance of the defects periods for a final settlement. This would leave half the value of the spares as a final 'sweetener'. The cost therefore of the final bargain on this basis would be £3,500.

READING III

The professional negotiating philosophy*

The professional philosophy is set around the following axioms:

1 In any major business transaction, both parties have a right and, indeed, an obligation to determine the goals and objectives that they wish to achieve in the transaction.
2 The goals and objectives desired by one party may create actual or potential costs or risks for the other party. Where this circumstance occurs, the party facing such costs or risks has a right and, indeed, an obligation to identify the costs and risks and to limit or protect against them or, alternatively, to require additional consideration for accepting them. (This statement may be a verbose method of communicating the old adage that 'there is no such thing as a free lunch'.)
3 Responsibilities, costs and risks should be discussed, understood and allocated in an honest and open business manner. Although the advocacy and sales process almost always results in the use of puffery and convincing argument, both sides should avoid efforts designed to foster or permit misunderstanding and deception, regardless of source or reason.
4 Honest mistakes and misunderstandings may occur in the negotiation of any complex business transaction. Neither party should falsely claim such problems, but where these problems occur both parties should work honestly towards their resolution.
5 The best contract is one which accurately sets forth the mutual understanding of the parties on all relevant issues. Such a contract invariably involves compromise, both in substance and specific language. This type of contract should be the negotiating goal. This axiom might be called the 'Holiday Inn' principle, to parody the advertising line used by that firm in the late 1970s: for both sides, 'a good contract should be like a good motel room: no surprises!'
6 A good contract must nevertheless contemplate that one or both parties may fail to perform their obligations under the agreement for any number of reasons, including reasons beyond their control. Therefore, the contract should include clear standards of performance and remedies. Such an approach may actually reduce the likelihood of litigation, by specifying the mutual obligations of the parties on all relevant issues.

* From J. Auer and C. E. Harris, *Computer Contract Negotiations*, Van Nostrand Reinhold, 1981. Reproduced with permission.

The professional negotiating philosophy recognizes that, in an ideal world, the best method of achieving optimum and mutual success at the bargaining table is for both parties to work together, in a professional atmosphere, to agree on how responsibilities, costs, and risks will be allocated, and to document the resulting compromise in a clear contractual agreement. The philosophy requires that each party treat the other as a professional to be respected for his or her honesty, expertise and mutual desire to fairly document and consummate the transaction. In this regard, the philosophy requires a cooperative negotiating environment rather than an adversarial one. It also requires that each party be willing to listen and respond to the concerns expressed by the other side, without becoming incensed or incited towards a 'killer' response. In the professional philosophy, neither side 'wins' in the traditional sense. Indeed, it might be said that neither side wins unless both sides win. As a result, negotiating factors such as aspiration level and psychological negotiating leverage must be directed away from achieving victory at all costs and toward achieving an acceptable, fully understood, and well-documented compromise. Ploys and manipulative strategies and tactics have no place in negotiations governed by the professional philosophy. Despite this fact, advocacy, sound reasoning, and effective, forceful communication play strong roles under the professional philosophy as well as under other approaches.

For example, in the professional philosophy, the tactic of picking off points for settlement one by one is replaced by what might be called an 'all-encompassing tactic'. In the latter approach, both sides theoretically avoid holding items back (only to spring them later once concessions on other related issues have been reached). Instead, both parties outline their respective goals and objectives in all areas, or at least major related areas, at one time. This approach optimizes the opportunity for understanding and for an honest assessment and trade-off of the specific responsibilities, costs and risks that may be involved.

Similarly, the professional philosophy mandates against a section-by-section review and discussion of the contract. Instead, it encourages consideration of broad concepts and, at a minimum, the discussion and review of groups of interrelated sections and obligations. In this regard, the philosophy recognizes and deals with one of the most basic and dangerous facts involved in negotiating provision and drafting computer contract provisions: the boundaries of any contract provision are more or less arbitrary; contract sections do not live in a vacuum — rather, they are invariably linked to one another in a flexible, working environment that may vary depending upon the obligations being considered at any given point in time. Because of this fact, it is neither sound nor professionally possible to allocate responsibilities, costs, or risks, or to draft actual contract language, unless all interrelated sections are identified and considered concurrently.

Where the professional philosophy is used, the parties generally follow a critical path that includes the steps shown below:

1 Each party reviews its own acquisition goals and prioritized negotiating objectives.
2 Each party in turn presents an overview of the responsibilities that it believes must be assigned in the transaction. (These responsibilities are generally based upon the goals and objectives of the parties.)

3 Each party announces the actual and potential costs and risks that it believes would be involved if it accepted the various responsibilities proposed by the other party.

4 The parties propose and negotiate alternative allocations of responsibilities, costs, and risks, striving to achieve a compromise on each issue or each group of inter-related issues.

5 The parties reach and announce a buy/no-buy decision on each proposed allocation of responsibilities, costs, and risks. For example, after all realistic alternatives have been proposed on a given issue or group of issues, the user must decide (through what amounts to a form of cost − benefit analysis) which, if any, of these alternatives is both technically acceptable and affordable.

6 The parties then agree upon and draft the specific contractual provisions necessary to document the understandings reached above.

In reality, of course, the professional philosophy is seldom as easy to apply as it is to describe. Several problems may arise.

First, the professional philosophy provides that the user's opponent should be treated as a respected professional, but the vendor may in fact be engaging in wholesale use of manipulative tactics, sometimes exploiting personal relationships and stretching the truth. This frequent occurrence is a serious blow to the user's ability to employ the professional philosophy in the contract bargaining process. Nevertheless, the user can still make an effort to use his advocacy of the professional principles noted above to seize and maintain control of the negotiations. This approach is most successful where the user firmly rejects all vendor ploys and other comments and formally announces that the user will continue to discuss contractual provisions and, indeed, continue to participate in negotiations, only if the parties mutually agree to proceed along the lines specified in the professional philosophy.

Secondly, where the vendor appears willing to pursue the professional philosophy, the user may be lulled into a false sense of security and, based primarily on a lack of information, agree to inadvisable compromises. Because of the innate information and negotiating advantages generally enjoyed by the vendor, the honesty element of the professional philosophy can pose serious risks for the user if the vendor wishes to be unethical or purposefully misleading. When these conditions occur, the user must be willing to abandon the professional philosophy and move to an approach that requires less mutual cooperation. (Note that the professional philosophy does not preclude use of hard-hitting tactics, for example, when progress seems unlikely.) When the vendor appears to be proceeding ethically, the user must nevertheless remain alert to the possibility of deception. Adequate user preparation is one of the best defences in this area.

Thirdly, the approach involved in the professional negotiating philosophy is often scorned by vendors and users alike, because it appears to require an inordinate amount of preliminary time and effort. Attorneys and other negotiators whose computer contract experience is more limited than they would like to admit may also attack the profes-sional philosophy on the ground that it fails to allow the hard-hitting approach that they believe is necessary to do the job. Because of these perceptions, the professional approach may be difficult. The only effective solution to this problem comes from experience — experience proving the value involved. In the interim, the user can only hope to outline the approach and express the fact that, despite any other appearances, the professional philosophy will save time in the long run (and probably in the short run) by resulting in an agreement that does an optimum job of reflecting and documenting the mutual understanding of the parties on all relevant issues.

Fourthly, the professional negotiating philosophy is somewhat like democracy: it is a fragile creature requiring both good conditions and universal participation for optimum success. As suggested above, the professional approach works best when both parties understand the philosophy and are dedicated to it. Because the professional philosophy eschews ploys and deceptive tactics, breaking deadlocks and disagreements often requires finer bargaining skills than many negotiators possess. Moreover, because the philosophy requires an overriding commitment toward honesty and compromise, it often creates psychological problems for negotiators who are overly concerned with pride and saving face. In essence, the professional philosophy is often a more difficult (and less flamboyant) negotiating approach than many users would like to admit. Because of this fact, effective implementation of the philosophy requires skill, dedication and practice.

CHAPTER 9

The agency/distributorship agreement

Channels of distribution and fundamental behaviours............................ 227
   Introduction 227
   Conflict and dependence... 227
   Power... 228
   Negotiation and resolution of conflict.. 229
Behaviours and agency/distributorship agreements............................. 230
   Agents — some common characteristics and differences.................... 230
   Relative power of parties... 231
   Inter-organizational cooperation... 231
   Interpersonal cooperation... 231
Negotiating original agreements... 232
   Negotiation and company objectives.. 232
   Objectives and information.. 233
   Information and internal negotiation... 233
   Deciding on the offer.. 233
   Establishing where the power lies.. 234
   Creating power.. 234
   Distributive bargaining stage.. 235
   Integrative bargaining stage.. 236
   Reaching agreement.. 239
   What has been agreed.. 240
Negotiating the maintenance and renewal of agreements...................... 242
   Environmental changes and the balance of advantage....................... 242
   Negotiations arising within agreements.. 246
   Cultural perceptions... 248
   Inter-organizational factors... 249
   Interpersonal factors.. 251
   Negotiation as an ongoing process... 251
Terminating agreements... 252
Summary 253
Reading... 256

CHANNELS OF DISTRIBUTION AND FUNDAMENTAL BEHAVIOURS

Introduction

The reduction of costs and the increase of efficiency brought about by specialization have provided the fillip to organizations to enter into trading relationships with other organizations. It is this establishment of relationships and the development of routinized operations which enables such specialized companies to increase the efficiency of joint operations. No longer do they need to seek a specialized supplier and negotiate a price each time a need is felt. When a course of dealing is established, procedures are built up which facilitate the exchanges by which needs are satisfied.

When two or more organizations acknowledge it is in their mutual interest to perpetuate a relationship, this is generally viewed as an indication that a channel of distribution has emerged. 'Open' or 'free-flow' marketing channels consist of relationships by which companies attempt to enjoy the benefits of specialization whenever and however possible. When the relationship loses its appeal arrangements can be readily dissolved. Such relationships can embrace a single transaction or take the form of short-term contracts to supply and to purchase. There is no expectation of further business when the sale is complete or the short-term contract expires. Procuring firms are at liberty to find other suppliers who can meet their immediate or short-term needs, whether it be on grounds of price or other consideration.

Quite apart from the degree of permanence in any channel arrangement, the rules for conducting business arise from negotiation. The logical outcome of a relationship of two or more organizations who perceive mutual gain from developing or continuing their relationship is mutual dependence. This will normally take place in vertical marketing systems. Mutual dependence is a basic concept which requires the management of a number of important behaviours (Bowersox *et al.* 1980).

Conflict and dependence

By the very fact of aligning themselves with other organizations in a relationship of dependence, organizations commit themselves to cooperative activities. Such cooperation takes the form of fulfilling a negotiated role in the channel of distribution. This role is likely to include the functions to be undertaken for agreed rewards. It is in effect a code of conduct which lays down the contribution of the channel members as is expected by other channel members. Since an adequate performance is critical to maintenance of harmonious relations within the channel, failure to achieve adequate performance can lead to frustration and conflict.

In developed markets, manufacturers of drugs can be expected to supply wholesalers or large retailers within a period of two or three days. Ordering patterns are arranged accordingly. If a manufacturer consistently fails to deliver within the expected period, then the wholesalers or retailers will experience frustration. In the industrial market, a company using specially designed thrust bearings may negotiate supply some eighteen months in advance of its needs for phased delivery over an annual period, allowing the manufacturer to produce in one economic batch. The customer's production is geared to the phased supply, and failure to perform as expected will cause dissension which must be resolved quickly.

The anticipation of a given channel member and other members in the channel of distribution may not coincide. Goal compatibility may not be good enough. The assumption that each channel member will achieve the desired level of profit through cooperation in achieving maximum channel profits is not always valid. Each organization has its own stakeholders and influence groups which dictate its expectations, and this may result in dissatisfaction at the way in which channel profits or costs are divided.

When channel members are located in different countries, with differing cultural, linguistic and ideological backgrounds, insensitive behaviour by one channel member can spark off a conflict which would be otherwise avoidable. A Mexican agent who had succeeded in effecting the sale of a major item of equipment felt discriminated against when his United Kingdom principal insisted on applying the terms of his own agreement with his credit insurers. Under this, the principal, in order to ensure the agent's commitment to the payment of long-term credit instalments, was required to hold a lien on the agent's commission. The agent was only to receive his commission on the payment of the instalments. Because of the custom of the country whereby the agent had to make payment for services rendered to persons instrumental in having the order placed, his outgoings did not begin to be recovered until receipt of the third instalment of ten, which was eighteen months after delivery. The two perceptions of the situation were different. Facts are likely to be interpreted in the light of prior experience.

Power

As we saw in considering sales/purchase agreements, power is a function of dependence in the channel system. Inter-organizational relations are more likely to be characterized by unequal than by equal power. One party to a relationship will therefore enjoy a relative power advantage.

In a channel of distribution those members perceived to possess relative power advantage may assume a position of channel leadership. Because wholesalers came together horizontally in West Germany before manufacturers could integrate vertically, they exert a greater influence today than wholesalers in other European countries, and are therefore able to influence intentionally the decisions and behaviours of other channel members. Leadership's objective is to contribute to a better level of performance for either the leader or the overall channel. German wholesalers, despite continuing erosion of their power, are still able to achieve this to a degree.

A firm's tolerance is related to its dependence on other channel members and the extent to which its objectives can be met by submitting to control. German manufacturers accept the situation of wholesaler channel leadership provided there is something in it for them, and in this case that is freedom from competition from foreign manufacturers. To enter the German market via a distributorship agreement can still be a problem in certain product areas. By exercising this kind of leadership and influencing the decisions of others, the channel leader is in a better position to undertake activities which will benefit the performance of the overall system.

The exercise of power over a channel member having a high level of resistance to control can result in conflict or stress. Nevertheless, most of the means by which conflict is resolved rely to a greater or lesser extent on some form of power or leadership.

Negotiation and resolution of conflict

In the literature relating to conflict, four power related processes have been identified (Bowersox *et al.* 1980). These are as follows.

Problem-solving

It is assumed that the parties involved have objectives in common, even if sub-objectives raise issues of conflict. It is further assumed that a solution can be found within the framework of these common objectives. Where alternative channels exist the incentive to resolve conflict can be great. Using these common objectives, a more efficient flow of communications can be devised and agreed which will assist channel members in their search for a solution.

Persuasion

This implies that institutions exercise the power bases available to them (see Chapter 2), or draw on their leadership potential through the communication skills which they possess.

Political solutions

By the development of conditions to alter the power structure within the channel, or by inducing the processes of mediation and arbitration, a resolution to the issues in conflict is sought.

Negotiation

It is claimed that this seeks to resolve a conflict episode, but not necessarily the fundamental stress which induced the conflict in the first instance. No attempt, it is further claimed, is made to refer to common objectives.

The concept of negotiation as solely a conflict resolution process is a very narrow one. Indeed, the four processes fit readily into the paradigm which interrelates the factors influencing negotiations at Figure 2.1, and the negotiation skills model at Figure 2.4 which accommodates these interrelationships.

The view of negotiation as a concept broader than bargaining subsumes these four processes. The negotiation skills model provides the framework for problem-solving, and Figure 2.1 shows how the problem-solving aspects are related to other factors influencing outcomes. Persuasion is included under influence strategies in Figure 2.1 and exercised as appropriate in the various stages of the negotiation skills model.

Bargaining, which is the definition of negotiation implied in a situation which emphasizes trade-off and compromise, is likewise embraced by the skills model. Political moves by channel members are no more than attempts to change the power structure, and as such are encompassed by the mutual dependence of the parties and the distribution of power between them which is part and parcel of the situational influences on the parties shown in Figure 2.1.

BEHAVIOURS AND AGENCY/DISTRIBUTORSHIP AGREEMENTS

Agents — some common characteristics and differences

Companies which elect to develop their markets through agents and distributors usually do so after considering alternatives which involve greater control and cost. In the overseas market agents and distributors account for more business than all other means put together. The agreements which give effect to suppliers' and intermediaries' interactions can therefore be of considerable importance to them.

The intentions of the parties are of necessity affected by the exact nature of the agreement. Legal perspectives distinguish between agents and distributors. An agent acts for a named principal, who then enters into a contract of sale with the agent's customer. A distributor acts on his own behalf and carries the economic risk of the transactions he enters into. In return the agent receives a commission on sales; or where circumstances justify it, as where sales are of large value but infrequent, on a retainer and reduced commission. Usually he also receives territorial exclusivity. Distributors receive exclusive or limited distribution in addition to the profits accruing from their efficiency in purchasing, from their estimates of their own markets, the price the product is sold at, and their effectiveness in managing their administrative costs. In return, they are expected to exert their best efforts in the sale of their supplier's products.

Some go further and distinguish an agent acting on behalf of an undisclosed principal. In Belgium and Italy, for example, this kind of agent is known as a *commissaire* or *comisario*.

A manufacturer does not usually have the choice between an agent and distributor. It is determined by the nature of the product. A distributor will normally be used by manufacturers of consumer goods, consumer durables, industrial consumables and low-cost capital equipment and products. Raw materials and high-cost capital goods are normally marketed through an agent, where not sold direct.

In practice the distinctions are not quite so clear cut. An agent may act as such for his principal's products but as a distributor for spares or consumables. A distributor may act as such for his supplier but may be paid commission when required to service accounts of competitive distributors being supplied by the same manufacturer. Indeed, twenty seven different types of agent/distributor have been identified (McMillan and Paulden 1974). Because of these wide variations, the use of specimen agreements is to be avoided. Companies should develop agreements which meet the needs of the specific situations in which they and their intermediaries are likely to find themselves.

Relative power of parties

Given that relationships between principals or suppliers and agents or distributors are rarely of equal power, then one or other of the parties will have a relative power advantage. This is usually, but not exclusively, the principal/supplier. In some jurisdictions public policy regards the agent as the weaker of the parties and provides for a goodwill compensation in certain cases on termination of the contract of agency. United Kingdom and US law — and other countries whose law is based on the Anglo-American system such as Australia, Canada and New Zealand — do not provide for such goodwill compensation. On the other hand the various systems of Continental European law do so to differing degrees. The view in some of these countries is extended to distributors, indicating a widespread view that the intermediaries are the weaker of the parties.

Under conditions of unequal power among negotiators the party possessing the greater relative power tends to behave exploitatively, while the less powerful tends to behave submissively. For the principal/supplier in agency/distributorship negotiations, the temptation to exercise that power has to be kept in check. The manufacturer or supplier who seeks to develop a market through agents or distributors depends on the performance of these intermediaries for the success of his plans. If a supplier from a position of strength arbitrarily sets targets at an unattainable level for a distributor, or negotiates an agency commission lower than the average for the industry and as a result provides what eventually operates as a disincentive for the intermediary, his actions will be counterproductive to his own interests. However, there will be occasions, and these are referred to below, when that power must be exerted in the interest of conflict resolution.

Inter-organizational cooperation

Because organizations wish to work with others to achieve their goals, cooperation is the most commonly observed form of behaviour in distribution channels, and hence in making agency and distribution agreements. It exists either on a voluntary basis or as a result of conflict resolution by the channel leader through the exercise of the power that he holds. While conflicts may arise, they normally do so within an overall desire to maintain cooperative relationships. This is consistent with the view that inter-organizational relationships should be conceptualized in a way which integrates exchange and power-dependency approaches, and suggests that these relationships be seen as a mixed motive situation in which each organization behaves in accordance with its own self-interests (Schmidt and Kochan 1977).

Interpersonal cooperation

If we take as read the need for inter-organizational cooperation, there is equal need for interpersonal cooperation. The decision to negotiate an agency/distributorship agreement cannot be divorced from the agency/distributor selection decision. All things being equal, wise suppliers select intermediaries with whom they feel they can operate the agreement on a continuing basis. Wise intermediaries take a similar view. What is important is not the agreement as such, but the foundation from which relationships can be built up within which the conflict which will inevitably arise can be effectively handled. Mutual goodwill is a prerequisite to the establishment of lasting relationships. An important concomitant is the ability to span the gap between one's own culture and that of the other party to the agreement (see Chapter 3).

Chinese negotiators differ from West European negotiators in so far as the latter tend to believe that human relations cannot stand still, that they should be continuously reinforced and should progress towards greater intimacy. The Chinese, on the other hand, accept that relations can remain on the same level for indefinite periods of time. What they want is a sense of reliability, not warmth. One authority, while pointing this out, derives the principle of restrained steadfastness (Pye 1982):

'It is easy to document that the most successful negotiators with the Chinese have been men who take an optimistic but reserved approach to their personal interactions with the Chinese and who provide ample evidence that they will be around for the indefinite future.'

The Japanese seek signs of sincerity and are much more sensitive to relationships than are Western businessmen. They often judge visitors by the way they can strike emotional chords in them. The relationship is of prime importance for them.

Most Arab executives have a preference for personal relationships and informality, and tend to dislike impersonal and transient relationships when conducting business. As with these other high-context cultures, its distinctive characteristics must be known so as not to offend unknowingly. It is difficult, indeed virtually impossible, for the majority of businessmen to act all the time in accordance with the rules of these cultures. Therefore, the negotiator seeking to lay the basis of sound relationships should still be true to his own culture, but should be able to adapt to the behavioural needs of the situation so that in the negotiation of agreements such as agency and distributorships the optimal circumstances are developed for the blossoming of these relationships.

Initial impressions are important at the formative period of the relationship. Hence there is a need, on the part of the individual acting on behalf of the party marketing the product of service, to be highly sensitive to these cultural aspects. Personal experience within the supplier/agent – distributor relationship is likely to shape future channel relations. Wise companies will ensure through their selection and training processes that those people nominated to negotiate agency/distributorship arrangements have the necessary skills. Even more crucial are the skills required in maintaining and operating the agreements negotiated.

NEGOTIATING ORIGINAL AGREEMENTS

Negotiation and company objectives

Negotiation is the process by which a firm positions itself in one or more channel arrangements. It is the means by which expression is given to company plans in markets where it has chosen to use these channels, and because of this it is a key process in channel management. These plans spring from company objectives, which will in turn be partly determined by policies laid down by top management and the philosophies which underly them or the processes by which they are arrived at.

A chief executive or top management team might decide to exploit multi-markets simultaneously and appoint distributors or agents around the world. Again, an interest group of influential executives might seek to promote the belief that markets should be exploited in depth, and therefore limited to those in which the opportunities were greatest and in which greater control would be exercised than through distributors. The appointment of intermediaries may be seen as only a step in the development of markets and in the development of channels of distribution.

A distributor or agent might decide that carrying yet another line would further spread the cost of overheads, or he might decide through his own political processes that a sufficient number of lines was already being carried. The decision taken by the manufacturer or the distributor/agent will have implications for the organization's objectives in the market and the commitment of its resources.

Objectives and information

Manufacturers and agent/distributor companies will develop their plans from their objectives. To do so they will require information. Well coordinated information is the cornerstone of good negotiations. Where a distribution channel crosses frontiers and presents problems associated with geographic, cultural and social distance, and where redress for perceived wrongs is not necessarily handled by familiar institutions, the exercise of judgment depends even more on a bank of relevant information. This will relate not only to the market and the prospective intermediary, but also to the match of the manufacturer's product to the market.

Information and internal negotiation

A manufacturer may have to decide whether the standardized product or a modified version for the market be produced, if that is what may issue from negotiation with a strong agent/distributor. This entails internal negotiation in connection with analysis of costs, revenues and profits, as well as the possible effect on the product. If there is a desired target distributor who may wish to negotiate specific procedures compatible with his computer system, this would have to be negotiated between the marketing and data processing functions of the manufacturer's organization.

A distributor who is likely to rely increasingly on the product of the manufacturer may have, for example, to modify his own accounting procedures to accord with those of the manufacturer, because of his likely stake in the operation of the agreement.

Largely because of their own perceptions of their relative weakness in relation to suppliers, aspiring agents and distributors do not often negotiate the terms offered by suppliers. Therefore there is less likelihood of internal negotiation to the extent practised by suppliers. Intermediaries are, however, stronger than they think.

Deciding on the offer

In considering the offer he will make, a principal/manufacturer has to be aware that the higher his expectations of what the distributor will accept, the more desirable it will be to him and the less attractive it will be to the distributor. The distributor's stake in the agreement will be determined by his view of resources put into such items as stockholding, advertising, and technical support equipment.

The distributor for his part will have equal concern for some of these aspects and may well have different ideas of how his resources should be allocated. In particular he is likely to want to bargain on price, or indirectly on the terms of agreement which affect price, such as special test equipment or commitment to local advertising. An agent will estimate his likely income less likely costs in support of the agency, and hence concentrate on the basis of his commission and expenditures likely to affect the net amount.

The offer in an original agreement negotiation is not affected by previous arrangements. Once an agreement has been made, however, precedents are established and a history of commitments and performance created which may affect later decisions.

Establishing where the power lies

Parties preparing to negotiate an original distributorship or agency agreement are affected by where the relative power lies, in that this will have a bearing on negotiation objectives. There is some evidence to suggest that where the distributor has the higher stake by dint of his dependence on the manufacturer, this confers power on the manufacturer which he uses to a greater degree than where the manufacturer is dependent on the distributor (Rosson and Ford 1982).

Power also derives, as we have already seen, from environmental and situational factors. When reputable agents are in short supply, as they often are, such scarcity value gives the apparently weaker agent/distributor a strong negotiating base. They will equally be strengthened if it is established before or in the course of negotiation, for example, that the distributor or agent has a special relationship with key customers or has special facilities or capabilities.

A manufacturer's hand is strengthened if his product is patented or has patented features. The credibility of the company will be another factor, so any presentation which can highlight this in terms of users or significant sales will reinforce this credibility. The credibility of the negotiators themselves, and their effect on each other in terms of creating a climate of confidence, can also affect the relative power situation.

Creating power

Where the manufacturer has seen fit to make space for himself for alternative courses of action, such as other candidates for distributorship or other means of distribution like a local sales office, and can subtly make this known to a candidate for distributorship, he creates a more powerful negotiating position for himself. Similarly, if distributors or agents can indicate competition for their services, they are performing a similar function. Unless such alternatives are consciously made, no effective balance of power will be available to the negotiating parties.

Power so held or generated must be real. Bluffing is often used as a tactic in sales/purchase agreements to obtain the best possible settlement. This can include such ploys as holding to a strong position which is not so strong in reality, or telling a downright lie with conviction. In negotiating agency and distributorship agreements it can be costly. The expectation which a negotiator has of his opposer is that he is acting in good faith, as both will be involved in operating any resulting arrangement over an extended period. Trust is an element of the relationship which is basic to its satisfactory functioning.

The exercise of power held or created is something that can only be achieved successfully with finesse. The crude use of power may be used when there is no alternative, but it will be used against the negotiator in a later round of bargaining when the power position may well have changed. It may be necessary to hint at the existence of such power, particularly where the true position is seen to be not wholly perceived.

Distributive bargaining stage

The trust which is expected of their opposers by negotiators makes it difficult for this stage of the negotiations to be as hard and competitive as some sales/purchase situations. This is likely to be because the extreme stances which sales and buying personnel can take up tend to be supported by behaviours and associated language which would be perceived to be at odds with the cooperation expected in the course of a manufacturer – distributor/agent agreement. Similarly perceived will be efforts designed to foster or permit misunderstanding and deception, regardless of the reason.

The whole tenor of the relationship is a cooperative one arising from agreement on the roles and rewards for joint marketing performance, and any action tending to undermine the trust condition implied in cooperative behaviour would be perceived as a threat to, and an unfavourable omen for, the establishment operation of a relationship.

Nevertheless, the cooperative nature of negotiation of distributorship and agency contracts does not mean that there cannot be a competitive element to the interaction. What might be considered an outrageously demanding proposal in mature channel negotiation conditioned by experience of already having operated an agreement, can be viewed much more tolerantly when the parties are strangers to each other and to the ways of each other's country and neither party has yet ascertained his stake in the relationship. To that extent there is scope for settlement within a bargaining area which is perceived to be reasonable, and for varying the bargaining area by reducing the opposer's aspirations. So the strategic function of the negotiation process, which is the information parties can elicit and use for mutual influence, can still hold good when negotiating these agreements for the first time.

It is therefore quite acceptable for the parties to original agreements to adduce the issues they consider important to them and the outcomes they would foresee in relation to these issues. It is possible for an agreement to be hammered out on the basis of competitive bargaining, but it remains a matter for conjecture whether such an agreement should be entered into in view of the need for problem-solving on a regular basis when business comes to be transacted on the basis of the agreement.

The likelier alternative is where the parties can state their positions and have the open communications and trust that allow them to move straight to the integrative bargaining stage. Here cooperative problem-solving can result in an agreement which addresses the real problems of the participants. This normally provides for full agreement as to who will perform the functions, the rewards available for risk and performance, and the procedures for regular modification of the agreement in the light of difficulties experienced.

Integrative bargaining stage

Because the cooperative problem-solving mode most suited to negotiating the agency/distributorship agreement precludes those factors which create the necessity of getting movement from entrenched positions, it is possible to move directly into the integrative bargaining stage of the 'negotiation skills model' (Figure 2.4).

Very often a large manufacturer will put his viewpoint in terms of a standard agreement, in which case it is the would-be distributor's or agent's responsibility to examine how it matches his own view of how the agreement should be framed. If necessary — and this will be in the vast majority of cases — offending clauses should be removed or amended through the negotiation process, and omissions should be likewise rectified. It is possible to standardize an agreement but not the situations which can arise from it.

Perceptions of issues

A manufacturer with experience of a variety of markets tends to standardize his roles and routines for ease of administration; for this reason an agent or distributor has usually a good idea of what is expected of him, for he will be dealing with a number of principals/suppliers in normal circumstances. He will also have an idea from his prior experience what he expects of the manufacturer. The following is an example of issues in agency and distributorship negotiations:

> An agent in Venezuela for machinery for supply to the chemical industries on a proposed exclusive agency might dispute the 10 per cent commission on ex-works price proposed by a British manufacturer, preferring it to be 12½ per cent FOB port, which would put it on a par with some other agencies for a similar category of product. He might also feel that the manufacturer, whose agreement includes a contribution of 25 per cent of advertising expenditure in Venezuela, should in fact pay 75 per cent of costs of advertising in the trade press, which some European suppliers already meet.
>
> Other issues on which he might be at variance with his British supplier might be in relation to the law under which the agency contract should be construed, the agent preferring the protection of his own law to that of England; also on whether he should purchase the fairly substantial spares as recommended by the principal, preferring that the manufacturer should supply these on consignment. For his part the manufacturer might be trying to instil some sense of the importance of market information and wishes to ensure that market data are supplied on a regular basis in relation to market size, company's share of imports, market share and imports and local production, and any other factors likely to bend the trend.
>
> It is assumed that there is no conflict on such items as the period of the agreement, the territory, terms of payment, sales/service support by the manufacturer, immediate break and termination proposals, responsibility for sales training costs, stock on termination and original equipment manufacturers.

Strength of commitment

Because of the long-term implications of an agency/distributorship agreement, and the pressures for cooperative behaviour stemming from this, the probing and testing of commitment to issues in the Venezuelan example, as in many others, will almost certainly be much less aggressive than in many sales/purchase situations. Loaded questions, or the introduction of surprise or emotional outbursts, are tactics likely to put off an opposer because of the need for harmonious relations, even to the extent of withdrawing from a possible relationship, particularly if alternative partners are available. And yet within a framework of cooperation the parties must be quite clear about all aspects of a transaction before operating as an inter-organizational unit.

Reason, then, is likely to be the preferred behaviour. In the above example the Venezuelan agent might open discussions by stating his position in relation to the manufacturer's proposed agreement, and follow that up with a reasoned statement on the individual issues: 'Ours is a very competitive market and this is recognized by other principals, some of whom are very well known companies as you can see. Many of them pay 12½ per cent on the FOB port price. There are expenses in this market arising from local practices of recompensing people who have influenced a sale, and we would hope you could match that figure'. The manufacturer's marketing man might respond by pointing out how his product differs from some others: 'Our 10 per cent commission is based on our concept of a fair reward for our agents. Our product is highly competitive on quality and price, and given the sales effort you claim your company makes, should result in sales which in their aggregate commission should far exceed that provided by some agencies offering a slightly higher unit margin'.

The agent might not wish to leave it at that: 'We are unhappy about your paying us on the ex-works price (FOB factory price in the USA), because our experience of this is that we as agents want to know just what our revenue as commission will be, and the only satisfactory way is to show the ex-works and extra for the FOB port separately. In our experience, the customer wants one price and can sometimes draw wrong conclusions from a comparison of different exporters' costs from factory to the ship's side at the port of shipment. As you know, these can vary from actual cost to a generous percentage to cover that cost'.

As the dialogue develops the manufacturer may become convinced that the agent has a strong commitment to his view and that there is a case for quoting FOB and perhaps for a slightly higher commission. Nevertheless, the manufacturer has to take into account the policies of the organization and whether these sometimes desirable changes from the point of view of the relationship are still desirable in the context of the company's global operations. While to operate standardized procedures as nearly as possible may be desirable from an administrative standpoint, it may not meet the needs of particular market partners. However if the conceding of changes — for example, to accommodate an agent or distributor in a given market — is likely to lead to pressure from agents or distributors in other markets for equal terms, he may be right to resist. This will depend on a number of factors, including the degree of uncertainty present which has been shown to lead to standardized routines, the changes taking place in the market, and the likelihood of agents exchanging information on their agreements.

Given that the manufacturer is prepared to consider going some way to meeting the needs of the Venezuelan agent, he might well relate the issues under consideration to other issues: 'If you are prepared to pay 75 per cent of a limited advertising outlay which we might eventually relate by mutual consent to sales volume, we might consider paying you commission on the FOB price. You will realize that we normally add 7½ per cent on our factory prices for FOB port of shipment. That would mean that your commission would in effect be nearly 11 per cent if you compare it with our normal ex-factory terms'.

The manufacturer might well raise other problem-related issues: 'We can't see at this stage that we can supply the different drive unit spares on consignment. We do, however, hold a stock of these items at our works and we can air-freight them to arrive in Caracas within forty-eight hours of notification. We could hope you would purchase one each of these three main drive units as part of what we consider to be a minimum spares holding in support of the agency'. The agent's commitment is now being tested, for this is related to the worth of the agency. One of the costs is the outlay of capital and the incurring of certain variable costs in relation to the likely revenue from sales. In considering this the agent might reserve his position until he knows if the principal is likely to make further demands on him: 'Perhaps we can come back to this when we have discussed the full range of your proposals.'

A further issue might be raised by the agent: 'We are strongly of the view that the clause in which you claim the right to deal directly with large customers is not in the spirit of the agreement we would envisage. We would want to maintain the exclusivity of our agency in the territory for which we have been appointed. In return for our best efforts on your behalf, we would expect our agreed commission on all goods sold into the territory by you. There are multinational companies whom we represent who purchase through central buying units in the USA and Europe for delivery here, and we would agree a reduced commission for us in these circumstances, just as we would agree a reduced commission where we delivered an order into another country. But where you are the seller direct we would want full cover. After all, government organizations here make more than 50 per cent of purchases in the chemical industry, and if you were to deal direct with them with nothing in it for us, your agency would not be worth while as far as we are concerned.' The manufacturer might come back with words like these: 'While we include this as a clause it is only because in our experience occasions have arisen where the alternative was 'no sale'. All that we are doing in these circumstances is to avoid that alternative. Should the need to exercise it ever arise, then we would do everything possible to assure some cover for yourselves and consult you before taking any action.'

'As far as your opposition to an agreement under English law is concerned, that is our company policy. The interests of the agent are taken care of through the International Chamber of Commerce arbitration clause'. The agent might go on to illustrate how other principals do agree to having Venezuelan law as the law of the agreement on the grounds that Venezuela is where the contract is to be carried out.

Thus far the protagonists have stated their positions on issues on which they are not in complete accord, have indicated the possibility of settlement of the issues of advertising and commission, are aware of each other's expressed commitments and reservations in respect of other issues, and now are in possession of some more information on which to reach some form of resolution.

Reaching agreement

Bargaining away the unacceptable

When commitments have been demonstrated and tested, the parties can seek an accommodation which will enable each party to be satisfied they have reached an equitable settlement.

In the above example the agent might assess the situation as one in which the manufacturer holds most of the shots but is prepared to go a little way to meet him. The manufacturer has demonstrated that he is unlikely to move from the position taken up on direct sales, but might just be amenable to helping in some way with the drive unit spares. The agent might now try for agreement: 'I think we might be prepared to agree to your clause on direct dealing now you have explained the circumstances, if you could see your way to helping us with the spares drive units which are heavy costs items which might not be needed for years.'

The manufacturer could come back with the argument that the cost of spares would be recovered in six months of expected sales which did not appear to be such a high cost when seen in relation to likely sales growth: 'However, we have not yet agreed what the sales target should be for the first year. Our own view based on the size of the market is twenty machines valued at x thousand Bolivars. If you feel that is agreeable, then we would provide six months' credit for the spare drive units.'

Assessing what is acceptable

By the moves and countermoves which the parties make in the course of the negotiation interaction, the area of conflict is reduced to the point where the possiblities of early agreement can be assessed. The available possibilities are known and the parties now have to decide what is or is not acceptable.

Either party may take the initiative to put forward a final package, which may or may not be accepted without amendment. If now the agent takes it upon himself to try to finalize the agreement, the dialogue might go something like this: 'We feel we would like to settle, but twenty machines in the first year seems a tall order, even with a very special effort. In the first place, interest rates are high and decisions to purchase machinery of the kind you make are readily postponable. Secondly, we need time to make an impact with your machines. Nothing succeeds like success, and given a few successful installations, we are certain we can well exceed twenty machines a year. If in the first year you will agree to fifteen machines, we shall agree to purchase the spare drive units on the six months' credit terms you have mentioned, which will get us off the hook as far as our cash flows are concerned.'

To which the manufacturer might reply: 'If we extend the credit for a period of six months, we feel you could try for twenty units as part of the contractual obligation.'

By using the word 'try' the manufacturer is indicating that he is really open to some revision, and the response from the agent should take this all into account: 'If you will accept eighteen units or y Bolivars for the first year, we would be pleased to accept English law as the law of the contract.'

The parties might now think they had something to shake hands on: 'Let's just summarize what I think we have agreed . . .'. An agency agreement is about to be made. The manufacturer might take it upon himself to impress on the agent the need for information as in the agreement. Should conflict arise in relation to its implementation, the manufacturer might not be so happy to find out that in Venezuela local law applied in these cases (Allen 1975). What the agent has conceded is a 'straw' issue; in other words nothing. Information is power, and in default of that information or the search which produces it a negotiator is to a very large extent dependent on what the other party says, or deliberately lets him think, is the situation.

The whole scenario of reaching agreement could be replicated with respect to distributorship. A distributor will be interested in price and discounts, the basis of the quotation in respect of payment terms, the period of credit, the stocks carried, freedom to set prices, and any other factors affecting the worth of the distributorship. Like the agent he will wish to have an exclusive agreement, a defined area, shared promotional expenses, unequivocal conditions under which the agreement may be terminated, and protection in the event of unresolved conflict.

A distributor will be constrained by the anticipated stake he will hold in the joint activity. If the stake is high and dependence correspondingly high, he may have to go some way to meeting the manufacturer's requirements. A manufacturer may see his competitiveness in the market to be dependent on the commitment of resources by the distributor.

A manufacturer of metallic and coloured pigment stamping foils which are supplied to the hot stamping foil industry worldwide for use on book cover titles among other applications found it difficult to compete on price with a number of its competitors. Prices could be reduced in the area of packing, cores, wrappers and carriage if distributors would take delivery of 'jumbo' rolls of 2,000 metres, which could then be spooled down by distributors. This involved distributorships investing in their own spooling facilities, which were an issue for negotiation in the process of appointing new distributors. An Italian manufacturer of recording and control instruments insists as one of his conditions that an instrument mechanic is employed by the distributor when accumulated sales into his market have reached a given volume.

What has been agreed

Inter-organizational relations

By reducing what has been agreed to writing, the parties are not entering a watertight contract. Such a legalistic view could have an adverse affect on the performance of the agreement. In any case no agreement could legislate for all contingencies. What is important is how it operates as a basis for the development of the relationship. An agreement of agency or distributorship is only as good as the difficulties identified in operating it and the steps taken to resolve them. The agreement formalizes the stated commitment of the parties and gives expression to their inter-organizational dependence.

In the examples above the agent undertook to commit resources to the spares necessary to operate as the arm of his principal, and the distributor undertook to invest in spooling facilities to keep down costs. The manufacturer likewise has committed resources to these joint undertakings by gearing to service the agreements and providing necessary services, such as the provision of credit for essential spares.

Interpersonal relations

The relationship between two companies exists at the interpersonal level as well as at the inter-organizational level. Personal experience within the manufacturer − agent/distributor relationship is equally likely to shape channel relations, through the familiarity and trust built up as a result of individual episodes within the relationship and the social interaction which takes place. Because of the possibility of relationships not being built effectively, and the development of avoidable conflicts, the importance of the key contacts in exporting firms is a critical one, for they stand between the organization and its partner. For the distributor/agent and ultimate user the exporting company representative often is the firm.

The cultural dimension

If effective relationships between organizations are largely a function of the inter-personal interactions of boundary spanning personnel, the exporting company which is moving continuously between cultures has a responsibility to itself to consider the implications for selection and education and training of personnel performing the tasks of negotiating distributorship and agency agreements.

The process of effective interaction is viewed as the implementation of at least three core interpersonal skills (Mangham 1979):

1 The ability to see what is appropriate in any given situation. Past experience, familiarity with overseas counterparts, and conversancy with the culture of similar people and interactions with them are all determining factors of the depth of insight into interaction situations. Familiarity with a culture is no guarantee of real conversancy. The cultural analysis approach begins with a knowledge of the traits of the negotiator's own culture and a similar level of understanding of the opposers culture (Lee 1966). It aims to isolate the 'self-reference criterion' and the bias contained in viewing behaviour of foreign negotiators in terms of one's own culture. Because of the nature of marketing work, those people negotiating agency and distributorship agreements are not always in a position to observe local behaviour and the cultural values governing it. There is therefore a need for an ability to adapt behaviour appropriately, as discussed in Chapter 4, and the ability to communicate with understanding via the parallel communication channels

discussed in Chapter 3.

2 The ability to consider the implications of the opposer's behaviour for oneself. This relates to the mutual role-taking discussed in Chapter 7, in which parties to an interaction situation must be able to assume that what others do or are perceived to do during an interaction are important clues to the definition of the situation. This is a measure of the technical interaction competence of the parties.

3 The ability to put the above skills into action: The development of interactive skills through the application of interactive skills training (Rackham *et al.* 1971), or through small group work whereby members can consider more directly the kinds of issues that arise at both organizational and individual levels in attempting to undertake collaborative work with others (Low and Bridger 1979). By such developmental means negotiators involved in managing relationships can widen their repertoires of appropriate behaviours.

NEGOTIATING THE MAINTENANCE AND RENEWAL OF AGREEMENTS

The self-determination of the parties which exists at the time an original agreement is made is complicated by factors of performance and commitment to the joint activity once it is put into operation. The original objectivity is clouded by the history of the growing relationship and the subsequent negotiations that take place within the original agreement. The stake anticipated in the agreement is given effect by the allocation of resources.

All relationships are subject to stress, and organizations in principal/agent and supplier/distributor relationships are no exception. This stress can be brought about by a number of factors.

Environmental changes and the balance of advantage

Environmental changes can very readily upset the balance of advantage implicit in the original agreement. While this balance is not necessarily delicately poised, it can be so in the perception of the people giving effect to the agreement. Even if one of the parties is getting more than the other in relative terms by virtue of good original nego-tiation, it is the way the parties themselves interpret situations and episodes affected by these changes that will colour their reaction to them.

Economic changes

The economic environment can change quickly. Variations in exchange rates are examples of this.

A manufacturer normally quoting the distributor and invoicing him as originally agreed in the manufacturer's currency may find his own currency depreciating in relation to the currency of the distributor's country. If the price elasticity of demand of the manufacturer's product is low, then there is no requirement on the distributor to pass on to the customer any part of the increase between the distributor's costs and his revenue occasioned by the relative movement of the currencies. The manufacturer will receive a decreasing proportion of the division of resources between the parties, unless he is aware of this and takes corrective action. That action will be to increase the price to the distributor, so that in terms of relative costs the distributor is not affected.

If the movement of the currencies over a short period is of such a magnitude that the increase in price under notifiable arrangements in the agreement is perceived by the distributor to be excessive, then negotiation is called for rather than administrative action aimed solely at ensuring that maximum advantage derives from the currency movements. The negotiation then might take the form of joint decision-making, where the manufacturer's proposal might have the objective of creating synergistic alternatives, by making available to the distributor demonstration products or increased advertising allocation, or other alternatives clearer perhaps to the distributor from his knowledge of the market; while ensuring that an adequate proportion is received for other possibilities, such as product development or payments to shareholders. Even more so than in negotiating original agreements, the cooperative problem-solving approach is seen to be the touchstone of inter-organizational performance of manufacturers and agents/distributors.

The pressure for change brought about by the growth aspirations of a company in the market, or by changes in the nature of competition, can affect channel arrangements in a number of ways. The very forces which provide the incentive to set up agencies and distributorships in the first instance can threaten their dissolution unless negotiators can identify mutually acceptable directions for their activities. A Dutch manufacturer of pumps was so successful in Mexico through the efforts of his Mexican distributor that he decided to set up a manufacturing unit in Mexico to exploit the Mexican market and the export potential arising from its Mexican location. The threat to the distributors left them in an apparently weaker position in relation to their supplier than when there was no sign of a Dutch presence in the country.

Political changes

Changes in the political environment can equally affect the balance of advantage between the parties. When a government decides to make a rule that all agents should be indigenous to the country, the power base of the manufacturer's negotiator is weakened because the choice open to him is restricted and there is not the leverage he might otherwise have where a larger number of alternatives is open to him.

When a country starts to provide incentives for joint-venture operations, perhaps in support of pioneer industries, existing distributor arrangements may well be threatened. See Reading I for an example of the interaction of environmental factors of which the political will is an important component, and the likely effect of this on manufacturer/agent relationships.

The possibility of preference being given to a company which sets up manufacture locally can be reinforced by the raising of tariff barriers which can further threaten the arrangement. Consideration of the possibility of taking advantage of government incentives might lead to negotiations of a joint venture with the agent/distributor. Where this is not feasible, but a more suitable company is considered, termination negotiations will have to be carried out with the existing distributor.

Legal changes

When government legislation is enacted which affects agency/distributorship agreements, these can affect the relative power between the organizations involved.

A decision of the European Commission or a judgment of the European Court of Justice can affect this balance of advantage as between supplier and distributor. When the EC Commission compelled Kawasaki UK Ltd.[1] to remove the restriction on its dealers which prevented them from exporting motor cycles to other EC countries, this opened up the export trade to the dealers, and created the situation in which the possibility existed that the company became more dependent on the dealers as the latter took advantage of increased export sales. In West Germany, where the comparative prices were higher, the possibility was created that the dealers might become dissatisfied as a result of inroads being made into their market, perhaps causing stress within their relationships with Kawasaki GmbH as a direct result of the Commission's decision.

One of the functions of management planning, of which negotiation of an agreement is often the implementation, is to make contingency plans which derive from possibilities of change in the environment. To negotiate the withdrawal from an agreement can be a strategic decision. The situation in the package tour industry in the United Kingdom at the time of writing is that package tour operators may only sell package tours through travel agents who are members of the Association of British Travel Agents. Travel agents may only sell foreign package tours of operators who are ABTA members. With Spain's accession to the European Communities, the interest of some Spanish property owners may not be seen to be best served by the arrangement, because it may be deemed to be restrictive and to affect trade between countries. This may well result in complaints to the Competition Office in Brussels that the practice is contrary to Article 85 of the Rome Treaty, which expressly proscribes restrictive practices as a general principle. A decision against ABTA would be likely to shift the relative advantage from the tour operator to the travel agent. Strong retail chains would be able to dictate to the tour operator what kind of tour and what level of price they would accept for sale. The organizations likely to be affected, namely the tour operators who had earlier integrated vertically with airline companies, hotel owners in the resorts who had long-term contracts with the tour operators, travel agents who were members of ABTA, and those travel agents outside ABTA, should be making contingency plans now. This would be not only as a preparation for negotiating future agreements, but against the possibility of negotiating out of existing arrangements.

With the completion of a single internal market within the EC by 1992, areas like financial services and air transportation are gradually being opened up to competition causing major changes in the structure of markets. For example, until a recent judgment of the European Court, French law required that only 20 per cent of hull and machinery business in the French marine insurance market could be placed overseas. French brokers, forwarders and shipowners are now well aware that their long-enjoyed protection will cease to have effect. French insurance interests will require to adjust to the liberalization, either by mergers to strengthen their position in a more competitive international environment, or by cooperation arrangements like joint ventures with foreign insurance interests like Lloyds brokers seeking a share of the new business.

Changes in competitive position

Very often the balance of advantage will be tilted one way or another as a result of technological, strategic and market developments. This will inevitably give rise to conflict, which will have to be negotiated away.

When a competitor to a supplier brings out a new product or process, as distinct from a variant which will give him only a very temporary advantage, then the situation changes for the parties to the agreement. An agent working on behalf of a centrifuge manufacturer serving the chemical industries who found that, because of developments in the continuous centrifuge, the batch machines of the supplier he represented were becoming increasingly limited in their application, urged his principal to develop or otherwise put on the market a continuous machine within a reasonable time. In the interim, the manufacturer became more dependent on the agent and his ability to convince customers of the advantages of continuing to use batch machines, or getting them to delay a decision until the manufacturer had a continuous model. The motivation of the agent to continue these efforts depended to a large extent on his perception of the supplier's efforts to get back to a competitive position.

When conditions are so adverse the ultimate insurance is the relationship, the agent's ability to influence action and the manufacturer's ability to take it.

Sometimes competition is experienced from other distribution channels which change the competitive position. In a situation in which a Japanese supplier of highly sophisticated technical equipment had changed his mode of operation in South Africa from operation via distributors to a local sales branch, the distributor of competing products of a European manufacturer saw a threat to his interests. The Japanese raised the standard of debate on the equipment to a highly technical level regarding design, application and performance — which the distributor could not match — thereby tilting the balance of advantage away from the European supplier in negotiations with the distributor.

Because the competitive environment is dynamic, shifts in power will take place over time and negotiations will focus on existing business arrangements. A British manufacturer supplying chocolate products on an international scale adopted a strategy of providing larger discounts to the growth area of supermarkets than to a symbol group purchasing equivalent quantities. Their argument was that the symbol group was not purchasing on its own account, but on behalf of a large number of small retailers. But weaker parties will always strive to protect their interests by strengthening their negotiation position, and the symbol group was no exception. It had organized on a West European basis and threatened to exclude the manufacturer from 11,000 retail units in Western Europe outside Britain. The threat was sufficient to move the chairman of the company to travel hot-foot to Amsterdam to negotiate new terms with the symbol group.

Changes in perceived strengths of parties

When an agreement is put into effect the parties begin to find out things about each other which they could not have known at the time the agreement was made. A distributor in Austria who was able to make switch arrangements for payment of goods by Eastern European countries through its knowledge of the trade and its connections with financial institutions made its Western European supplier more dependent on it as a result.

A Thai agent of Chinese extraction, whose principal customers were Taiwanese Chinese in Thailand who dominate the sugar industry there, provided his customers, who were largely technical people, with commercial expertise. On items attracting extended credit terms he was able to obtain confirmed, irrevocable Letter of Credit terms covering the whole contract, where normally this could only be obtained on the first 10 per cent shipped of the contract value. As a result there was no need for credit insurance charges to be incurred. Since indemnification to his principal would be received from a bank whose reliability was undoubted, the principal would therefore increase his margin of profit by the amount of the premium saved which on extended terms of payment can be considerable. The agent was thus able to eliminate the risk element in payment and put himself in a position to ask for special terms, either for himself or a customer by removing the need for export credit insurance. The apparently weaker of the parties if not without power.

Negotiations arising within agreements

Occasionally, operation of agreements highlights differences in approach and philosophy not always uncovered at the stage of concluding them. The interests of a manufacturer seeking widest possible distribution through his agents are at odds with an intermediary view which sees the sale of only one or two items a year from a wide number of agencies as a factor which can induce greatest profit from minimum resource commitment.[2] Expectations of manufacturers in respect of market information may be seen as an unnecessary requirement or unprofitable, resource-consuming activity by a distributor. Such basic differences once resolved allow the parties to concentrate their energies on those conflicting issues for which an agreement cannot specifically legislate.

Most of the issues which must be negotiated during the operation of an agreement are largely concerned with aspects of the marketing mix, and are likely to have been induced by the change factors discussed above. Many are minor adjustments in which negotiation is minimal, but some can be of major significance. Acrimonious and protracted disputes have begun with minor adjustments to an agreement.

Product issues

In the course of servicing an agreement a manufacturer may find that his distributor wishes to make minor packaging modifications, or decides that he wishes to introduce his own label of goods produced by the manufacturer, or wishes modifications to be carried out to suit his market. All such changes require to be negotiated, for the benefits of providing satisfaction to a customer who is in a long-term business relationship has also costs incurred by the allocation of resources to solving the problem. A Finnish manufacturer of agricultural machinery, in modifying his forage harvester to the much muddier Irish conditions, had to negotiate the nature and cost of the modification with his Irish distributor.

Service and product warranty is an area in which negotiation frequently takes place. Even where goods have been subject to parallel imports, the manufacturer has to honour the warranty within the EC. The motor vehicle industry is one in which the form of reimbursement to the dealer has changed several times. Now that UK laws have complied with EC product liability directives and responsibility for product defects rest with the manufacturer rather than the seller, new agreements will require to be entered into between manufacturers and distributors and basic functions and rewards negotiated.

Distribution issues

The question of physical distribution is one which goes far beyond the actual cost of transporting goods from A to B — it spans inventories, warehousing, alternative physical distribution means, and involves the costs of performing or not performing a specific function.

The concept of 'land bridge' is right in the middle of physical distribution. A Japanese motor cycle manufacturer can decide to ship his products by short sea crossing to Canada, across the Canadian continent by rail and by air from Canada to Europe. In so doing, he must negotiate the terms with the importing distributor, who will have a new series of costs related to customs clearance, delivery from airport to depot and associated accounting functions.

In the situation instanced earlier in which a Dutch supplier was so successful in Mexico through the efforts of his agent that he decided to set up his own manufacturing facility there, the distributor prevailed on the Dutch company to employ them as selling agents. The changes negotiated in the distributor's channel role resulted in this case in a favourable outcome for him.

Communication issues

During the course of a relationship, change factors can require renegotiation of joint advertising or promotion arrangements. A whisky manufacturer who developed a secondary brand as a 'mixer' with lemonade or other soft drinks, with the object of using less mature and hence cheaper stocks to generate cash flows in a price-elastic South American market, found his requirements of his distributor had changed. The secondary brand introduced to get rid of excessive stocks called for advertising and personal selling to the trade in the distributor's market. However, the end objective of creating the secondary brand was to create the funds to support the more price-inelastic primary brand aimed at the status-conscious middle-class consumer. A shift of financial resources to the secondary brand had therefore to be negotiated, while not neglecting the advertising media for the primary brand. Changing a strategy implies adjustment in intermediary actions.

In the situation illustrated earlier — in which a Japanese supplier set up a direct operation in South Africa in which technical personnel raised the issues considered to a higher level of debate than before — the distributor whose sales were threatened was able to prevail on his supplier to respond effectively. The negotiated outcome was that the manufacturer commissioned a programmed learning package which enabled the distributor the better to match the local sales operation of the Japanese company.

Distribution agreements cannot be divorced from joint communication efforts towards the ultimate consumers of a product. A promotional package marketed for a limited time has to be stocked and distributed to the point of sale in advance of the promotions period. Such arrangements may have to be negotiated with distributors.

Price issues

Price is the focal point of any agreement, in that it takes or should take into account all other aspects of a negotiation. When discount structures are revised, or terms of payment changed, or product modifications made, or amended distribution or communication arrangements introduced, price is rightly seen as the value placed on the overall package. It is incumbent on the parties to these changes to know the implications of each change so that the negotiation does not have an outcome that is much more favourable to the other party.

Cultural perceptions

From time to time issues can be coloured by transference to them of the values of one's own culture. Conflict can arise on ethical issues. Nowhere is this more evocative than in the subject of corruption. Corruption can arise worldwide, but when put into a cross-cultural context can be interpreted very differently in different countries.

In Latin America, black Africa, parts of Asia and in the Arab countries, the use of family and friendship ties is widespread and is a necessary and important means of doing business. The use of agents and distributors raises the question of commission and bribery. This has been well put (Muna 1980):

> 'To the Arab business mind using personal ties and connections, because of their reciprocal nature, means using up old "credits" or accumulating new "liabilities" depending on one's "balance sheet" of reciprocal transactions. Either way there is usually a value attached to the use of personal connections which is not always an economic value. When a foreign organization employs an agent on its behalf, the agent/middleman will incur several costs, one of which might be the cost of capital; his personal "ties/connections" capital. For these services the agent feels entitled to a commission. Thus while there is one line between commission and bribery for a Westerner doing business in the Arab world, the dividing line may be drawn differently for the Arab businessman. The line of demarcation of the Arabs is a clear one. He may or may not use a proportion of his commission for bribery; that for him represents a fee for services rendered. This is how one Arab businessman differentiated between corruption and commission:
>
> > "If one offers money to a government to influence it, that is corruption. But if someone receives money for services rendered afterwards, that is a commission. . . . If one-sided or greatly unequal in value or given with the purpose of inducing favourable treatment, then such gifts become bribery. . . . While some Arab executives may regard with disfavour the use of personal ties and connections, it is often the only viable alternative.

Both the society's values and its institutions strongly encourage the use of these means of doing business." '*

In a study conducted among American and Japanese companies which had done business with the People's Republic of China, the main differences between American and Chinese businessmen were (1) that Chinese Communist culture puts emphasis on ethical and moralist principles, whereas Americans were thought to be very legalistic; and (2) culture and politics are inextricably intermingled in the PRC, while the American view is that politics, economics and social relations occupy separate spheres (Pye 1982).

The Chinese have less feeling for the drama of agreement than do Westerners. A formal contract is not the end of negotiations. Indeed the lack of finality about agreements with the Chinese, and the prospect of continuous negotiation, suggests the kind of ensuing relationship being advocated here. It is the relationship that is important, not so much the agreement, because the agreement cannot anticipate the changes and consequent problems surrounding the relationship. The system is effective because changes can be made after the agreement has been struck. The message is 'Don't hesitate to ask for changes after the contract has been made.' The Chinese will certainly not hesitate.

Inter-organizational factors

Negotiations relating to the marketing mix elements are illustrative of how the operation of agreements reach right into the various functions or departments of the negotiating parties. Where manufacturing and buying organizations are in direct contact their interaction is basic to their successful achievement of objectives. Where the supplying and buying organizations are linked by intermediaries, the importance of communication and information to facilitate the interaction of the parties is underlined. It is all very well and necessary to write into the original agreement the provision of technical and market information by the intermediary, and corresponding provision of information, particularly technical, by the manufacturer for promotional purposes by the intermediary. But it is only in the operation of the agreement that the real needs of the parties can be determined.

While the original agreement may have established the basis on which the parties would undertake to do business, it does not necessarily determine the competence of the intermediary in undertaking his agreed functions, particularly in view of the fact that market conditions change, technologies change and products are modified or replaced. There is therefore a need for the intermediary to update himself in order to satisfy his customer's needs. It is equally necessary for the supplier to provide the necessary training. Good analysis of the internal and external environment will pinpoint the need for the interacting organizations, open communications will highlight each party's needs for the other, and subsequent negotiation will determine how the problem will be resolved and the costs shared.

In the process of operating agreements companies learn a great deal about each other's needs. The production personnel of a factory get to understand that failure to deliver

* From F. A. Muna, *The Arab Executive*, Macmillan, London and Basingstoke, 1980. Reproduced by permission.

on schedule may or may not affect the ultimate user's plans; but it will almost certainly affect his costs, as where production asks for a Letter of Credit raised by the customer to be extended. Again communication and information must interact in order to establish acceptable procedures for processing orders.

Sometimes changes in the environment require inter-organizational adjustments which are effected through negotiation. A North American agent for a German company found that his principal's product was becoming less competitive against similar equipment manufactured elsewhere and supplied by competing distributors owing to the general appreciation of the German currency. The manufacturer sought to reduce the agent's commission, while reducing his own price. The agent maintained that his percentage commission was inviolate. It was only the threat of withdrawal of the agency which eventually drove the agent to settle by negotiation. The principal was aware of the importance of his product in the range which the agent offered, and of the probable unavailability of a competing agency. He exerted his channel power to provide a solution, and the ensuing negotiation hinged on what constituted equal sacrifice in the mutual interest. The cooperative nature of the relationship between the organizations was threatened by an issue of apparent principle. When the agent reviewed his operations at the end of the first year under the new arrangement, he appreciated that his income was higher than it would have been had he maintained his position.

Information becomes crucial to the relationship, but it is only in the course of interacting that overseas intermediaries and suppliers realize fully their mutual needs. In pursuing their own objectives each may require information not considered important by the other. A distributor may consider that his best efforts should be directed to increasing his sales, measuring them in comparison with the comparable period in the previous year, and estimating the future in relation to the potential growth of existing customers. In devising his strategy the manufacturer may wish to know the total market, total imports, distributor's share of the overall market as well as of imports of products supplied by him.

An Italian exporter of recording and control instruments, in seeking to impress on his Mexican distributor the need for market awareness, highlighted this when he provided him with locally produced statistics which purported to show that the market was increasing at a greater rate than the distributor's sales. In the event, the agent investigated the figures and found that they included such items as clinical thermometers, and that in fact his performance in terms of market share just about matched the growth in the market. The Italian had, however, made his point. A negotiation had been completed without the disagreement being voiced.

In the interest of the maintenance of good relationships with his agents and distributors, a manufacturer should not only keep them informed of developments within his own organization which may affect them, but also to remember that these intermediaries have other organizations to which they relate and with which they also have relationships.

If, for example, the manufacturer is in direct touch with a user because of an urgent problem, then he should remember the distributor or agent's function in servicing the user, and remember to advise him in good time of all developments.

> **High and dry**
>
> A European manufacturer of machinery mistakenly sent an Australian customer machinery with a rotating component designed for a lower speed than the Australian customer would be using. Because of the inherent danger, the manufacturer communicated direct with the user to replace the component and hold up production. The agent arrived to find a difficult situation he had neither anticipated nor been advised of. In a letter to the manufacturer he described his feelings in one heartfelt sentence: 'I felt like a shag on a rock.'

Interpersonal factors

When organizations interact, the effectiveness of their interaction is largely determined by those individuals involved in boundary-spanning activities — marketing executives, export managers, distributor executives and the like. It is they who are responsible for building up the trust necessary to initiate and nurture agreements. Not only must they be capable of judgment in relation to inter-organizational factors — for example, when to bring in functional specialists; they must also go beyond task factors. It is they, by and large, who interpret the relationships for people within their own organizations.

It is therefore essential for them to bridge the cultural/linguistic barriers on which relationships often founder. Indeed, it is the supplier organization which ought to take the initiative in these matters. It is the marketing function of these organizations which has the experience of working in different cultural milieux, and therefore the responsibility to develop the sensitivity necessary to communicate effectively. Relationships can hang on such abilities.

The implications for the supplying organization's recruitment and training policy are considerable. Not only do the people responsible for making and maintaining agreements have to have a high task orientation; they must also be able to adapt to the different nature of relationships within different cultures. While such matters are outside the scope of this book, selection of these key personnel is an important decision.

They need to be suited to the work, be high self-monitors in terms of learning from the experiences to which they are exposed, be amenable to the appropriate cultural and communication training, and have the kind of personality which takes enjoyment from the activities involved.

Negotiation as an ongoing process

It will be seen from the foregoing that in mature relationships between a manufacturer and his distributors or agents, negotiation is an ongoing process. It depends for its effectiveness on the continuing cooperation of the organizations involved, which in turn hinges on the interpersonal skills of those people who must operate the agreements on a continuing basis.

It depends also on the ability of these people to read the ebbs and flows of relative power, for the foundation of negotiation strategy is power which will not necessarily be exercised except when conflicts cannot be resolved without it.

As the company marketing a product or service to and through other organizations is the one which actively moves across cultures, there is, in the vast majority of cases, an onus on that company to bridge the cultural gap. The basic objective of negotiation is to reap the benefit of the joint opportunities that exist, and that can only be done by continuous feeding of the relationship and an active search for creative solutions to the problems which must arise in the course of it. It is no coincidence that a study on manufacturer/overseas distributor relations and export performance showed the intensity of the relationship and the readiness of the parties to adapt their roles and routines to be critical factors in performance (Rosson and Ford 1982).

TERMINATING AGREEMENTS

Sometimes agreements are terminated because the manufacturer concerned has been successful in the market and market factors are such that a new form of distribution is appropriate, as where a subsidiary is established. Takeovers of either the manufacturer or the distributor/agent, particularly when done by an organization supplying competitive products, can lead to a collapse of the common objectives on which the original agreement was formed, and lead to termination. But probably the most frequent reason is the continuing unsatisfactory performance of the distributor or agent.

Whatever the reason for wishing to end an agreement, there are problems to be resolved in its dissolution. If a distributor or agent holding stocks of spares has his agreement terminated by the supplier, he should not have to be left with stocks to dispose of as he can. A good agreement will have made provision for this, for example, by stating that in the event of termination by the supplier they will be bought back at the price paid plus any charges such as carriage if they are quoted in the supplier's standard catalogue. Yet, this does not resolve everything. A distributor or agent may be carrying stocks which are obsolete, but are held as a service to customers using old equipment and could be held to represent a goodwill element.

When an agreement is terminated by the distributor or agent, it is not unusual for a clause in the original agreement to have anticipated this by conceding the right to the supplier to repurchase, in such an eventuality, such stocks as are currently catalogued and in a good saleable condition. This does not provide answers to such questions as what payment is to be made for past services. Sometimes the law under which the agreement is operative will provide the answer, as in Belgium where a specific law relating to distributorship exists and provides for recompense under specific rules for the goodwill which the outgoing distributor is assumed to have built up for the manufacturer.

Just as in the approach to any negotiation, the preparation of information bearing on the negotiation is important. If the agent or distributor has consistently failed to meet targets written into the contract but subject to periodic agreement, that has to be established. The manufacturer's position is weakened if he terminates but has failed himself to meet the terms of the agreement, such as failing to deliver outstanding orders.

The objectives for termination will vary. The first is to ensure that any litigation is avoided. This involves legal information and advice so that a threat of legal action can be seen for what it is — and that very often is a bluff. The second is to terminate in such a way that the outgoing distributor or agent assists in the transfer, for example of stocks, customer enquiries, and if possible information on customers and markets.

At the end of the day, termination of an agreement is a confession of failure either to identify the right candidate in the first place, or to exercise the best strategies in relation to situations with which the manufacturer is confronted. The accumulated experience of the parties to it should be used to make a new agreement more successful than the one that preceded it. That is a function of information, communication and training.

SUMMARY

Specialization has promoted trading relationships which, once the relationships are perpetuated, are indications of the emergence of channels of distribution. Mutual dependence is the outcome and requires the management of important behaviours, including conflict and power. Examples were given in the cross-cultural context, and this was related to negotiation in terms of the resolution of conflict and the exercise of channel power. Negotiation is isolated as a key process in conflict resolution, subsuming the four power-related processes identified in the literature — namely problem-solving, persuasion, political solutions and bargaining.

The differences between agency and distributorship were pinpointed but seen in practice to be less clear cut. The relative power of the parties was examined and the dangers of exploiting channel power highlighted. Cooperation is seen to be the most commonly observed form of behaviour in inter-organizational and interpersonal terms. Experience at these levels within the manufacturer/agent distributor relationship is seen to be likely to shape future channel relations. Relationships are seen to vary in their nature and function according to the cultures across which they are developed.

In the negotiation of original agreements, the process is seen to be the means by which a firm positions itself in one or more channel arrangements. In deciding on first offers, both parties have invariably different ideas of how resources will be allocated to any agreement. The locus of power has a bearing on negotiation objectives. Power is also seen to derive from situational and environmental factors and can be created by the establishment of alternative courses of action.

Because the tenor of agency/distributorship agreements is cooperative, the problem-solving mode induced precludes those factors which make necessary the movement from entrenched positions. It is therefore possible to move directly into the integrative bargaining stage of the negotiation skills model. Perceptions of issues within this stage were looked at in relation to an agent in Venezuela and a supplier in the United Kingdom, and a scenario drawn of a typical negotiation exchange. A trade-off across the issues reflected the power balance as mediated by environmental and situational factors. The able negotiator is one who, in addition to task-related abilities, can bring about effective relationships and can implement core interpersonal skills which hinge on cultural sensitivity for their effectiveness.

In the negotiation of the maintenance and renewal of agreements, the situation is complicated by the prior experience of the parties. The balance of advantage is seen to be affected by changes in the economic, political, legal and competitive environ-

254

ments. Most of the issues to be negotiated in the operation of an agreement are concerned with product, distribution, communication and price issues.

Issues can be coloured by transference to them of the values of one's own culture. This was looked at particularly in relation to views of corruption. Differences in interpretation arise in cross-cultural contexts, and nowhere is this more evident than in the different approaches in Western and Arab cultures. The essential difference is seen to be in the use of family and friendship ties in the Arab countries, where the culture requires these to be necessary and important means of doing business.

It is only in the course of interacting that overseas agents/distributors and their suppliers realize fully their mutual needs. The effectiveness of these inter-organizational interactions is dependent on the people operating at the organizational boundaries — executives of distributor companies, agents, marketing executives, export sales managers, and the like.

Negotiation then is an ongoing process in mature channels of distribution. It depends for its success on the continuing cooperation of the organizations involved and the cross-cultural and interpersonal skills of the people whose tasks require them to operate the agreements. It also rests on the ability of these people to read the ebbs and flows of relative power.

But even long-standing relationships can be brought to an end by changes in circumstances, just as unsatisfactory relationships are terminated by a specific act of one of the parties, usually the supplier. When agreements are being dissolved a similar process is gone through as in negotiating original agreements and maintenance issues.

Notes

1 See the Official Journal of the European Communities No. L16/9 of 23 January 1979, Commission Decision of 12 December 1978 relating to a proceeding under Article 85 (IV/29.430 — Kawasaki).
2 This is an example of how alignment of goals can be seen to diverge in practice. Some manufacturing firms can, depending on a number of factors, opt for developing a few salient markets in depth while others may be more suited to operating in a wide number of markets at a low level of penetration. See Piercy (1981) for a discussion of the factors which determine which of the options is the more appropriate in different circumstances.

Questions

1 What are the fundamental behaviours in distribution channels and how are they related to each other?
2 Identify the factors which affect the power relationship between a manufacturer and his distributor/agent. How can that power be used to the benefit of channel members?
3 What is the function of an original agreement and what are the principal features that distinguish it?

4 Give examples of environmental changes, other than those given in the text, which can lead to the requirement to modify or change an agreement.

5 To what extent is the maintenance of agency/distributorship agreements an ongoing negotiation process?

6 Is there room for gift-giving and confidential and special payments to agents/distributors?

7 Why should the termination of an agreement benefit from being a negotiated one?

READING

Environmental factors and the renegotiation of manufacturer/agent relationships *

The following extract from a letter from the President of a German manufacturing company to his Mexican agents was the culmination of a series of events leading to apparent breakdown in relationships between the parties. His retrospective review of the history of the relationship given in the extract illustrates the culturally-induced strains on it; for example, coping with the pressure to compromise when compromise is associated with the loss of personal honour as has been indicated by Fisher (1980). It also shows how economic factors, assisted by the political will to improve the situation, can impact strongly on distribution channel arrangements.

'You will recall that in our export manager's letter of 17 September 1981, we reviewed the history of our recent competitive position in Mexico. In that letter we went to the trouble of explaining that, over the years since the floating of the German mark, our competitive position had been eroded by the strengthening of the mark in relation to most world currencies. We invited you at that time to accept a reduction in your percentage commission which would be matched by an equivalent reduction by ourselves. The object of this combined reduction was to counter the effect of the appreciation of the deutschmark on our business. The combined reduction would in fact have made our prices more competitive. Nobody should be more aware of the opportunities in the Mexican market than yourselves, for we have lost a fair number of orders on price. Our market is a highly competitive international one and it was our belief that the price reduction to the customer would stimulate demand which could give us a greater total sales and yourselves a greater aggregate commission than you have obtained up to now.

Your own view at the time was that you did not wish in any way to prejudice the rate of commission agreed in our agency agreement. Recent problems of the Mexican economy were made clear to me while I was on a visit to the United States. Because of the deterioration of your country's external accounts and subsequent borrowings from the IMF, your government, hampered by weak oil prices, has had to devalue the peso twice and close the exchange market. However, among the current plans to meet the IMF conditions of repayment is an envisaged increase of the petrochemical market by two and a half times in the next eight years, brought about by a burgeoning of demand

* Extract from the case study 'Case Avila S de RL' by J. B. McCall, Open Business School, 1984. Reproduced by permission of the Open University.

in the domestic market and major thrust in export markets. This could have been to our joint advantage. That is what prompted me to visit Mexico City. It was my intention in the short time at my disposal to discuss with you these latest developments. I was hopeful of re-opening the subject in our mutual interest and of being successful in getting you to move from the uncompromising position you had taken up. In the present situation the issue of import licences is virtually certain to be related to price.

In the middle term we may have to consider some sort of manufacturing operation in Mexico to meet your government's aspirations of developing a broadly-based capital goods sector which until now has been slow to develop by comparison with the consumer goods sector. We have no doubt that the long-term prospects of the importation of equipment of the kind we supply will be restricted due to the need to conserve foreign exchange.

You will further recall that we were of the opinion that the negotiation of the sale of glass-lined vessels to Allones Hermanos y Sucesores could well have been handled by yourselves. While we are always prepared to help on the more substantial contracts (at no cost to yourselves) we do feel that you could have negotiated the small reduction which our representative had to concede. Had it been negotiated by yourselves and you had conceded a similar amount I think we would probably have met the cost of this in any case. However, there is a mutuality in all these things and more and more we get the impression that any concession should, in your opinion, be made by us.

Perhaps if we had met while you were in Germany we might have worked out a formula agreeable to both of us, but Herr Schumann was on an overseas visit and I was on holiday. Perhaps if you had scheduled your visit for earlier or later in the year I should not have missed you.

We cannot really continue to do business in this way and perhaps it would be more satisfactory if we were to discontinue immediately our relationship. I feel certain that in the circumstances you will not put any obstacle in our way.

May I thank Sr Martin for his attention and hospitality during my brief visit. He was an excellent host in what must have been for him, very trying circumstances.'

CHAPTER 10

The licensing agreement

Licensing and the transfer of knowledge... 258
What licensing is.. 258
Factors affecting licensing.. 259
Choosing partners.. 260
Organizational access.. 261
Secrecy and confidentiality... 262
Financial considerations... 263
Costs and benefits.. 263
Assessing the worth.. 264
Exclusivity.. 266
Improvement clauses... 267
Cross-licensing... 267
Communications and inter-organizational relationships......................... 268
Termination clauses.. 269
Licensing and the 'negotiation skills model'...................................... 270
Pre-negotiation stage.. 270
Distributive stage.. 270
Integrative bargaining stage.. 271
Decision-making and action stage... 271
Post-negotiation stage... 272
Cultural context of the agreement.. 272
Summary 273
Reading.. 275

LICENSING AND THE TRANSFER OF KNOWLEDGE

What licensing is

Licensing agreements are essentially concerned with a sale of knowledge, access to that knowledge and the means to exploit it. See Chapter 6 for a fuller description.

In terms of entering foreign markets, exporting and direct investment (in terms of an operational unit) come readily to mind. However, they are not the only methods of entering a foreign market. Licensing represents another approach which may be as profitable as, or possibly more so than, other alternatives. The reasons cited in the next chapter for a likely growth in joint-venture agreements apply equally to licensing. As less developed countries become more economically nationalistic, more doors to autonomous direct investment are going to close. Organizations wishing to expand their markets will be provoked to examine the alternative methods available more closely. As Contractor (1984) suggests, 'Licensing agreements are receiving increased attention particularly for areas of the world where the environments for foreign investment has become more restrictive.'

Although statistics for the UK for 1983 indicate that almost 55 per cent of unrelated royalty receipts are derived from North America and the rest of Western Europe — indicating clearly the direction of licensing traffic — almost 28 per cent is derived from less developed countries. It is the relationships which are at the basis of this 28 per cent which have seen a slightly greater degree of growth over the last five years, and which are likely to grow further, as less technically advanced economies, and organizations within these economies, seek access to advanced technologies as part of their programme of increasing the rate of economic development.

Licensing agreements are characterized by a range of alternative possibilities. The licensor can grant to the licensee patent rights, rights to trademarks, copyrights or know-how rights. In addition, assistance with production may be agreed, together with arrangements regarding the extent of the licensee's rights to the marketing of the end product.

Factors affecting licensing

Depending on the nature and extent of the rights granted, the focus of the negotiation of the licence will change. Virtually all the research evidence, and the views from licensing executives operating in the field, suggest that, whatever the arrangement under negotiation, the licensing operation to be successful must be mutually beneficial and must allow both parties to profit from the agreement.

The drawing up of a licensing agreement is a particularly complex procedure, since an array of contingencies must be considered and accounted for. Against a background of anti-trust legislation, whether in Europe or America or elsewhere, parties to an agreement must guard against exposing themselves, by the provisions of the agreement, to legal sanctions. At the same time parties to the agreement want to ensure that, in the case of some dispute arising, the terms which have been agreed are legally enforceable. No matter what the circumstances, however, it is not possible to draft agreements to cover all contingencies, no matter how sharp the lawyer's pencil.

In essence a licence may be described as a contract by which the owner of a proprietary product or process grants another company the right to produce that product or process, in exchange for financial compensation. As has been indicated, the negotiation of such agreements in an international setting across cultural boundaries is characterized by a number of similarities, particularly in the manner in which negotiations proceed through the various stages. Equally, each particular agreement type has unique features, giving the negotiator a fresh challenge in each case. This is no less the case when the negotiation involves licence and technical assistance agreements.

In many respects the negotiation of such agreements provides the negotiator with a whole array of different circumstances, depending on the nature of the licence sought. It is not difficult to appreciate how different the negotiating arena might be if what is being negotiated is the grant of a licence to a prospective licensee as a result of that licensee's infringement of patent rights. In this case the licence is being granted as part of a settlement in lieu of litigation. Compare this with negotiating access to production rights and know-how for a highly advanced technology.

Alternatively, consider a negotiation in which a licensor is influenced by time pressures, exerted by technical obsolescence and expiry of patent rights, to reach an agreement quickly to ensure that an innovation is brought rapidly to the market.

There are so many variables involved in a licensing arrangement that it is extremely difficult, and perhaps not a little dangerous, to talk in terms of some standard format or approach. By spelling out the major issues, however, and then placing those issues into the context of the 'negotiation skills model' of Figure 2.4, general lessons may be drawn which can be of value to the prospective negotiator.

Choosing partners

In terms of licensing policy, companies would appear to fall into two broad categories. Firstly, there are those companies (which represent the majority) which do not pursue an aggressive marketing policy with regard to selling rights to their products and processes. In general, these companies with desirable technology tend to adopt a fairly passive role, responding as necessary.

The second category are those companies who more than likely have a major commitment to research and development activity. They are constantly on the lookout for opportunities to underwrite development costs, and to identify partners who can provide the technology and financial resources necessary to exploit an invention commercially.

Regardless of the particular category that an organization falls into, the first step is to evaluate the prospective partner. A licensing arrangement is likely to involve a fairly long-term relationship, and therefore choice of licensee or licensor is going to be crucial to the success of the enterprise.

As part of this evaluation, there should be a rigorous analysis of potential markets, distribution costs and benefits, commercial practices in the prospective partner's locality, the legal situation (particularly with regard to patents), and the general technological climate which may well affect the successful marketing of the licensed product.

Following this evaluation, consideration must be given to the extent to which such an arrangement might fit into the future development of the business. Even what appears as a favourable arrangement or deal may not be worth establishing if it does not make sense within the framework of wider corporate operations and objectives. This means that before negotiations begin, and then while they are proceeding and details are unfolding, senior executives within the business should be evaluating the nature of the deal to ensure some degree of corporate fit. This means that the negotiator will be required to provide clear statements of the proposals, for guidance of senior management or the board.

It is important to point out, however, that in a limited but nevertheless significant number of cases a company may not be able to adopt such a rational posture. This is particularly so when events force the company to adopt a defensive strategy. This occurs in those cases where the licensing executive feels that if he refuses to grant a licence requested by a foreign organization, then that organization will eventually use the patent anyway without paying anything for it. For the licensing company, refusing to grant a licence means no royalties, and raises the question of litigation. Litigation tends to be a less profitable alternative. It is an expensive exercise and the costs involved, even for the successful, are seldom recovered in full, even when possible damages so awarded are taken into account.

This means that one of the major reasons an organization takes action in this way is to act as a deterrent to intending infringers. Although this shift in power between licensor and licensee can generate feelings of frustration and injustice within the licensor's organization, it is perhaps worth reflecting on the view that many organizations are somewhat passive in their approach to licensing and its role as an income generator.

Organizational access

The next factor for the organization to turn attention to is the implementation of the licensing arrangements once an agreement is reached. If only patent rights are licensed, such that it is then up to the licensee to use or develop his own processing know-how, and design and procure his own plant, then access by the licensee is extremely limited and any arrangement may be somewhat at arms length. When, however, know-how and technical assistance are involved, then the licensor's expertise will be used and the licensor's plant is likely to be reproduced as part of the agreement. The nature of the implementation of the licence is such that the agreement involves not only the patent, but also involves uplifting know-how from one organization and implanting it in another. Such a process involves giving the licensee's organization access to the licensor's organization. In negotiating such an agreement, however, it is important to delineate the nature and extent of that access.

As well as the immediate agreement, considerable thought will also have to go into the nature and extent of future relationships between the licensor and the licensee. The whole question of the implementation of an agreement implies not only an understanding between the parties; it also implies that within the licensor's organization there has been adequate liaison between those responsible for negotiating the agreement and those eventually responsible for implementing the letter of the agreement.

In cases where know-how is being exported, the licensing agreement involves much more than the simple transfer of drawings and specifications. More substantial technical support is usually required. The extent of the technical assistance depends on the complexity of the product and processes involved, and the capabilities of the licensee with respect to both technology and managerial and marketing skills.

The situation may be such that the licensor has to send technical personnel to advise on production processes and help set up the operation, involving the licensor in considerable costs, not least in terms of managerial time. For example, the secondment of managers may be necessary in order to set up the production process and begin operations. Secondment of operatives may be necessary to provide a level of informal know-how which has been built up on the licensor's shop floor. These key individuals might be described as the 'technological gatekeepers'. Research has suggested that in many cases it is difficult to transfer information across the boundaries between different organizations unless these key individuals are on hand to help.

Other costs of this nature might be associated with quality control. When the negotiated agreement is such that the licensed product must bear a reference to the licensor — for example, 'made under license from . . .' — then the agreement is likely to contain details of how the licensor is to satisfy himself that the licensed product is up to the required standard. This may mean negotiating access to the licensee's plant, with perhaps some licensor's personnel being on station. It may also mean a commitment on the part of the licensor's organization to give substantial training to the licensee's staff — on a periodic basis, as well as at the commencement of the arrangement. In these circumstances it is as well to stipulate in the course of the negotiations the actual number of licensee's personnel who will be permitted into the licensor's works at any one time.

Access in the form of various exchanges of personnel raises the important question of security during the negotiation and implementation of a licensing agreement. In ensuring appropriate disclosure as a legitimate element of the licence, and in ensuring effective communication, a balance has to be struck between regarding one's partner's personnel as potential industrial spies and exercising a degree of prudence in keeping them away from confidential matters of no direct interest to the venture under negotiation.

Secrecy and confidentiality

Considerations of secrecy and security almost have the impact of making a licensing negotiation something of a two-stage affair. Once a potential partner has been agreed on, then inevitably there must be some disclosure of information as part of the process of discussions of a possible licensing agreement. At a very early stage during these preliminary negotiations it will be necessary to reach a secrecy agreement such that if no deal results the company approached will not use or disclose any of the information revealed up to that stage in the discussions.

Questions of disclosure of information arise particularly in the case of the so called 'option'. The option provides a potential licensee with a period during which he can make up his mind whether or not to proceed with the licence. It is quite useful in new industries where market potential may not be easily assessed, or where a process or product is in the early stages of development.

The option usually takes the form of the disclosure of significant information. The option period is usually from one to three years, and the licensor is given a lump sum in respect of the period. The negotiation of this charge is important since to set the charge too low might encourage the prospective licensor not to adopt a particularly active approach to eventual exploitation of the invention. It also might well encourage malpractice by a potential licensee who, because of involvement in a similar field, regards it as a means of suppressing or delaying the marketing of the invention.

These considerations must be balanced against the desire by the potential licensee not to be paying high fees during a period of possibly no marketing activity. The major advantage to the potential licensor is that he may be able to gain some contribution to the development costs. The major disadvantage is, however, associated with the disclosure of information, since if the option stage leads to nought the licensor has the immediate concern as to whether the information will remain safe in the hands of the potential licensee. Thus if an 'option' is negotiated it is vital that there is a clear statement of how respective parties stand in regard to the disclosure of confidential information in the event of the option arrangement not leading to a more permanent agreement.

FINANCIAL CONSIDERATIONS

Costs and benefits

The payment of a fee for products, processes and know-how has one major justification. It is in many respects a payment for the risks associated with the initial development effort. In addition it also represents a payment for the surrender of access to possible large rewards which would result from vigorous exploitation of the temporary monopoly position gained as a result of that development effort.

In weighing up the cost and benefits of extending the possibility of potential gains to others, and the resultant possible losses to himself, the licensor has to consider whether he possesses the resources for the extended monopoly exploitation. How long would it be before that position was eroded by other parties entering the arena, either by way of a close imitation or by direct infringement? As the rate of technological change increases, there is a need to start recovering the investment as soon as possible; there is the ever-present danger that, either independently or otherwise, a competitor may be working on a similar project aimed at a similar market. Against the background of such environmental factors, licensing may be one way for the licensor to overcome the marketing weaknesses in his own organization, thereby enabling him to ensure at least some rapid exploitation of the market, albeit for a reduced return in the form of a royalty payment rather than market receipts.

It has to be admitted, however, that such rational economic criteria only infrequently provide the basis for the negotiation of a licensing agreement. Most companies' approach can be characterized by comments like the following: 'We use the back of an envelope to compute profitability'; or 'I just try to get a rough feel for the attractiveness of the deal'; or 'My approach is intuitive'. Such an approach is undoubtedly indicative of most organizations' approach to licensing, which is essentially passive, with many licensors granting a licence simply because they have been approached; then the licence fees are regarded as 'gravy income'. The original research and development was never intended to be a source of foreign royalty income, and any revenues subsequently derived are considered as a bonus.

Many organizations involved in international business will also admit to having accepted licence arrangements on an interest free basis, or at least they have seen it as an opportunity for 'cross-licensing' — granting rights in exchange for other licensing rights.

For many other companies, however, the negotiation of the financial arrangements relating to the licence assumes the position of 'centre stage'.

Since so much depends on the nature of the product, the nature of the negotiators and the economic climate, it is difficult to establish any simple rules about how royalty payments should be negotiated. The licensing executive of a large chemical organization suggested that the negotiation of licensing compensation was pure 'horse trading' with licensing fees being determined according to the nature of the technology and the vagaries of the market-place. Financial considerations are likely to vary depending upon whether the technology was 'standard', reasonably sophisticated, or 'high-tech'. In the case of 'standard technology' an initial lump-sum payment may represent 5 per cent or less of the overall plant costs. In the case of sophisticated technology the lump-sum could well exceed 20 per cent of overall plant costs. In the same way 'running royalty' payments might vary between ½ per cent and in excess of 5 per cent. Such dynamic, and at times fairly intangible, issues are at the heart of this element of the negotiations. Inevitably, during the pre-negotiation stage the two parties are likely to disagree in their evaluation of the economic environment and their evaluation of the technical and legal worth of the licence. From this point of view their respective skills and the manner in which they proceed through the various stages of the negotiation are likely to be among the determining influences affecting the agreed royalty payment.

Assessing the worth

The first thing for the negotiators to estimate is the cost of the alternatives available assuming no licence agreement. In addition to such estimates, consideration should also be given to manufacturing costs, estimated selling price, and a forecast of sales. Once such estimates have been agreed on, the outcome in terms of royalty rates should be such as not to effect materially the competitive situation of either the licensor or licensee.

This serves to highlight one major issue with regard to the negotiation of a licence agreement — the recognition that for a licence agreement to operate successfully it must allow both the licensor and the licensee to make a profit. Among licensing executives there appears to be almost unanimous agreement that it is far more important that both parties to an agreement be pleased with its provision than to press too short-sightedly for a one-sided agreement during negotiations. In establishing the royalty rate it is therefore as important for the licensor to calculate, and then attempt to ascertain, the potential profit or savings of the agreement to the licensee, since in the final analysis it is this that represents the realistic measure of the commercial value of this licence granted, and influences the nature and level of potential power that the licensor can bring to bear at the negotiation.

The licensor's power is limited by the fact that if he attempts to be prohibitive (from the licensee's perspective) in his demands concerning the royalty payments, then the licensee may be provoked to explore ways around any proprietary rights; or alternatively, depending on the legal environment of the licensor, it may be interpreted that his demands are an abuse of the related monopoly power. This has been borne out by the research of Root and Contractor (1981):

'Managers do not make systematic assessments of opportunity costs, and they do not assign R & D costs to particular licensing agreements. Furthermore, managers seldom make quantitative estimates of a licensee's prospective incremental profits in order to calculate a ceiling price prior to negotiations. Indeed our interviews reveal that licensors do not want to obtain a ceiling price because they believe that efforts to maximize licensing revenues would be counterproductive. Instead they stated a willingness to accept a minority share of economic rent for several reasons: the entrepreneurial risk borne by the licensee, the dependence of a successful agreement on a good relationship [royalties are dependent on the licensee's performance and therefore on his incentive to perform], and the ability of a licensee to cheat on an agreement if he becomes dissatisfied with it.'

The wide variety of possible financial transactions within a licensing agreement provide the licensor with something of an opportunity to 'package' the arrangements. It has become commonplace for a down-payment to accompany the grant of the licence. This is usually taken to be the licensee's contribution towards the initial research and development expenditure. As a result the amount tends to vary with the stage of development of the item subject of the licence. If little development effort is required, other than perhaps local modification, then lump-sum payments are likely to be higher than if an amount of effort is still to be deployed to ensure successful start up.

In cases other than when an outright sale of technical know-how is paid for by means of a lump-sum payment, royalties may be based on output, sales, value-added or profits. In addition to flat-rate royalty payments, a situation might be negotiated in which a payment is made to make up the difference between royalties actually accruing and some minimum level of payment agreed on. If the nature of royalty payments proposed by the licensor proves to be unacceptable to the licensee, then the licensor might place emphasis on such factors as service fees, or a payment system to cover assistance provided by the licensor's personnel.

Another factor influencing the power relationships within the agreement, and therefore consequences in terms of the financial arrangements, is the time the patent has to run. It is not legally possible for a licensor to require royalty payments on a patent after its expiration. The position may become somewhat more complicated in circumstances where some patents have expired and others that come within the agreement are still in existence. This may mean that, within the context of the negotiations, it is necessary to consider some system of reduction in royalty rates for those parts of the agreement covering items for which the patent has expired or is due to expire.

This is not to suggest that when patents expire payments cease. As has been pointed out, there are frequently many other non-royalty obligations included in agreements which influence the financial arrangements. Direct and indirect costs associated with licensing cover such items as engineering services, laboratory and pilot plant activity. Any licence becomes more valuable as activity is scaled up from laboratory tests through to pilot plant operations. The most valuable asset then in licensing, for example, a manufacturing operation, is the possession of successful operational data for a full-scale plant. The advertising and promotional activity which has already been undertaken, together with that planned, might influence or form part of the agreement and also effect the evaluation of royalty payments.

Another factor is secrecy. Clearly the know-how implicit in a licence cannot be guaranteed, since it is open to any party with the research and development capability to discover the technology. With this in mind, given that there is something of an obligation on both parties to maintain a degree of secrecy, it is not uncommon in an agreement for a reduced royalty rate to be negotiated and applied if technical details become public property. Relationships between licensor and licensee are likely to become particularly difficult if a licence holder, paying a licence fee and appropriate royalties, sees an infringer, because of leakages of information, able to achieve similar market results without making any payments.

The nature and extent of exclusivity may also affect the royalties agreed. Consequently, an exclusive licence in which the licensor agrees not to grant further licences or to work the licensed property himself typically commands a higher royalty rate than a non-exclusive licence. A sole licence is something of a half-way house in which the licensor continues activity in his own right but agrees not to grant additional licences.

Exclusivity

The extent and nature of exclusivity is likely to be a major bargaining issue in many licensing agreements.

The difficulties for a licensor in deciding on the most appropriate policy for the issue of exclusivity are amply illustrated by the following somewhat different views (Lovell 1968):

> 'A major pitfall that our company has often seen in the practices of other companies is a refusal to license or a tendency to license on such a basis (i.e. exclusive licensing) that the benefits of patented inventions do not become available to the public, or are restricted in such a way that these benefits do not become available in a truly competitive situation. This mistake is often made by licensors who rate more highly an immediate or guaranteed return from their patent than the perhaps significantly larger return that would result from development of a market for an invention on a broad competitive basis.'

On the other hand an aircraft company executive thinks that one major licensor pitfall is the:

> '. . . failure to provide a degree of exclusivity in the marketplace sufficient to permit the licensee to make a profit commensurate with the risks involved.'

Whichever view prevails in a particular case is likely to be significantly influenced by the nature of the business environment against which the negotiations take place, the nature of the products or processes involved, overall company policies, the degree of power accorded to respective parties according to product/market circumstances, and finally the extent to which the respective parties are committed to reaching an agreement.

The now somewhat famous story of Pilkington's float-glass process is an example which serves to illustrate many of the points raised with regard to licensing and the question of market power. Such was the innovation in terms of glass production that manufacturers sought to license the process for defensive reasons. The structure of the glass industry was such that many manufacturers shared the worldwide market, but were limited to specific areas by transport considerations. As far as the licensor was concerned, there was no advantage to be gained from attempting to maintain a worldwide monopoly, since the capital requirements of establishing the requisite overseas manufacturing and marketing infrastructure was prohibitive; and any attempt to operate from the home base would simply have eroded the benefits associated with the new process. Consequently there were mutual benefits to be derived from establishing a multiplicity of licences, each with certain territorial limitations. Licences were granted to a limited number of manufacturers. These licences involved the now common feature of a down payment and running royalties of sales dropping on a time scale. The nature of the licences also contained an interesting continuing know-how improvement provision. The licensor agreed to pass on to all licensees all the improvements the licensors made, and in return they were to receive from each licensee details of each improvement devised by the licensee. When the licences expired the licensor was the sole holder of all the improvements that had been made, whereas each licensee had only a limited amount of the information made available to him by right. In this way, each licensee was encouraged to continue to work on process improvement, since all licensees had a common interest in being completely up-to-date in the latest refinements of processing technique in order to keep their advantage over competitors using different processes or making somewhat different products.

In this case the nature of the market, the product and the extent to which the innovation was a major advance on previous technology were determining influences on the nature of the arrangements agreed on.

Improvement clauses

The above example also serves to raise issues relating to the negotiation of improvement clauses. It is usually in the licensor's interests to negotiate a clause requiring complete particulars relating to any improvement by the licensee to be communicated to him. If patents are granted in respect of the licensee's developments, a licensor may attempt in the negotiation process to require that licences — possibly exclusive licences — are granted to him in respect of those patents.

The extent to which such arrangements or clauses can be invoked may be to a large measure directly related to the level of cooperation already established between the licensor and the licensee. If invoked, such clauses may create an abrasive situation which is unlikely to be particularly profitable for longer-term relationships. Such arrangements might also carry with them legal consequences in terms of anti-trust legislation, where it might be interpreted as giving rise to a restraint on competition. This would certainly be the case in the USA, where it would be illegal for a licensor to insist on the exclusive right to use and benefit from inventions produced as a result of his licensee's efforts.

Cross-licensing

In addition to one-way traffic, so to speak, there is the so-called cross-licence agreement in which two parties license each other under one another's patents and/or know-how. This may be practised where one party has a patent which he cannot employ without the cooperation of another patentee. In such cases the respective patentees may grant each other licences which will allow them both to exploit the process or the complete end product without the fear of infringing the other's rights. In nearly all such cases of cross-licensing, however, a package of items is involved such that the exchange covers a patent with different expiry dates. This means that it is necessary to negotiate the arrangement for a stipulated time period, not necessarily related to the expiry date of any of the patents, or indeed to the life of what might be regarded as the most important patent.

Further complications can arise in cross-licensing activity where it becomes beneficial to agree on an exchange of licences between several companies. Although arrangements of this nature add another dimension to the agreement, they do not change many of the essential principles. One that does not change — if anything it becomes of increasing concern the more companies that are involved — is the question of communication and inter-organizational relationship within the context of the licensing agreement.

COMMUNICATIONS AND INTER-ORGANIZATIONAL RELATIONSHIPS

Good communication is a vital consideration for both companies that are party to a licensing agreement. This is so not only from the perspective of inter-organizational relationships and communications, but also from intra-organizational considerations. It is particularly the case with regard to the actual implementation of the licence agreement.

The smooth running of the licence agreement implies that within the licensor's organization there has been adequate liaison between those responsible for negotiating the agreement and those eventually responsible for implementing the letter of the agreement. In a large organizational setting this is particularly vital, since different personnel may be responsible for carrying out the respective functions.

As well as being of obvious importance to the licensor's organization in that operational personnel are aware of the demands likely to be placed on them, it is also important from the point of view of communications between the licensor and licensee. A set of technical drawings hardly constitutes the transfer of technical know-how. In most cases it will be necessary to transfer design information, manufacturing data, process know-how, application information, sales and after-sales information, and a host of other factors. This in effect requires an effective and continuing dialogue between the licensor and licensee.

Personnel in the respective organizations must be kept attuned to each other. For example, it might be crucial for a licensee that the right engineer or department of the licensor's organization be kept aware of the particular stage reached by the licensee's engineers, so that they may be warned of particular problems and pitfalls which the licensor, through experience, had learnt to avoid.

In some cases the requirements for an on-going dialogue might be built into the actual licensing agreement. An example might be the marine engineering field when a particular ancillary piece of equipment that is to be fitted to a vessel depends for its configuration on the particular characteristics of the vessel to which it is to be fitted.

Experience from the licensor's organization might be vital to ensure that the engineering requirements of the equipment are appropriate for the vessel in question. In addition, ultimately the reputation of the licensor's organization might also depend on the correct equipment being fitted. Such eventualities can be accounted for in clauses in the licence agreement which spell out the licensee's responsibility in the following way:

> 'On receipt of an enquiry the licensee shall disclose to the licensor the technical particulars of the vessel. Thereafter the licensee may not offer to supply equipment other than as defined by the licensor.'

It is perhaps consideration of such communication issues which serves to emphasize that interchanges between engineers and key personnel from the respective organizations are at the heart of every licensing relationship, and are the key to the ultimate success of such agreements. Building into the agreement the necessary communication systems is never easy. Exchange of personnel is one possibility, but not without its disadvantages in terms of security. Success depends on personal relations, the quality of intra-corporate relationships as a basis for satisfactory inter-organizational relationships, and a mutual awareness of a community of interests between licensor and licensee.

Termination clauses

There is always the possibility that relationships can sour, so it is well to ensure that appropriate termination conditions have been negotiated into the agreement.

Ensuring that such contingencies exist is necessary not only in case of a breakdown in relationships, but also in case of changing fortunes within the organizations party to an agreement. One of the most common causes of a breakdown in a licensing relationship is that of merger activity, in which the licensor's company is taken over. A new management team may not necessarily endorse the policies of its predecessors. For example, a licensor's organization that is merged into a larger international organization might find that the enlarged corporation of which they are now part possess the market outlets which it once lacked, and which were in fact part of the reason for negotiating a licensing agreement in the first place.

Non-payment of royalties by the licensee might create conditions for termination.

Premature termination of the agreement for whatever reason raises once again the thorny issue of secrecy and confidentiality of the know-how already transferred. Clauses in the agreement which state that 'the provisions as to confidentiality of the technical information shall survive the termination of this agreement for a period of ten years' are one way of attempting to come to terms with issues of this nature. Whether such clauses would ever be tested in terms of litigation if contravened is likely to depend on the costs involved and the estimate of achieving a successful outcome.

It is worth pointing out that termination clauses and their associated sub-clauses add nothing in terms of support to a licensing relationship. At best they might provide a quick release mechanism. If, however, the vital working relationship between licensee and licensor has been impaired, there is little that enforcements of a legal nature can provide.

LICENSING AND THE 'NEGOTIATION SKILLS MODEL'

Pre-negotiation stage

The pre-negotiation stage within the context of a licensing agreement is a very real and fairly discreet stage during which the prospective parties are deciding how much detail to disclose at this point.

At this stage the parties tend to be preoccupied with issues relating to the extent of information to provide in case the negotiation should get no further. The balance lies in giving just enough detail to enable the pre-negotiation stage to proceed smoothly and not disclosing information that might be of commercial significance if the parties agree to proceed no further.

As the negotiations progress and broad financial considerations are raised, the two parties are likely to disagree in their evaluation of the economic environment. As trust is built up and the parties begin to feel increasingly comfortable about the fact that the negotiations could proceed further, then further disclosures enable the parties to present their evaluation of the technical and legal worth of the proposed licence. As these issues have a major bearing, it is again likely that licensor and licensee will attach different weights, and therefore different values, to influencing factors.

It is at this stage that the level and nature of dependency and power within the relationship will become clear. This will depend on the extent to which the licensor regards licensing activity as an opportunity to gain access to markets, or to gain access to the financial and production resources of the licensee. It will depend on the time the patent has to run before expiry. It will also depend on the extent to which what is being licensed is either the result of laboratory activity, pilot plant work, or full production activity. From the licensee's point of view it will depend on his evaluation of investing in research and development, as opposed to the costs involved in gaining access to the results of someone else's. It will depend on market forces and the nature and strength of competitive activity, and it will depend on the economic value placed on the technology, in terms of anticipated returns, by the licensee.

Each party to the negotiation will begin to make some judgment of the other's position and perspective as a basis for establishing negotiations.

Distributive stage

The factors influencing relative positions of power will next be spelt out in more detail, and the nature and extent of movement by the parties is also likely to be established.

The parties to the agreement at this stage will begin to identify whether cooperative or competitive strategies should be adopted. It must, however, be stressed that all the evidence points to a ready recognition that, if mutual benefits are to result from the arrangement, cooperative as opposed to competitive strategies are likely to be the most appropriate.

It is also during the distributive bargaining stage that the actual requirements of the parties in terms of the agreement will be established. The respective objectives in granting and seeking a licence must be made quite clear. If the licensor's aim is to reach an agreement with a licensee who will shoulder part of the financial burden, contribute technical effort and management skills, then the extent of this involvement should be spelt out. Likewise the requirements of the licensee must be spelt out. It may be that the objectives of the licensee are to defend or augment an existing product line. Such defensive licensing, however, places the licensee in a particularly vulnerable position from the negotiating point of view, since it will be well recognized that the product or process for which the licence is sought could pose a marketing threat to the licensee.

In other cases the licence may be sought for reasons of technological diversification. Whatever the reasons the balance of power will be different, but objectives must be stated as the basis for moving the negotiations through to the integrative bargaining stage.

Integrative bargaining stage

Now the respective parties should attempt to obtain some insights into the opposer's mode of behaviour. To what extent does the negotiating behaviour reflect the style of operations that might be expected during the life of the agreement when the parties will have to work together?

At this stage it is necessary to try to elicit information on the intangible issues. This can be very important in a licensing agreement, particularly with regard to know-how and technical assistance. This is because technical assistance can be extremely difficult to define specifically, yet it is very much at the heart of the prospective agreement. The following goes some way towards providing at least some terms of reference which might be used to identify the boundaries and the extent of such assistance:

> 'It is possible to distinguish between knowledge which is system specific (related to a particular product or process), that which is firm specific and that which is general. . . . It can be useful to distinguish between personal skills which can be transferred by individual action independent of a firm possessing it, and corporate skills, the transfer of which requires the direct and continuous participation of the supplying organization.' (Brooke and Buckley 1983)

The nature and extent of know-how involved in the agreement will have a major impact on the nature and extent of the licensor's organizational involvement, the distribution of power within the relationship, and the consequent financial arrangements ultimately established. The decision-making stage of the negotiating model is the stage during which understanding of these factors can be tested.

Decision-making and action stage

It is during this phase of the negotiation that the parties can present and evaluate a package of items. Packaging activity within the context of a licensing agreement is likely to be fairly difficult to achieve, since the extent of detail that might be involved in the agreement makes the task of keeping issues linked together complex.

It is during this phase, however, that an attempt should be made to summarize the discussions and outline the nature of the concessions which are required to enable a contract to be drawn up. Because of the ground that must be covered, and the variety of factors involved in the licensing agreement, it is inevitable that specialist legal advice will be required to ensure that the negotiating efforts of the sales and technical specialists are not dissipated owing to ambiguity creeping into the agreement.

It is also important to ensure that the details of the licence agreement are enforceable, and that they do not expose the parties to legal sanctions or other penalties. This is particularly important owing to the existence of anti-trust legislation.

The individual handling the licence needs to be backed up by supporting services. He will need to call on technical people and obtain advice on financial matters. Before negotiations, ideally, he should be briefed by these services, and options should be available to introduce them into the negotiations as required.

Post-negotiation stage

Finally the parties draw up and agree a contract which clearly establishes what has been agreed. Typically such a contract will cover issues relating to the licence itself, the territory, the technical information, the royalties and fees and the payment details. In addition the responsibilities of licensor and licensee are likely to be spelt out, together with details relating to the duration of the agreement, its termination and its possible extension. As with all such agreements, reference should be made to the provisions for arbitration and the nature of the laws by which the agreement should be governed.

CULTURAL CONTEXT OF THE AGREEMENT

The cultural setting will have a major bearing on almost all aspects of the process. The licence agreement can pose a number of problems in this respect, particularly when one of the parties is from a high-context culture, such as the Japanese or Chinese.

General criticisms of the UK and US based agreements tend to suggest that typical licences are too complex and too full of verbiage. As well as tending more to confuse than clarify, this also creates suspicion because nuances and shades of meaning are not immediately obvious to a non-native speaker (and, incidentally, quite often to a native speaker).

This places far greater emphasis on the spoken word during the negotiations. Negotiators should therefore explain fully and state exactly what is meant, rather than place reliance on formal documentation.

The formal contract should be regarded as the embodiment of a mutually beneficial relationship. At the time of drawing up the formal licence agreement it should not be too difficult to go some way to accommodate something of both parties' styles. As well as highly structured detailed clauses, the licence can also include clauses such as:

'The parties will amicably consult with each other in the event of substantial changes of any circumstances relevant to the mutually acceptable operation of the agreement.'

Clauses of this nature should be designed to encapsulate the principle of mutuality. Obviously in subsequent arrangements between the same two companies, against the background of a history of successful working relationships, any preoccupation with the need for detail is likely to diminish.

SUMMARY

In the negotiation of a licensing agreement the question of the balance of power between the two parties are not immediately obvious. It would be inappropriate to infer that because a licensee is doing the requesting, so to speak, that he is necessarily in the weaker bargaining position. Many factors have an impact on the balance. Factors such as the threat of patent infringement, the respective resources of both parties, the nature of the market, the nature of the technology, and the position with regard to patents.

The sanction for the patent holder to get involved in protective litigation does not add substantially to the licensor's power, since the costs involved tend to deny litigation as an option for financial recovery.

The patent or patent rights, the nature of the market and the particular resources of the parties to the agreement all have a bearing on the negotiations of the agreement and the financial arrangements.

The parties must have established their key objectives in adopting a licensing approach and must have determined the exact nature of how the arrangement is designed to fit into organizational plans. Although such a rational approach is less likely in the case of passive licensors, attention must be given to the way in which the agreement should be implemented. Factors affecting implementation are the result of intra-organizational and inter-organizational considerations.

Attention in most cases will have to be given to the exchange of personnel, not only as part of the policy of transplanting know-how, but also as part of the policy of quality control.

This inevitably involves discussion of fees and royalties relating to the agreement. With regard to the level of royalty payments, the balance of power is not immediately obvious owing to the requirement for the arrangement to be mutually profitable.

The final value of the licence to either party will be the result of arrangements made regarding exclusivity and improvement clauses, as well as prevailing market conditions.

Regardless, however, of the details of the licence or the prevailing environmental conditions, one factor above all else seems to be vital to ensure the successful operation of a licensing agreement. That is the recognition by both parties that the other party must benefit by the arrangement.

Questions

1 What are the factors which affect the negotiating range between an intending licensor and a would-be licensee?
2 If you decided to license the manufacture of your product or the provision of your service abroad, what conditions would you seek to impose? What might make it difficult to impose some of these conditions? If you are not presently working in an organization, choose a product or service.
3 What factors determine the price to be paid? Examine this from the viewpoint of
   (a) the licensor
   (b) the licensee.

4 To what extent can a licensee's ability to contribute to the continuing improvement of the licence subject be written into the agreement?

5 How far should an intending licensor or licensee be competitive in his behaviour? In making your evaluation, compare the appropriate behaviours in licensing with those in sales/purchase agreements.

READING

Licensing negotiation, agreement, and outcome

This is an analysis of negotiations between 'Metro Corporation' and 'Impecina Construcciones, S.A.' of Peru for the licensing of petroleum-tank technology. Corporate identities have been disguised. Other facts, such as the countries involved, have also been modified without detracting from the essential depiction of events or the education context.

THE LICENSOR FIRM

Metro Corporation is a diversified steel-rolling, fabricating and construction company based in the midwest. It considers itself to be in a mature industry, where innovations are few and far between. With transport and tariff barriers and the support given by many governments to their own companies, exporting as a means of doing foreign business is rather limited. Similarly, given the large investment, modest return and political sensitivity of the industry, direct foreign investment is all but a closed option. In a global-strategic sense then, Metro Corporation has far more frequently focused on licensing as a market-entry method, with technologies confined to processes and engineering of peripheral processes (for example, mining methods and coke-oven-door designs) and applications of steel in construction and other industries (petroleum-tank design, welding methods, thermo-adhesion, and so forth).

All of Metro's licensing is handled by its international division, International Construction and Engineering (ICE), which is beginning to develop a reputation in Western Europe and South America as a good source for specialized construction technology.

THE PROPOSED LICENSEE

Impecina, a private firm, is the largest construction company in Peru and operates throughout Latin America. Impecina has a broad range of interests, including residential and commercial buildings, hydraulic works, transportation and maritime works. The company employs several thousand engineers and technicians, and its sales had doubled in the last five years. It was still primarily a Peruvian business, with most of its turn-over in Peru, but it was in the process of expanding into Colombia, North Africa, Argentina, Brazil, and Venezuela. Impecina has advanced computer capacity, with a large IBM system at its main office and other computers at its branches. In oil-storage tanks, Impecina's experience was limited to the smaller fixed-cone roof designs under 150 feet in diameter.

* From Farok J. Contractor, *International Technology Licensing: Compensation, Costs and Negotiation*, Lexington Books, 1981. Reproduced by permission of D. C. Heath & Co.

THE TECHNOLOGY

National Tank, Inc., a fabrication division of Metro, had developed a computerized-design procedure for floating-roof oil-storage tanks, which minimized the use of steel within American Petroleum Institute standards or any other oil-industry standards. Particularly for the larger tanks (for instance, 150 feet in diameter and above), this would confer upon a bidding contractor a significant cost advantage. National Tank had spent one man-year, at a direct cost of $225,000, on the computer program alone. Patents were involved in an incidental manner — for the seals on the floating roof only — and Metro had not bothered to file for this patent except in the United States.

THE MARKET

Peru's indigenous oil output is very low, but it imports and refines 50 million tons annually, mostly for domestic demand. Following the escalation of oil prices and the tightening of supplies, the Peruvian government determinedly set about to formulate a programme to augment Peru's oil-storage capacity. Impecina's representatives, at a preliminary meeting with ICE at ICE's US headquarters, said that their government planned to spend $200 million on oil-storage facilities over the next three years (mostly in large-sized tanks). Impecina's 'ambition' was to capture a one-third share of this market. That this appeared to be a credible target was illustrated by Impecina's existing 30 per cent share of the market for the fixed-cone type of tank less than 150 feet in diameter. Additionally, they estimated that private-sector construction value over the next three years would total $40 million.

Approximately half of a storage system's construction cost goes for the tank, the remainder being excavation, foundation, piping, instrumentation and other ancillary equipment, all of which were very familiar to Impecina's engineers.

Neighbouring Colombia was building a 12 million ton refinery, but the tank-installation plans of other South American nations were not known, according to the Impecina representatives.

Each of Impecina's competitors for this business in Peru was affiliated with a prominent company; Umbertomas with Jefferson, Inc., in the United States; Zapa with Philadelphia Iron and Steel; Cosmas with Peoria-Duluth Construction, Inc.; and so on. Thus, association with Metro would help Impecina in bidding.

THE FIRST MEETING

In the past year, National Tank had bid jointly with Impecina on a project in southern Peru. Although that bid was unsuccessful, Impecina had learned about Metro's computerized-design capabilities and had initiated a formal first round of negotiations, which were to lead to a licensing agreement. The meeting took place in the United States. Two Impecina executives of sub-director rank were accompanied by an American consultant. Metro was represented by the vice-president of ICE, the ICE attorney, and an executive from National Tank.

Minutes of this meeting show that it was exploratory. Both genuine and rhetorical questions were asked. Important information and perceptions were exchanged, and the groundwork was laid for concluding negotiations. Following is a summary of important issues gleaned from the somewhat circular discussion.

Licensee market coverage

Impecina tried to represent itself as essentially a Peruvian firm. Its executives reviewed their government's expenditure plans and the hoped-for market share. Yet, throughout the meeting, the issue of the license also covering Libya, Algeria, Morocco, Colombia, Argentina, Brazil, and Venezuela kept cropping up.

Exclusivity

Metro negotiators had no difficulty conceding exclusivity for Peru. They mentioned that granting exclusivity to a licensee for any territory was agreeable in principle, provided that a minimum-performance guarantee was given. The question was then deferred for future discussion. At one point, a Metro executive remarked, 'We could give Impecina a nonexclusive license — and say, for example, that we wouldn't give another [licensee] a license for one year [in those nations],' thus proposing the idea of a trial period for Impecina to generate business in a territory.

Agreement life

Impecina very quickly agreed to a ten-year term, payment in US dollars, and other minor issues.

Trade name

The Impecina negotiators placed great emphasis on their ability to use Metro's name in bidding, explaining that their competition in Peru had technical collaboration with three US companies. They were asked rhetorically if that meant that National Tank could compete with Impecina in Peru. (Actually, both sides seem to have tacitly agreed that it was not possible for Metro to do business directly in Peru.)

Licensee market size

Attention turned to the dollar value of the future large (floating-roof) tank market in Peru. Impecina threw out an estimate of $200 million in government expenditures and $40 million in private-sector spending over the coming three years, of which they targeted a one-third share. Later, a lower market-size estimate of $150 million (government and private), with a share of $50 million received by Impecina over three years, was established. (Memories are not clear on how the estimates were revised.) 'Will Impecina guarantee us that they will obtain one-third of the market?' brought the response, 'That's an optimistic figure, but we hope we can realize it.' Impecina offered as evidence their existing one-third share of the fixed-roof, under 150-foot tank market, an impressive achievement.

Product mix covered by licence.

It became clear that Impecina wanted floating-roof technology for all sizes and fixed-roof technology for sizes over 100 feet in diameter. They suggested that the agreement cover tanks over the 100-foot size. They were asked if Impecina would pay on all tanks, of any size, to simplify royalty calculations and monitoring. After considerable discussion, Metro seems to have acceded to Impecina's proposal to cover both types, but only those over 100 feet in diameter, based on consensus on three points:

1 The competition probably does not pay their licensors on small tanks, and therefore Impecina would be at a disadvantage if they had to pay on small tanks also.
2 The market in floating-roof tanks was usually for those over 100 feet anyway.
3 Impecina claimed that customers normally dictated the dimensions of the tanks, so Impecina could not vary them in order to avoid paying a royalty to Metro.

Compensation formula

Metro proposed an initial lump-sum payment (in two instalments, one when the agreement is signed, the second on delivery of the computer program and designs), plus engineers and executives for bid assistance on a per-diem rate, plus royalty on successful bids, based on the barrel capacity installed by Impecina. Impecina's American consultant countered with the idea of royalties on a sliding scale, lower with larger-capacity tanks, indicating talk about 1-million-barrel-capacity tanks. A possibly rhetorical question regarding Peru's oil capacity seems to have brought the discussion down to earth and veered it off on a tangent, while both sides mentally regrouped.

On returning to this topic, when they were asked, Impecina executives ventured that, as a rule of thumb, their profit markup on a turnkey job was 6 per cent. (However, when excluding the more price-sensitive portions, such as excavation, piping, and ancillary equipment, which typically constitute half the value, Impecina conceded that on the tank alone they might mark up as much as 12 per cent, although they kept insisting that 5 to 6 per cent was enough.)

Impecina executives later offered only royalties (preferably sliding) and per-diem fees for bid assistance from Metro executives and engineers.

Metro countered by pointing out that per-diem fees of, say, $225 plus travel costs amounted at best to recovering costs, not profit.

The compensation-design question was left at this stage and deferred for later negotiation, the broad outlines having been laid. Metro's starting formal offer, which would mention specific numbers, was to be telexed to Lima in a week.

The royalty basis

Metro entertained the idea that Impecina engineers were very familiar with excavation, piping, wiring and other ancillary equipment. Metro was transferring technology for the tank alone, which typically comprised half of overall installed value.

Government intervention

Towards the end of the discussions, Impecina brought up the question of the Peruvian government having to approve the agreement. This led to their retreat from the idea of a ten-year term, agreed to earlier, and Impecina then mentioned five years. No agreement was reached. (Incidentally, Peru had in the last two years passed legislation indicating a guideline of five years for foreign licences.)

INTERNAL DISCUSSION IN METRO LEADING TO THE FORMAL OFFER

The advantages derived by the licensee would be acquisition of floating-roof technology, time and money saved in attempting to generate the computerized-design procedure in-house, somewhat of a cost and efficiency advantage in bidding on larger tanks, and, finally, the use of Metro's name.

It was estimated that National Tank had spent $225,000 (one man-year = two executives for six months, plus other costs) in developing the computer program. Additionally, it might cost $40,000 (three-quarters of a man-year) to convert the program into Spanish and the metric system and adapt it to the material availability and the labour-cost factors peculiar to Peru. Simultaneously, there would be semi-formal instruction of Impecina engineers in the use of the program, petroleum-industry codes and Metro fabrication methods. All this had to be done before the licensee would be ready for a single bid.

It was visualized that Metro would then assist Impecina for two man-weeks for each bid preparation and four man-weeks on successful receipt of a contract award. Additionally, if Metro's specialized construction equipment were used, three man-months of on-site training would be needed. As the licensee's personnel moved along their learning curve, assistance of this type would diminish until it was no longer needed after a few successful bids.

Additional considerations that went into a determination of the initial offer were as follows:

1 Metro's obligations (and sunk costs) in computer-program development were fairly determinate, whereas their obligations to provide bidding assistance depended on the technical sophistication and absorptive capacity of the licensee's engineers, their success rate in bidding, and so on.
2 If Impecina's market estimates were used, over the next three years they would generate large tank orders worth $50 million, on which they would make a profit of $3 million (about 6 per cent of 50 million or 12 per cent on half the amount).
3 The market beyond three years was unknown.
4 Exclusive rights might be given to Impecina in Peru and Colombia, with ICE perhaps reserving the right of conversion to a non-exclusive licence if minimum market share was not captured.

280

5 Although Impecina's multinational expansion plans were unknown, its business in the other nations was too small to justify granting exclusivity. They might be satisfied with a vague promise of future consideration as exclusive licensee in those territories.
6 Metro would try for an agreement term of ten years. It was believed that Impecina's computer and engineering capability was strong enough that they would not need Metro's assistance after a few bids.

Surprisingly, the discussions reveal that no explicit consideration was given to the idea that Impecina might emerge someday as a multinational competitor.

In view of the uncertainty about how successful the licensee would actually be in securing orders, and the uncertainty surrounding the Peruvian government's attitude, a safe strategy seemed to be to try to get as large a front-end fee as possible. Almost arbitrarily, a figure of $400,000 was proposed. (This was roughly 150 per cent of the development costs, plus the initial costs of transferring the technology to the licensee.) There would be sufficient margin for negotiations and to cover uncertainties. In order that the licensee's competitiveness not be diminished by the large lump-sum fee, a formula might be devised whereby the royalties for the first five years could be reduced.

THE FORMAL OFFER

The formal offer, communicated by telex a week later, called for the following payment terms:

1 A $400,000 lump-sum fee, payable in two instalments.
2 A 2 per cent royalty on any tanks constructed that were over 100 feet in diameter, with up to one-half of the royalties owed in each of the first five years reduced by an amount up to $40,000 each year, without carryovers from year to year. The royalty percentage would apply to the total contract value, less excavation, foundation, dikes, piping, instrumentation, and pumps.
3 An agreement life of ten years.
4 Metro to provide computer program conversion and training services to Impecina in consideration of the lump-sum and royalty fees.
5 For additional assistance in preparing bids, Metro to provide, on request, personnel at up to $225 per day, plus travel and living costs while away from their place of business. The per-diem rates would be subject to escalation, based on a representative cost index. There would be a ceiling placed on the number of man-days Impecina could request in any year.
6 All payments to be made in US dollars, net after all local, withholding, and other taxes.
7 Impecina to receive exclusive rights for Peru and Colombia only, and non-exclusive rights for Morocco, Libya, Algeria, Argentina, Venezuela, and Brazil. These could be converted to an exclusive basis on demonstration of sufficient business in the future. For Peru and Colombia, Metro reserves the right to treat

the agreement as nonexclusive if Impecina fails to get at least 30 per cent of installed capacity of a type covered by the agreement.

8 Impecina to have the right to sublicense only to its controlled subsidiaries.

9 Impecina to supply free of charge to ICE all improvements made by it on the technology during the term of the agreement.

10 Impecina to be entitled to advertise its association with Metro in assigned territories, on prior approval of ICE as to wording, form, and content.

THE FINAL AGREEMENT

ICE executives reported that the Peruvians 'did not bat an eyelid' at their demands, and that an agreement was reached in a matter of weeks. The only significant change was that Metro agreed to take a lump-sum of $300,000 (still a large margin over costs). Other changes were minor: Impecina to continue to receive the benefit of further R & D; ICE to provide, at cost, a construction engineer if specialized welding equipment was used; the per-diem fee fixed at $200 per day (indexed by an average-hourly-wage escalation factor used by the US Department of Labor); and the $300,000 lump-sum fee to be paid in instalments over the first year.

In other respects, such as territory, royalty rate, exclusivity, and travel allowances, the agreement conformed with Metro's initial offer.

AN UPSET

The Peruvian government disallowed a ten-year agreement life. By then, both parties had gone too far to want to re-open the entire negotiation, and Metro appears to have resigned itself to an agreement life of five years, with a further extension of another five years subject to mutual consent. Given Impecina's in-house engineering and computer capability, extension of the agreement life was a very open question.

CHAPTER 11

The joint-venture agreement

Joint ventures... 282
    Variety of types... 282
    Propensity to failure... 283
    Growth of joint ventures.. 284
    Power in the joint venture.. 284
The context.. 285
    Yugoslavia... 286
    Japan.. 287
    China.. 289
Inter-organizational factors... 290
    Organizational relationships.. 290
    Interpersonal relationships... 292
    Joint ventures and the 'negotiation skills model'............. 292
    Face-to-face... 293
Intra-organizational relations.. 296
    Environmental changes affecting joint ventures................ 296
    Conflicts arising out of the joint venture........................ 297
    The political interface: the key..................................... 297
Summary 299

JOINT VENTURES

Variety of types

The term 'joint venture' is used to refer to a multitude of arrangements and relation-ships, some fairly loose, others characterized by formal equity participation in a new third entity. It involves organizations in collaboration of a more far-reaching nature than with the commercial arrangements thus far discussed. A joint-venture agreement is therefore based upon partnership in which the respective parties are committed to working towards common goals. Morris (1987) provides an appropriate definition when he suggests that, 'A joint venture relationship can be described in general terms as an agreement involving the cooperative efforts and utilization of the resources of two or more entities working together to accomplish agreed-upon goals.'

An arrangement conducted between a New York restaurateur and the authorities in Sichuan Province in China provides one example of a fairly loose 'joint venture' arrangement. The Sichuan Province provided a chef and the American partner paid his salary and living expenses. In addition the restaurant was committed to buying materials and decorations through the Vegetable and Food Catering Service of Sichuan Province. At the end of each financial year Sichuan Province authorities would receive between 15 per cent and 20 per cent of the profits.

At the other end of the spectrum, the arrangement most frequently associated with the term joint venture is that involving two parties who make an equal or nearly equal investment in both money and management to establish a jointly owned production unit. The relationship between International Nickels of Canada and Daido Steel Company of Japan is one such example, in which the two parties to the agreement came together with the objective of producing a special alloy.

Although these examples differ widely, both relationships have the potential for complexity such that the decision-making process can be a drawn-out affair. It is the inherent complexity, together with the requirement of the joint-venture agreement to span a broad area of activity and interest, that goes some way to explaining the fact that such agreements, in their implementation, tend to be characterized by considerable turbulence. Virtually all of the research work on classical joint-venture agreements indicates a high failure rate in terms of the longevity of the partnership.

'Private enterprise has definitely been given a boost by the summit. An Astro Pizza truck, with Texas licence plates and the slogan "It's fresh, it's fast, free delivery" painted on its sides, has set up shop behind the onion domes of St Basil's Cathedral. The American and Russian partners in the joint venture have agreed to split the profits 50−50. At 1.25 roubles (£1.80) per pizza slice and a roaring trade of 290 customers an hour, this promises to be a good deal.'

'Fresh paint but no fireworks as President visits Moscow' (*Financial Times*, Tuesday, 31 May 1988. Reproduced by permission of the *Financial Times*.)

Propensity to failure

Given the usual high initial investment in management time and physical assets, the reasons for failure are worthy of comment and the resultant consequences for the negotiation of such arrangements are worthy of investigation.

Larger companies have been no less immune to the potential for failure. Names like Avis, Sterling and General Mills were among ninety or so joint-ventures participants in Japan reported by the Boston Consulting Group as having collapsed between 1972 and 1976.

More recently, an article by Killing (1982) in the *Harvard Business Review*, reporting on thirty seven joint ventures involving North American and Western European companies, indicated almost 35 per cent failure, with seven of those investigated involving total collapse and five requiring drastic reorganization.

It is not difficult to appreciate why many managers are sceptical of the idea of entering into a joint venture which they might regard as too complex, too ambiguous and which, from an operational point of view, can be regarded as too inflexible.

Growth of joint ventures

Despite such problems, however, the incidence of joint-venture activity is likely to increase. One of the major influencing factors is technological change. As a result of the technological considerations, projects are likely to increase in size, complexity and their resultant financial costs, to the extent that many individual projects will prove too much of a burden to be shouldered by one company.

Other factors are market considerations. Companies from the industrially advanced nations will wish to further protect their existing foreign markets, and at the same time search for new opportunities as they seek to take advantage of production economies arising from new technology. This search will be matched by the desires of developing nations for economic development and access to rapid routes to technologies which appear to offer opportunities for accelerated development.

These forces will be acting against a background of growing nationalism as recently independent Third World countries reject the neo-colonialism frequently associated with simply playing host to an autonomous multinational subsidiary. In these circumstances the joint-venture agreement offers an acceptable alternative. In fact it is increasingly likely to be the only method that Western organizations have available for getting access to a growing number of foreign markets.

A manufacturer of surgical sutures with a policy of operating solely through distributors found himself excluded from the Malaysian market when a competitor set up a joint venture with a local company. The identification of the local company with Malaysian enterprise resulted in large government contracts being diverted to the new venture. Such pressures force manufacturers to consider joint ventures.

Power in the joint venture

The notion of power within relationships can be used as a conceptual framework to explain the propensity of joint ventures to failure. With joint-venture agreements, organizations can be regarded as being in a state of high mutual dependence. In other words, each party has the potential to move the other party a considerable way from its initial bargaining point.

If discussions have progressed to a stage where a joint venture is seen as the major option, and both parties see prospects for high-level returns, the bargaining distance they may be provoked to move on any one individual issue is likely to be quite considerable. However, excessive movement by either party might well sow the seeds for future antagonism. Research evidence has also shown that the less the total power within the relationship, the greater is the possibility for acceptable outcomes. Joint ventures with their high degree of mutual dependence are therefore characterized by potential for stress.

As demonstrated in the context of sales/purchase agreements and agency/distributorship agreements, power is a function of dependence, as is the consequent potential for conflict. Obviously parties proposing to enter a joint-venture agreement will attempt to resolve potential conflict, as with all such agreements, within an overall wish to reach agreement, albeit against the background of the level of concessions they are prepared to extend to reach such agreement.

In any bargaining and negotiation situation the power of one party is directly related to the strength of the desire that the other party has to reach agreement. In certain instances hands can be strengthened by a demonstration of power. For example, if one partner is a company from an industrialized country while the other is a government of, or a company within, a less developed country, then the latter might seek to strengthen its hand if it can create alternatives and show these alternatives to be active. The government of India has invited companies interested in an oil venture to indicate their degree of interest and has visibly entered into and continued negotiations with more than one company. This is a ploy that is also well used by certain shipbuilding yards when making purchases. Obviously it is a permissible strategy when dealing with a depressed industry such as marine engineering, with companies desperate to make a deal almost at any price.

Information and intelligence constitute power. The information might relate to the economy, the project, the companies involved, and any other aspect of an objective nature. This emphasizes again the requirement to undertake as much research as possible prior to entering discussions and negotiations for a joint venture. It is, however, important to point out that 'intelligence' is coloured by the subjective views and attitudes of both individuals and organizations. In this respect, from a negotiating perspective, knowledge of the attitudes of key opinion-forming groups is therefore often more important than factual information, which might be the basis of those subjective variations. Lack of information/intelligence can give rise to unrealistic expectations, which in turn can lead to conflict at a later stage of the agreement, especially if not highlighted during the original negotiations.

When an international organization is considering a joint venture, its efforts in terms of intelligence gathering and creating appropriate perspectives can be enhanced by developing local affiliations, such as enlisting the support of other companies. This is an approach adopted by the Japanese in seeking joint ventures in Malaysia. Connections are sought with Chinese partners, because of their commercial strengths and their long-standing business relations.

THE CONTEXT

The key issues of joint-venture negotiation will be examined in the light of experiences and information derived from operations in Japan, Yugoslavia and latterly China.

Despite the large degree of political autonomy enjoyed by the Yugoslavs, it is still very much a socialist country. The autonomy it enjoys, however, has meant that its methods of doing business are perhaps the most 'Western' in nature. As a result many businessmen look on Yugoslavia as a 'half-way house' which provides access to other socialist bloc economies of Eastern Europe.

Japan is an extremely well documented and reported market; yet despite this coverage its culture and consequent management style remain something of an enigma.

China's entry on the commercial stage is of more recent origin, since it was only in July 1979 that the laws governing joint ventures with the People's Republic of China were adopted by the Fifth National People's Congress. As yet reported experience with the PRC are few and far between; however, long-term prospects in that market make it one which cannot be ignored.

Yugoslavia

Of the socialist economies, Yugoslavia is in the forefront of joint-venture activity with Western parties (Gupta 1978). A restriction in Yugoslav law permitting foreign investors to hold up to only 49 per cent of the total equity of the venture has now been abolished and amendments to the constitution are being made to facilitate further liberalization.

The exact form and nature of the joint venture can differ according to particular circumstances, but the partnership agreed on tends to be formalized in a contract covering the usual matters of equity participation, technical assistance, management control, circumstances relating to organizational profits, and the repatriation of capital.

Despite the abolition of 49 per cent limit, the average equity share taken by most Western companies to date has been less, with figures between 20 and 30 per cent being suggested as the norm. However, power within a joint venture is not necessarily directly correlated with the level of equity held. As might be expected, all of the arrangements have involved manufacturing enterprises, with automobiles, chemicals and electrical and mechanical engineering being the major industries. The emphasis in favour of manufacturing is partially accounted for by the fact that outside involvement is not permitted in trading firms, banks and insurance businesses.

Physical proximity has been a major determinant for the source of joint-venture partners, with Italian companies having the largest number and West Germany the second largest. Together, companies from these two countries account for a little over 50 per cent of all foreign direct investment of this nature.

The law governing the degree of equity participation is not the only regulation that organizations considering involvement in the Yugoslav economy have to contend with. Prospective partners face an array of regulations involving day-to-day management issues as well as policy considerations. In many respects this is hardly surprising in a country characterized by a firm commitment to the principle of worker participation. Western partners must expect to have to deal with the embodiment of this principle in the form of a Joint Operations Board. In addition, regulations govern the export of the joint-venture output and the consequent convertibility of the resultant dinar earnings.

Not surprisingly the Yugoslavs prefer firm contractual terms to cover all aspects of the joint venture. Despite this commitment to spelling out the detail of arrangements, Yugoslavia has proved no exception in having its share of joint-venture difficulties. The major areas of conflict have been with the establishment of channels of distribution and after-sales service, the choice of export markets, and to a lesser extent considerations of price.

Difficulties in terms of distribution channels no doubt reflect the differing marketing approaches that the partners are used to, with the Western partner being more sophisticated, more aggressive and more consumer-oriented. The Yugoslav, on the other hand, is somewhat more familiar with a target system and is obviously more production-oriented.

With regard to export markets, it is not difficult to appreciate how problems have arisen. Italian partners are unlikely to acquiesce in the manufacture of joint-venture products which are likely to find their way into the Italian home market.

The difficulties reflect the differing, and at times almost diametrically opposite, goals and objectives that partners entertain. To the Western businessman the objective of involvement in the Yugoslav market is to gain access to other socialist markets. For the Yugoslav partner, as well as access to technology and managerial know-how, the aim may be to gain outlets to more developed markets as a means of earning somewhat harder foreign currency than can be derived from their other socialist neighbours. Despite these difficulties, it is likely that Yugoslavia will continue as one of the more attractive of the socialist countries for joint-venture activity.

Japan

The post-war Japanese 'economic miracle' has ensured that the economy has not wanted for candidates to share in the growth. This can be highlighted by the level of foreign investment attracted to Japan since the 1950s. In 1955 it was estimated that foreign direct investment stood at $52.2 million; by 1975 this had risen to $4500 million. Today it is estimated at more than four times that figure and is still growing at an impressive rate despite barriers. Much of the growth has been in the form of joint-venture activity, and much of it has been American sourced.

Japan may have been one of the most attractive of foreign markets, but it has also proved to be one of the most complex. The history of joint ventures with the Japanese has been far from tranquil. For many, the difficulties have finally ended in the total collapse of the relationship. See Reading I at the end of this chapter for an insightful account of the problems of setting up a joint venture in Japan and making it work to the satisfaction of both parties.

The reasons for failure are complex, and searching for root causes is difficult. Having said that, however, it is important to point out that many of the difficulties undoubtedly derive from cultural differences and an inability by both partners to understand the cultural basis of each other's managerial perspective.

Some of these differences have manifested themselves in the different weight that the respective partners accord to basic organizational goals. Other problems have arisen in response to communication difficulties and the resultant misunderstandings.

For the Western partner organizational goals tend to find expression in a high priority being placed on profitability and a fairly rapid return on investment. On the other hand the Japanese partner, in response to the general business environment in Japan, is more concerned to ensure growth, with a greater emphasis being placed on increasing market share.

Other problems arise as a result of somewhat more latent differences. The Japanese partner, for example, may often view the investment in the joint venture as a means of generating growth elsewhere within what might well be an associated group of companies.

The Japanese orientation towards growth of sales volumes and market share stems from several conditions unique to the Japanese business system. Because of the lifetime employment tradition in most large Japanese companies, continued growth in the size of the company is important to maintain motivation and morale. Conflict has arisen when, particularly during the current recessionary period, the Western partner would have preferred to see employees laid off. The Japanese partners have clearly been reluctant to accomplish this.

This commitment to employees is one manifestation of one aspect of the Japanese notion of power and dependence. The dependence of one party on the other is important in explaining relationships in Japanese society. The dependency relationship of employees towards their bosses is viewed as arising from antecedent parent – child and other culture-bound relationships. While the Japanese do not believe that one can make all situations determinate, much of the activity of Japanese executives is in using power to reduce the indeterminateness for both their organization and its employees.

In terms of communications, the lack of fluency by both partners' executives in each other's language frequently leads to a feeling that they are unwilling to openly discuss problems. The problems of communication, however, go much deeper than simply an inability to understand each other's language, and arise in response to different cultural parameters.

Both Western and Japanese businessmen recognize the need for decision-making, given the uncertain and dynamic nature of the business environment. However, they differ radically in their approaches. The typical Western approach is to gather information, seek advice, argue the consequences forcibly and then arrive at a decision. The Japanese approach is first to decide whether there is a need for a decision, and what the decision is about. Emphasis is given to the process, and defining the question is seen as an important part of the process. Once the question is framed and it is clearly established what the decision is about, then the all important matter of 'consensus' on the decision is more likely (Sullivan *et al.* 1981).

Another area of possible conflict arises in relation to the actual formalizing of the joint venture. Western businessmen prefer to minimize possible sources of ambiguity and misunderstanding by agreements; relationships are subsumed under the letter of a contract, and arrangements for arbitration provide a formal apparatus to resolve conflict. The Japanese, on the other hand, clearly prefer that disputes be worked out through mutual discussion. Generally speaking the Japanese view the use of legal documents as evidence of mistrust; if the partners have mutual trust, then it is unnecessary to cover all contingencies through formal legal contracts (Sullivan and Peterson 1982). As a result, Japanese businessmen do not commonly use formal detailed contracts in their domestic business relationships. They prefer flexibility in responding to problems. Any documents governing relationships are much shorter in nature than the Western equivalent, and are characterized by such phrases as: 'All items not found in this contract will be deliberated and decided on in a spirit of honesty and trust.'

Detailed written contracts are too precise to be used comfortably in the Japanese system. When conditions of a legal contract are violated, responsibility must fall on one party or the other, violating the important principle of 'face-saving'.

Arbitration is not unknown in Japan, and there is in existence the Japanese Commercial Arbitration Association. However, its role is a little different in that the emphasis is not on the differences but rather on compromise, and only a few cases coming before the Association end in binding arbitration.

As one negotiating intermediary said to a Canadian negotiator who was particularly frustrated by the inability to come quickly to precise written agreements: 'As long as the music plays and the heart is in the right place, you will make a deal. Just listen to the music, not the words' (Wright 1979).

Consequently, for the Japanese partner any form of formal contract is then subsumed under the developed relationship 'friendship first, business second'. This means that the actual agreements arrived at for the joint venture tend to be extremely brief; the keynote of the related interpersonal relationship is one of trust. Because of this desire for harmony, many Western businessmen reflect on the fact that in Japan conflicts and problems tend to be kept beneath the surface, and confrontation is avoided.

The question of relationships also spills over into such apparently simple items as selling methods. Conflicts over selling methods arise in response to the Japanese custom of building a longer-term intimate relationship with a customer, as opposed to the high-pressure quick-sales approach of his Western partners. The Japanese method clearly requires there to be more contact with the customer before the sale is made, less pressure to sell, and more follow-up activity to cultivate the long-term relationship.

It is differences of this nature which have tended to mean that business relationships between Western and Japanese partners have been particularly turbulent. If joint-venture agreements are going to be maintained, both Western and Japanese partners will have to develop a far greater understanding of their respective approaches to doing business and the way in which the differing approaches are reflected in their negotiation styles.

China

In terms of prospects for future business activity via joint-venture agreements, China could have much to offer. The publication and establishment of the Joint Venture Code in July 1979 signalled China's emergence from isolation and the establishment of economic policies designed to enable the country to begin its programme of the so-called four modernizations.

Although there are wide cultural differences between the Japanese and the Chinese, a number of underlying characteristics are similar, particularly with regard to attitudes towards relationships. The Chinese Joint Venture Code provides a manifestation of these characteristics; and as a result its fifteen articles are short on detail, merely establishing a basis on which foreign capital can participate in setting up a joint venture in the People's Republic. Thus the law on joint ventures is best regarded as an enabling act permitting potential foreign parties to work out a comprehensive agreement through negotiations with their Chinese counterparts. The joint-venture law opens up the possibility for expanded international economic cooperation and technological exchange on the basis of the principle of 'equality and mutual benefit' which is seen by the Chinese as fundamental, and applicable to relationships with all potential partners.

As far as approval of agreements is concerned, the joint-venture Law offers little in the way of administrative detail; however, the Chinese are known to be considering a three-stage process beginning with a non-binding letter of intent signed between the parties. This letter is likely to specify the scope and terms of the joint venture, the capital structure, the technologies, if any, contributed by the foreign partner, the production methods, and the sale and distribution of products. If after the Chinese have carried out a feasibility study the situation still looks promising, then the parties proceed to the conclusion of a general agreement (*xieyi*). This establishes the basic outlines of the venture, and the Foreign Investment Commission will be asked to approve it. If the Commission signals a go-ahead, the parties will then negotiate stage three, which will be the final documentation. The joint-venture agreement, and articles of association and related contracts, must then be submitted to the Foreign Investment Commission for final approval.

To date the most popular foreign ventures have been processing work agreements and compensation trade agreements. In the former the foreign businessman pays the Chinese factory a processing fee. In the latter, the Chinese party waives part of this processing fee in exchange for a factory financed by the foreign (to date usually Hong Kong based) firm and/or equipment together with appropriate technological knowledge and instruction.

So far the Chinese would appear to have demonstrated something of a preference for compensation deals. The reason is that they offer the possibility of technical training for the Chinese, yet they impose minimal budget commitments in that no foreign exchange needs to be provided by the Chinese side. In addition, they offer a built-in export market in that marketing is usually the responsibility of the foreign partner, and there is flexibility in the contract concerning the time period in which the commitment is made.

These are still early days for the establishment of commercial arrangements with the Chinese. The Joint Venture Code essentially provides a set of principles, and legislation governing much of the detail of such commercial arrangements is non-existent or only recently promulgated. As a result there is much likely to be left to the individual negotiators of the joint ventures to clarify, and in so doing establish some manner of working with the Chinese.

INTER-ORGANIZATIONAL FACTORS

Organizational relationships

Of all the agreements that organizations in an international marketing setting can enter into, perhaps none has as much potential for giving rise to difficulties and disputes as the joint-venture agreement.

As an arrangement it does not involve a company in yielding its identity, as in a full-blown merger. Nevertheless it usually involves more deep-rooted relationships than those reflected in sales/purchase agreements, with the exception of some complex episodes with extensive relationships (see Chapter 8).

The commitment of resources is usually much higher than in agency/distributorship or licensing agreements. It follows that the parties have a high stake in a joint venture, and therefore the mutual dependence of the parties is high, as is the total power involved. Each party has the potential to move the other through a wide range of outcomes. Where control of the joint venture is equal, it can be said that in theory the parties can move each other through an equivalent range of outcomes. In such situations equal power can be said to exist. As indicated in Chapter 2, research points to the fact that equal power results in more effective bargaining than does unequal power, and that the greater the total amount of power in the system the less effectively bargainers are likely to function.

Given that it is only rarely that equal power exists, and that the parties to a proposed joint-venture arrangement have potential to do great damage to each other, it is not surprising that possibilities for conflict abound. Even more so than in other types of agreement, the joint-venture agreement depends on the relationship between the parties for the quality of performance arising from it. No two or more parties are likely to embark on a venture of high resource commitment without some kind of exploratory discussions and a considerable amount of prior research to provide the information on which to base decisions. These serve to highlight the issues that each party considers important and underline the gap to be bridged. The process can be considered to be the pre-negotiation stage of the 'negotiation skills model'. There is an opportunity for would-be joint venturers to go away and consider their own and other's expectations, and reflect on creative possibilities in relation to the gap which separates their thinking.

The parties to a negotiation already have relationships with other organizations. They may operate through a particular channel of distribution, which is now perceived to have served its purpose. Interest in a joint venture may be a response to a new dimension in the market, as has confronted suppliers to the offshore industries as new oil resources have been identified and exploited; or where a company is seeking to improve its market penetration by more direct involvement, as where two European suppliers to the laundry industry established a joint sales company in Italy. In the latter case one of the companies considered replacing the Italian part of one of its divisions serving the chemical industry, but found in the process that there was no structural fit. The skills of the personnel in the Italian sales company, which was based on the existing organization of the other venture member, were very much geared to the laundry industry. So the two companies were able to enter negotiations without having to consider further the chemical interests.

Because the parties to an intended joint-venture agreement must identify all these capabilities, strengths, weaknesses and intentions of the companies involved, and the attitudes and preferences of the individuals comprising the teams, the atmosphere within which the parties conduct negotiations is of prime importance. Atmosphere affects and is affected by the kinds of experiences the parties have had with each other, the relationships established which these experiences will reflect, and the climate of trustworthiness created. Equally it affects and is affected by the market environment. Where the market is such that a switch of allegiance to another organization is difficult and costly, considerable resources can be put into the relationship, all things being equal.

Interpersonal relationships

Cooperation has to be the keynote of a relationship in which resources are likely to be invested on a relatively heavy scale. When negotiators meet with a view to a long-term relationship, they cannot afford to be seen to be competitive and self-seeking, for fear of driving their counterparts away from the relationship. The importance to the organizations of continuing to negotiate until an agreement is finalized, or a decision is taken not to proceed — especially where alternative candidates are few or unavailable — inhibits the negotiators from taking up the extreme positions often evident in sales/purchase negotiations. This behaviour is matched by the use of language which is moderate. Influence will almost certainly be exercised, but it will be through processes which are unlikely to cause offence. An opposer who is perceived to be aggressive will not be the most favoured candidate for partnership in a joint venture.

All things being equal, an opposer who is perceived to be reasonable and cooperative is likely to have his organization considered seriously as a suitable partner, provided other criteria are satisfied (such as structural fit in terms of a match of technology, skills, operating routines and world views of the participants).

Joint ventures and the 'negotiation skills model'

Pre-negotiation activities

Because of the long-term, resource-intensive nature of most joint venture agreements, and the potentially far-reaching consequences for the parties, information gathering and analysis will be an important activity to identify the resources needed for the venture. It will also involve, as already indicated, pre-negotiation contact between parties to establish subjective elements, such as attitudes and feelings of opposers, for their perceptions will be important determinants of outcomes. Information will be required on the assistance needed by the would-be partners.

Because of the demonstrable difficulties in operating joint ventures, other possibilities must be exhausted before the decision to embark on one is made. Very often the organizational and commercial features of the host environment strongly influence the structure and control of the joint venture. So much is this the case for the Japanese environment that some Western businessmen with experience of joint venture activity with the Japanese suggest the best policy is to allow them to run the show. However, in most cases such an approach will be regarded as neither feasible nor desirable. Such are the inherent difficulties that organizations would do well to consider whether or not they really need such a form of direct investment before taking the plunge.

An agreement is probably most satisfactorily established after a period of involvement with the partner via slightly more 'arm's length' arrangements, such as licensing or distributorship. Thus the advice would be to enter a joint venture slowly in the case of both Japanese and Chinese partners. This is likely to accord with their requirements for general business relationships to build up over time and so allow mutual trust to develop. It will also allow a gestation period during which prospective partners can attempt to come to terms with each other's culturally based perspectives.

From a negotiating perspective it is less the actual nature of the agreement and the parties to it that is important than the stability in the interaction. Sometimes a joint venture is a step on the way to a full merger of organizations.

Face-to-face

When negotiators meet in circumstances where much hinges on the outcome, it is advisable to agree an agenda and the basic ground rules for the negotiations. In joint ventures in which there is considerable resource commitment, as where a corporate joint venture is established, negotiations can take some time to complete. If either of the parties wishes special procedures to apply, this is the time to hammer out the basis for them.

In negotiations with the Chinese over the supply and installation of power equipment, a Scottish-based company as a matter of policy negotiated a procedure whereby its negotiators would operate up to two weeks at a stretch. After that they would take a week's break away from the negotiating table, a very necessary step in the view of the company management, because of the pressures of working in an unaccustomed culture, the long drawn-out nature of the negotiations, and the austere nature of Chinese provincial life. Such an 'oil-rig' system of working has a number of advantages in these circumstances. It does mean, however, that accurate records are vital to ensure continuity. It also means that Chinese negotiators will be deprived of the reassurance of continuity in personnel they appear to need.

In countries like Japan and China where the adoption of such written and agreed records of proceedings can be construed as lack of trust, it is as well to negotiate the question of records as a procedural issue. When this has been done it will be up to the foreign negotiators to ensure that these records of what has been agreed are not perceived to be used as a manipulative device.

Distributive bargaining stage

Despite the fact that the relationship is paramount, it does not follow that the parties do not voice disagreement strongly or advocate a particular course of action. On the contrary, the relationship should encourage open communication to identify likely issues and problems. The language used may be couched in less than contentious terms (see Chapter 3), but it is only through expressing expectations that possible difficulties can be resolved. If not, they are certain to surface after the establishment of the venture when expectations will be somewhat different and perhaps attitudes less tolerant from those held when the position is still fluid.

In negotiations between parties in Western cultures, the kinds of behaviour learnt in assertiveness training in the USA and the interactive skills approach in the United Kingdom would appear to be particularly suited to joint-venture negotiations, where it is a prerequisite to agreement to uncover all the information necessary in connection with positions, attitudes, interests and reservations (Rackham and Morgan 1977, Tennant 1982). Where skilled negotiators are involved, these behaviours assist in clarification and the correction of what could otherwise remain misperceptions.

In view of the need to promote sound relationships, uncover hidden issues and generally create the climate within which these relationships can flourish, the distributive bargaining phase is very low-key. Because extreme positions are not taken up, there is little possibility of 'attack – defend' spirals developing, and the situation created whereby parties fear loss of position or image if they are seen to make concessions. The transition to the integrative bargaining stage in the negotiation skills model is made quickly and smoothly.

Integrative bargaining stage

At this stage the issues have been identified, often in prior discussions where what was agreed was recorded and became the first item on the agenda in the next round of negotiations. The issues are likely to be so numerous or complex that a number of meetings may be required. Because of the protracted nature of the process, issues are explored and problems identified which may require further information or joint action before negotiations can proceed further. When they resume, objectives may be restated in the light of new clarifications and hidden or implicit goals revealed which may, in turn, require further information or action before further progress can be made towards agreement.

Such lengthy proceedings would indicate patience as a necessary quality in the pursuit of a joint-venture agreement. Such a counsel is particularly true of 'consensus' cultures. Foreign executives bent on concluding joint ventures swiftly tend to become frustrated by the apparent delaying tactics of their opposite numbers, who appear either unwilling or unable to make a decision. This is because they do not come to decisions until such time as they have put together the whole picture. Hence the emphasis on information in Asian negotiations.

Decision-making and action stage

When the questions have all been asked and responded to, the parties are in a position to agree to what their inputs will be, a statement of corporate policy, and objectives, and to questions of day-to-day management.

Such can be the complexity of some joint-venture arrangements that the agreement on issues cannot be spelt out as a single package. This kind of situation can be handled by sub-dividing the issues into a variety of packages within which different trade-offs can be identified. This is very similar to an arrangement referred to as the 'contractual joint venture', in which a number of separate contracts are concluded, with each contract covering a specific issue. The question of profits might be treated in one contract, that of management control in another, and technical considerations in yet another. Each contract is completely independent of the others and as such creates an opportunity for a degree of flexibility and manoeuvre in particular areas without jeopardizing the whole arrangement. If there is a certain inevitability in this, it is probably best to establish agreement in principle on the main issues at the outset as a preliminary to detailed discussions in a number of separate areas.

The fine-tuning of an overall package or the individual elements constituting the overall agreement may require adjournments for consultation with specialists. The language used will reflect the cooperative behaviours that have been adopted; for example, 'Given the possibilities of agreement in the broad areas of distribution strategy, perhaps it would be in our joint interest to adjourn and finalize the technical details. If we can find an acceptable formula for this, then there would appear to be very little difficulty in finalizing our arrangements.' This gives nothing away, provides an opportunity for consolidation, and provides for clarity in terms of the final agreement. Provided the negotiations have proceeded on the basis of demonstrated commitment to the venture, individual issues can be linked to the total package or packages.

The output of the agreement is the detailed resource commitments of the participating companies, the agreed policies, objectives and strategies and the procedural agreements on day-to-day running and control. The basis of board composition, and distribution of profits, will be stated. Where the host government places a limit on the amount of profits which can be repatriated, this will normally also be stated. The agreement should be cross-checked for understanding in the same way as for the issues in the earlier stages of the negotiation.

Some cultural factors

Majority control is not always what it seems to be. In Java, the most heavily populated island of the Indonesian archipelago, there is a cultural dislike of professional trading which has resulted in a status system based on ethnic groups which leaves trade to the Chinese. The ruling junta of today has adopted aristocratic values. They use selected Chinese who are permitted to indulge their traditional commercial skills to accumulate wealth. They have no inclination or head for business, but collect tribute in return for the granting of privileges. The fees paid by one person for trading rights that are officially allotted to another are known as 'Ali Baba money'.

Current investment policies, which are dominated by economic nationalism and xenophobia, have reserved more and more business sectors for Indonesians. Rules have been established that businesses should be 51 per cent owned by non-Chinese Indonesians within ten years of their establishment. In the view of one authority on the area, the 51 per cent majority holding is just a piece of unworkable pedagogy. No normal business would achieve a return which would enable half of it to be controlled by partners who would have nothing to contribute. What is likely to happen, he claims, is that serious Western investors will diminish and the Japanese, who are much more sensitive to such problems and who know how to handle them, will adapt to the 'Ali Baba' system. The indigenous entrepreneur may get his 51 per cent control on paper, but will accept much less in practice for fear of getting no returns at all (May 1978:383).

The assertiveness which can be a strength in uncovering problematic issues in the negotiating of joint-venture agreements between parties of Western origin can be a positive drawback when interacting with nationalities who do not respond to these approaches. Scandinavians, who have a much quieter style than Americans, Germans or even British, and in any case are very much concerned with working as a team and making team decisions, will find it difficult to establish relationships with people exhibiting assertiveness. The Japanese will view it an aberrant behaviour and find it difficult to connect. Australians will tend to interpret it as overbearing and react accordingly.

Differing perceptions of a basic situation will have different cultural responses. If the relationship is important, as it is in the negotiation and operations of joint ventures between parties of differing cultures, then there is an onus on the party moving across cultures to act and react in a way that causes least discomfort and creates an atmosphere in which relationships can thrive. In doing this a negotiator must possess the cross-cultural skills which enable him to adapt his behaviour to the situation. That is a function of education and training. Differing perceptions can also arise in terms of communications. This is particularly the case in countries like the USSR and other Soviet bloc countries where the opportunity for misunderstanding is enormous. This can be the case with such concepts and terms as 'profit' and 'loss'. Although *glasnost* giving rise to increased democratization together with the consequences of *perestroika* may go a long way to break down barriers to understanding, one suspects that differences in management style, and management perceptions which are the consequences of deep-rooted cultural traits are likely to be the source of much misunderstanding.

INTRA-ORGANIZATIONAL RELATIONS

Environmental changes affecting joint ventures

Changes can take place in the environment of the joint venture which change the climate for the foreign company and affect its negotiating strength. The election or self-election of a new government can adversely affect operations if that government decides to implement new policy. A government can arbitrarily change the rules whereby, for example, profits are repatriated. The figure can be set at an amount below the limit existing or agreed at the time the joint venture was formed. Sometimes a government will make the granting of permission for, say, a factory extension, contingent on acceptance of a change in the original rules. Changes in the tax situation, investment rules and procedures, delays in decision-making, violation of contract terms, are all changes in the environment which affect operations. Sometimes these can be negotiated by the joint venture, but that will depend very much on its negotiating strength, both within the organization in obtaining unanimous support for the proposed action, and in terms of the benefits the joint venture is seen to continue to bring to the host country. Sometimes these problems are compounded by changes in the economic environment, as where a deteriorating balance of payments position can bring pressure to stop outflow of funds.

Changes within the political and social climate and consequent discriminatory legislation and action can equally affect the implementation of the joint-venture agreement. Some companies have preferred to operate in Malaysia with Chinese partners or in East Africa with East African Asians as partners, because of the generally accepted belief that these people were the best businessmen to associate with. The negotiating strength of the joint venture is reduced with the effectiveness of local Chinese or Indian partners because of government's resentment of Chinese or Indian businessmen in these countries and consequent discriminatory legislation against them.

Conflicts arising out of the joint venture

Once a joint venture has been set up, issues of conflict must be settled within the organization. However good an agreement may be, certain problems will only be identified under operational conditions.

Where nationals of both countries have to work together to meet stated objectives, there are certain to be misunderstandings owing to cultural differences, both in terms of national and organizational cultures. American or European executives operating a joint venture in association with an Arab partner may find that the Arab insistent on operating through personal ties and connections is at odds with his own professionalism, unless he is aware of the Arab social values and institutions which promote this.

Personnel from a German company may find the ambiguity in relationships with officers from the Japanese partner hard to bear, or may challenge the Japanese selling approach which may be perceived to emphasize sales volume at the expense of profitability. A Nigerian partner company may view European criteria of performance as irrelevant, as where one measure is the number of sales calls made per week in a country where relationships and the time needed to maintain them are not consistent with the measures applied.

In joint ventures with overseas governments, company officers may have to work beside civil servants. If the company officers come from Western countries, where subordinates are encouraged and expected to take initiatives, and rewards and penalties attach to this responsibility, this may seem outside the job remit of the civil servant in the relevant Ministry who does not normally have such motivations. Where direct initiatives are expected of the civil servant, there can be a clear cultural void which has to be spanned or otherwise filled.

Despite the difficulties of joint-venture operations, particularly in relation to 'fade-out' policies and the period over which investment would be recovered, the difficulty of adjusting to partners with differing world-views, and the vagaries of the environment which tend to diminish the joint venture's negotiating strength, there remain positive advantages. It is frequently the only means of adequate market access, it is often a useful hedge against political action, and it is a means of developing a market where the finance or local expertise is not available to go it alone. Good negotiation practice as a complement to sound judgment can provide the best basis for development of the relationships necessary for effective continuing operations.

The political interface: the key

The foregoing discussions serve to emphasize the point that of all the arrangements that have been discussed it is the negotiation of a joint-venture agreement that is most likely to bring an organization and its personnel into direct contact with a potential host country government. This is, obviously, particularly likely to be the case in less well-developed economies, especially when the nature of the proposed investment could effect the general economic equilibrium, either within the country itself, or a region of the country. It is also likely that in such environments encouraging the introduction of foreign technologies will be part of some structural plan for the economy which has been drawn up to increase the rate of economic development.

Because the entry of foreign capital through the medium of a joint venture may assume such significance in national economic terms, the venture is also likely to attract political attention. The level and nature of this political attention depends on the importance attached to foreign investment by the host government. Although many of the underlying threads of political activity are inspired by economic need, when the environment within a country is turbulent then a political force rather than an economic force can dictate the nature of policy towards foreign investment — particularly if by focusing attention on foreign investment, attention is also diverted from other issues. Such can be the swing of these political forces that what is welcomed under one regime can so easily be severely criticized and limited under another.

The exposure of an organization to the vagaries of such forces means that in many circumstances key personnel in the foreign element of a joint-venture agreement may be continually having to negotiate a position in a somewhat fluid environment. It is only in this way that a degree of stability can be established for the joint-venture investment.

This means that there is likely to be an on-going dialogue of bilateral bargaining as government and the enterprise engage in two-way trade-offs — each giving and getting. Arguments concerning economic benefit and loss may have varying degrees of impact with the host government. It may not be enough, however, to outweigh the strength of political arguments which can quickly build up once incited.

The foreign enterprise partner has, however, a number of arguments that can be invoked, and which in the long run are demonstrably powerful arguments.

First, the foreign enterprise is likely to bring much needed technology, together with the resources to assist in the transfer of that technology. Secondly, the foreign enterprise is likely to have a degree of choice in terms of its geographic location, and therefore it has a degree of power associated with its ability to chose a possible host. Thirdly, this also means that the foreign enterprise's assessment of the host environment and its willingness to advise others of the nature of the climate can have a major bearing on the power relationships within a negotiation. Publicity is thus a powerful weapon. Whilst a host government with control over the media can exert certain pressures when negotiating, the foreign enterprise can also exert pressure via its network of associations with other companies and international banking groups.

It is important for an enterprise's negotiators to recognize, however, the different weight that the host government attaches to the political as opposed to the economic. An example might serve to illustrate this point, and to emphasize the extent of preparatory research an enterprise should undertake prior to entering a joint venture. In Indonesia an American company was granted timber tracts on one of the outlying islands. The military governor of the island had entered into an arrangement with Chinese interests for the same tract. Central government did not care to enforce its agreement, because the armed services and the politicians had a delicate balance and termination of the military governor's agreement could have had serious domestic political consequences (Kapoor 1975).

It must also be recognized by the enterprise that the weight the host government attaches to political as opposed to economic factors will change at certain points in the duration of a project. At the early stages of the project the economic aspects will be emphasized by the host government, because it wishes to attract the resources it requires for its development aspirations. As the project becomes increasingly operational and the impact of the activity begins to be felt, then indigenous groups representing potential political pressure ensure that growing weight is attached to political considerations. In most cases the enterprise's response is to reiterate economic arguments.

Although involvement with a local organization in the form of the joint-venture agreement certainly assists in reducing the weight of undesirable attention that the organization receives, it is still nevertheless important for the foreign enterprise to include in its overall planning for negotiations the importance attached to non-economic contributions by the host government. During the negotiations with the indigenous partner the negotiators must try to recognize the nature of the 'hidden agenda' which in these circumstances could well be influenced by political factors. The negotiators from the in-coming enterprise must adopt a broader outlet.

Because the foreign enterprise associates itself with a local enterprise in the form of a joint venture, it does not necessarily imply that from a political perspective all its troubles are over. In an environment of shifting political fortunes it is possible for the indigenous enterprise to fall from grace.

All these factors mean that the personnel from the international enterprise must possess significant negotiating skills, since a great deal of their time could be spent in this activity. As Kapoor (1975) points out: 'Studies in some Asian countries indicate that the country manager of an American international corporation devotes as much as 50 per cent of his time directly or indirectly in interacting with the host government.' He further goes on to stress the importance of establishing meaningful relationships with the host governments, and he suggests that: 'To make any significant progress in this area the international corporation must develop executives with skills in dealing with host governments. The art of negotiation will be one of the essential skills of an executive dealing with developing countries'.

SUMMARY

The term 'joint venture' has been used as an umbrella term for a wide variety of business arrangements between partners across cultural boundaries. Regardless, however, of the specific details of the arrangement, they have a high propensity to failure and collapse. This can be related to the nature of mutual dependence and power within the relationship, and directly to cultural misunderstandings, particularly in those cases where there is significant cultural divergence.

Despite the high failure rate, this form of business relationship is likely to increase as emerging nations seek rapid routes to technologies for development purposes, and the sheer resource commitment of many projects requires some form of syndicated financing activity. In many cases it is the only way in which organizations can gain access to an increasing number of markets. Examples of such a policy are the diverse cultural settings of China and Yugoslavia.

The joint-venture arrangement is characterized by a complexity of inter-organizational factors and relationships which have a bearing on the agreement and the negotiation of the agreement. Parties to such an agreement are therefore advised to engage in substantial information gathering activity as a prerequisite to the negotiations. The complexity of the arrangements also mean that the negotiations could well be long drawn-out affairs as issues need to be clarified and relationships are established and power plays are indulged in.

As parties proceed through the negotiations, the keynote must be patience, particularly when dealing with 'high-context' cultures which place a high premium on personal relationships being the key to good business relationships.

The extent of corporate issues involved in the joint-venture agreement means that a 'total package' is difficult to accomplish and keeping issues linked almost impossible. Inevitably some sub-dividing must go on, and the so-called 'contractual joint venture' is one such approach.

As well as cultural factors greatly influencing the negotiating behaviour, they also have a major bearing on the choice of partners, and on government attitudes towards the venture. This is particularly the case where cultural sub-groups are regarded as the business force in a particular environment.

As the dominating forces in such an environment change, so too can the fortunes of the joint venture. Such changes, which might be politically inspired, highlight perhaps the most significant issue in the negotiation of a joint venture — that is, the whole question of the political interface. Despite a host country's requirements for resources, technology and managerial skills, in the final analaysis political forces outweigh economic considerations. Joint-venture negotiators would do well to reflect on this issue and ensure that appropriate energy is devoted to a satisfactory political balancing act.

Questions

1 Compare the nature and complexity of joint-venture agreements with any of the agreements treated in earlier chapters.
2 Prepare a list of the factors salient to your interest on which you would seek to obtain a positive outcome if you were a surgical appliances manufacturer seeking to set up a joint venture with a Hong Kong Chinese company.
3 What might the Chinese view of the situation be in Question 2 above? What difficulties would you expect in negotiations and how might you handle them?
4 To what extent do you think joint-venture negotiations with a private business organization differ from negotiations with a government or quasi-government organization?

READING I

Negotiating joint ventures with the Japanese: the timescale of patience*

The Japanese prefer to resolve difference through discussion, and the US partner should respect the Japanese wishes. Should conflicts arise, these are usually discussed between the parties in *lengthy* sessions. Both sides will wish to reach amicable conclusions that will be mutually beneficial. In the process, various trade-offs will be made. In short, both partners have to learn to give and take. In Japan issues are always resolved through negotiations. Casanova (Chairman of Sperry) stated emphatically that it is important for US businessmen to realize that 'in dealing with Asia, matters are not resolved through votes. In Japan and Asia in general, if I have three votes on the board and someone else has four, it does not mean that the other partner will win on the issues. All our business in Japan has really been handled through *lengthy* discussions, from middle management all the way up to top-management.' The chairman of Sperry and the vice-presidents of the various divisions are usually actively involved in the negotiations. 'These issues are resolved through *many, many* meetings, which could be very *lengthy*. Through the numerous *lengthy* sessions we *finally* arrived at a form of company that is mutually beneficial to the parties.' According to Omata (Japanese-American in charge of the joint venture) the company, fortunately, has never been confronted with an issue that could not be negotiated; both sides have always been able to resolve their differences. Large companies like Mitsui or Mitsubishi are cosmopolitan in their outlook and hence are very accommodating to differing perspectives.

From the Japanese standpoint if an issue can be resolved, both parties *will continue to negotiate* until common ground is reached and the differences ironed out. An example of a problem that would require negotiations between the two parties is how to respond to the product needs of the Japanese market. Recently there arose a need in Japan to produce computers capable of processing Japanese characters (*kanji*). To operate as a native industry, the joint-venture company had to develop a *kanji* processor. The US partner had to understand that and work with them. As a result NUK developed a processor with *kanji* capability. This development was possible only after *innumerable* sessions between Sperry's development people and those of NUK.

Another type of problem that requires negotiations is the issue of quality . . . the Japanese are obsessed with quality; the zero-defect movement is strong in Japan. Sperry has to work with NUK's technical people *constantly* to respond to consumers' specifications. To resolve such issues, both sides must engage in *long discussion* sessions. Such negotiations may take *a year or longer*.

* From R.L. Tung, *Business Negotiations with the Japanese*, Lexington Books, 1984. Reproduced with permission of D. C. Heath & Co. The italics are those of the authors.

Casanova noted that in a joint venture some issues might be unresolvable: 'if the issue cannot be resolved and we arrive at a confrontation point, we will sell out or we will buy them out.' Even here, both parties would go through a *long discussion* period until it became obvious to one side that there was no solution. At that point the venture disintegrates. Some US—Japanese ventures have, unfortunately, arrived at this stage. The Japanese process of conflict resolution is *time-consuming* and *more drawn out* than in the United States, where both parties bring in their attorneys and begin suing each other. That is unlikely to happen in Japan. Casanova believes that 'the Japanese system works better where there is a possibility for solution because *once you arrive* at a decision, then you obtain total support from the two sides. But in a confrontation process where there is really no solution, the Western way is much better. Where there is a way to work out the difference, the Japanese system is better. We could here, use the analogy of a divorce. In America you might get a divorce that you really did not have to.'

READING II

First and foremost South Koreans want to be number one:
But attitudes can be counter-productive*

Korean policy-makers are intent on welcoming foreign investors and making it worth-while for them to stay, but foreign businessmen in Seoul express doubts that the rest of the Government or society at large wants to go along.

'There is a powerful bias against foreigners,' one says. He described a seminar last year of foreign and Korean businessmen and government officials which produced a unanimous response from foreigners that profit was the purpose of joint ventures. The Koreans had a very different idea. They looked for increased market share, acquisition of technology, more employment and greater exports.

When one foreign participant suggested that his company wanted at least a 15 per cent return on investment, the Koreans loudly protested.

. . . The attitude runs deep. Some companies have months of struggle to repatriate dividends that the foreign investment law says should be automatic. The first problem is with the joint-venture partner who probably wants to re-invest profits. Several joint ventures have split over this kind of quarrel.

The next hurdle can be the Korean banks who may refuse to release money because it exceeds unpublished guidelines for dividend distribution. Although companies eventually get their money, it may require many trips to government ministries to receive authorization.

. . . Many foreigners find the pervasive role of the Government extremely onerous. It is present at every stage, from approval and licensing to operations and finally to dissolution. One businessman says, 'Investors who come are totally unprepared for it.'

---

* From Steven Butler, 'Outsiders face bias over profits', *Financial Times*, 15 May 1985. Reproduced with permission.

CHAPTER 12

Managing the negotiation process

Management and negotiation.. 304
Planning and preparing for the negotiation.. 306
Implementation: the bargaining and decision-making stages.................... 307
Review: post-negotiation stage... 310

Consideration of 'managing' the negotiation process begins from the assumption that management is about exercising a range of skills, carrying out of a series of tasks, and creating an appropriate climate within the organization. This combination of skills and tasks is geared towards facilitating, in an effective and efficient manner, the achievement of predetermined organizational goals. It is against this background within the context of negotiations that this final chapter attempts to highlight some of the key management issues and so draw together many of the strands presented in the previous chapters.

MANAGEMENT AND NEGOTIATION

The management of the negotiation process has a number of aspects. First, it involves the acquisition and exercise of a range of skills. Implicitly throughout many of the previous chapters this action-oriented approach has been adopted and rather than present another so-called instant recipe book on 'how to negotiate across cultural boundaries', an attempt has been made to present concepts and insights which might enable negotiators (and would-be negotiators) to develop from these insights and so extend their skills, enabling them to develop successful strategies to achieve preferred outcomes. Secondly, in addition to the acquisition and exercise of such skills, the management process involves taking account of the organizational environment and consequent organizational activity which, as well as providing the basic task support, also creates the appropriate climate and ethos. In so doing it facilitates the creation of opportunities to ensure such skills can be exercised to the full. The requisite cluster of negotiating skills involves information, interpretation, influencing skills, problem-solving skills, decision-making skills and an ability to manage the complex and uncertain. The model of effective job performance outlined by Boyaztis (1982) as the context for the exercise of managerial competencies, provides a useful insight into an appropriate approach to presenting negotiating skills in a management context. No matter how successful an organization might be in either recruiting individuals with the appropriate negotiating skills, or alternatively exposing individuals to training in the field of negotiations, if this duality of requisite skills and the exercise of supporting tasks is not recognized and the process is not properly managed, then the outcomes are likely to be sub-optimal.

It could be argued that such statements might be made about any aspect of management. However, in the case of the commercial negotiation process it represents the arena in which an organization's sales/marketing and purchasing strategy is operationalized and implemented and, as such, outcomes stand in stark relief and cannot be masked by either organizational procedures or other organizational 'noise'. It therefore provides a very clear representation of management in action. In spite of this limelight position it is still a little difficult to talk in isolation about the application of sound management principles to one aspect of an organization's activities. The management of any process or task occurs within a specific organizational context and hence is influenced by an organizational culture. It is obviously a truism that well-managed organizations are typified by sound management practices. Therefore, in this discussion of the management of the negotiation process, the necessary assumption is made that the process takes place against the background of a soundly managed organization.

It might be suggested that within the context of negotiations across cultural boundaries that stating such a caveat about the overall organizational context is not necessary, since in many organizations it is not unusual for those who operate in an international setting to have a fair degree of operating autonomy. The negotiating process can therefore be well managed regardless of the rest of the organization. If this were the case then negotiators would be freed of what might well be the management vagaries of other parts of the organization. In almost all cases, however, the negotiating activity interacts with other organizational processes. For example, in the case of the negotiation of sales/purchase agreements, licensing agreements and other contracts, there is of necessity interface with a range of other business activities. The fulfilment of any contract depends upon conformity by a range of organizational activities. As has already been indicated in Chapter 11 the all-embracing nature of joint-venture activity means that the negotiations of a joint venture has implications for the total organization. In a similar vein in a time dimension, it does not pay to lose sight of the fact that the manner in which contracts are fulfilled and business conducted has implications for the success of future deals and future business. This emphasizes yet again the significance of the relationship between the management of the organization and the management of the negotiation process. It is therefore not really possible to separate out the management of the negotiation process from overall organizational management. This chapter attempts to highlight those elements of management activity which, within the context of negotiation activity, require emphasis.

The previous chapters have highlighted the key processes involved in cross-cultural negotiations and indicated where appropriate the manner in which to proceed. This final section of the book attempts to draw many of these strands together in a manner consistent with the action-centred format already adopted. The framework adopted for this approach is standard to much management activity and that is one based on the key steps of *plan and prepare, implement or operate* and *evaluate or review.* This approach and the resultant review also attempt to accommodate the fact that sound management is the result of the successful meshing of skills and tasks or activities. This framework is also congruent with the negotiating skills model (see Figure 2.4) which highlights as the key stages the pre-negotiation stage, the stages of negotiation and the post-negotiation stage. It is against the background of the negotiating skills model that this review will be undertaken.

PLANNING AND PREPARING FOR THE NEGOTIATION

The need for planning and preparation cannot be overemphasized as being part of the key management tasks which must be undertaken. Initially, a great deal of this planning is going to involve information-gathering both at the macro-environmental level and at the level of the individual organization, either in relation to the opposing organization with which the negotiation is planned to take place or in relation to competitive organizations which might be involved in pitching for business. At the macro-environmental level this may invlove information-gathering with regard to country and cultural profiles, socio-economic considerations, political and legal considerations. Understanding with regard to political issues or socio-economic issues can provide a commercial edge. This was well illustrated in Chapter 8 (p. 187) where preparation and intelligence gathering with regard to forward currency movement projections resulted in the well-informed European party gaining an edge and agreeing to payment in US dollars. Being thus well-informed served to shift power in favour of the European negotiators. It pays to be well-informed about key environmental factors which are likely to have a bearing on the outcome of a negotiation since relative power can change quickly in response to changes in the environment of interacting organizations. Those activities bearing on outcomes for which pre-negotiation planning is a prerequisite, have been addressed in detail by Morrison (1985).

As was suggested in the negotiation skills model the pre-negotiation stage is very much concerned with determining objectives in relation to environmental and known or likely situational factors. Recent research and writings on negotiations in an international setting emphasize the point that negotiations must be seen as a process occurring within a much larger social system. As has been indicated by Hopmann and Walcott (1977), 'this approach to the analysis of negotiations has emphasized the effect that stresses and tensions emanating from the environment may have on both the processes and outcomes of negotiations' and indicate clearly the importance of preparatory activity and planning as a key element of the pre-negotiation stage.

At the micro or individual organizational level it is vital to attempt to gather as much information as possible about the opposition, their level and seniority, the nature of their business and the overall operating environment. The level of such activity obviously varies as between negotiating an agency agreement or a licensing agreement or a joint venture. It must be stressed, however, that it is a difference of degree rather than a difference of kind.

It is vital to establish clearly the purpose of any possible visit as and when it becomes necessary to establish contact. It is necessary to establish who will be met in the other organisation. Is the person the 'decision-making unit' or is the decision-making unit a committee. If, for example, the decision-making unit is a committee then this could have major implications for the overall nature of any presentation made.

It is perhaps worth emphasizing that within the context of licensing activity a great deal of this preliminary information is vital to the planning of an encounter since, as the negotiations proceed, it is often necessary to give out more and more sensitive and commercially confidential material. One needs to be assured in such circumstances that the exercise is a serious encounter. In many cases a great deal of this information can be clarified in preparatory correspondence.

This preparatory stage might also extend to the task of attempting to establish the agenda for the negotiation. As has already been indicated, control over the agenda, as with access to quality information, can give rise to a certain degree of power and control over the decisions since it can be used to position a seller and require him to outline his commitments and as such should not be overlooked.

This level of preparation and careful attention to detail wherever possible should also extend to the nature of the physical environment of an encounter. Even if it takes place on neutral ground, such as a hotel room, consideration should be given to the seating since research has indicated that proximity and bodily orientation can affect participants' reaction to situations and outcomes.

Data collection by itself is insufficient. Facts need to be turned into useful information. Negotiators are operating in an uncertain, threatening environment in which they must use whatever resources are available to make sense of what is going on around them. This task could be facilitated by the establishment of a systematic intelligence-gathering and maintenance system which is regularly updated. One valuable way in which such a system might be added to is by cumulatively building up information based on the careful recording of negotiating behaviour, together with the key issues and outcomes of a negotiation. As well as a key source of intelligence for each future interaction it could also become a key element of the vital process of post activity reflection. Reviewing the process is a key element in almost all management activity.

IMPLEMENTATION: THE BARGAINING AND DECISION-MAKING STAGES

The negotiation skills model (see Figure 2.4) indicates that it is during the stages of distributive bargaining, integrative bargaining and decision making that strategy with regard to the goals of the respective negotiators, is attempted to be implemented. From the perspective of the organization this is a very important phase which requires skilful management. It is well to remember that each move a negotiator makes within a negotiating situation not only affects the substantive question it also helps structure the rules of the negotiations. Therefore proceeding according to a predetermined strategy can influence the actual way that the negotiation progresses. At this stage of the negotiations process it is likely that a great deal of information is passing between the parties. It is inevitable that cues and signals (which to a large extent are culturally specific) may be missed or misinterpeted. A well-founded, well-informed strategy may help to minimize any resultant problems. It is during this phase that the process must be properly managed to ensure that agreements are not concluded which are contrary to the objectives of the organization. This might occur because of a lack of understanding of resultant legal interpretations of the process which is subsequently highlighted should a dispute arise. As was suggested in Chapter 6 (p. 123) parties to a negotiation can very often enter into a contract by the very fact of accepting a tender or an order, or even by conducting themselves in a way that the courts would assume that they had intended to be legally bound.

It is during this stage of the negotiations process that the negotiator must try to empathize with the opposition in an attempt to ensure a real understanding of the areas of difference. Such understanding might be facilitated by an organization's team of negotiators, undertaking a role-playing exercise, as part of their preparatory activity, in an attempt to explore and establish possible lines of strategy and arguments likely to be pursued and presented by the opposition team.

Despite such preparation the unexpected may still occur. The effective negotiator considers a wider range of options and is more likely to think in terms of a range of possible outcomes rather than think in terms of rigid objectives. Before embarking on this exercise it is perhaps valuable to recognize at the outset that no matter how prescriptive we might wish to be, it is important that a negotiator or a negotiating team maintain a degree of flexibility. Flexibility is necessary to accommodate the behavioural activity of others. An effective plan is one which survives contact with the opposition and does not require a mental change of gear when they fail to react as they should. In the terms of Rackham and Carlisle (1978), effective negotiators use plans which are independent of sequence; by addressing issue planning rather than sequence planning, means are made flexible but ends are likely to remain fixed.

In order for negotiators to be in a position to undertake such responsive planning activity prior to the negotiations, the senior management of an organization must ensure that they provide their negotiators with sufficient latitude to make effective plans and conduct negotiations. Managing the implementation of strategic objectives through the negotiation process depends upon a negotiator having the authority to be sufficiently flexible in the negotiations to ensure an appropriate outcome. In many cross-cultural negotiation situations there is an expectation on the part of the opposing organization that the person they are dealing with has the appropriate level of authority to carry out the negotiations. Continual interruptions to seek advice and authority from home can destroy credibility and reduce the chances of success. Consequently, it is important for the negotiator or the negotiating team to have clearly established limits of authority before proceeding with any negotiations.

Negotiations are very much concerned with the distribution and consequent exercise of power be this sapiential, personal or positional. In many negotiations power is divided differentially. It is likely, during this stage of the negotiations process, that the differential power-bases become somewhat clearer. Even such factors as being on home ground can add a dimension of power to the home team. This power differential needs to be recognized, and the process needs to be so managed as to ensure that if a negotiator recognizes that he possesses greater relative power, that he does not tend to use it exploitatively. A rein must be kept on the temptation to exercise the power in this way. As was suggested in Chapter 9 (p. 234) the crude use of power may well be used against a negotiator in a later round of bargaining when the power position may well have changed.

Perhaps the key management task at this stage is to create an atmosphere of interpersonal trust. Failure to do so at best ensures that the process is protracted and at worst increases the likelihood of the negotiation not coming to a satisfactory outcome. One way as has already been indicated that such trust can be established is by increased levels of pre-negotiation contact, enabling parties to come closer together in interpersonal relationships. Such contact may need to be managed with time set aside to provide an opportunity for such contact to take place. It has been stressed in 'high-context' cultures such as the Japanese and the Chinese that such contact and the opportunity to establish relationships appears vital to the success of the negotiation. Consequently, when dealing with such cultures, it is important to manage time in such a manner as to enable such relationships to be established.

This bond of trust can be confirmed and developed further if all stages of the negotiating process are characterized by a management philosophy which recognizes that the best method of achieving mutual success at the bargaining table is for both parties to work together in a professional manner. This is not to deny the fact that no matter how highly on-going relationships are valued, it will always be necessary to face the reality of interests that conflict. Such is the very heart of the negotiation process.

A professional approach to negotiations should be based on trying to settle differences and conflict on the basis of objective criteria rather than on the basis of the will of either side. The approach is based upon trying to achieve a solution based on principle not pressure. Negotiations characterized by a constant battle for dominance threatens relationships. It is far easier to negotiate when both parties are discussing issues on the basis of objective criteria rather than simply trying to force each other to back down. As has been suggested in Chapter 8 (p. 224), indeed neither side wins unless both sides win'. This clearly infers that energies should be directed away from an approach characterized by a win at all costs' towards a solution which is acceptable to both parties. This means that ploys and manipulative strategies of the kind identified by Steiner (1981) are not appropriate behaviour to ensure the development of long-term successful business relationships. Managing to maintain such an objective and professional approach in what at times can become an emotionally-charged atmosphere is not easy.

Above all else the development of such a 'professional' philosophy depends upon the extent to which the parties to the negotiation are willing to listen and respond to the concerns expressed by the other side. Listening is a key management skill. Nowhere is it more important than in the context of the negotiation situation. In this respect it is perhaps not inappropriate to suggest that 'the cheapest concession you can make to the other side is to let them know you have heard'. The opportunity for misunderstanding (particularly when different languages are involved) is enormous. The process of communicating in such situations, even with opposing parties in the same room, might be likened to the process of 'sending smoke signals in a high wind'. Thus the process must be so managed as to ensure clarity in communications.

As well as listening being an important skill in this matter of ensuring clarity of communication so too is the act of 'summarizing' at regular points in the negotiations. This is part of the process of 'testing understanding'. This is a necessary step to ensure that the parties do not leave the negotiating table with a different perception of what they believe they have agreed. The maxium is to summarize what has been agreed and get agreement that what has been summarized was agreed. Failure to test understanding and so clarify could well result in further negotiations in the future arising from differing interpretations of an orginal agreement. Such unfortunate recall to the negotiating table can hardly be regarded as effective management. As part of avoiding misunderstanding the well-managed negotiation is punctuated by points of summary.

REVIEW: POST-NEGOTIATION STAGE

Sound management of the negotiation process ensures that both parties leave the negotiations with a common understanding of what has been agreed. It is this process which lays the ground for the final stage of the negotiations process which is concerned with managing the process of recording the bargain and/or drawing up a legal contract which reflects the established understanding.

It is likely that in most situations the negotiations may have been conducted thus far without significant recourse to specialised legal minds. This may be due to a number of factors such as the negotiations taking place against the background of some set of 'standard conditions' or contract. It may be due to seasoned negotiators being aware of the legal boundaries, or it may reflect the result of only selective reference back to legal help. Whatever the reasons, the principles of an agreement so established during the negotiations process need to be encapsulated in appropriate legal terms. If the negotiations process has been well managed then the key principles and areas of agreement will not be altered by legal draftsmanship.

From a managerial perspective signatures on an agreement should not be regarded as the end of the process. Time should be taken to review and evaluate the process of the negotiation, the nature of the resultant outcome and the relationship and interaction between the two. Any lessons drawn from the encounter should be recorded and form part of the information bank on the negotiation thus ensuring the accumulation of a body of knowledge relating to the organization's experience of negotiating. Details of this nature can add to the organization's collective experience and so provide valuable information for the preparation and conduct of future negotiations.

This final chapter has attempted to draw many of the strands of the negotiation process together. In so doing an approach has been adopted which recognizes that the achievement of strategic goals via negotiations is the result of effective management action. Success is seen to arise from the exercise of skills, which can be regarded as describing a sequence of behaviours which are functionally related to attaining some performance goal, and from the completion of a range of tasks, which are aspects of the job rather than aspects of the individual negotiators capabilities or competencies. In describing this duality, emphasis has been given to planning and preparation, to the exercise of interpersonal skills in a professional manner during the key stages of the negotiation, and to the need to review the exercise as part of a process of moving up the learning curve and so enhancing requisite skills. It is only by adopting such a professional approach to business negotiations that effective agreements can be established enabling marketing strategies the better to be implemented.

Bibliography

Abell, P. (1975), 'Organizations as Bargaining and Influence Systems' in Abell, P. (Ed.) *Organizations as Bargaining and Influence Systems*, Heinemann.

Adams, J. B. (1957), 'Culture in an Egyptian village', *American Anthropologist*, **59.**

Alderson, W. (1971), 'The analytical framework for marketing' in Lawrence R. E. and Thomas M. J. (Eds), *Modern Marketing Management*, Penguin.

Allen, P. (1975), *The Practice of Exporting*, Macdonald and Evans.

Almeney, A. J. (1981), 'Cultural traits of the Arabs: growing importance for international management', *Management Review International*, **3.**

Ardagh, J. (1977), *The New France*, Penguin Books.

Ardagh, J. (1982), *France in the 1980's*, Penguin Books.

Argyle, M. (1975), *Bodily Communication*, Methuen.

Argyle, M. (1981), 'Intercultural communication' in Argyle, M. (Ed.), *Social Skills and Work*, Methuen.

Argyle, M. (1983), *The Psychology of Interpersonal Behaviour*, Penguin Books.

Auer, J., and Harris, C. E. (1981), *Computer Contract Negotiations*, Van Nostrand Reinhold.

Bacharach, S. B., and Lawler, E. J. (1981), *Bargaining: Power, Tactics and Outcomes*, Jossey-Bass.

Balint, M. (1965), *Primary Love and Psychoanalytic Technique*, Liveright NY.

Banks, A. S., and Texter, R. B. (1967), *A Cross-Polity Survey*, MIT Press.

Bass, B. M. (1966), 'Effects on the subsequent performance of negotiations of studying issues or planning strategies alone or in groups', *Psychological Monographs General and Applied* No. 614.

Berger, P. L., and Luckman, T. (1971), *The Social Construction of Reality*, Penguin Books.

Bernstein, B. (1972), 'Social class, language and socialisation' in Giglioli, P. P. (Ed.), *Language and Social Context*, Penguin Books.

Birdwhistell, R. L. (1973), *Kinesics and Context*, Penguin University Books.

Blake, R. R., and Mouton, J. S. (1977), *The Grid for Sales Excellence: Benchmarks for Effective Salesmanship*, McGraw-Hill.

Blake, R. R., and Mouton, J. S. (1980), *The New Managerial Grid*, McGraw-Hill.

Blois, K. J. (1972), 'Vertical Quasi Integration', *Journal of Industrial Economics*, Vol. 21.

Bonoma, T. V. (1982), 'Major sales: Who really does the buying?', *Harvard Business Review*, May/June.

Bonoma, T. V. (1985), *The Marketing Edge: Making Strategies Work*, The Free Press.

Bowersox, D. J., Cooper, M. B., Lambert, D. L., and Taylor, D. A. (1980), *Management in Marketing Channels*, McGraw-Hill.

Boyaztis, R. E. (1982), *The Competent Manager: A Model for Effective Performance*, John Wiley.

Brislin, R. W. (1982), *Cross-Cultural Encounters*, Pergamon Press.

Brooke, M. Z., and Buckley, P. J. (1983), *The Handbook of International Trade*, Kluwer.

Brunner, J. A., and Taoka, G. M. (1977), 'Marketing and Negotiation in the Peoples Republic of China', *Journal of International Business Studies*, Fall/Winter.

Cawthra, B. I. (1978), *Patent Licensing in Europe*, Butterworths.

Chertkoff, J. M., and Esser, J. K. (1976), 'A review of experiments in explicit bargaining', *Journal of Experimental Psychology*, **7.**

Clyne, M. (1977), 'International communication breakdown and communication conflict' in Molony, C., Zobl, H., and Stölting, W. (Eds), *German in Contact with Other Languages,* Kromberg Scriptor.

Conrad, C. (1985), *Strategic Organisational Communication: Cultures, Situations and Adaptations* Holt, Reinhart and Winston.

Contractor, F. J. (1981), *'International Technology Licensing: Compensation, Costs and Negotiation,* Lexington Books.

Cropp, J. A. D., Harris, D. C., and Stern, E. S. (1970), *Trade in Innovation,* John Wiley.

Crystal, D. (1975), 'Paralinguistics' in Benthall, J., and Polhemus, T. (Eds), *The Body as a Means of Expression,* Allen Lane.

Diamantapoulos, A. (1987), 'Vertical Quasi Integration Revisited: The Role of Power', *Managerial and Decision Economics,* Vol. 8.

Doi, L. T. (1973), *The Anatomy of Dependence,* Tokyo Kodansha International.

Douglas, A. (1962), *Industrial Peacemaking,* Columbia University Press.

Doyle, P. (1979), 'Management Structures and Marketing Strategies in UK Industries', *European Journal of Marketing,* Vol. 13, No. 5.

Drucker, P. F. (1971), 'What we can learn from Japanese management?', *Harvard Business Review,* March/April.

Druckman, D. (1968), 'Pre-negotiation experience and dyadic conflict resolution', *Journal of Experimental Social Psychology,* **4.**

Dunn, D. T. (1979), 'Agents and distributors in the Middle East', *Business Horizons,* October.

Eggers, E. R. (1977), 'How to do business with a Frenchman' in Weinshall, T. D. (Ed.), *Culture and Management,* Penguin Books.

Ekman, P., and Friesen, W. V. (1969), 'Non-verbal leakage and clues to deception', *Psychiatry,* **32.**

Evans, J. M. 'America: The View from Europe', Stanford, The Portable Stanford, Stanford Alumni Association, quoted in Watzlawick (1976).

Everton, A. R. (1978), *Trade Winds,* Alan Osborne and Associates.

Farmer, R. N., and Richman, B. M. (1965), *Corporate Management and Economic Progress,* Irwin.

Fisher, G. (1980), *International Negotiation: A Cross-Cultural Perspective,* Intercultural Press.

Fisher, R., and Ury, W. (1983), *Getting to Yes: Negotiating Agreement without Giving In,* Hutchinson.

Flynn, P. J., and Kynoch, W. S. (1983), *Scotpack Developments (B) Case Study,* Case Clearing House, Cranfield, England, No. 583-011-2.

French, J. R., and Raven, B. H. (1959), 'Bases of social power' in Cartwright, D. (Ed.), *Studies in Social Power,* Ann Arbor, Michigan.

Galbraith, J. K. (1975), *Economics and the Public Purpose,* Penguin Books.

Goffman, E. (1972a), *Interaction Ritual,* Allen Lane.

Goffman, E. (1972b), 'The neglected situation' in Giglioli, P. P. (Ed.), *Language and Social Context,* Penguin Books.

Graham, J. L. (1981), 'A hidden cause of America's trade deficit with Japan' *Columbia Journal of World Business,* Fall.

Gumperz, J. (1966), 'Linguistics repertoires, grammars and second language instruction', *Monograph No. 18: Report of the Sixteenth Annual Round Table Meeting on Linguistics and Language Study,* Washington, D. C., Georgetown Press.

Gupta Dipak, K. (1978), 'Multinational investment in Yugoslavia: an appraisal', *Columbia Journal of World Business,* Spring.

Guyerot, J. (1976), *The French Law of Agency and Distributorship Agreements,* Oyez Publishing.

Hakansson, H. (Ed.) (1982), *International Marketing and Purchasing of Industrial Goods: An Interaction Approach,* John Wiley.

Hall, E. T. (1959), *The Silent Language,* Doubleday.

Hall, E. T. (1969), *The Hidden Dimension,* Bodley Head.

Hall, E. T. (1976), *Beyond Culture,* Anchor Press/Doubleday.

Hall, E. T. (1983), *The Dance of Life: The Other Dimension of Time*, Anchor Press/Doubleday.

Hammarkvist, K.-O. (1983), 'Markets as Networks' in Christopher, M., McDonald, M., and Rushton, A. (Eds), *Back to Basics: The 4 Ps Revisited*. Proceedings of Marketing Education Group Conference.

Handy, C. P. (1985), *Understanding Organizations*, Penguin Books.

Harris, P. R., and Moran, R. T. (1987), *Managing Cultural Differences*, Gulf Publishing.

Hill, R. W., and Hillier, T. J. (1977), *Organizational Buying Behaviour*, Macmillan.

Hofstede, G. (1984), *Culture's Consequences: International Differences in Work-Related Values*, Sage Publications.

Hogarth, R. M., and Makridakis, S. (1981), 'Forecasting and Planning: An Evaluation', *Management Science*, Vol. 27, No. 2.

Honey, P. (1978), *Face-to-Face: Business Communication for Results*, Prentice-Hall.

Honnold, J. O. (1982), *Uniform Law for International Sales under the 1980 United Nations Convention*, Kluwer.

Hopman, P. J., and Walcott, C. (1977), 'The Impact of Internal Stresses and Tensions on Negotiations', in Druckman, D., *Negotiations: Psychological Perspectives*. Sage Publications.

Hornstein, H. A., and Deutsch, M. (1968), 'Tendencies to compete and to attack as a function of inspection, incentive and available alternatives', *Journal of Personality and Social Psychology*, **4.**

Horowitz (Ed.) (1939), 'The language and ideas of ancient China'. *The Collected Essays of C. Wright Mills*, Oxford University Press.

Hovland, C. L., Janis, I. L., and Kelley, H. H. (1953), *Communication and Persuasion*, Yale University Press.

Kahn, H. (1971), *The Emerging Japanese Superstate*, André Deutsch.

Kapoor, A. (1975), *Planning for International Business Negotiations*, Ballinger Publishing.

Karrass, C. L. (1974), *Give and Take*, Thomas Y. Crowell.

Kasulis, J. T., and Spekman, R. E. (1980), 'A Framework for the Use of Power', *European Journal of Marketing*, Vol. 14, No. 4.

Kelman, H. C. (1961), 'Processes of Opinion Change', *Public Opinion Quarterly*, **25.**

Kennedy, G., Benson, J., and McMillan, J. (1980), *Managing Negotiations*, Business Books.

Killing, P. (1982), 'How to make global joint ventures work', *Harvard Business Review*, May/June.

Kotter, J. (1985), *Power and Influence*, The Free Press.

Lakoff, G., and Johnson, M. (1980), *Metaphors We Live By*, Chicago University Press.

Lawrence, P. A. (1980), *Management in West Germany*, Croom Helm.

Lawrence, P. A. (1982), *Swedish Management: Context and Character*, Report to the Social Science Research Council.

Lax, D. A., and Sebenius, J. K. (1986), *The Manager as Negotiator: Bargaining for Co-operation and Competitive Gain*, The Free Press.

Lee, J. A. (1966), 'Cultural analysis in overseas operations', *Harvard Business Review*, March/April.

Lewis, I. M. (1976), *Social Anthropology in Perspective*, Penguin Books.

Lidstone, J. (1977), *Negotiating Profitable Sales*, Gower Press.

Lovell, E. B. (1968), *Domestic Licensing Practices*, The Conference Board.

Low, K. B., and Bridger, H. (1979), 'Small group role in relation to management development' in Babington Smith, B., and Farrell, B. A. (Eds), *Training in Small Groups*, Pergamon.

MacMillan, I. C. (1978), *Strategy Formulation: Political Concepts*, West Publishing.

Magenau, J. M., and Pruitt, D. G. (1979), 'The social psychology of bargaining' in Stephenson, G. M., and Brotherton, C. J. (Eds), *Industrial Relations: A Social Psychological Approach*, John Wiley.

Mangham, I. L. (1978), *Interactions and Interventions in Organizations*, John Wiley.

Mangham, I. L. (1979), *The Politics of Organizational Change*, Associated Business Press.

Marsh, P. D. V. (1984), Contract Negotiation Handbook, Gower.

314

Marwell, G., and Schmitt, D. R. (1967), 'Dimensions of Compliance Gaining Behaviour', *Sociometry*, **30.**

May, B. (1978), *The Indonesian Tragedy*, Routledge and Kegan Paul.

Mazzolini, R. (1974), *European Transnational Concentrations*, McGraw-Hill.

McCall, J. B. (1984), *Casa Avila*, Case Study, Residential School Booklet P672, Open University.

McCall, J. B., and Cousins J. Y. (forthcoming 1989), *Communication Problem Solving: The Language of Effective Management*, John Wiley.

McCall, M. W., and Kaplan, T. E. (1985), *Whatever It Takes: Decision Makers At Work*, Prentice-Hall.

McMillan, C., and Paulden, S. (1974), *Export Agents*, Macmillan.

Miller, G. A. (1966), 'The Magical Number Seven Plus or Minus Two: Some Limits on our Capacity for Processing Information', in Miller, G. A. *The Psychology of Communication*, Penguin Books.

Miller, G. R. (1983), 'On Various Ways of Skinning Symbolic Cats: Recent research on persuasive message strategies', *Journal of Language and Social Psychology*, Vol. 2, Nos 2, 3 and 4.

Mills, C. W. (1939), 'Language, logic and culture' in Horowitz (Ed.) *The Collected Essays of C. Wright Mills*, Oxford University Press.

Morgan, G. (1986), *Images of Organization*, Sage Publications.

Morley, I. E., and Stephenson, G. M. (1977), *The Social Psychology of Bargaining*, Allen and Unwin.

Morris, D. (1978), *Man-watching*, Triad Granada.

Morris, J. (1987), *Joint Ventures: An Accounting Tax and Administrative Guide*, John Wiley.

Mueller, R. K. (1986), *Corporate Networks: Building Channels for Information and Influence*, The Free Press.

Muna, F. A. (1980), *The Arab Executive*, Macmillan.

Nakane, C. (1973), *Japanese Society*, Penguin Books.

Negandhi, A.R. (1980), 'Multinational corporations and host governments relationships: comparative study of conflicts and conflicting issues', *Human Relations*, **33.**

Parris, J. (1982), *Retention of Title on the Sale of Goods*, Granada.

Patai, R. (1973), *The Arab Mind*, Scribner Books.

Pedler, M. J. (1977a), 'Negotiation skills training', *Journal of European Industrial Training*, **1,** 5.

Pedler, M. J. (1977b), 'The resolution of conflict and the negotiating process', *Journal of European Industrial Training*, **1, 6.**

Pennington, R. R. (1982), 'French, German and US law' in Parris, J., *Retention of Title on the Sale of Goods*, Granada.

Peters, J. I. (1977), 'The new industrial laws in Mexico and Brazil – implications for multinational operations', *Columbia Journal of World Business*, Spring.

Peters, T. J. (1988), *Thriving on Chaos*, Macmillan.

Pettigrew, A. M. (1973), *The Politics of Organisational Decision-Making*, Tavistock Publications.

Pfeffer, J. (1981), *Power in Organisations*, Pitman.

Phillips-Martinsson, J. (1981), *Swedes as Others See Them: Fact, Myth or Communication Complex*. Affars Forlaget.

Piercy, N. (1981), 'Export strategy: concentration on key markets *v* marketing spreading', Journal of International Marketing, Vol. 1, No. 1.

Piercy N. (1985), *Marketing Organisation: An Analysis of Information Processing, Power and Politics*, Allen and Unwin.

Pockney, B. P. (1978), 'Languages for the 1980s and 1990s' in *Does Britain Need Linguists?* (Conference sponsored by the Royal Society of Arts, University Of Surrey, and British Overseas Trade Board), BOTB.

Pollzien, G. M., and Langen, E. (1973), *International Licensing Agreements*, Bobbs Merrill.

Pondy, L. R. (1967), 'Organisational Conflict: Concepts and Model', *Administrative Science Quarterly*, Vol. 12, No. 2.

Poppleton, S. E. (1981), 'The Social Skills of Selling', in Argyle, M. *Social Skills and Work*, Methuen.

Porter, M. E. (1985), *Competitive Advantage: Creating and Sustaining Superior Performance*, The Free Press.

Pye, L. W. (1982), *Chinese Commercial Negotiating Style*, Oelgeschlager, Gunn and Hain.

Rackham, N., and Carlisle, J. (1978), 'The effective negotiator: the behaviour of successful negotiators', *Journal of European Industrial Training*, **2**, 6.

Rackham, N., Honey, P., and Colbert, M. J. (Eds) (1971), *Developing Interactive Skills*, Wellens Publishing.

Rackham, N., and Morgan, R. G. T. (1977), *Behavioural Analysis in Training*, McGraw-Hill.

Razzouk, N. Y., and Harmon, R. (1985), 'The Information Content of Magazine Advertising in the Islamic Culture', in Shaw, S., Sparks L., and Kaynak, E. (Eds), *Marketing into the 1990's and Beyond*, Proceedings of the Second World Marketing Congress, University of Stirling, Scotland.

Redding, S. G. (1980), 'Cognition as an aspect of culture and its relation to management processes: an exploratory view of the Chinese case', *Journal of Management Studies*, May.

Reischauer, E. O. (1977), *The Japanese*, Belknap Press of Harvard University Press.

Ritter, L., and Overbury, C. (1977), 'An attempt at a practical approach to joint ventures under EEC rules of competition', 14 *Common Market Law Review*.

Roberts, K. H. (1970), 'On looking at an elephant: an evaluation of cross-cultural research related to organisations'. *Psychological Bulletin*, **74.**

Robinson, P. J., and Faris, C. W. (1967), *Industrial Buying and Creative Marketing*, Allyn and Bacon.

Robles, F. (1984), 'Buying in a Matrix Organisation', *Industrial Marketing Management*. Vol, 13, No. 3.

Robock, S. F., and Simmonds, K. (1983), *International Business and Multinational Enterprises*, Irwin.

Root, F. R., and Contractor, F. J. (1981), 'Negotiating Compensation, in *International Licensing Agreements*', Sloan Management Review, Winter.

Rosson, P. J., and Ford, I.D. (1982), 'Manufacturer-overseas distributor relations and export performance', *Journal of International Business Studies*, Fall.

Rubin, J. Z., and Brown, B. R. (1975), *The Social Psychology of Bargaining and Negotiation*, Academic Press.

Salaman, G. (1980), 'Organisations as Constructors of Social Reality', in Salaman, G., and Thompson, K. (Eds), *Control and Ideology in Organisations*, Open University Press.

Schein, E. H. (1985), *Organisational Culture and Leadership*, Jossey-Bass.

Schmidt, S. M., and Kochan, T. A. (1977), 'Inter-organisational relationships; patterns and motivations', *Administrative Science Quarterly*, June.

Schmitthoff, C. M. (1986), *Schmitthoff's Export Trade: The Law and Practice of Export*, Stevens.

Seaton, A. V. (1976), 'Language and the secondary socialisation of employees in the multinational corporation: the occupational world-picture of the marketing executive' in Baker, M. J. (Ed.), *Buyer Behaviour* (Proceedings of the Marketing Education Group Conference).

Shouby, E. (1951), 'The influence of the Arabic language on the psychology of the Arabs', *Middle East Journal*, 5.

Simmonds, K., and Smith, H. (1968), 'The first export order: a marketing innovation', *British Journal of Marketing*.

Simon, H. (1979), 'Information Processing Models of Cognition', *Annual Review of Psychology*.

Snyder, M. (1974), 'The self-monitoring of expressive behaviour', *Journal of Personality and Social Psychology*, October.

Spillard, P. (1985), *Organisation and Marketing*, Croom Helm.

Steiner, G. (1975), *After Babel: Aspects of Language and Translation*, Oxford University Press.

316

Stern, L. W. (1976), 'Managing conflicts in distribution channels' in Evan, W. M. (Ed.), *Inter-Organisational Relations*, Penguin Books.

Stern, L. W., and El-Ansary, A. I. (1982), *Marketing Channels*, Prentice-Hall.

Stern, L. W., and Eovaldi, T. L. (1984), *Legal Aspects of Marketing Strategy: Anti-Trust and Consumer Protection Issues*, Prentice-Hall.

Stevens, P. B. (1983), 'Ambivalence, modernisation and language attitudes: French and Arabic in Tunisia', *Journal of Multilingual and Multicultural Development*, Vol. 4, No 2 and 3.

Strauss, A. (1978), *Negotiations: Varieties, Contexts, Processes and Social Order*, Jossey-Bass.

Sullivan, J., and Peterson, R. B. (1982), 'Factors associated with trust in Japanese-American Joint ventures', *Management International Review*, **22**, Part 2.

Sullivan, J., Peterson, R., Kamanda, N., and Shimada, J. (1981), 'The relationship between conflict resolution approaches and trust – a cross cultural study', *Academy of Management Journal*, **24.**

Tennant, C. (1982), 'Assertiveness training – a practical approach', *Journal of European Industrial Training*, **6.**

Terpstra, V. (1978), *The Cultural Environment of International Business*, Southwestern.

Thomas, K. W. (1976), 'Conflict and Conflict Management', in Dunette, M. D. (Ed), *Handbook of Organisational and Industrial Psychology*, McNally.

Thompson, K. (1980), 'Organisations as Constructors of Social Reality', in Salaman, G., and Thompson, K, (Eds), *Control and Ideology in Organisations*, Open University Press.

Tung, R. L. (1982), 'US-China trade negotiations: practices, procedures and outcomes', *Journal of International Business Studies*, Fall.

Tung, R. L. (1984), *Business Negotiations with the Japanese*. Lexington Books.

Turnbull, P. W., and Cunningham, M. T. (1981), *International Marketing and Purchasing*, Macmillan.

Turner, B. (1971), *Exploring the Industrial Sub-Culture*, Macmillan.

Turpin, C. (1972), *Government Contracts*, Penguin Books.

Van Zandt, H. R. (1970), 'How to negotiate with the Japanese', *Harvard Business Review*, Nov/Dec.

Warrington, M.B., and McCall, J. B. (1983), 'Negotiating a foot into the Chinese door', *Management Decision*, **21**, 2.

Watzlawick, P. (1976) *The Language of Change: Elements of Therapeutic Communication*. Basic Books.

Webber, R. A. (1977), 'Convergency or Divergence', in Weinshall, T. D. (Ed.), *Culture and Management*, Penguin Books.

Webster, F. E., (1984), *Industrial Marketing Strategy*, John Wiley.

Webster, F. E., and Wind, Y. (1972), *Organisational Buying Behaviour*, Prentice-Hall.

Weinshall, T. D. (1977), 'Communication, Culture and the Education of Multinational Managers', in Weinshall, T. D. (Ed.), *Culture and Management*, Penguin Books.

Weitz, B. (1981), 'Effectiveness in sales interactions', *Journal of Marketing*, Winter.

Wright, R. W. (1979), 'Joint venture problems in Japan', *Columbia Journal of World Business*, Spring.

Zartman, I. W. (1976), *The Fifty Percent Solution*, Doubleday.

Author index

Abell, P. 6
Adams, J. B. 47
Alderson, W. 8
Allen, P. 240
Almeney, A. J. 167
Ardagh, J. 67, 73, 208
Argyle, M. 52, 53, 54, 58, 167
Auer, J. 190, 214, 222

Bacharach, S. B. 6, 20, 177
Bacher, T. J. 207
Baker, M. J. 315
Balint, M. 61
Banks, A. S. 120
Bass, B. M. 199
Benson, J. 39
Benthall, J. 312
Berger, P. L. 101
Bernstein, B. 66
Birdwhistell, R. L. 61
Blake, R. R. 93, 159, 166
Blois, K. 19, 177
Bonoma, T. V. 7, 107–8, 111, 113, 162
Bowersox, D. J. 227, 229
Boyatzis, R. E. 305
Bradford, D. L. 115
Bridger, H. 242
Brislin, R. W. 190
Brooke, M. Z. 271
Brotherton, C. J. 313
Brown, B. R. 8, 16, 18, 21
Brunner, J. A. 90
Buckley, P. J. 274
Butler, S. 303

Carlisle, J. 29, 30, 45, 46, 308
Cartwright, D. 312
Cawthra, B. I. 133
Chertkoff, J. M. 177
Clyne, M. 50
Cohen, A. R. 115
Colbert, M. J. 242
Conrad, C. 112
Contractor, F. R. 259, 264, 275
Cooper, A. B. 227, 229
Cousins, J. Y. 43, 44, 109
Cropp, J. A. D. 132–3

Crystal, D. 47
Cunningham, M. T. 48

Deutsch, M. 28
Diamantopoulos, A. 177
Doi, L. T. 61, 90
Douglas, A. 39
Doyle, P. 106
Drucker, P. F. 80
Druckman, D. 28, 313
Dunette, M. D. 316
Dunn, D. T. 139

Eggers, E. R. 71
Ekman, P. 54
El-Ansary, A. I. 145
Eovaldi, T. L. 145
Esser, J. K. 177
Evan, W. M. 315
Evans, J. M. 52
Everton, A. R. 138

Faris, C. W. 161
Farmer, R. N. 91
Fisher, G. 256
Fisher, R. 29, 111
Flynn, P. J. 183, 218
Ford, I. D. 234, 252
French, J. R. P. 23, 24, 39
Friesen, W. V. 54

Galbraith, J. K. 6
Ghauri, P. N. 212
Goffman, P. 56, 57, 58
Graham, J. L. 80, 87, 88, 96
Gumperz, J. 48
Gupta, D. K. 286
Guyerot, J. 136

Hakansson, H. 4, 163, 166
Hall, E. T. 58, 63, 78, 91
Hammarkvist, K.–O. 4
Handy, C. P. 68
Harmon, R. 50
Harris, C. E. 190, 213, 222
Harris, D. C. 132–3
Harris, P. R. 114
Hermann, A. H. 147
Herzberg, F. 93
Hill, R. W. 162

Hillier, T. J. 162
Hofstede, G. 92, 98
Hogarth, R. M. 100
Honey, P. 46, 242
Honnold, J. O. 143
Hopman, P. T. 306
Hornstein, H. A. 28
Horowitz, L. 260
Hovland, C. L. 61

Janis, I. L. 61
Johnson, M. 60

Kahn, H. 79
Kamada, N. 282
Kaplan, T. E. 100
Kapoor, A. 298
Karrass, C. L. 180
Kasulis, J. T. 23
Kaynak, E. 315
Kelley, H. H. 61
Kelman, H. C. 23, 24
Kennedy, G. 39
Killing, P. 283
Kochan, T. A. 231
Kotter, J. 107–8
Kynoch, W. S. 183, 218

Lakoff, G. 60
Lambert, D. M. 227, 229
Langen, E. 143
Lawler, E. J. 6, 20, 177
Lawrence, P. A. 62, 74, 167
Lax, D. A. 6, 106
Lee, J. A. 91, 241
Lewis, I. M. 92
Lidstone, J. 121
Lovell, E. B. 266
Low, K. B. 242
Luckman, T. 101

MacMillan, I. C. 6, 191
Magenau, J. M. 203
Makridakis, S. 100
Mangham, I. L. 168, 241
Marsh, P. D. V. 178, 183, 194, 206, 219
Marwell, G. 42, 43, 109
May, B. 298
Mazzolini, R. 145
McCall, J. B. 43, 44, 59, 109, 256
McCall, M. W. 100
McMillan, C. 230
McMillan, J. 39
Miller, D. L. 80

Miller, G. A. 100
Miller, G. R. 23, 42–44
Mills, C. W. 104
Molony, C. 312
Moran, R. T. 114
Morgan, G. 99
Morgan, R. G. T. 308
Morley, I. 26, 39, 188, 199
Morris, D. 53, 55
Morris, J. M. 282
Morrison, W. F. 306
Mouton, J. S. 93, 159, 166
Mueller, R. K. 107
Muna, F. A. 195, 248

Nakane, C. 50, 58, 67, 80, 92, 94, 200
Negandhi, A. R. 51

Overbury, C. 141

Parris, J. 143
Patai, R. 50
Paulden, S. 230
Pedler, M. 18
Pennington, R. R. 143
Peters, J. I. 133
Peters, T. J. 8
Peterson, R. 288
Pettigrew, A. M. 188
Pfeffer, J. 106
Phillips-Martinsson, J. 190
Piercy, N. 7, 106–7, 254
Pockney, B. P. 58
Polhemus, T. 312
Pollzien, G. M. 143
Pondy, L. R. 111
Poppleton, S. E. 159
Porter, M. E. 5
Pruitt, D. G. 203
Pye, L. W. 206, 232, 249

Rackham, N. 29–30, 45–6, 242, 308
Raven, B. H. 23, 31
Razzouk, N. Y. 50
Redding, S. G. 59, 90
Reischauer, E. O. 80
Richman, B. M. 91
Ritter, L. 141
Roberts, K. H. 78
Robinson, P. J. 161
Robles, F. 162
Robock, S. F. 130
Root, F. R. 167
Rosson, P. J. 234, 252
Rubin, J. Z. 8, 16, 18, 21

Salaman, G. 103
Sathe, V. 113
Schein, E. H. 100–1
Schmidt, S. M. 234
Schmitt, D. R. 42–3, 109
Schmitthoff, C. M. 125–6, 143
Seaton, A. V. 71, 104
Sebenius, J. K. 6, 106
Shaw, S. 315
Shimada, J. 288
Shouby, E. 49
Simmonds, K. 130, 188
Simon, H. 100
Smith, H. 188
Snyder, M. 160
Sparks, L. 315
Spekman, R. 23
Spillard, P. 6, 101–2
Steiner, G. 47
Steiner, C. M. 299
Stephenson, G. M. 26, 39, 188, 199, 313
Stern, E. S. 132–3
Stern, L. W. 12, 145
Stevens, P. B. 48
Stölting, W. 258
Strauss, A. 6
Sullivan, J. 288

Taoka, G. M. 90
Taylor, D. A. 227, 229
Tennant, C. 293

Terpstra, V. 71
Texter, R. B. 120
Thomas, M. J. 314
Thomas, K. W. 25–6
Thompson, K. 101
Todd, J. 153
Tung, R. L. 71, 80, 90, 207, 301
Turnbull, P. W. 48
Turner, B. 105
Turpin, C. 129, 212

Ury, W. 29

Van Zandt, H. F. 50, 80

Walcott, C. 306
Warrington, M. B. 59
Watzlawick, P. 52
Webber, R. A. 202
Webster, F. E. 162, 163
Weinshall, 63, 313
Weitz, B. 160
Williamson, O. 8
Wind, Y. 162
Wright, R. W. 289

Zartman, W. 6
Zobl, H. 261

Subject index

agenda
   agreeing the, 190–1, 293
   negotiating the, in Sweden, 190
   seller's proposals defining the, 192
   using the, to influence outcomes, 190
agreement
   and relationships, 199, 234–5, 251–2, 272, 292
   assessing possibilities of, 207
   concessions and, 88, 192
   getting movement towards, 196–7, 210
   in principle, 190
   memorandum of, 208–9
   on agenda, 190
   on rules of meeting, 189
   pre-negotiation contact in assisting, 28, 34, 185–7, 209–10, 292
   reaching the, 30–1, 46–7, 207, 239–40, 274–5, 297–8
   recording the, 36–7, 47, 209, 244, 274–5
agreements
   cross-licensing, 267–8
   disputes arising from, 214
   environmental changes affecting, 242–6, 296–7
   licensing
      assessment of worth in, 264–6
      exclusivity of rights in, 132–3, 134–5
      improvement clauses in, 270
      prevention of competition in, 134–5
      restrictions on grant-back in, 135
      US legislation affecting, 135
   manipulation of minutes in negotiating, 208, 296
   negotiations arising within, 213–5, 246–8
   of agency
      as distinguished from distributorship, 135–6, 233
      in French law, 136
   of distributorship, 136, 226–255
      as constrained by EC law, 137–8
      as constrained by US law, 138–9
      in Arab countries, 139
   of joint venture, 282–300
   of minor significance, 6, 141
   of purchase/sale, 153–217
   parallel, 213–4
      restrictive in EC, 137–8
      restrictive in US, 138–9
      terminating, 252–3, 272
anti-trust laws, 133
arbitration, 128–9, 175
   awards, invalidity in law of, 147–9
   clause, ICC, 238
   ICC Court of, 128
   in Arab countries, 129
   in British–American contracts, 129
   in government contracts, 210–1
   in Japan, 129
   provisions in standard conditions, 175
   UNCITRAL rules of, 129
attitudes, 17
attitudinal structuring, 18
authority limits, 201

bargaining
   area, varying the, 181
   concession close in, 31, 60, 88, 191
   decision stage in, 30–1, 207–9, 234–40 271–2, 294–5
   distributive, 24–6, 35, 192–6, 210, 235–6, 270–1, 294
   early competitive or cooperative, 27
   framework, 180–1
   integrative, 26–30, 35–6, 197–203, 236–9, 271, 294
   linking of issues in, 28, 200, 203–6, 239–40, 265, 294
   parcelling of proposals in, 30
   price and worth in, 203–4
   reducing aspirations in, 195
   step-by-step, 190
   testing commitment in, 197–8, 205, 237–9
   testing of limits in, 24–5, 192
   trading off in, 28, 194, 204–5
behaviour
   adaptive, 78–9
      contingency selling as, 159–60
      cultural clusters as points of reference for, 93–4
      deception in, 54–5
      detection of deception in, 54–5
      frameworks for, 90–4

behaviour (*cont.*)
    how much, 78–9
    collaborative, 25–6, 235–6
    competing, 23
    compromising, 24
    contradictory signals in, 54–5
        a believability scale for, 55–6
        under- and over-reactions in, 56
    intra-organizational, joint ventures and, 296–302
    negotiating
        fear of image loss in, 26
        fear of position loss in, 26
        promises and threats in, 21–3
    organizational buying, factors affecting, 162–3
    skilled negotiators', 41–7
bid bond, 210
buyer
    evaluation of target objectives by, 176–7
    government as, 209–12
    increasing power of, 161
    modifying objectives of, 175–6
    positioning of seller by, 190
    setting of level of first offer by, 179–80
    style, 159

communication
    and handling of conflict, 111–2
    and negotiation
        with Americans, 52
        with Arabs, 49–50, 129, 139, 191, 195, 199, 204, 232, 248–9
        with Chinese, 205, 206, 232, 249
        with East Europeans, 47, 68–9, 171, 190, 197
        with Frenchmen, 48, 67, 72–3, 190, 208
        with Germans, 50, 62, 67–8, 94–6
        with Japanese, 50–1, 56, 61–2, 81–9, 178, 207, 232, 301–2
        with Koreans, 51, 202, 303
        with Scandinavians, 50, 57, 60, 93, 167, 178, 190
    and persuasion, 42–4
    and shared meaning, 113
    as multi-channel system, 61
    breakdown, 50
    conveying without commitment in, 26, 44, 196
    cultural – linguistic barriers in, 49–52
    integrational aspects of, 61
    managing impressions of self in, 56–7
    non-verbal, 52–7
        expression of emotion in, 52–3
        personal attitudes and feelings in, 53–4

of interpersonal attitudes and feelings, 53–4
    perspectives assisting interpersonal, 65–9
        education, 67–8
        group or individual orientation, 66–7
        growth processes of firm, 65–6
        ideological background, 68–9
    prerequisites for oral,
        over-assertion by Arabs in, 49–50
        overstating case in, 50
        receiving signals in, 196
        sending signals in, 196
        strategies, 112
        understating case in, 50
concession
    and agreement, 88
    close, 31
    rate, initial, 191
    rates, commitment and, 201
    setting a value on, 202–5
conflict
    arising from agreement, 214, 246–8
    as function of mutual dependence, 228
    methods of avoiding, 127–8
    mutual interest and, 12, 169–70, 231
    negotiation and resolution of, 229–30
    of laws, 127–8
contract
    applicable law in, 127
    change of circumstances in, 126
    Chinese perception of, 60
    force majeure clauses in, 127
    formation of, 122
    forms incorporating standard conditions, 171
    frustration of, 126–77
    Japanese interpretation of, 86–7
    model terms for, 127–8, 130
    of purchase/sale
        the counter offer in, 124
        the offer in, 122–3
    performance of, 124–6
    price adjustment clauses in, 172–3
    with governments, 129–30
cross-licensing, 267–8
cultural
    analysis, 91, 241–2
    assessment
        a four-dimensional framework, 92–4
        matrix approaches to, 91
        structural analysis in, 91–2
    behaviour, learning other people's, 64
    bias, overcoming, 63–4
    dimension in making agency agreements, 241–2
    factors in joint venture control, 295–6

influences on level of offer, 177–8, 195–6
orientations in persuasion, 88
perceptions
of corruption, 218–9
of meaning, 272
of time limits, 191
roles and scope for misinterpretation, 169
sensitivity and interpersonal communication, 63–9, 85
snares in sales/purchase agreements, 195–6
culture
and implications for negotiators, 40–76
and negotiation, 37
and social relations, 81–3
cognition
in Chinese, 59–60
in Western, 59
concept of harmony in, 59, 84–5
concepts
of space in, 57–8
of time in, 57–8
differences in cognitive structures in, 59–60
group formation in, 81
group maintenance in, 82
high and low context, 57–8
Japanese
importance of, 79
uniqueness of, 79–81
vertical principle in, 81–7
organizational
and national culture, 98–9
and organization of thought, 104
civil servants and, 211–2, 300
corporate language in, 104–5
government departments and, 209–12
linguistic protocol and, 104
propensity to development of, 5
role models and, 104
universe of discourse in, 104–5
ranking of organizations in, 87
social context and, 57–60
customer grid, 159

damages, liquidated, 126, 204
deception, 54
detection of, 54–6
decision-making
as stage of negotiation, 30–1, 36, 207, 212, 239–40, 271–2, 294–5
Chinese, 59–60, 86
group consensus in, 60, 86, 93
Japanese, 86

negotiation as basic process in, 6–7
disputes, arising from agreements, 214–5, 219–21, 246–8

franchising, 131
in the EC, 135
free-flow/open distribution channels, 7–8, 165, 230

guarantees, 97
of delivery, 144
of performance, 144

IMP Group, 4–5, 48–9, 163–5, 166
Incoterms, 121, 128, 171
and American Uniform Commercial Code, 121
and CEMA General Conditions of Delivery 1968–75, 121
information
additional, for clarification, 59
and internal negotiation, 200, 236
and objectives, 235–6
and supplier/agent relationships, 250–1
and termination of agreement, 252–3
as interorganizational power, 19, 21, 185–7, 234–5, 288
as intra-organizational power, 19, 21, 106–7, 107–8
Chinese and Japanese propensity to absorb, 59, 88
extraction as strategic function of negotiation, 20–1, 186
–structure–power (ISP) model, 106–7
task-related exchange of, 20–1, 88
interaction (interorganizational)
and atmosphere, 165
and preferred supplier concept, 8
and transaction-specific investments, 8
and work interactions within the organization, 14
differing perspectives in, 169–70
environment effects in, 164–5
personal contact at heart of relationships in, 166, 292
processes in, 163–5
value chains and, 5
interaction (interpersonal)
as basis of interorganizational effectiveness, 202–3, 241, 292
as basis of intra-organizational coordination, 103–4, 106–8, 111–2
competitive mode of, 15–6, 202
concept of face in, 57, 59–60, 86–7, 206

interaction (interpersonal) (*cont.*)
  cooperative mode of, 15–6, 202, 231–2
  core skills in, 168–9, 241–2
  definition of situation in, 168
  importance of Japanese language for, 61–3
    amae, 61–3, 74–5, 80
    giri, 63
    honne, 78–9
    ninjo, 63
    on, 63
    oyabun/kobun, 84
    tatemae, 88
  mutual role-taking in, 168
  performing dimensions in, 169
  relationships in, 15–6, 66–77, 85–7, 202–3, 254, 292
  technical competence in, 168
interaction (intraorganizational)
  and the political use of information, 106–7
  and the selective use of language, 104
  and the effects of organizational logics, 102–3
  and the self-interest of groups, 105
  and the self-interest of individuals, 106
  and the effects of information, structure and power, 106–7
  and the use of networks, 107–8
  and negotiation, 111–2
  and persuasion strategies, 109–11

Japanese
  market
    approaches to, 80–1
    problems of, 79–80
  negotiation styles, interpersonal relations and, 87–8
  patterns of emotion, 85–7
  pre-occupation with interpersonal relations, 84–5
joint ventures
  as direct investment alternatives, 131–2
  conflict in, 297
  constraints on, 140
  cultural context of, 295–6
  in China, 289–90
  in EC, 140–1
  in Indonesia, 298
  in Japan, 246–8
  in Yugoslavia, 286–7
  political interface in, 297–9
  susceptibility of, to environmental changes, 297
  tendency to failure in, 283–4
  varied nature of, 139–40, 282–3

language
  and commitment in negotiation, 41–5, 197–8, 205
  and social relationships, 49–50
  and accomplishment of tasks, 103–4
  and the literate Arab, 48–50, 199–200
  as macro-culture, 61–3
  as micro-culture, 103–5
  as organizational culture, 103–5
  as pico-culture, 103–5
  as vehicle for influencing behaviour, 41–7
  foreign, decision to use or not, 48–9
  in organizations, role models and, 104
  non-verbal mediation of, 53–7
  overstatement of case in, 50
  paralinguistic features of, 44–5, 47
  probing, 193
  protocol of, 104
  situation and communication in, 57–8
  social context and, 57–60
  'tall poppy syndrome' and, 57
  understatement of case in, 59
  use
    for flagging behaviour to come, 45–6
    for summarizing, 30–1, 46–7, 207
    for testing understanding, 30–1, 46, 207
    in checking out ambiguities, 46
    of affirmatives as negatives, 50, 86
    of negatives as affirmatives, 49
law
  code, 120
  common, 120
  diversity of the, 120
  individual businessman and the, 121–2
  international, the harmonization of, 120–1
  international trade, the custom of merchants as, 121
  Muslim, 120
  pervasiveness of the, 119
  supranational, 120
  unity of the, 120–1
laws
  choice of, 128
level of first offer, 177–9, 233–4, 264–6
licensing
  agreements,
    improvement clauses in, 267
    negotiating organizational access in, 261–2
    patent, price-fixing in, 133
    royalties in, 133, 264–6
  and copyright, 133–4
  and know-how, 133–4
  and patents, 133–4

and trademarks, 133–4
compulsory, 132
costs and benefits in, 263–4
cross–, 267–8
defined, 131, 258–9
EC constraints on,
factors affecting, 259–60
negotiations
    assessing worth in, 264–6
    security in, 262–3
liquidated damages, 126, 204
logics, organizational, 101–3

macro-culture, 41–71
marketing
    as cross-cultural activity, 5
    face-to-face element in, 5
    plans as agreements for negotiation, 6
    strategy implementation
        as agreements, 1
        skills, 6
message strategies, compliance-gaining, 42–5, 109–11
micro-culture
    and language in organizations, 103–5
    and macro-culture, 98–9
    and pico-culture, 99
    and social reality in organizations, 99–103
    and ways of looking at issues, 105
motivational orientation, 19

negotiation
    and company objectives, 175–6
    and modification of objectives, 176
    and networks, 107
    and organizational reality, 111
    approach to marketing, 1, 6–10
    as focus for buying and selling, 165–9
    as on-going process, 111, 251–2
    attack/defend spirals in, 45
    centrality of relationships in, 166
    communication in, 41–2
    communication issues in, 247–8
    contract, business as, 7
    cross-cultural constraints on, 56–60
    definition of, 15
    distribution issues in, 250
    environmental influences on, 20, 185–6, 242–6
    envisaging ultimate bargain in, 193–4
    face-saving in, 201, 206
    face-to-face element in, 5, 181, 189–91
    fundamental strategic issues in, 20–1
    incompatible expectations in, 13

influence channels in, 188–9
influence strategies in, 20–4
    explicit persuasion, 21–3
    initial proposals, 21
    moves and counter-moves, 21
influencing behaviours in, 41–4
interaction-dependent outcomes in, 14
language in, 42–5, 109–11
    checking out ambiguities in, 46–7
    flagging behaviour to come in, 45–6
    paralanguage in, 44–5
    use of foreign languages in, 44–52
    use of irritating language in, 45
lowering of aspirations in, 27–8
maintaining flexibility in, 29, 200, 203–6, 211, 239–40, 265, 295–6
misperception in, 56–60
mixed motives in, 12, 234
multiple packages in, 28, 212
mutual role taking in, 168
nature of, 12–5
negotiating rules for, 189
non-verbal sign systems and, 52–7
of agenda, 190–1
of rules of meeting, 189, 296
outcomes, influencing, 9–10, 19–24, 31–37, 40–60, 78–9, 184–215, 232–256, 236–9, 292–6
package in, 28, 46–7, 203–4
pervasiveness of, 6–7
philosophy of, 215, 222–5
planning system and, 7–8
presentation in, 188
price issues in, 203–4, 248
principled approach to, 29
product issues in, 246–7
selling and, 161
setting of time limits in, 191, 195, 204–5
shaping predictable reactions in, 46
situation and status relationships in, 47–9, 59–60
situational influences on, 18–20, 186, 227–8
stages in, 10, 24–31, 192–209, 235–40, 270–2, 293–8
strength of case in, 188
skills model, 10, 31–4, 88–9, 187–209, 232–240, 270–2, 292–5
social context in, 59–60
social structural constraints on, 58
table, getting to the, 187–9
varying situations in, 12–3
with governments, 209–12
with government-sponsored agencies, 212–3

negotiation (*cont.*)
 with local authorities, 213
 with public corporations and services,
  212–3
 within organizations, 111
Negotiation Skills Model, 10, 31–4, 88–9,
  187–209, 232–40, 270–2, 292–5
 accommodation of organizational selling
  and buying in, 165–9
 and negotiation with Japanese, 88–9
 as framework for problem-solving and
  bargaining, 229–30
 cultural de-emphasis in, 32–33, 195–6
negotiators
 concession dilemma of, 26, 41
 home organizational constraints on, 200
 implications of culture for, 54–60
 selection and training of, 168–9
 skilled behaviours of, 42–7
 social structural constraints on, 53
 use of authority constraints by, 201
 use of legitimate power by, 203
 use of moral rules by, 203

objectives
 evaluating buyer's target, 176–7
 evaluating seller's target, 176
 modifying, 175–7
 negotiation and company, 175
 negotiation and marketing, 175
 negotiation and purchasing, 175
 negotiation and sales, 175
offer and acceptance, 93–5
 setting aside of, 141
open or free-flow channels, 7–8, 165, 230
 defined, 230
 market system and, 7–8
organizational buying, 161–5
 as cross-functional process, 161–2
 as multi-stage decision process, 131–2
 buying centre concept in, 161–2
 buy-phases model in, 161
 dependence on sellers in, 163
 interactive dimension in, 163
 key decision points in, 162
organizational culture, 5, 13, 99–114
 analysing the, 112–3
 and group self-interest, 105
 and individual self-interest, 101
 and organizational rationalities/logics,
  101–3

parallel
 agreements, 213–4
 exports, 137–8

imports, 143–4, 150–2
patents
 and differing views of patentability, 132–3
 and strengthening of negotiating position,
  132
 differing philosophical and legal perspectives on, 133
 requirements for working of, 132
 rights of third parties in relation to, 133
 selection of markets for cover of, 133
performance bonds, 171, 174, 210
persuasion
 American and Japanese approaches to,
  87–88
 as strength of case, 188
 by appeal to legitimate power, 203
persuasive message strategies, 42–4, 99,
  109–11
pico-culture, 99, 101, 103–5, 106–7
power
 and conflict, 160, 185–7, 228–30
 and information, 106–7
 and structure, 106–7
 as function of interdependence, 18,
  228–30
 as situational influence on behaviour, 18,
  186
 bases of social
  coercive, 22
  communicative, 23–4
  expert, 22
  information, 21
  legitimate, 22
  referent, 22
  reward, 21–2
 building in, 186–7
 environmental forces of, 185–6
 objective, 19
 relative, forces of change affecting, 185,
  242–6
 subjective, 19–20
problem-solving
 as face-saving, 201, 206
 as integrative bargaining, 26–31, 35–6,
  197–203, 211–2, 236–42, 274, 294
 as pre-negotiation interorganizational
  contact, 28, 34, 187–8, 209–10
 as pre-negotiation intra-organizational
  contact, 31–4, 175–6
 'close' in, 30–1, 60, 88, 207, 212, 239–40
 conveying without commitment as, 26–7,
  31, 197
 cooperative, 24–30, 202, 236
 effecting movement from stage to stage as,
  34–7

overcoming the concession dilemma in, 26, 196–7
signalling behaviour in, 26–7, 44–5, 196–7
trading of concessions in, 28, 88
property, passing of, 125–6

rapport
establishing non-task behaviour in, 88
language reflecting intention to establish, 182
rationalities, organizational, 101–3
reality (organizational)
external physical reality and, 100
individual reality and, 101
social reality and, 100–1
relations (interpersonal)
and consensus in decision-making, 60, 86–7, 93
and negotiation styles, 16–7, 87–8
as function of nature of agreements, 231–2, 292
face and, 54, 56–7, 206
in and between Japanese groups, 85–7
individualism as measure of, 92–3
intercultural aspects of, 166–8
Japanese patterns of emotion in, 86–7
power distance and authority in, 92
uncertainty avoidance as factor in, 92
relations (interorganizational), 234, 249–51, 268–9
see also Interaction
relations (intra-organizational)
and conflict arising from joint ventures, 298–9
in joint ventures, changes affecting, 298
role
obligations, 13, 17
of the tender, 170–1
model, 104
perceptions, 17, 68
relationships, 66–7
taking, mutual, 168

seller
and adaptive behaviour, 159–60
aspiration level of, 177–9
evaluation of target objective by, 176–7
level of first offer set by, 177–9
positioning a, 190
style, 159–60
undertakings given by, 126
selling to organizations
and negotiation, 161

contingency approaches to, 159–60
the formula model in, 157–8
the need satisfaction model in, 158
the problem-solving model in, 158
the traditional selling process in, 159
Weitz contingency model and, 160, 166
social influence
compliance and, 23–4
identification and, 23–4
internalization and, 23–4
standard conditions,
delivery in, 174
main areas covered by, 172–5
need for, 170
patents, trademark and copyright in, 174–5
payment in, 172–3
performance in, 174
price in, 172
various kinds of, 170
straw issues, 180, 197, 240
structural analysis, 58, 81–5, 89–90

Technik, 74–6
tender bond, 139

vertical organization
concept of attribute not apparent in, 81
concept of frame in, 81
consensus decision-making in, 86
group emphasis and interpersonal relationships in, 83–5
group leadership and change in, 84–5
mutuality in personal relationships in, 86
oyabun/kobun relationships in Japanese, 84–5
structure of, 84

Warranty, product and service, 215
Weitz contingency model, 160, 166